PSYCHOANALYSIS AT ITS LIMITS

PSYCHOANALYSIS AT ITS LIMITS

NAVIGATING THE POSTMODERN TURN

Edited by

Anthony Elliott
and Charles Spezzano

'an association in which the free development of each
is the condition of the free development of all'

FREE ASSOCIATION BOOKS / LONDON / NEW YORK

First published 2000 in Great Britain by
Free Association Books Limited
57 Warren Street, London W1P 5PA

ISBN 1 85343 464 7 hbk; 1 85343 465 5 pbk

A CIP catalogue record for this book is available from the British Library

Designed and produced for Free Association Books Ltd by
Chase Production Services, Chadlington, OX73LN
Printed in the EU by T.J. International, Padstow

Contents

Acknowledgements

The idea for this book arose out of a collaborative research effort. It was some years ago that we uncovered important emerging connections between psychoanalysis and postmodernism. The article which resulted from our research, 'Psychoanalysis at its Limits: Navigating the Postmodern Turn', unleashed dialogue and debate between various schools of the discipline; since then, many people encouraged us to extend our work in this area by putting a book together comprising academics and psychoanalysts, in order to consider the changing configurations of psychoanalysis, postmodernism and contemporary theory.

There are several individuals that we must thank at the outset. We are grateful to David Stonestreet at Free Association Books for supporting the project and providing helpful advice throughout. In the early planning stages, Michael Moskowitz offered constructive encouragement; also Ed Rawlings offered much steadfast help in assembling the manuscript. We owe a particular debt to Anthony Moran, who assisted with the final stages of editing and played a crucial role in turning the manuscript into a book. Finally we are grateful to the contributors for responding to our many queries, and for providing essential links between psychoanalysis and postmodernism in the material analysed and debated in this book.

We are grateful to the following publishers for their permission to republish some of the material in this collection:

Anthony Elliott and Charles Spezzano, 'Psychoanalysis at its Limits: Navigating the Postmodern Turn', *The Psychoanalytic Quarterly*, 1996, Vol. LXV, No. 1: 52–83. Reprinted in O. Renik (ed.), *Knowledge and Authority in the Psychoanalytic Relationship*, Northvale, NJ: Aronson, 1998: 59–92.

Jane Flax, 'Final Analysis: Can Psychoanalysis Survive in the Postmodern West?', in her *Disputed Subjects*, New York: Routledge, 1993.

Stephen Frosh, 'Postmodernism and the Adoption of Identity', adapted from themes developed in his *For and Against Psychoanalysis*, London: Routledge, 1998.

Jessica Benjamin, 'The Shadow of the Other Subject: Intersubjectivity and Feminist Theory', from her *Shadow of the Other*, New York: Routledge, 1998.

Thomas Ogden, 'The Dialectically Constituted/Decentred Subject of Psychoanalysis I and II', *The International Journal of Psycho-Analysis*, Vol. 73: 517–26 and Vol. 74: 613–26. Copyright © Institute of Psycho-Analysis.

Anthony Elliott, 'The Ambivalence of Identity', slightly revised version of chapter from his *Subject to Ourselves: Social Theory, Psychoanalysis and Postmodernity*, Cambridge: Polity Press, 1996.

Charles Spezzano, 'The Struggle to Imagine', slightly revised version of chapter from his *Affect in Psychoanalysis*, Hillsdale, NJ: The Analytic Press, 1993.

Anthony Elliott and Charles Spezzano
Melbourne and San Francisco
April 1999

Notes on Contributors

Jessica Benjamin is Professor on the Faculty of the New York University Postdoctoral Program in Psychoanalysis and Psychotherapy. Her most recent books are *Like Subjects, Love Objects* (1995) and *Shadow of the Other: Intersubjectivity and Gender in Psychoanalysis* (1998). She practises psychoanalysis in New York City.

Mark Bracher is Professor of English and Director of the Center for the Psychoanalysis of Culture and Society at Kent State University. He is the author of *The Writing Cure: Psychoanalysis, Composition, and the Aims of Education*, and *Lacan, Discourse, and Social Change: A Psychoanalytic Cultural Criticism*. He is co-editor of *Lacan and the Subject of Language* (1991), *Lacanian Theory of Discourse: Subject, Structure, and Society*, and *Lacan, Language and Literature*, and editor of *The Journal for the Psychoanalysis of Culture and Society*. He received his psychoanalytic training at the Cleveland Psychoanalytic Institute.

Anthony Elliott is professor of Social and Political Theory at the University of the West of England. His books include *Psychoanalytic Theory: An Introduction* (1994), *Subject to Ourselves: Social Theory, Psychoanalysis and Postmodernity* (1996), *The Mourning of John Lennon* (1999), and *Social Theory and Psychoanalysis in Transition* (1999, second edition). He is co-editor, with Stephen Frosh, of *Psychoanalysis in Contexts* (1995), and editor of *Freud 2000* (1998) and *The Blackwell Reader in Contemporary Social Theory* (1999).

Jane Flax is Professor of Political Science at Howard University and a psychotherapist in private practice. Her books include *Thinking Fragments* (1990), *Disputed Subjects* (1993) and *The American Dream in Black and White: The Clarence Thomas Hearings* (1999).

Stephen Frosh is Professor of Psychology at Birkbeck College, University of London, and Consultant Clinical Psychologist and Vice Dean in the Child and Family Department at the Tavistock

Clinic, London. He is the author of numerous academic papers and several books, including *For and Against Psychoanalysis* (Routledge, 1997), *Sexual Difference: Masculinity and Psychoanalysis* (Routledge, 1994), *Identity Crisis: Modernity, Psychoanalysis and the Self* (Macmillan, 1991) and *The Politics of Psychoanalysis* (Macmillan, 1987; second edition 1999). He is joint author, with Danya Glaser, of *Child Sexual Abuse* (Macmillan, second edition 1993) and co-editor with Anthony Elliott of *Psychoanalysis in Contexts* (Routledge, 1995). He is currently, with Ann Phoenix, involved in a research project on 'Emergent Identities: Masculinities and 11–14-year-old Boys'.

Stephen Mitchell is training and supervising analyst at the William Alanson White Institute and supervisor of the New York University postdoctoral program in psychoanalysis. He is the author of *Relational Concepts in Psychoanalysis* and *Hope and Dread in Psychoanalysis*; and co-author, with Jay Greenberg, of *Object Relations in Psychoanalytic Theory*.

Thomas Ogden MD, is co-director of the Center for the Advanced Study of the Psychoses, supervising and personal analyst at the Psychoanalytic Institute of Northern California, and faculty at the San Francisco Psychoanalytic Institute. He is the author of many books, including *Subjects of Analysis* (1996).

Karen Peoples works in psychotherapy in San Francisco.

Charles Spezzano is a training and supervising analyst at the Psychoanalytic Institute of Northern California, and a member of both the Los Angeles Institute and Society for Psychoanalytic Studies, and the International Psychoanalytic Association. He is the author of *What to Do Between Birth and Death* (1991) and *Affect in Psychoanalysis: A Clinical Synthesis* (1993). He is co-editor of *Soul on the Couch*, and contributing editor to the journal *Psychoanalytic Dialogues*.

Introduction: Rethinking Psychoanalysis in the Postmodern Era

Anthony Elliott and Charles Spezzano

The portrait of psychoanalysis developed in this book circles around multiplicity, pluralism and ambivalence. This is not only, as one might expect, because of the diversity of contributions contained in the volume; and nor is it simply a consequence of reflecting upon the Freudian understanding of human subjectivity as passionate, fractured and divided. Rather it is because the key issues of modernity and postmodernity are riddled with ambiguity and controversy, and demand the rediscovery of psychoanalysis itself.

The postmodern in psychoanalysis, as in other discourses, involves second-order reflections upon the limits and limitations of the modern project of making the unconscious conscious, putting the ego where the id was, or simply helping the patient to become more reasonably passionate. The postmodern edge of psychoanalysis takes issue with modern reason and its consequences; it questions and deconstructs the ideas, assumptions and objectives which derived into psychoanalysis from the Enlightenment. The postmodern is modern psychoanalytic practice coming to terms with itself, pushing its ideological and moral beliefs to the limit, all in an attempt to think the unthinkable.

Some theorists, analysts and therapists have heard such notions as arguments that everything about psychoanalysis as they have known it is over – that to allow postmodern ingredients into the psychoanalytic stew is to stop trying to create better understandings of psyche or better images and accounts of insight, healing and transformation. We take issue with this. Following the French philosopher, Jean-François Lyotard, we argue that the notion of the postmodern should not be understood as implying sequentiality, that is, as an epoch which comes after modernity. All attempts to play the postmodern off against the modern and to assign these epochs historical periodization, according to Lyotard, must fail. For we have not taken leave of the modern. Instead, the problem of postmodernism is that of an intensely critical relationship with the modern which is coming into view everywhere – for example, in our responses to technology, the environment, the family, gender relations, identity and personhood. This viewpoint is also strongly endorsed by the cultural theorist Zygmunt Bauman. 'Postmodernity', writes Bauman (1990: 272), 'does not necessarily mean the end, the discreditation or the rejection of modernity. Postmodernity is no more (but no less either) than the modern mind taking a long, attentive and sober look at itself, at its conditions and its past works, not fully liking what it sees and sensing the urge to change.'

Similarly, postmodernism is not an attack upon, or reading of, psychoanalysis from outside the discipline. In fact, the origins of postmodernism are not infrequently rooted by postmodern philosophers in Freud's unseating of rationality in favour of dreaming as the dominant state of mind, dislocating the psyche from the private realm into a more transferential space, and fragmenting of the ego through identifications and splittings. Lyotard, for example, analyses the postmodern self-reflection on modernity in terms of concepts borrowed from Freud: 'remembering', 'repeating', and 'working through' (see Lyotard, 1988). Here the typically postmodern encounter is one of the modern mind remembering its past actions, fantasies and thoughts; repeating their implicit assumptions and affects in the act of self-examination; and working through such psychological states in a movement towards alternative selves and alternative modernities. From this perspective, as we suggested, Freud can be credited, albeit *avant la lettre,* as 'postmodern': his discovery of the repressed unconscious, and with it his critique of consciousness, helps initiate a thoroughgoing scepticism about Enlightenment reason, a scepticism which will eventually fall to the terrain of postmodernists such as Lyotard. But this, as it stands, is too simple, primarily because it suggests that it is psychoanalysis – as theory and as practice – which can be dragged across into current intellectual debates about modernity and postmodernity and illuminate the stakes of such debate through the deployment of its own operational categories (repression, displacement, fantasy and the like).

Yet what the modernity/postmodernity debate uncovers is a two-way traffic between psychoanalysis and contemporary theory; that is, it is the operational categories of psychoanalysis too that will be called into question – one upshot of which is the restructuring, re-invention, transformation, or transmutation of the discipline. Take, for example, Freud's thesis in *The Interpretation of Dreams* that all dreams are wish-fulfilments. Freud presents this thesis in the course of discussing his famous dream of Irma's injection. Yet is it not possible to turn Freud's generalization back upon itself, in suitably postmodern fashion? Indeed, this is precisely what the French psychoanalyst Didieu Anzieu does in commenting that Freud's thesis is itself a wish-fulfilment – the wish that Freud should uncover the enigma of dreams (see Anzieu, 1986).

The development of a postmodern orientation to psychoanalysis is intended to draw attention to the decline of traditional, modernist approaches to knowledge and experience. Such a decline, however, is not coterminous with its disintegration. On the contrary, the contributions in this book highlight that what is emerging today is a kind of *psychoanalysis of psychoanalysis*: a running together of modernist and postmodernist psychoanalytical currents, the rediscovery or reinvention of psychoanalysis as a vibrant theory and practice, the sharpening and differentiation of models of mind, the restructuring of methodology, and the rethinking of interactional configurations in which the self is understood in relation to others (see Elliott, 1996, for extended discussion of these points). Three key contrasts demarcate modernist and postmodernist orientations to psychoanalysis.

First, linear models of the psychic subject as complete, layered and continuous are challenged by multiplex and multi-layered models of multiplicity and fracturing. This occurs, not only in the problematization of psychic space, but also in the rise of intersubjectivity as a constructive dialectic for analysing the links between unconscious desire and otherness.

Second, while traditional psychoanalysis locates the transformation of unconscious fantasy into rational understanding as the key to the analytic process, the more reflexive, postmodern version underscores the centrality of imagination, desire and affect to the creation of personal meaning and intersubjective understanding. The impersonal forces that Freud labelled the 'it' in his 1923 theory are not only made personal through the ego's sublimating capabilities but are also made personal and transpersonal through the ego's capabilities for what Thomas Ogden (1994) has called 'the analytic third' and what one of the present authors – Spezzano (1996) – formulates as the co-creation of consciousness.

Third, the problem of whether psychoanalysis is (or might become) a science is replaced by problems of internal critique, cross-linking and fusion of existing paradigms. That is, the issue of epistemology is now becoming central to psychoanalysis, but this time psychoanalysis is seeking to incorporate its own understanding of the emotional inner world into the development of a scientific worldview geared towards the needs of analysts and analysands for the twenty-first century. The resulting epistemological position of psychoanalytic investigation resembles that summed up by Smith (1996: 7) in this way:

> I accept that the 'hermeneutical situation' from which we *start* our attempts at understanding is not to be construed as an unsullied, self-grounding Cartesian detachment; but this does not imply that we are thrown blind into a situation we can in no way bracket. It is inappropriate to conceptualize the interpretive act as one of an autonomous subject completely extricated from the concrete present. But it is equally inappropriate to see it as hopelessly historical. There are many possibilities between those two poles; this is not an either/or choice.

This does not mean that nothing of the traditional, modern vision of how psychoanalysis might develop (that is, through analysts formulating hypotheses, observing how patients react to interpretations based on them, and then writing up papers to communicate these empirical findings to colleagues) is finished, but that it is not enough to keep analysis evolving in the most vital and clinically useful way.

Opening and Closing Freud: Modern Constructions, Postmodern Revisions

In this section we explore the question of the subject in psychoanalysis through a reconsideration of the nature of human imagination – in particular, the imaginative processing of emotional experience. In what follows we discuss some grey areas of human subjectivity in psychoanalysis. We argue that the question of the subject in psychoanalysis is always a question about the nature and limits of thinking itself (thinking being understood, following Bion, as the processing of affect), or of what can be psychically processed and thus transformed.

The navigation of alternative selves and states of mind is the psychoanalytic location – or so we shall propose – of the *subject in question* (see Elliott, 1995, 1996). For Freud, psychoanalysis involves an opening out of unconscious psychic life to reflection and deliberation; a recovery of the past which is accessed through looking at what goes on in the psyche. It is worth wondering about the structure of our internal world, says Freud, since it is precisely through human imagination – at the levels of language and intersubjectivity – that the internal landscape of the subject opens itself to self-understanding and transformation. In Freud's famous phrase: '*Wo Es war, soll Ich werden*' ('*Where id was, there ego shall become*'). There is a profound connection here between remembering and forgetting – the imagined links between identity and difference that can be recovered and processed, repressed and forgotten. Certain core questions arise in this respect. What is the project of questioning, psychoanalytically speaking, the realm of subjectivity? In psychoanalysis, what are the limits and transformations of the subject? What is the signification of the subject itself, as theory and as practice? And, crucially, in what ways does the advent of the postmodern transform psychoanalytic accounts of subjectivity?

Let us begin addressing these questions by considering Freud's remarks on the therapeutic action of psychoanalysis. There are three dominant discourses (no doubt, other competing discourses could be mentioned) which have emerged about the aims of analysis, typically labelled post-Freudian, post-Kleinian, and post-Lacanian. We position them heuristically on a continuum from the more modern to the more postmodern, although we wish to suggest that all three interpretations open and close the implications of psychoanalysis too hastily.

The first view is essentially a rationalist one. It holds that Freud (topographic model of psyche) argues for the possibility of making the unconscious conscious and that Freud (structural model of psyche) argues for the possibility of helping the ego sublimate the id. The topographic vision suggests that the paralysing grip of unconscious repression can be undone through reason and self-mastery. The structural vision suggests that the ego can be transformed from primarily defender against libidinal and aggressive anxieties to primarily integrator of sexual and aggressive affects. Especially this structural view of the aim of the psychoanalytic process – that the id can be effectively sublimated by the ego – became deeply entrenched, of course, in American ego-psychology, but significantly it has also been evident in the European social theory and philosophy of Jürgen Habermas and others (Habermas, 1972; Lorenzer, 1976). In this theory of an ego that sits at the centre of mental conflict, 'the patient's task is to negotiate the conflict [between the ego and forces from the id and superego or between the life and death instincts] and when unable to do so he develops symptoms as a compromise and uses maladaptive mental mechanisms to defend himself and his [internal] objects' (Steiner, 1996: 1074).

The second view of the aims of psychoanalysis radiates from the Fairbairnian notion of ego splitting and the Kleinian notion of projective identification: splits in the object are followed by splits in the ego and then these split-off ego fragments are fantasmatically experienced as being parts of someone else. This view was argued by Klein, and now by neo-Kleinians to be a natural extension of Freud's project – since Freud (1924) had amended his overall psychology of conflicted whole persons with the notion of the ego anxiously trying to avoid either being overwhelmed by or losing contact with the id or the superego 'by deforming itself, by submitting to encroachments on its own unity and even perhaps by effecting a cleavage or division of itself' (Freud, 1924: 152–3). As Steiner argues, however, the Kleinian vision of the ego/self goes well beyond Freud's ego psychology: 'The radical nature of this theory has to do with the self no longer being seen as a unitary structure, so that a coherent sense of self has to be achieved through the regaining and integration of lost and dispersed elements' (Steiner, 1996: 1075).

The third view of Freud's aims for psychoanalysis is more critical than the first two (not so much a radical revision as a turning on its head), and is associated with Jacques Lacan's 'return to Freud'. Lacan interpreted Freud's maxim not as a therapeutic injunction to promote conflict-free spheres of self-identity, but as a formula which underlines the primacy of the unconscious. Lacan's critique of American ego-psychology, in particular, rejects the notion that the object of analysis is that 'the ego must dislodge the id' (Lacan 1977: 45). In working out a specular theory of personality formation, Lacan argues that the ego is 'an imaginary identification or, to be more accurate, an enveloping series of such identifications' (Lacan 1966: 8). Accordingly, any attempt to strengthen the ego is simply a re-inforcement of the illusions and deceptions of a narcissistic mirage. By contrast, Lacanian and post-Lacanian analysts argue that the unconscious always-already precedes the 'I', and that the object of analysis involves a radical decentring of the self, such that it is understood that the subject will always remain bound to the Other. In other words, the id punctuates the imaginary discourse of the ego which must recognize itself being taken by surprise.

Any theory as innovative and complex as Freud's is bound to open itself to multiple interpretations. But, in contrast to these three dominant developments of Freud's seminal work, we would like to offer an alternative construction of the transformation of the subject in analysis. By our reading, the aim of analysis for Freud is what Bion called 'K' (understood by us as imaginative elaboration of, immediately, affect, and, ultimately, 'O' or being, beyond the closures of repetition) and an opening up of Winnicott's transitional space where human psychological life evolves (individually and collectively) in the interchange of affect, image, and idea. A combination of free association, the mapping of memory, the intersubjective crossings of transference and countertransference and reflection upon unconscious fantasy: these are the principal means by which we are to become more open to ourselves and to others. By this open-endedness, we mean to underscore a questioning of the links between identity and non-identity, the turning back of fantasy upon itself in order to glimpse the inner complexity of the different states of mind of which we are capable. This scanning of fantasy and desire lies at the core of the transformation of the relation between conscious and unconscious psychic streams to which Freud refers, and which Matte Blanco describes as a continuum of mental states composed of varying blends of consciousness and unconsciousness, primary and secondary process thinking, symmetrical and asymmetrical logics. In addition, as the Kleinians especially stress, it is through the reflection upon disowned parts of the mind that the subject achieves an alteration of mental functioning.

In Freudian psychoanalysis, the reflective articulation of the subject's psychic representations occurs in and through language. The dynamics of transference and counter-transference, following Lacan's integration of post-Saussurian linguistics into psychoanalysis, are variously characterized as a heterogeneous set of grammatical and logical 'structures' (obsessional, paranoid, hysterical, schizophrenic). In fact, perhaps the most widely recognized aspect of the signifying capacities of the human subject – particularly in contemporary critical theory – concerns 'discourse' and 'speech', at both the individual and interpersonal levels. But this zoning of language – or of 'being in language' – captures only one dimension of psychic representation, that of symbolization. The pleasures and restrictions of sublimation are of central concern here: the turning of 'private', unconscious enjoyment into some kind of figuration that is valued as part of the socio-symbolic bond, and which can be communicated and translated within the languages of culture. But to see this dimension of symbolization as exhausting the question of the subject is, of course, a dramatic over-simplification.

In an important essay, the French psychoanalyst Julia Kristeva poses the following question: 'Is the destiny of the speaking being reducible to speech and language, or should even other *systems of representation* be taken into consideration in order to think this being's logical particularities and/or in order to reach the very psychical level, on which sense reveals itself to the subject?' (1994: 18). Kristeva – notwithstanding coming to psychoanalysis from linguistics – argues that it is essential for contemporary psychoanalysis to attend to the heterogeneity and polyvalence of psychic representatives; of the erotization of lost primary involvements which dislocate the subject's capacity to use words:

> [T]he development of semiology has led to the conception of different signifying systems (iconic code, musical code, etc.) that

> are irreducible to language (the latter being envisaged as a structure or a grammar, a language or a discourse, a statement or an utterance). This has shaken 'linguistic imperialism'. Concurrently, a return to Freud, and in particular to the Freudian concept of representation, takes into account a plurality of psychic representatives: thing-representation, word-representation, representation of drive, representation of affect. The ensuing result is a 'laminated' model of the psychic signifying process with heterogeneous *traces* and *signs.* (1994: 18)

What, exactly, are these psychical traces and signs – radically heterogeneous – of which Kristeva speaks? Kristeva's own response to this question has been to displace the Lacanian emphasis on language and intersubjectivity with the notion of a 'semiotic' signifying process, a realm of prediscursive experience (including the tone and rhythm of infant utterances, gestures, affects and bodily rhythms) which is necessarily prior to symbolic representation and entry into cultural processes. This semiotic is construed here as the most direct appearance in consciousness of the drives. Kristeva thus suggests there is a connecting track between the semiotic displacement, or unconscious rupture, of language, and the folding back of repression into a symbolic signifying process through which the eroticization of language perpetuates and normalizes itself.

In pursuing this construction, we propose to draw some linkages between human subjectivity and the systems of representation that can be taken into consideration in order to think the limits of psychical processing. The ideas of postmodernists are very useful in this context because of the acceptance and underlining of the multiplex, fragmentary and discontinuous nature of systems of representation and signification. Embracing the fragmentation and dislocation inherent in human experience implies much about the character of psychic life and intersubjective relations, and indeed many of the contributions contained in this book examine the implications of this for the reconstruction of psychoanalysis as theory and as practice. But, at this point, we wish to underline the importance of the postmodern condition (fragmentation, discontinuity, dislocation and turbulence) for analysing the nature of the unconscious, and especially the systems of representation to which it gives rise. It is true that modernist approaches to the question of representation also give some prominence to the fragmented and divided nature of psychic life and human experience. But whereas modernists propose a tight correspondence between what is being thought (the signified) and the fantasies which circle around such thoughts (the signifier), postmodernist thinking sees these connections as much more open-ended and creative. One significant upshot of this is that, whereas modernists tended to privilege language or rationality in the framing of systems of representation, postmodernists understand meaning as also rooted in non-verbal or pre-symbolic modes of generating experience. Thus, Winnicott and Bion might be seen as early voices of the postmodern impulse in psychoanalysis.

These various modes of generating experience carry rich implications for the analysis of human subjectivity, and demand a radical rethinking of the dominance of the concept of narcissism as it has been elaborated by theorists such as Lacan, Kohut and Lasch. Narcissism and the ego may be closely paired, but from the viewpoint of postmodernism the question of their precise relationship remains contentious, and it is from this angle that analysts influenced by postmodern theory attempt to prise open a more reflective space for human subjectivity. The problem with Lacan's version of the narcissistic genesis of the ego is that it equates rigidified forms of ego formation into the self as such. The alternative offered by postmodernism is that of a complex, contradictory relationship between the ego and unconscious representation, self and other, autonomy and heteronomy. In postmodern terms, Freud's therapeutic maxim demands, not only that unconscious sources of motivation become the object of conscious self-reflection, but that affects (viewed by Freud as the primary drive-derivatives) come to full expression in both the life of the subject and society at large. Ultimately, then, postmodernism underscores the importance of passion and the affects, subjective resources necessary for rethinking the subject in the aftermath of recent upheavals (Winnicott's writings on the use of the object; intersubjective theory; self-psychology; Ogden's positing of the analyst and patient creating a third subjectivity; and so on and so forth) – in psychoanalysis.

In This Book

Over the last fifteen years or so, the critical discourse on postmodernism in its relation to psychoanalysis has proliferated dramatically. The majority of critiques, however, are one-dimensional refutations that have failed to seriously confront the challenges and provocations of the postmodern for psychoanalytic theory today. The articles collected in this book, by contrast, enter into a reflective encounter with the legacies of the modern and postmodern, trace specific psychoanalytic phenomena in the light of these discourses, and develop sustained critiques of the contributions and limitations of postmodern theory. Many of the authors have undertaken serious engagements with postmodern theory, and have developed powerful arguments for the restructuring of psychoanalysis in the light of postmodernism.

In Chapter 1, Anthony Elliott and Charles Spezzano develop an analysis of how the postmodern condition in its different contexts relates to psychoanalysis. They begin their chapter, 'Psychoanalysis at Its Limits: Navigating the Postmodern Turn', by pointing to conflicting notions of modernism and postmodernism, from which they suggest that there are in fact 'three faces of postmodernism': the aesthetic, the social-theoretic and philosophical, and the private and intersubjective. Against this more differentiated backdrop, they critically examine recent psychoanalytic critiques of postmodern theorizing, from which the argument is developed that the postmodern turn in contemporary psychoanalysis has generally been poorly conceptualized. Elliott and Spezzano, by contrast, suggest the fruitfulness and vitality of postmodern theorizing for psychoanalysis. To do this, they develop a number of key hypotheses about the nature of human subjectivity, psychic fragmentation and dislocation, the realms of representation and signification, and the like. Throughout the chapter Elliott and Spezzano put psychoanalysis and postmodernism into a reflective encounter.

In Chapter 2, 'Final Analysis: Can Psychoanalysis Survive in the Postmodern West?', Jane Flax also takes up these issues, but in a somewhat different theoretical context. Drawing from the work of the French social theorist Michel Foucault, Flax argues that psychoanalysis is best understood as a complex, contradictory 'discursive formation' in which knowledge and power are produced and reproduced, generating autonomy and resistance in equal measure. Flax argues that when psychoanalysis is seen in this light the claims of postmodernists, and postmodern feminists in particular, become particularly disturbing for the psychoanalytic profession/discipline. She contends that postmodernism radically challenges the epistemological underpinnings of psychoanalytic truth claims.

The issue of convergences and divergences is also taken up in Stephen Frosh's chapter, 'Postmodernism and the Adoption of Identity' (Chapter 3). Tracing psychoanalytic accounts of psychic flux, Frosh reworks the postmodernist thesis that identities refer to the outside (the socio-symbolic network) rather than the inside (psychic interiority, self or ego). In Lacanian terms, Frosh notes that the subject's fantasized perception of others is precisely this underscoring that identity comes from without, the locus of the field of the Other. Through a consideration of the work of the European psychoanalyst Cornelius Castoriadis, however, Frosh argues that psychic flux (as an ever-erupting core of unconscious representations) requires the 'prop' of external reference points ('the institution' or 'society') in order to seek out a name, an identity. This is why identity can never be self-identical: because there is always some leftover, namely the unconscious, which dislocates the realm of consciously perceived selfhood. In the latter part of the chapter, Frosh pursues these themes further through consideration of the ways in which the roller-coaster ride of postmodern hyperspace intensifies the search for the adoption of identity and its attendant discarding.

In Chapter 4, 'The Shadow of the Other Subject', Jessica Benjamin argues that our psychic condition is defined by our dialectically oscillating perception/experience/use of the other as object and as subject. Her version of postmodern intersubjectivity critiques the tendency to dichotomize mind as defined by relationship versus relationship as defined by mind, or the primacy of recognizing the other versus being recognized by the other. Instead narcissism and difference, perhaps the cutting-edge problems in contemporary discussions of mind and clinical process, are treated by her as partners in a dance where each leads and each follows.

The issue of how psychoanalysis engages with theories of modernity and postmodernity is directly taken up by Anthony Elliott in Chapter 5, 'The Ambivalence of Identity'. Tracing connections between the global transformation of social practices on the one hand and changes at the level of self-identity on the other, Elliott explores modernity and postmodernity as contrasting object-relational configurations. He argues that the object-relational configuration of modernity supports a mode of fantasy in which security and enjoyment are derived by attempting to control, order and regulate self, others and the social world. The object-relational configuration of postmodernity, by contrast, supports a mode of fantasy in which reflective space is more central to psychical life, the creation of 'open spaces' to embrace plurality, ambiguity, ambivalence, contingency and uncertainty. Viewing modern and postmodern object-relational configurations as tangled and interlocked, Elliott concludes that postmodernity opens new paths for psychoanalysis to respond to, and cope with, psychic turbulence and dislocation.

In Chapter 6, 'Lacanian Psychoanalysis and Postmodernism', Mark Bracher places Lacan's work in the broader context of theoretical debates about semiotics, poststructuralism and postmodernism. Bracher argues that the tendency in mainstream psychoanalysis is to view Lacan as either an exemplar or an opponent of postmodernism. But this is too reductive. According to Bracher, Lacan's 'return to Freud' incorporates both Enlightenment and postmodernist assumptions about human subjectivity, and in so doing raises various ontological and epistemological challenges. Developing a succinct exegesis of the Lacanian psychoanalytic model of subjectivity, Bracher examines the centrality of the imaginary and symbolic processing of experience in the wider frame of postmodern systems of technology, visual-spatial environments and virtual spaces.

Many theorists have argued that postmodernism has dealt a devastating blow to modernist forms of knowledge, such as psychoanalysis. As a consequence, it is further argued that the imaginative vision which underpins psychoanalysis cannot remain within the normalizing constraints of classical theory. To speak of the imagination in relation to psychoanalysis in the postmodern epoch requires greater attention to ambiguity and ambivalence than most theorists have been willing to permit. In Chapter 7, 'From Ghosts to Ancestors', Stephen Mitchell finds a prefiguring of today's radical postmodern imagination in the psychoanalytic writings of Hans Loewald. Loewald's psychoanalytic formulations engage contemporary concerns, says Mitchell, since they press beyond the binary dualisms of classical psychoanalysis. A key example is language. Whereas classical theory draws sharp distinctions between the preverbal and verbal realms, primary and secondary mental processes, Loewald sees language as deriving from an original 'primordial density' in which self, others, perceptions and affects are intricately interwoven. On this view, language separates out between sound (as a global, dense undifferentiated experience) on the one hand, and signification (when the semantic aspects of language take precedence over its affective features) on the other. At work in this approach to language, with its stress on plurality and density, is the influence of Loewald's mentor, Martin Heidegger – a significant figure in the emergence of post-metaphysical thinking and postmodern social theory and philosophy.

In Chapter 8, Thomas Ogden frames 'the psychoanalytic subject' in the light of dialectical processes – at once conscious and unconscious – through which signification is created, sustained and decentred. Beginning with Freud's theory of the subject, Ogden analyses the evolution of ideas concerning the dialectical constitution and reproduction of being and signification in post-Freudian psychoanalysis. The key theorists he identifies in this connection are Klein, Winnicott, Bion and Lacan. Drawing upon and refashioning these psychoanalytical approaches, Ogden argues that the self is simultaneously centred and decentred, an occupant of multiple and dialectically related psychic positions rather than the final step in a series of developmental stages. So, too, the analytic process is a dialectically creative process in which three subjectivities (that of the analyst, that of the patient, and a 'third' created by them and through which they are also created) give form to the experience of the analysand.

Karen Peoples explores in Chapter 9, 'Why the Self Is, and Is Not, Empty', recent thinking about selfhood and subjectivity from a psychoanalytic frame. She argues that both psychoanalysis and constructivist-driven versions of postmodernism have failed to grasp the creative-adaptative functions of psychic emptiness. Psychoanalysis has tended to treat the state of emotions as the pathological outcome of early environmental failures or as useless and dreadful holes left where evacuated parts of the self might have been. Social constructivist thinking, with its phobic avoidance of the notion of intrinsic universals, imagines that the sense of emptiness results from an empty culture insinuating itself on the mind and then defensively colluding with the emptiness-ridden psyche that is has produced to conceal and fortify the social practices from which the emptiness originated. Instead, Peoples suggests, the sense of emptiness often reflects a universal, creative-adaptive capacity for opening up psychic space within which generative mental activity can be initiated.

In the concluding chapter, 'The Struggle to Imagine', Charles Spezzano puts forward the notion that psychoanalysis has always been the pursuit of affective truth, a type of truth that overlaps scientific and hermeneutic truth but is also distinct. We discover this truth through unconscious affective communication and projective identification (as understood by Bion) and through imaginative understanding (as described by Winnicott). In this intersubjective-affective psychology, the holding, communicating, containing, thinking about, and interpretation of affect define the psychoanalytic situation and process.

References

Anzieu, D. (1986), *Freud's Self-Analysis*, London: Hogarth Press.

Bauman, Z. (1990), *Modernity and Ambivalence*, Cambridge: Polity Press.

Elliott, A. (1995), 'Psychoanalysis and the seductions of postmodernity: reflections on reflexive thinking and scanning in self-identity', *Psychoanalysis and Contemporary Thought* 18 (3): 319–61.

— (1996), *Subject to Ourselves: Social theory, Psychoanalysis and Postmodernity*, Cambridge: Polity Press and Cambridge, MA: Blackwell.

Freud, S. (1924), 'Neurosis and Psychosis', *SE* XIX: 147–53.

Habermas, J. (1972), *Knowledge and Human Interests*, London: Heinemann.

Kristeva, J. (1994), 'Psychoanalysis in times of distress', in S. Shamdasani and M. Munchow (eds), *Speculations after Freud: Psychoanalysis, Philosophy and Culture*, London: Routledge.

Lacan, J. (1966), *Écrits*, Paris: Editions du Seuil.
— (1977), *Écrits: A Selection*, New York: Norton.
Lorenzer, (1976), *Symbol und Verstehen in Psychoanalytischen Prozess*, Frankfurt: Suhrkamp Verlag.
Lyotard, J.-F. (1988), *Reecrire la Modernite*, Paris: Lille.
Ogden, T. (1994), *Subjects of Analysis*, Northvale, NJ: Aronson.
Smith, G.B., (1996), *Nietzsche, Heidegger, and the Transition to Postmodernity*, Chicago: University of Chicago Press.
Spezzano, C. (1996), 'The three faces of two-person psychology: development, ontology, and epistemology', *Psychoanalytic Dialogues* 6: 599–622.
Steiner, J. (1996), 'The aims of psychoanalysis in theory and practice', *International Journal of Psycho-Analysis* 77: 1073–84.

1 Psychoanalysis at its Limits: Navigating the Postmodern Turn

Anthony Elliott and Charles Spezzano

In a 1929 essay, T.S. Eliot wrote about Dante that 'he not only thought in a way in which every man of his culture in the whole of Europe then thought, but he employed a method which was common and commonly understood throughout Europe' (cited in Trachtenberg, 1979: 1). Dante may have been the last writer to enjoy this guaranteed rapport with his audience. Certainly no psychoanalytic author can expect anything like it. Quite the contrary, it is guaranteed that all psychoanalysts writing for their 'colleagues' today will encounter, among at least some readers, disbelief at their failure to grasp basic principles, headshaking over their hubris in imagining that what they have written contains new ideas, or disinterest from readers not of their 'school' because they talk 'another language' that is too 'old fashioned' or 'not really psychoanalysis'.

Further, in the theorizing and clinical reports contained in contemporary analytic journals one does not only find authors whose work is intended to advance (or fits neatly into) a project called ego analysis, self psychology, object relational theory, or Kleinian analysis. One also finds authors whose work seems harder to pigeonhole; but, as philosopher Iris Murdoch (1993: 1–2) has suggested: 'We fear plurality, diffusion, senseless accident, chaos, we want to transform what we cannot dominate or understand into something reassuring and familiar, into ordinary being, into history, art, religion, science.' We want to say: 'That is classical analysis, self psychology, relational psychoanalysis. The author is an element of one of our reassuring unities.'

As the individual voices in psychoanalysis proliferate, we need more unifying labels to maintain order and ward off chaos. 'Postmodernism' is the most recent. As with other labels, it relies for its appearance of usefulness and validity on the availability of a contrary perspective: 'modernism'. In this case, for the first time in the history of psychoanalysis, the duelling labels have been imported from other disciplines. This has tended to increase the confusion about their usage beyond the level that has beset the use of other psychoanalytic dichotomies. The aim of our chapter is not so ambitious as to clear up this confusion, but rather simply to describe it. We will argue, in fact, that it might be a good idea to allow it to remain confusing.

Modernism and Postmodernism: The Alleged Dichotomy

The 'thing' against which postmodernism is most often described as setting itself – the thing called modernism – was midwifed into existence by Kant's angry reaction to the blindness of metaphysics and the emptiness of empiricism. Although he championed it with some qualifications, what Kant offered in place of these pretenders was that most precious child of the Enlightenment: reason. Through reason (and only through reason) 'could the universal, eternal, and the immutable qualities of all humanity be revealed' (Harvey, 1990: 12). As such knowledge accumulated, 'rational modes of thought promised liberation from the irrationalities of myth, religion, superstition', and, especially, 'release from the arbitrary use of power as well as from the dark side of our own human natures' (*ibid.*).

As might be expected, once such a monolithic entity as modernism has been constituted, it becomes convenient and compelling to write as if everything that is not it is one other thing, in this case postmodernism. If modernism has been a quest for truth and reality and if its modus operandi has been positivism or objectivism, then everything that is not positivistic and objectivist is assumed to be thoroughly antagonistic to truth and reality. If, however, modernism itself was a cubist painting – with ambiguously related surfaces of reason, truth, certainty, objectivity, and positivism made to look like a unified whole – then a contemporary theorist who takes issue with one of these points might not take issue with all of them. This, it turns out, might well be the messy truth of postmodern thinking in psychoanalysis and other disciplines. Consider the following epistemologies.

British philosopher Roger Scruton (1994) argues that Kant's take on human beings knowing the world is not the final word, but it is the best one. We cannot look at the world from outside our concepts and know the world as it is. We cannot see it from no particular point of view, as God might. In fact, we could not even begin to think about the world if we did not believe that we were viewing it through concepts of objectivity and that our judgements of it would represent reality.

German critical theorist Jurgen Habermas argues that all human beings possess the same faculty of reason. We experience the results of reason's successful application when we find ourselves with dialogical consensus or in co-ordinated action with others. 'The intersubjectivity of the validity of communication rules is confirmed in the reciprocity of actions and expectations. Whether this reciprocity occurs or fails to occur can be discovered only by the parties involved; but they make this discovery intersubjectively' (1970: 141).

In his highly readable introduction to postmodernism, John McGowan (1991: ix) uses the term 'to designate a specific form of cultural critique that has become increasingly conspicuous in the academy since about 1975'. He understands postmodernism as referring to an antifoundationalist critique, but adds to this a positive dimension: a search for freedom and pluralism that accepts the necessity, if not the virtue, of norms to which people, institutions and practices are responsive.

American philosopher Simon Blackburn (1993: 4) takes what he calls a 'quasi-realist' position: 'that truth is the aim of judgment; that our disciplines make us better able to appreciate it, that it is, however, independent of us, and that we are fallible in our grasp of it'.

Jacques Derrida suggests that we read all texts deconstructively. We must 'work through the structured genealogy of its concepts in the most scrupulous and immanent fashion, but at the same time to determine from a certain external perspective that it cannot name or describe what this history may have concealed or excluded' (1981: 6). We might paraphrase Norris (1987), in his excellent account of Derrida's philosophical project, and say that the effect of Derrida's philosophy is to render 'intensely problematic' much of what passes for 'rigorous thought in psychoanalysis' (as well as in philosophy and literary theory). 'But this effect is not achieved by dispensing with the protocols of detailed, meticulous argument, or by simply abandoning the conceptual ground on which such arguments have hitherto been conducted' (Norris, 1987: 20).

Barnaby Barratt (1993), in his book *Psychoanalysis and the Postmodern Impulse*, offers a vision of psychoanalysis as a process of free-associative deconstruction – 'deconstructive and negatively dialectical in a subversively postmodern sense' rather than 'insight establishing and reflective in the modern philosophical sense' (Barratt, 1993: xiv).

Italian philosopher Gianni Vattimo (1980: 43), during a discussion of Nietzsche's reduction of truth to morality, takes the following position: 'Whenever a proposition seems evident, there operates a series of historical premises and predispositions towards acceptance or rejection on the part of the subject, and these predispositions are guided by an overriding interest in the preservation and development not simply of "life" as such, but of a particular form of life.'

Neopragmatist philosopher Richard Rorty (1982: 92) argues that there 'are two ways of thinking about various things'. We can think of truth 'as a vertical relationship between representations and what is represented'. We can also think of truth 'horizontally – as the culminating reinterpretation of our predecessors' reinterpretation'. He adds: 'It is the difference between regarding truth, goodness, and beauty as eternal objects which we try to locate and reveal, and regarding them as artifacts whose fundamental design we often have to alter' (*ibid.*).

In *The Postmodern Condition: A Report on Knowledge* Jean-François Lyotard (1984: xxv) writes: 'I define postmodern as incredulity toward metanarratives.' For Lyotard, the postmodern world is made up of Wittgensteinian language games and 'the social subject itself seems to dissolve in this dissemination of language games' (*ibid.*). Even science needs to have rules that prescribe what moves are admissible into its language game. These prescriptions are the same sorts of presuppositions that form the foundation of any language game.

Where would one draw a line, on this roughly arranged continuum of perspectives, to separate modern from postmodern given the blend of continuities and breaks that simultaneously link and separate each one from its neighbours? 'Modernism' and 'postmodernism' are not homogeneous or unambiguous facts, but only partially successful attempts to locate and define intellectual centres of gravity. Psychoanalysts looking to this epistemological debate, in their effort to assess their attitudes toward their own interpretations, must tolerate greater heterogeneity than they might have hoped to find.

Three Faces of Postmodernism

The modernity/postmodernity debate can be seen to fall into three realms, each of which must be fully considered when tracing the impact of postmodernity upon psychoanalytic theory and practice. First, there is the aesthetic debate over modernism and postmodernism, which concerns above all the nature of representation in the contemporary epoch. Postmodernism, in this particular sense, concerns a particular set of aesthetic or cultural values which were first given expression in the domains of architecture, the plastic and visual arts, poetry and literature. In contrast to the high modernist ambitions of uncovering an inner truth behind surface appearances, postmodernism exhibits a new playfulness, a mixing of previous aesthetic distinctions of content and form, high and low culture, the personal and public realms. The modernist attempt to discover a 'deeper' reality is abandoned in the postmodern in favour of the celebration of style and surface. The preoccupation of modernism with principles of meaning and rationality is replaced with a tolerance for diversity and difference, the characteristics of which are reflected in a postmodern criticism which values irony, cynicism, pastiche, commercialism, and, in some cases, relativism (see Jameson, 1991). To portray the complexity of aesthetic surfaces and signs in the postmodern, Deleuze and Guattari (1977) invoke the metaphor of 'rhizome': a peculiar rootstock that is multidirectional, chaotic, and random in its expansion. In this new aesthetic experience, postmodernism is a self-constituting world, determined by its own internal movement and process.

The second area of debate has focused on the philosophical and cultural concepts of modernity and postmodernity. Here it has been argued that a postmodern approach is necessary to avoid the realist assumptions of the Cartesian–Kantian–Hegelian tradition. Perhaps no other text has marked the intellectual terms of reference here as much as Lyotard's (1984) short treatise *The Postmodern Condition: A Report on Knowledge*. Postmodernism, writes Lyotard, 'designates the state of our culture following the transformations which, since the end of the nineteenth century, have altered the game rules for science, literature and the arts' (1984: xxv). The 'game rules' to which Lyotard refers involve a letting go of the grand narratives of traditional philosophy and science and an acceptance of the 'heteromorphous nature of language games'. Reason comes in many varieties. Two groups applying it effectively and adaptively to the same situation might well end up inventing, and living in, different Wittgensteinian language games without common ground rules. Here, the emphasis is away from forms of thought that promote uniformity and universality, and toward an appreciation of particularity, especially as regards the holding in mind of ambiguity and difference. Lyotard's position on postmodernism has been described as extreme insofar as it presents a radical separation of the nature of language games from their sociocultural context, and, as such, is said to threaten a complete fragmentation of subjectivity (see Norris

(1993) and Eagleton (1990) for critical appraisals of Lyotard's more recent work).

Under postmodern theories of knowledge, there has been a profound questioning of foundationalism. Derrida (1978) argues that Western metaphysics is haunted by impossible dreams of certitude and transparency. Derrida, and the deconstructionism that his work has promoted, draws attention to the binary oppositions of textual practices and rhetorical strategies, using a poststructuralist conception of language as a differential play of signifiers to uncouple language from the world it seeks to colonize through acts of description. There will be in everything a writer writes or a patient says a contradiction that the author of the statement cannot acknowledge. As Stanley Fish (1989: 215) sums up the goals of a Derridean deconstructive reading, it will 'surface those contradictions and expose those suppressions'. As a result, such a reading will expose those ideas or feelings which have been suppressed (repressed or dissociated, we might add). These exposures 'trouble' the apparent unity of the text. We say that this unity has been defensively constructed. Deconstructivists say that such a unity was achieved in the first place 'only by covering over all the excluded emphases and interests that might threaten it'. According to Fish, Derridean deconstruction does not uncover these contradictions and dialectic hiding operations of rhetoric in order to reach 'the Truth; rather it continually uncovers the truth of rhetorical operations, the truth that all operations, including the operation of deconstruction itself, are rhetorical' (1989: 215). From this standpoint, there is no philosophical or ideological position that is able to claim *ultimate* authority or justification. On the contrary, the justification of knowledge, as the postmodern pragmatist Richard Rorty has argued, is always a matter of argumentation from different positions and perspectives, such that our beliefs about the world are necessarily local, provisional, and contingent.

The third area of debate is concerned more explicitly with the personal, social, and cultural aspects of postmodern society. Here the issue concerns the way in which postmodernity affects the world of human selves and of interpersonal relationships. And it is at the level of our personal and cultural worlds, we suggest, that postmodernism most forcefully breaks its links with the ontological premises of modernity. By this we mean to focus attention on contemporary culture and its technologies, and in particular the ways in which globalization and instantaneous communication are transforming self-identity and interpersonal relationships. Globalization, transnational communication systems, new information technologies, the industrialization of war, universal consumerism: these are the core institutional dimensions of contemporary societies, and most students of contemporary culture agree that such transformations carry immense implications as regards selfhood, self-identity, and subjectivity (Frosh, 1991; Giddens, 1991; Thompson, 1990). The transformation of personal experience that postmodernity ushers into existence concerns, among other things, a compression of space and mutation of time, rapid and at times cataclysmic forms of change, an exponential increase in the dynamism of social and economic life, as well as a growing sense of fragmentation and dislocation. Such transformations, to repeat, are not only social in character; on the contrary, they penetrate to the core of psychic experience and restructure unconscious transactions between human subjects in new, and often dramatic, ways (see Elliott, 1996).

It is from this flux and turmoil of contemporary social life that many commentators have branded postmodernity as antihistorical, relativist and disordered. Postmodernism, in this reading, represents the dislocation of meaning and logic, whether of society or of the mind. It is possible to hold a more optimistic view of this apparent cultural disorientation, however, once the irreducibility of the plurality of human worlds is accepted. The social theorist Zygmunt Bauman (1990, 1991, 1992, 1993), for example, argues that postmodernity represents a new dawning, rather than a twilight, for the generation of meaning. 'Postmodernity', Bauman (1991: 35) writes, 'is marked by a view of the human world as irreducibly and irrevocably pluralistic, split into a multitude of sovereign units and sites of authority, with no horizontal or vertical order, either in actuality or in potency.' This emphasis on plurality and multiplicity highlights that postmodernity involves a rejection of the typically modernist search for foundations, absolutes and universals. Postmodernity is a self-constituting and self-propelling culture, a culture which is increasingly self-referential in direction. From cable TV to the information superhighway: postmodern culture is a culture turned back upon itself, generated in and through reflexive systems of technological knowledge.

The strength of Bauman's interpretation is that it demonstrates that modernity and postmodernity are not dichotomous. Culturally, we have not transcended modernity, nor have we entered a postmodern society writ large. Instead, it can be said that contemporary Western societies deploy modern and postmodern cultural forms simultaneously. Postmodernity is better understood as 'modernity without illusions'. It is a form of life, or perhaps state of mind, in which the messiness of life is directly embraced and dealt with as challenge. Pluralism, contingency, ambiguity, ambivalence, uncertainty: these features of social life were assigned a negative value – they were seen as pathologies to be eradicated – in the modern era.

For Bauman, however, these are not distortions to be overcome, but are the distinctive features of a mode of social experience which has broken with the disabling hold of objectivity, necessity, law.

Thus, the picture that we are presenting is that modernity and postmodernity are not homogeneous or unambiguous facts; nor are they dichotomous entities. Rather, as modes of contemporary experience, modernity and postmodernity locate and define cognitive-affective centres of gravity for individuals seeking to come to terms with the difficulties of day-to-day life. As a result, psychoanalysts looking to this epistemological debate, in their effort to assess their attitudes toward their own interpretations, must tolerate greater heterogeneity than they might have hoped to find.

In the following section of this chapter, we will consider two typically reductive critiques of the postmodern turn in psychoanalysis, reductive in that postmodernism is reduced to a single meaning, and thus the complexity of postmodernity is screened from view. We will argue, in contrast to much recent thinking on the subject, that there are indeed alliances between certain thinkers known in their own fields as postmodern and some contemporary psychoanalysts. We will also argue that, contrary to dominant assumptions concerning the inescapability of fragmentation, all but the most extreme forms of postmodernity permit an 'opening out' to reflective psychical activity, a space for the thinking or processing of uncertainty, ambivalence, otherness and difference. Similarly, although some postmodern thinking is relativistic, it is perspectivism and not relativism that is essential to postmodernism. Acknowledging the viability and plausibility of multiple perspectives does not consign one to accepting that any interpretation is as good as any other.

James Glass's Critique of Postmodern Theorizing

In *Shattered Selves: Multiple Personality in a Postmodern World*, James Glass (1993) accepts that many of the objectivist ambitions of modernity should be renounced. He supports the postmodern critique of all-inclusive and dominating metanarratives, and he underscores the importance of recent French psychoanalytic feminist critiques of the phallocentric values and assumptions of modernity in promoting personal and political change in the contemporary epoch.

Glass, however, also sees a costly price tag on this postmodern agenda. If the identity of the self, as some postmodernists assert, following the French psychoanalyst Jacques Lacan, is imaginary – a kind of papering over of the indeterminacy of desire itself – then the human subject is fully desubjectivized. That brand of postmodernism isolates the self and argues that there is nothing hidden or split off in psychological experience, nothing inaccessible to ideological explanation. We share that concern about Lacanian and similar brands of postmodernism, but since Glass assumes that postmodernism is homogeneous, he believes that all postmodernists carry this subject-destroying virus:

> In their insistence on freeing the self from any historical or structural conception of what the self is, the postmodernists reject, in coming to an understanding of what identity 'is,' the influence of infancy, the psychoanalytic notion of the preoedipal, the Freudian conception of the unconscious (drive theory), and the idea that actions of the self may be represented in severe forms of internal psychological conflict whose origins lie in primitive emotional symbolization. (1993: 5)

Postmodernist theories, in this reading, are not only attempting to destabilize modernist conceptions of subjectivity, meaning, and truth, they are out to do away with the basic tensions or contradictions of self and world altogether. As a result they must all end up criticizing and rejecting everything modern in Freudian psychoanalysis: 'multiplicity of self' will lead to the psycho-logical repudiation of difference and of language; the fragmentation idealized in the postmodernity discourse is really multiple personality disorder and schizophrenia; flux threatens the self, subjectivity and identity.

Finally, we are presented with a list of postmodern theorists, a list which includes Derrida, Lyotard, Baudrillard, Cixous, Irigaray and others (all quite different) who are all said to be indifferent to the harm or injury of psychological fragmentation as well as ignorant of the post-Freudian stress on relationality and intersubjectivity. (That some of these theorists have produced some of the most important critiques of psychoanalysis in France since the Second World War is something that seems to have escaped Glass's attention; as well as the point that some of them are practicing analysts.)

Kimberlyn Leary's Critique of Postmodern Theorizing

For most clinicians questions about selves, subjects and truth become important insofar as they suggest options to be considered and decisions to be made in the analytic situation. Kimberlyn Leary, in her essay 'Psychoanalytic "Problems" and Postmodern "Solutions"' (1994), argued that 'postmodern solutions' suggest illusory answers to real clinical problems. She used the writings of Hoffman and Schafer as examples of postmodernism.

The 'implication that follows' from postmodern writings, Leary argues, 'is that we can, at will, assume a self that suits us if the proper audience can be assembled' (1994: 454). This is a hyperbolic rendering of the postmodern argument that, given a different social context, we might imagine people coming to have other senses of what it means to be a self than the sense they now have in our culture. This is especially the case, in that the postmodern deconstruction of subjectivity is precisely an attempt to criticize and rethink modernist notions of the will, intention, agency, and the like. Leary, however, argues that there is no difference between imagining that one might be whomever one wants to be if only the right audience could be assembled (or that one is only stuck being who one is because one has always had the wrong audience) and being diagnosable as borderline or narcissistic.

Before considering whether Schafer or Hoffman might be construed, from anything either has written, to have ever embraced a 'choose your own self' position, we want to note that, as many readers might have noticed, Leary's marriage of Hoffman and Schafer is itself problematic. She recognizes that there are significant differences between the various positions they take in their writings, and she details some of these. Yet, she cannot resist the temptation to conclude, after all, that, despite these differences, their theoretical projects are variations on the postmodern theme of relativism about truth and fragmentation of the self.

This lumping together of Hoffman and Schafer under the postmodern label glosses over the unique features of their quite different theories that are crucial if one wants to use them as examples of postmodern theorizing in psychoanalysis (and it also buries the modernist features of both men's work). Hoffman sees analysts' participation as a function of their subjectivity (countertransference, in the broadest sense). They will neither be aware nor want to be aware of every aspect of this unconscious subjectivity. Thus, they ought to remain (or realize that they are) more uncertain of what they mean and what they are doing than many analysts – of all the major schools – have been. If a patient claims to know or suspect something about the analyst's personality or experience, then the analyst does not necessarily affirm or deny, but shows interest in the patient's observations and wonders what conclusions the patient might draw from them.

Schafer, by contrast, emphasizes that the way in which the analyst understands and interprets is always partly a manifestation of the analyst's theory. He says little or nothing about the analyst's unconscious psychology. For example, Schafer (1992: 52) writes of a teacher, S.M., who 'derives pleasure from regularly treating his students cruelly'. In Freud's psychosexual language, the patient is sadistic. 'He, however, thinks that he treats his students fairly, dispassionately, professionally.' As Schafer points out, we, as analysts, along with many other observers, might conclude that he is deceiving himself. 'The attribution of self-deception is, however,' Schafer argues – and here is where he becomes postmodern – 'based on a number of unstated assumptions, interpretations, and evidential claims.'

> Far from this deception being an unmediated perception by an 'objective' observer of what S.M. is 'really' doing, it is a rather elaborate construction. (1992: 52)

> ... it is the storylines that establish the facts of the case, which of these facts are to be taken as significant (for example, as evidence of sadism), and how these facts are to be situated ... The case of S.M. could be told differently; it often is. (1992: 55)

Yet, as if in anticipation of critiques like Leary's, Schafer adds: 'I am not proposing that any account is as acceptable as any other.' What he does propose, in a hermeneutically postmodern argument, is that 'when we speak of true and false accounts of actions, we are positioning ourselves in a matrix of narratives that are always open to examination as to their precritical assumptions and values and as to their usefulness in one or another project' (1992: 56).

Where Schafer is interested in how the analyst's theory reshapes the patient's account of her or his history (which account is itself already one of many possible narratives), Hoffman talks about how the analyst chooses to shape the evolving relationship with the patient by doing or not doing, saying or not saying certain things at specific junctures. The analyst can no longer be certain that unwavering adherence to a specific technical stance (whether empathy or resistance analysis) simply serves to bring forth a clear picture of what has been inside the patient's psyche or guarantees the most effective route to what has been called structural change. Further, such unwavering adherence does not mean that the analyst is not deciding over and over to shape the analytic relationship in a specific way.

As an example of a specific decision he made in his own work, Hoffman (1994) reports that when he called an angry patient's internist during a session in response to the patient's demand that he do something immediately to help her get Valium, the

> enactment helped me and the patient to begin to see how much she wanted me to be frantic about her in a way similar to how she thought her mother was frantic about [a sister], the difference being that my 'getting hysterical' was also an object of curiosity and

> critical reflection. Thus there was reason to believe that the quality of my attention, taken as a whole, was better than what either the patient or [the sister] got from their mother. (1994: 212–13)

What Hoffman emphasizes here is his awareness that his choices are rooted in his subjectivity, which includes countertransference even when it is theoretically informed. The choice therefore invites critical reflection as to its meaning in the relationship. The countertransference is not condemned since the entire transference–countertransference enactment is an object of critical reflection.

Neither Schafer nor Hoffman has been implying that analysands have no enduring unconscious psychology, nor that people are an endless flow of abruptly appearing selves unrelated to each other in time and space. What each, in quite different ways, has argued at times is that his clinical observations have led him to think that one enduring feature of human unconscious psychology is a greater sense of discontinuity and contingency than was recognized by previous theories.

By the time Leary was ready to move from Hoffman and Schafer to the realms of body and gender, she was in high positivist and objectivist gears. Postmodernists, she says, forget that people have bodies and that these bodies come in male and female versions – an especially intriguing criticism, given that the contemporary focus on the body and its pleasures by the social sciences and the humanities is generally understood to derive from postmodernism (see Butler, 1993). Having forgotten this, they probably talk to their female patients as if these patients are free to forget those realities as well. Further, she suggests, postmodernists probably tell patients that death is just another version of life, just as they must believe that Terry Anderson could have made anything he wanted out of his captivity once he got past putting too much stock in treating as real such facts as his captors' controlling when he could use the toilet (Leary, 1994: 458).

Hoffman, after briefly considering it, Leary tells us, gives up on the idea of an external reality. He does not. He simply argues that the variations of what we claim is out there are not constructed privately by each mind but by minds in interaction. Similarly, Hoffman's emphasis does not argue that every account of the analysand must be treated by the analyst as credible and tenable. He suggests a shift in technique in which the analyst is much more likely, than was once (in the history of psychoanalysis) the case, to treat as plausible that the patient did in fact evoke and then find some element of the analyst's experience (including unconscious experience) or behaviour on which to hang the enduring representation of a ragefully attacking other. Further, Hoffman nowhere says that he automatically agrees with his patients that everything they say about him is true. He portrays himself as doing exactly what Leary suggests analysts should do: he appreciates the patient's view of the analyst by more often treating it as plausible than theories of transference-as-distortion had encouraged us to do. He argues, however, that such appreciation has been crude when embedded by analysts in clear statements that while they appreciate the patient's infantile view of them, there is simply not a shred of current truth in it.

If an analyst was persuaded by Hoffman's writings and if that analyst gradually internalized a constructivist attitude, we might expect a shift to more often and more automatically considering the possibility that a patient's statement about the analyst's experience (including the analyst's unconscious experience) has captured something true not only about the analyst but also about the patient's ability to evoke experience in others and the patient's selective attention to certain aspects of the experience of others. Similarly, such an analyst might also feel more free to judge (out loud) the patient's assessments of the analyst's experience with the proviso that the analyst understands such judgements as arising out of subjective experience and as having the potential to contribute in part to the enactment of transference–countertransference patterns. What makes the difference in Hoffman's view is that the analyst appreciates that his or her judgement is born out of his or her full subjective participation in the process.

What is unfortunate about articles such as those by sceptics of 'postmodern psychoanalysis' like Glass and Leary is that they raise important issues about the psychical and social implications of postmodernism in such a divisive and dismissive way. Their respective critiques of the 'inescapable fragmentation' which postmodernity promotes does specify quite well a dilemma which psychoanalysts face today: the contemporary world is marked by constant turmoil and dislocation, yet to embrace the insights of postmodernism risks a further escalation of fragmentation itself – of knowledge, expertise and meaning.

In our view, such an understanding of postmodernism is misplaced (even if the anxiety registered is expressive of a fear of 'not-knowing'). In fact, the critiques made by Glass and Leary are critiques that many postmodernists would make against the extreme forms of postmodernism that Glass and Leary set up for criticism. Leary, especially, having set things up this way, then simply claims that any nonpositivist, nonobjectivist theorist of the analytic process must, prima facie, be one of those extreme postmodernists; since she can see only those two places for a theorist to stand. Because, as we have said from the start, those points of view labelled as postmodern are heterogeneous; postmodernity permits other conceptual options than those imagined by Glass and Leary.

In the next two sections of this chapter we want to go beyond the specific arguments of Glass or Leary and take up two general categories of critique written against attempts to use postmodern discourse to reshape psychoanalytic theory: that it forces on us an untenable notion of the self as inescapably fragmented, and that it leaves us with no hope or even ambition of finding the truth about anything. In each case we hope to show that these criticisms should not frighten away or deter interested analysts from pursuing the possibility that a study of postmodern ideas will enhance their clinical effectiveness. In considering each of these criticisms, we offer distinctions between what is and what is not being said about selfhood and subjectivity in the postmodernity discourse. In brief, postmodern thought does not force upon us the notion that the self is incoherently fragmented (rather, it is decentred); and, postmodern thought does not leave us lost in the belief that any interpretation is as good as any other (rather, all views are interpretive and perspectival).

The Critique of 'Inescapable Fragmentation'

Postmodern conceptions of plural selves and worlds are informed, in broad terms, by the poststructuralist notion of the decentring of the subject. This is a decentring initiated by Freud himself, who suggested in the strongest theoretical terms that the ego is not master in its own house, and this is an insight that has been fruitfully extended by Lacan to include a focus on the creative and coercive effects of language.

The central point to note at this stage is that this decentring should not be equated with a disintegration of the human subject. The criticism that the postmodernist decentring of selves amounts to a wiping out of subjectivity is perhaps better seen as a defensive reaction to the dislocation of modernist fantasies of self-control and mastery. The postmodernist stress on ambiguity, ambivalence, difference, plurality and fragmentation, on the contrary, underlines the psychical capacities and resources that are needed to register such forms of subjectivity, or, psychoanalytically speaking, to attach meaning to experience in open-ended ways.

Seen in this light, postmodern conceptions of multiple selves actually situate the subject in a context of heightened self-reflexivity, a reflectiveness that is used for exploring personal experience and fantasy. This intertwining of experience, fantasy and reflexivity is conceptualized in terms of the capacity to think about – that is, to symbolize and to process – unconscious communications in the interpersonal world, of projective and introjective identifications, splitting, denial and the like. Broadly speaking, what is being stressed here is the prising open of a space between fantasy and words (the chain of significations) in which meaning is constituted, such that the subject can reflect upon this self-constitution and creatively alter it.

In some circumstances, of course, self-reflexivity is debilitating rather than emancipatory. An openness to multiple worlds of fantasy can produce extreme pain and anxiety, as well as a dislocation of the capacity of the mind to register thinking itself (Bion, 1962; Ogden, 1989). In general terms though, and in a diversity of contexts, it produces the contrary: an 'opening out' to the multiplicity of fantasy and imagination at the intersection of self and world. This is conceptualized, as we will examine later in this chapter, in differing ways by postmodern analysts. Cornelius Castoriadis speaks of a self-understanding of 'radical imagination', Julia Kristeva of 'semiotic subversion', and Christopher Bollas of our 'personal idiom'. This focus highlights a reflexive awareness of imagination, and of the key role of ambivalence, difference and otherness in human relations.

Criticisms of the Postmodern Collapse of Signification

What about 'reality' and 'truth'? Some critics of postmodernism have reached the erroneous conclusion that so-called hermeneutic, relational, deconstructionist, intersubjective or constructivist perspectives imply that the conditions of interpretation are such that no true or correct interpretations are possible – a position that some philosophers (Bohman, 1991) label 'interpretive skepticism' (136) or 'strong holism' (130). These terms refer to the arguments by certain postmodern thinkers that all cognitive activity is interpretive and so warrants deep scepticism and that it is holistic in the sense of always taking place against the background of all our beliefs and practices. 'Together these two theses imply that no interpretation can be singled out as uniquely correct, since the assertion that it is so would itself be an interpretation within a particular context' (Bohman, 1991: 130) – the so-called hermeneutic circle.

A number of philosophers and literary critics have strongly identified with this epistemological claim while others have partially or moderately embraced it at times in their writings. We do not, however, believe that postmodern analysts have to embrace this strongly sceptical and strongly holistic position on interpretation. To varying degrees Schafer and Hoffman (who are as much modern as postmodern), along with other analysts who work within the modern/postmodern dialectic, seem to agree that interpretation is indeterminate and perspectival, while also maintaining that interpretations can produce revisable, shared knowledge based on identifiable evidence. Thus, in the clinical situation a postmodern attitude does nothing so radical as to force the abandonment of the quest for truth about the patient's unconscious psychology. It does, however, question and make problematic any rigidly modernist pursuit of this truth. Consider, for example, this clinical event:

> A 25-year-old woman fell silent after I made an interpretation. After a few minutes, she said she felt my voice was too 'insistent,' and she became silent again. (Busch, 1995: 47)

One could easily imagine any analyst influenced by postmodern trends asking the patient to tell him or her about his or her insistence. Busch almost does that, but the contrast is vital. He reports: 'I immediately recognized what she was responding to' (1995: 47). Postmodernism would urge a little less certainty about what the patient was responding to until the patient had a chance to elaborate (or associate to) her representation of the analyst as too insistent.

What happens next is, at first, a bit confusing. We might expect that Busch would tell us, the readers, what it was that he immediately recognized; but he only tells us that the 'interpretation was one that I had speculated about for some time, and the analysand's associations confirmed it in a way that she seemed ready to understand' (1995: 47). We read this in two ways. First Busch wants us to know that he has waited until the patient was already saying whatever it was he told her in the interpretation she claimed he made too insistently. Second, he wants us to know that he was not speculating about the unconscious wishes that make her anxious. This matters because in most of his writings Busch identifies himself as working along the lines suggested by Paul Gray, and Gray has made it clear throughout his writings that he does not think analysts should do that sort of speculating about what *absent content* catalyses defences – just interpret resistance, especially in the form of superego projections onto the analyst, and the patient will get to the anxiety that triggers the resistance and the sexual excitement or rage that triggers the anxiety. Busch has to make this apologetic because sooner or later he will say something about that *absent content*, and he does not want to emphasize the subjective nature of the judgement call involved in deciding when one is simply pointing to it in the patient's associations and when one is getting it from one's own thought. Like Leary, he wants there to be a ground in the data of the patient's associations upon which we stand free of constructions or narratives.

Having made these points, Busch then tells us that what he immediately recognized was that he, too, thought there had been a shift from his more questioning voice to another kind of voice. It is crucial here, however, that he does not label that new voice. It is hard to imagine that he does not have a label for it in his mind, just as the patient has the label 'too insistent' attached to it in hers. He does, after all, have a label for the voice he shifted from: it was 'questioning'. What a postmodern analyst might say at this point is that Busch has his shift in voice constructed one way in his mind and the patient has it constructed another. How can Busch be so positive (as in positivistic) that her construction ('too insistent') is wrong? This does not mean that Hoffman or Schafer thinks every construction is as plausible here as any other, simply that if Busch shifted from questioning to telling or from questioning to asserting, there is a range of constructions that might make sense of what he had done.

What Busch does next is return to his questioning voice. A bit later in his article he complains that object relational analysts, whom he believes he is critiquing in his essay, might simply 'turn down the volume' of their voice to make the patient feel safe, so we assume he wants us to understand that, while he too did that, he also did more. No object-relational analyst whose work we have read has suggested that if the patient complains about something we are doing, we simply stop doing it and do not try to work with the patient to understand the complaint.

What matters here is that Busch, too, changed his voice but attributes little or no significance to this as influencing what happens next. Further complicating things, his lack of attention to how he is participating in constructing this complex relational event with his patient allows him to say simply in passing that the first thing he did after returning to his *questioning* voice was to *tell* her something: that he could see how she heard his voice as 'different'. Finally, he has been forced to do what we have been suggesting, from a postmodern perspective, cannot be avoided: he tells us how he has constructed his changing of his voice. He has applied the word 'different' to it. He will implicitly claim that anything more descriptive than that is entirely the patient's resistance. We believe that this is precisely the sort of clinical work, in counterpoint to which theories such as Hoffman's stand. Leary's use of the extreme example of a patient's claiming the analyst is always ragefully attacking her, when he has never overtly done so, masked this problem of the clinical position her stance implies.

What Critics of Postmodernism Such as Glass and Leary Fail to Do

Some of the most important changes taking place in postmodern culture concern the restructuring of emotional relationships, sexuality, intimacy, gender and love (Beck and Beck-Gernsheim, 1995; Giddens, 1992). In the light of the postmodernist critique of the grand narratives of Western rationality, how can psychoanalysts rethink the relationship between subjectivity, unconscious desire, and interpersonal processes? (For an extended treatment of these issues, see Elliott (1999).)

Critiques such as those of Glass and Leary, in our opinion, occlude the epistemological interest of postmodernism in psychoanalysis. That is, they fail to deal with what is most important and significant in the postmodernity debate as regards psychoanalysis.

Glass focuses on the work of Michel Foucault and his thesis that 'subject positions' are determined by networks of power/knowledge relations. He then makes the criticism against Foucault – quite rightly – that unconscious and libidinal desires are rendered mere products of wider social forces, of power and knowledge. But the critical point here is that this is not a criticism of postmodernism: Foucault was not a postmodernist, and in fact rejected the notion of a transition from modernity to postmodernity (see Macey, 1993).

Leary makes use of the term 'postmodern' to marginalize the potential usefulness to analysts of the theorizing of Hoffman and Schafer (rather than, say, showing how their clinical work links them to specific modern or postmodern thinkers). She then implies that because they are postmodern, they would be inclined to do various absurd things during analytic hours. Her suggestion – that if we consider Schafer and Hoffman as gadflies for positivistically inclined analysts (rather than purveyors of clinical theories of their own), then maybe they are useful after all – hardly mitigates her previous severe criticizing of them, which is based on having first linked them, via labelling them 'postmodern', with total fragmentation of the self and total relativism in the assignment of meaning to experience.

Postmodernity and Psychoanalytic Heterogeneity

Whereas Glass and Leary proceed by bundling very divergent postmodern social theories together and then developing a negative assessment of this shift in thinking as regards psychoanalysis as a discipline, we propose a different tack. In our opinion, it is too simple, and indeed erroneous, to imagine that divergent postmodern theories can either be imported into, or excluded from, psychoanalysis at the level of theory as well as the level of clinical practice. Such an approach treats the very nature of psychoanalytic thought as something that develops outside of our general culture. That thing known as 'postmodernism' appears as something that does not really affect the structure of mind; and if its conceptual and practical implications seem a little too threatening, then it is something that psychoanalysis would also do well to avoid. Postmodernity and psychoanalysis, in this reading, have absolutely nothing to do with each other, unless it is decided otherwise by the psychoanalytic community at some point when the profession might more actively consider a radical change in its system of beliefs.

In our view, the development of psychoanalysis is not so self-contained. On the contrary, recent trends in psychoanalysis indicate a transformation in theorizing as regards subjectivity, the status of the unconscious, the nature of intersubjectivity, and of thinking in terms of what analyst and patient know about themselves and each other (Elliott and Frosh, 1995; Mitchell, 1993; Spezzano, 1993). Such changes in theorizing take many forms throughout contemporary psychoanalytic literature, and it is a central aspect of our argument that this direction in psychoanalytic theorizing is part of our post-modern worldview.

Consider, for example, the question of epistemology. In traditional psychoanalysis, practitioners tended to pride themselves on their knowledge of the unconscious as a distinct psychical system. The unconscious, having been fully explored and colonized by Freud, was seen as a realm of mind that can be known and subsequently placed under rational control, once patient and analyst are brave enough to face sexual repression and its difficulty. In post-Freudian psychoanalysis, however, there is a range of approaches to thinking of the unconscious and the anxiety-provoking nature of desire which generally displace this emphasis on certitude toward more open-ended forms of knowledge and of experience. Indeed, the capacity to tolerate periods of 'not-knowing', at both subjective and theoretical levels, is positively valued in some contemporary versions of psychoanalysis (see Hoffman, 1987; Ogden, 1989).

Here the focus is on a suspension of preconceived thoughts and beliefs, coupled with the intersubjective exploration of fantasy and desire. Human knowledge is no longer understood as being subject to singular, rationalistic control (once the secrets of the unconscious are unlocked); on the contrary, knowledge is regarded as perspectival and decentred. Knowledge, of the self and of others, is discovered, according to Winnicott, in that 'transitional space' of intermediate experience; the connections between subjectivity and truth unfold at the margins of thinking and in intersubjective reverie, according to Bion; and fantasy is embedded in human relationships through a dialectical interplay of paranoid-schizoid and depressive positions of generating experience, according to Klein. We mention Winnicott, Bion and Klein in this context to highlight the beginnings of that psychoanalytic shift away from understanding knowledge as rationality and control. The point is not that any of these psychoanalysts may, at the current historical juncture, be reread as 'postmodern'. Rather, the point is that the development of psychoanalytic theory, to which their contributions are seminal, at once contributes to and reflects our postmodern worldview and culture.

Many psychoanalysts have been contributing to a shift away from realist aspirations or impersonal objectivity. They have rejected the traditional view that the clearest form of understanding occurs when secondary-process thinking is separated out from the unconscious fantasy. Instead, they pay explicit attention to the creative power of human imagination as regards issues of subjectivity, intersubjectivity, truth, desire, fantasy and personal meaning, and authenticity. As Stephen Mitchell (1993: 21) summarizes this rescaffolding of the discipline:

> What is inspiring about psychoanalysis today is not the renunciation of illusion in the hope of joining a common, progressively realistic knowledge and control, but rather the hope of fashioning a personal reality that feels authentic and enriching. ... The hope inspired by psychoanalysis in our time is grounded in personal meaning, not rational consensus. The bridge supporting connections with others is not built out of a rationality superseding fantasy and the imagination, but out of feelings experienced as real, authentic, generated from the inside, rather than imposed externally, in close relationship with fantasy and the imagination.

It is this explicit attention given to fantasy and the imagination that, in our opinion, helps to define the stakes of contemporary psychoanalysis. The stakes are necessarily high if only because no one knows with any degree of certainty how, and with what success, contemporary selves and societies will frame meaning and truth based on an appreciation of the ambivalence, ambiguity and plurality of human experience.

All of this raises the thorny question: has psychoanalysis, whether it likes it or not, become postmodern? Is there such a thing as 'postmodern psychoanalysis'? To this, we would respond with a qualified 'yes'; save that the issue cannot really be understood adequately if put in such terms. To grasp the trajectories of psychoanalysis today, we suggest, it is necessary to understand that the self-reflexivity which psychoanalysis uncovers and promotes (and which, according to Jurgen Habermas (1968), is Freud's central discovery) is radicalized and transformed in postmodern culture. With the eclipse of custom and tradition as embedded in modernity, the relationship between self and society becomes self-referential in postmodern times. Without the binding cultural, symbolic norms of modernity in arenas such as sexuality, love, relationships, gender and work, people become increasingly aware of the contingency of the self, of relationships, and of society itself. They also become profoundly aware of the contingency of meaning and of the sign; they see that meaning is not fixed once and for all, but rather that signification is creatively made and remade by desire and anxiety-driven human relationships. In this sense, postmodern culture can be said to directly incorporate certain core insights of psychoanalysis into its framing assumptions, especially as concerns the role of fantasy as being at the root of our traffic with social meaning. (For a detailed discussion of the intricate connections between postmodernity and psychoanalysis see Elliott (1996).)

There are strong indications that this cultural self-awareness of contingency, ambivalence, and plurality – key features of the postmodern worldview – are theorized in contemporary psychoanalytic dialogues. In contemporary psychoanalysis, in the work of its most radical clinicians and theoreticians, the subjectivity of the self is approached as comprising multivalent psychical forms, embedded in a field of interpersonal relationships, and in close connection with unconscious fantasy. In recent years, such writers as Castoriadis, Kristeva, Anzieu, Ogden and Bollas have radically reconceptualized the nature of psychic processing, and in particular of the constitution of psychic meanings. It is beyond the scope of this chapter to discuss in any detail the specific contributions of these authors, or the significant conceptual differences between their approaches to psychoanalysis. However, some of the common threads in their visions of psychoanalysis, and of their understandings of psychic constitution and meaning, will be briefly touched on here, in order to draw out the wider cultural links to postmodernism.

Cornelius Castoriadis (1987, 1995), an analyst living in Paris, theorizes subjectivity in terms of a 'radical imaginary', by which he means an unconscious architecture of representations, drives, and affects in and through which psychic space is constituted and perpetuated. The precondition for the self-reflection upon subjectivity, says Castoriadis, is fantasy: the capacity of the psyche to posit figuration *ex nihilo*. 'The original narcissistic cathexis or investment', he writes, 'is necessarily representation ... (otherwise it would not be psychical) and it can then be nothing other than a "representation" (unimaginable and unrepresentable for us) of the Self' (1987: 287).

In Castoriadis's reading of Freud, the unconscious is not so much the psychic depository of that which cannot be held in consciousness, but rather the essential psychical flux which underpins all representations of the self, of others, and of the social and cultural world. Such psychical flux, necessarily plural, multiple and discontinuous, is that which renders identity nonidentical with itself, as Adorno would have it, or, in more psychoanalytic terms, it is that which means that every self-representation is intrinsically incomplete and lacking since the subject arises from a primary loss which remains traumatic at the level of the unconscious. Here Castoriadis's emphasis on the radically imaginary dimensions of self and society parallels the postmodernist stress on the demise of external foundations as an anchoring mechanism for thought, and his stress on psychical flux mirrors certain postmodernist themes which highlight the ambiguity, ambivalence and radical otherness of contemporary social life.

So too Kristeva (1984, 1989) underscores the profoundly imaginary dimensions of unconscious experience in terms of her notion of the 'semiotic', a realm of prelinguistic experience (including drives, affects and primal rhythms) which is necessarily prior to symbolic representation and entry into cultural processes. Seeking to account for an internally disruptive presence as regards the space of the Other in Lacanian psychoanalysis, Kristeva argues that contemporary psychoanalysis is increasingly concerned with the complexities of semiotic displacement, or unconscious rupture, as that point of otherness which derails symbolism and intersubjectivity. One way of understanding Kristeva's reconceptualization of the unconscious in post-Lacanian theory is as an explicit attempt to account for the multiplication of fantasy (and of multiple selves) in its trading with received social meanings, or external reality.

Extending Kristeva, Elliott (1995) argues that this multiplication of fantasy is underlined by a 'representational wrapping of self and other', a preliminary ordering of pre-self experience, otherness, and difference. Such wrapping lies at the core of intersubjective space – indeed it is the unconscious investment in the shapes, textures, surfaces and pre-objects that comprise psychic space itself – and it functions as a kind of perpetual self-constitution, or what is termed 'rolling identification' (1995: 45–7). In a Kleinian vein, Thomas Ogden (1989) also speaks of such a preliminary ordering of pre-object relations as the 'autistic-contiguous mode of generating experience' (1989: 30), the sensory floor of psychic space which underlies paranoid-schizoid and depressive processes.

Along similar lines, Anzieu (1985) links fantasy and interpersonal experience with the notion of a 'skin ego', an imaginary registration of maternal holding. Influenced by Klein and Winnicott, Anzieu argues that the skin ego is constituted in relation to maternal bodily experiences, a contact from which the beginning separation of inner and outer worlds takes place through introjective and projective identification. The skin ego is thus a kind of 'containing envelope' for the holding of emotional states in fantasy, from which human experience can become known, symbolized and developed. So too Bollas (1992) argues that selfhood is generated in and through our 'personal idiom', a psychical grid (or unconscious space) between experience and fantasy.

In the preceding accounts, psychical life is portrayed as a nonlinear movement of fantasies, containers, introjects, representational wrappings, semiotic sensations, envelopes and memories. Such a focus has much in common with postmodernist theory insofar as the radical imagination of the psyche is treated as central to the constitution and reproduction of subjectivity; a self-reflexive subjectivity. This is not to say, however, that the subject of contemporary psychoanalysis is without grounding, set adrift within the logics of disintegration. On the contrary, the multivalent psychical forms of contemporary selves are said to be patterned in and through an interpersonal field of interactions with significant others, theorized variously as the Lacanian Symbolic Order, the Kleinian depressive position, or social imaginary significations.

Beyond Hermeneutics and Constructivism

The hermeneutic and constructivist perspectives of Hoffman and Schafer are not the whole story of a 'postmodern turn' in psychoanalysis. We emphasized their work because authors such as Leary (1994) and Glass (1993) had risked leaving an impression that might easily limit interest not only in the important work of these two analysts but also in anything else associated with postmodernism. As we argued above, psychoanalysts cannot remain impervious to the postmodern ideas swirling around them – any more than any domain of twentieth-century Western thought was able to decide not to be bothered by psychoanalysis.

Psychoanalysts believed, for most of this century, that we could choose not to study outside our discipline. We needed only to master our techniques and theories. Then came a period of time during which some analysts looked to philosophy, neuropsychology, infant research or literary criticism to adjudicate our theoretical and clinical debates. Leary's essay, although we disputed it, might be treated as a harbinger of a third phase in the relationship between psychoanalysis and other disciplines. In this emerging third phase, we would neither ignore nor annex ideas from, say, contemporary philosophy. Instead, we would recognize that as broad cultural shifts occur in our way of viewing the human condition (and in our way of understanding our ways of viewing the human condition), then psychoanalysis will both contribute to and be moved by these shifts. As a result we would understand that we are thrown into relationships with activities in other disciplines – from rereadings of Hegel to studies of affect and intersubjectivity by neuropsychologists and infant researchers – through which psychoanalysis (clinical and applied) both reacts to and shapes the human world.

References

Anzieu, D. (1985), *The Skin Ego*, translated by C. Turner, New Haven/London: Yale University Press, 1989.

Barratt, B.B. (1993), *Psychoanalysis and the Postmodern Impulse: Knowing and Being since Freud's Psychology*, Baltimore/London: Johns Hopkins University Press.

Bauman, Z. (1990), *Modernity and Ambivalence*, Cambridge: Polity Press.

— (1991), *Intimations of Postmodernity*, London: Routledge.

— (1992), *Mortality, Immortality, and Other Life Strategies*, Cambridge: Polity Press.

— (1993), *Postmodern Ethics*, Oxford: Blackwell.

Beck, U. and Beck-Gernsheim, E. (1995), *The Normal Chaos of Love*, Cambridge: Polity Press.

Bion, W.R. (1962), *Learning from Experience*, New York: Basic Books.

Blackburn, S. (1993), *Essays in Quasi-Realism*, Oxford: Oxford University Press.

Bohman, J. (1991), 'Holism without skepticism', in D. Hiley, J. Dorman, and R. Shusterman (eds), *The Interpretive Turn*, Ithaca: Cornell University Press, pp. 129–34.

Bollas, C. (1992), *Being a Character*, New York: Hill & Wang.

Busch, F. (1995), 'Resistance analysis and object relations theory', *Psychoanalytic Psychology* 12: 43–54.

Butler, J. (1993), *Bodies That Matter*, New York: Routledge.

Castoriadis, C. (1987), *The Imaginary Institution of Society*, translated by K. Blamey, Cambridge, MA: MIT Press.

— (1995), 'Logic, imagination, reflection', in A. Elliott and S. Frosh (eds), *Psychoanalysis in Contexts: Paths between Theory and Modern Culture*, London: Routledge, pp. 15–35.

Deleuze, G. and Guattari, F. (1977), *Anti-Oedipus: Capitalism and Schizophrenia*, New York: Viking.

Derrida, J. (1978), *Writing and Difference*, translated by A. Bass, Chicago: University of Chicago Press, 1980.

— (1981), *Positions*, translated by A. Bass, Chicago: University of Chicago Press.

Eagleton, T. (1990), *The Ideology of the Aesthetic*, Oxford: Blackwell.

Elliott, A. (1995), 'The affirmation of primary repression rethought: reflections on the state of the self in its unconscious relational world', *American Imago*, 52: 55–79.

— (1996), *Subject to Ourselves: Social Theory, Psychoanalysis and Postmodernity*, Cambridge: Polity Press.
— (1999), *Social Theory and Psychoanalysis in Transition: Self and Society from Freud to Kristeva*, London: Free Association Books.
— and Frosh, S. (1995), *Psychoanalysis in Contexts: Paths between Theory and Modern Culture*, London: Routledge.
Fish, S. (1989), 'Rhetoric', in F. Lentricchia and T. McLaughlin (eds), *Critical Terms for Literary Study*, Chicago: University of Chicago Press, pp. 203–22.
Frosh, S. (1991), *Identity Crisis: Psychoanalysis, Modernity and the Self*, New York: Routledge.
Giddens, A. (1991), *Modernity and Self-Identity: Self and Society in the Late Modern Age*, Stanford, CA: Stanford University Press.
— (1992), *The Transformation of Intimacy: Sexuality, Love, and Eroticism in Modern Societies*, Stanford, CA: Stanford University Press.
Glass, J.M. (1993), *Shattered Selves: Multiple Personality in a Postmodern World*, Ithaca, New York/London: Cornell University Press.
Habermas, J. (1968), *Knowledge and Human Interests*, translated by J.J. Shapiro, Boston: Beacon, 1971.
— (1970), *On the Logic of the Social Sciences*, translated by S.W. Nicholson and J.A Stark, Cambridge, MA: MIT Press, 1988.
Harvey, D. (1990), *The Condition of Postmodernity*, Cambridge, MA: Blackwell.
Hoffman, I.Z. (1987), 'The value of uncertainty in psychoanalytic practice', *Contemporary Psychoanalysis*, 23: 205–15.
— (1994), 'Dialectical thinking and therapeutic action in the psychoanalytic process', *Psychoanalytic Quarterly*, 63: 187–218.
Jameson, F. (1991), *Postmodernism, or, the Cultural Logic of Late Capitalism*, Durham, NC: Duke University Press.
Kristeva, J. (1984), *Revolution in Poetic Language*, translated by M. Waller, Ithaca, NY: Cornell University Press.
— (1989), *Black Sun: Depression and Melancholia*, New York: Columbia University Press.
Leary, K. (1994), 'Psychoanalytic "problems" and postmodern "solutions"', *Psychoanalytic Quarterly*, 63: 433–65.
Lyotard, J.-F. (1984), *The Postmodern Condition: A Report on Knowledge*, translated by G. Bennington and B. Massumi, Minneapolis: University of Minnesota Press.
Macey, D. (1993), *The Lives of Michel Foucault*, London: Hutchinson.
McGowan, J. (1991), *Postmodernism and Its Critics*, Ithaca, NY: Cornell University Press.

Mitchell, S.A. (1993), *Hope and Dread in Psychoanalysis*, New York: Basic Books.

Murdoch, I. (1993), *Metaphysics as a Guide to Morals: Philosophical Reflections*, New York: Viking Penguin, 1994.

Norris, C. (1987), *Derrida*, Cambridge, MA: Harvard University Press, 1988.

— (1993), *The Truth about Postmodernism*, Oxford: Blackwell.

Ogden, T.H. (1989), *The Primitive Edge of Experience*, Northvale, NJ/London: Aronson.

Rorty, R. (1982), *The Consequences of Pragmatism: Essays 1972–1980*, Minneapolis: University of Minnesota Press.

Schafer, R. (1992), *Retelling a Life: Narration and Dialogue in Psychoanalysis*, New York: Basic Books.

Scruton, R. (1994), *Modern Philosophy*, London: Sinclair-Stevenson.

Spezzano, C. (1993), *Affect in Psychoanalysis: A Clinical Synthesis*, Hillsdale, NJ: Analytic Press.

Thompson, J.B. (1990), *Ideology and Modern Culture: Critical Social Theory in the Era of Mass Communication*, Stanford, CA: Stanford University Press.

Trachtenberg, A. (1979), 'Intellectual background', in D. Hoffman (ed.), *Harvard Guide to Contemporary American Writing*, Cambridge, MA: Harvard University Press.

Vattimo, G. (1980), *The Adventure of Difference: Philosophy after Nietzche and Heidegger*, translated by C. Blamires and T. Harrison, Baltimore: Johns Hopkins University Press.

2 Final Analysis: Can Psychoanalysis Survive in the Postmodern West?

Jane Flax

> If – which may sound fantastic today – one had to found a college of psycho-analysis, much would have to be taught in it which is also taught by the medical faculty: along-side of depth-psychology, which would always remain the principal subject, there would be an introduction to biology, as much as possible of the science of sexual life, and familiarity with the symptomatology of psychiatry. On the other hand, analytic instruction would include branches of knowledge which are remote from medicine and which the doctor does not come across in his practice: the history of civilization, mythology, the psychology of religion and the science of literature. Unless he is well at home in these subjects, an analyst can make nothing of a large amount of his material. By way of compensation, the great mass of what is taught in medical schools is of no use to him for his purposes.
>
> Freud, 1927: 93–4

Can psychoanalysis survive in the postmodern West? To answer this question, I will first define psychoanalysis, since the meaning of this term is controversial and ambiguous (Brenner, 1955; Chodorow, 1989; Fairbairn, 1952; A. Freud, 1966; Goldberg, 1990; Kernberg, 1975; Klein, 1975; Kohut, 1984; Lacan, 1973; Langs and Stone, 1980; Lowenstein *et al.*, 1966; Schafer, 1983; Spence, 1982; Sullivan, 1953; Winnicott, 1989). My definition draws upon certain postmodernist ideas, especially the notion of a discursive formation. I will locate the discourse of psychoanalysis within its social-political context. Only then can we begin to understand and evaluate the current dilemmas and possible futures of psychoanalysis.

A discourse is a system of possibilities for knowledge, practices and power. Discursive formations include sets of usually tacit rules that enable members to identify some statements as true or false and to construct a map, model or classification system to organize these statements. The rules provide the necessary preconditions for the formation of meaningful statements and the production of truth. They also identify and authorize truth speakers. These rules also necessarily and simultaneously exclude other participants, prohibit other operations and confine both within delimited systems. Conformity to the necessarily restricted set of discursive rules determines the validity of statements and truth claims within the discourse. Truth is an effect of discursive rules and practices. A discourse as a whole cannot be true or false, because truth is always contextual and rule dependent. Discourses are local and heterogeneous, and they may be incommensurate. Discourse independent or transcendental rules cannot exist. No master rules or decision procedures are available that could govern all discourses or resolve conflicts among or choices between them. Truth claims are undecidable outside of specific discourses, and they may be irresolvable between conflicting ones.

Knowledge claims cannot exist or be understood unless situated within complex networks of disciplinary practices through which power circulates. These networks are also the loci of the legitimation of and resistance to power. Power is a productive force and an intrinsic aspect of all discursive formations. Repression or domination (power over others; power from the top down) is not the only or even most important form of power. It does not 'only weigh upon us as a force that says no but traverses and produces things, it induces pleasure, forms knowledge, produces discourse' (Foucault, 1980a: 119). The will to knowledge cannot be separated from the will to power even though, as presently constituted in our culture, 'the fact of power [is] invariably excluded from knowledge' (Foucault, 1977: 221–2). In our culture we must produce the truth; there can be no exercise of power without its concomitant production of truth.

One of the effects of power within and between discourses is to produce the appearance of an objective or neutral resolution of competing truth claims. Power can produce this effect by eliminating, ruling out or effacing certain truth claims. Discursive practices situate some voices as authoritative and worthy of attention and respect and marginalize or silence others. The place, function, and character of the knowers, learners, authorities, subjects/objects and audiences of a discourse are functions of discursive rules. Naming individuals as authorities also invests them with further power as legitimate bearers, teachers, articulators and judges of knowledge.

1. Mapping the Terrain: Psychoanalysis as a Discursive Formation

Within the discursive formation of psychoanalysis, we can distinguish at least three, not necessarily compatible, projects: perpetuating and constructing theories or positing truth claims, providing clinical treatment, and conserving a profession with particular practical and disciplinary interests. Different people in divergent intellectual and practical locations may pursue these projects. The audience, purposes and modes of legitimation for and within each may also vary. While my primary interest here is in the character and status of the first (theoretical) project, I will briefly discuss the others as well.

1(a) Theory

Like all discourses, psychoanalysis marks out a domain within which it claims authoritative or privileged knowledge (or the means to obtain and judge it). Authorities put forward and use various theoretical positions. They claim these hold true not only within the domain of psychoanalysis but outside it as well. The domain claimed by psychoanalysis includes the nature of subjectivity, the appropriate methods to investigate it, and the most accurate or useful theoretical languages to interpret or represent it. Psychoanalysts vigorously contest such claims among themselves. Nonetheless, there is probably a broad area of consensus among analysts about which claims are false, irrelevant or unworthy of attention.

There is less consensus among analysts about the most desirable location of their discursive practices and who their external audiences are, should or could be. One of the contemporary paradoxes confronting American psychoanalysis is the lack of reciprocity in its allegiance to and identification with the medical model. These have not been particularly fruitful, either theoretically or practically. Devaluation of psychoanalysis pervades much of scientific writing on the topic. Psychoanalysis is all but invisible within its traditionally desired discursive location – the institutions and practices of medicine and medical research. Yet, at the same time, within the humanities and social sciences and in professions such as psychology and social work, interest in and writing on psychoanalysis is widespread, lively and diverse. None of these discourses, however, has the status or privilege that medicine enjoys within the knowledge/power systems of the United States. This discursive rejection, loss of status and boundary confusion have had and will continue to have profound effects upon all three aspects of psychoanalysis.

The discursive domain claimed by psychoanalysis overlaps with terrain shared and contested by others – for example, philosophers, neurologists, sociologists and anthropologists – who are not psychoanalysts. For a variety of political and philosophical reasons, some of which I will discuss below, subjectivity is one of the most salient and contested questions within contemporary postmodern culture. Therefore, analysts ought to expect fierce battles for territory and control to continue indefinitely.

The other contestants have no particular reason to cede privilege to the analyst when he or she makes claims about subjectivity. At minimum they will await acknowledgement that their own claims exist and have implications for the analysts' projects. More likely, they will expect the analyst to follow their own discursive practices and norms concerning knowledge claims. If, for example, an analyst claims to put forward a general 'science of mind', the neurologist will expect him/her to follow the rules of science as practised by neurology. Within the neurologist's discursive frame, the analyst's claims will probably seem meaningless unless translated into the language of neurology and tested by its methods. The analyst, of course, can ask what authorizes or legitimates the neurologist's judgements. Since there is no neutral decision procedure both share, argument is likely to reach an impasse.

1(b) Clinical Treatment

The second aspect of psychoanalysis, clinical treatment, is also controversial. Analytic practices and justifications/legitimations vary, even among practitioners authorized by a widely acknowledged, official agency such as the International Psychoanalytic Association. In addition, the number of people who are not graduates of official training institutes yet claim to practice psychoanalysis continues to increase. Simultaneously, psychoanalysts have little influence or control over those with the discursive legitimacy to question the clinical efficacy of analysis. Medical researchers and public officials who evaluate health care to determine if it is effective (and reimbursable) have become increasingly sceptical about its worth.

From Freud on, analysts have relied upon certain truth claims to legitimate analytic practices as a source of knowledge and as a form of treatment. Claims about the relationship between facts and theories and about the nature of science have had an especially foundational role within psychoanalysis (Flax, 1990, Chapter 3). Freud's own accounts of the mind undermine many of these assumptions, yet psychoanalysts perpetuate and refuse to abandon them. These ideas are a curious mixture of empiricist assumptions, especially about the nature of 'observation' and the relationships between theory and data, and Enlightenment ones concerning the neutral yet beneficial character of reason and science.

Enlightenment philosophers privilege reason as the unique means of access to and voice of the Real and science as the ideal form of knowledge. In science, rationality manifests itself in the origination of a 'logic of discovery'. This logic is universal and binding on all scientific practitioners. It is neutral in that it affects neither the subject/investigator nor the object/data. Science's 'successes' (discoveries) are due to the adherence to this logic by its practitioners. The 'scientific method' enables all those who use it to dis-cover (not construct) the truths of its objects – bits of the Real that exist independent of the scientist and the scientific modes of investigation (Kuhn, 1962).

Analysts rely on this set of beliefs to provide accounts of the location, meaning and epistemic value of the clinical situation. The analyst gathers bits of 'data' from the object/patient and gradually assembles these into more general ideas that constitute a theory. He or she then 'tests' the validity of these ideas or theories in subsequent analytic encounters. If the analyst complies with the analytic rules, the treatment can be epistemologically and politically neutral. Analytic procedure or the social/political context in which both participants and process are embedded will not contaminate the resulting data or treatment of the patient.

Many analysts from Freud on would probably agree with statements like these: 'by testing thoughts against reality, science helps liberate inquiry from bias, prejudice, and just plain muddleheadedness' (Hoover, 1988: 3–4). They accept the Enlightenment belief that science is the ideal form of knowledge, the exemplar of the right use of reason, the guarantor of political neutrality and the methodological paradigm for all truth claims. Even today, analysts present clinical vignettes as if these can support or demonstrate the validity of an analytic idea or theory.

The plausibility, coherence, or even intelligibility of these claims requires a set of unstated background assumptions. There must be a neutral language available to report our discoveries. The 'logic of discovery' can operate independent of and without distorting either its subject or object. The background assumptions the researcher posits do not contaminate or predetermine data gathering. The 'scientific' process is self-correcting and -governing. The process contains the intrinsic capacity to eliminate biases or false knowledge. The real of science has an unchanging and universal character. Humans do not create or transform it in the process of doing science. Like the physical world, the social one is stable, homogeneous and lawfully structured. Its laws are benign and lack irresolvable contradictions. They work to the equal benefit of all.

If these conditions exist, there will be no fundamental disjunction between clinical treatment and the discovery/administration of truth. Psychoanalysts can make claims for their expertise (and its funding) based simultaneously on its 'scientific neutrality' and its contributions to health and public welfare. Action grounded in scientific/expert knowledge is an innocent form of power whose operation and effects are as transparent and universally accessible as the scientific enterprise. Expert rule generates neither privilege nor domination in its exercise. It results in the good for all.

1(c) Discipline and Training

These assumptions about knowledge and authority underwrite the disciplinary practices of psychoanalysis, including training and legitimation. The legitimacy of analytic institutes requires a belief among both 'candidates' and 'training' analysts in the doctrine taught. Members of institutes generally do not question the truth value of analysis as a method of acquiring knowledge about one's self and others. They do not challenge the right of particular organizations to mark out and regulate their domain and their authority to train and evaluate others.

One of the most important aspects of a discursive formation is the process of producing, reproducing and regulating the production of 'experts' as well as their attendant knowledges. Discourses seek a monopoly over the production of certain sorts of experts and practices. This process requires power and is one of its main circuits and modes of replication or extension. Discourses also attempt to normalize their construction of and control over certain domains. Successful normalization obscures the power/knowledge practices through which this occurs. Power can then flow more freely and productively.

On the other hand, certain kinds of questions are particularly dangerous to discursive formations. Most perilous are questions concerning the validity of their production of knowledge and its truth, their control over a domain and the right to train, regulate and produce expert practitioners. Generally these three aspects are interdependent and reinforcing; a challenge to one eventually puts the entire discursive formation at risk. Challenges to either theory or monopoly control produce crises of power and legitimation. Internal challenges, especially by those already named as experts, are most immediately threatening. If serious enough, the challengers may face expulsion (withdrawal of authority) or excommunication (declarations of heresy) (Clement, 1983; Gay, 1988; Grosskurth, 1986; Turkle, 1981). Contestants from outside the discourse are less threatening to those within it, since such others lack the discourse-specific power/knowledge to speak. Yet to the extent a discourse lacks autonomy either financially or in its capacity to generate prestige or produce truth, challenges by these others can undermine it.

Within certain cultural contexts, psychoanalytic discourse has been remarkably successful in achieving normalization. For example, imagine a situation in which a white, middle-class sixteen-year-old is not attending school. What description and treatment would this person encounter? First, the sixteen-year-old would receive the classification of an 'adolescent' – a 'life stage' unknown 150 years ago. The psychological and sociological discourses that produced this 'stage' also created the experts who investigate and treat it. Second, authoritative people will define the situation as a problem. No one is likely to question whether this person should attend school. Third, this now established problem may be categorized as a 'psychological' one, e.g. 'school refusal', and as a possible symptom of a more serious 'mental illness'.

The description/diagnosis determines the treatment. In white, middle-class culture, experts generally characterize 'psychological' problems as individual attributes and as consequences or symptoms of people's subjective states. The appropriate experts should examine the 'inner' or subjective workings of this person. This expert will 'specialize' in 'adolescence', and one of his or her prerogatives is to determine if the person is deficient or deviant (according to the standards generated by experts' discourse). If this is the case, the discourse stipulates who should 'treat' the problem and how. The expert must 'help' the person to alter the problematic subjective state or at least her or his behaviour.

It is easy to see how this process recreates and reaffirms the knowledge and expertise it assumes and how it creates the object/pathology that then becomes its legitimation. In other social contexts, one might describe this situation in different ways. Alternative possibilities include: (1) a moral failure by someone who must be held accountable for his or her actions by religious authorities; (2) a failure of the school to hold a student's interest and hence a problem for educators to investigate; (3) a refusal by the individual to uphold his or her obligation to the community and hence a matter for legal intervention; (4) a mark of shame on the family that requires action by the appropriate kinship group; (5) a failure of the community to find the proper place for the person about which proper political deliberation must occur.

2. Psychoanalysis and Western Legitimation Crises

Psychoanalytic discourse has attained considerable success in normalizing its domain. However, challenges to its legitimacy are strengthening. Lacan is not alone in his questioning of the authority of the analyst, the training and legitimation procedures within psychoanalysis and the status of its knowledge. Psychoanalytic theory, clinical treatment and disciplinary practices all face strong intra- and extra-discursive challenges. The social-political context of psychoanalysis compounds its difficulties. Profound crises of cultural identity, subjectivity, meaning, authority and place pervade the postmodern world. Contemporary political and intellectual developments are especially disruptive to the white, relatively rich Westerner's sense of identity and confidence. These persons have been the primary subjects/objects of psychoanalytic discourse.

Americans suffer from a particular sort of disillusionment. The fantasy that our social history is exempt from the disorder and tragedy experienced by others is dissolving. The long string of events beginning with the assassinations of (among others) President Kennedy, Robert F. Kennedy, Martin Luther King and Malcom X, urban uprisings, the war in Vietnam, Watergate and the resignation of President Nixon continue to affect us. The accelerating decay of civility and urban life also disrupts this fantasized sense of immunity and intensifies our sense of inefficacy. The United States no longer appears as the 'land of promise' free from the suffering and mistakes of other cultures. The Holocaust, challenges to Western political-economic hegemony by Japan and other countries, the rise of nationalist and anti-colonialist movements in the Third World, women's movements everywhere, and anti-racist struggles have further disrupted the expected order of things. These political shifts alter the circulation of knowledge and power in many ways. The meanings – or even existence – of Enlightenment ideas (reason, history, science, self, knowledge, power, gender and the inherent superiority of Western culture), including those upon which psychoanalysis depends, are subject to increasingly corrosive attacks.

Internal dissent has further disrupted the epistemological security of Western thinkers. Postmodernists and feminists undermine the foundations of Western thought by challenging their essential and interdependent girders. They expose the essential contestibility of its constituting notions. This exposure creates a crisis of innocence, since these notions then appear as mere humanly created artifacts for whose effects and consequences we alone are responsible. If knowledge is an effect of discrete, historical human action, it can no longer underwrite or guarantee political neutrality. The circuits of power and their relations with the production of truth are more evident.

As we will see, these philosophic and political developments pose profound challenges to some of the most cherished and legitimating psychoanalytic ideas. Two foundational notions now appear particularly problematic. One notion is the belief that because it can rely on clinical 'data' to validate theory, psychoanalysis is an empirical science. The other is that analytic treatment (or its legitimating theories) is politically neutral.

2(a) Postmodernism and the Powers of Knowledge

Postmodernists challenge Enlightenment ideas about truth, knowledge, power, history, self and language still predominant in the West (Flax, 1990). According to postmodernists, most Western philosophers took as their task the construction of a philosophic system in which something Real is re-presented in thought (Derrida, 1978; Rorty, 1979). Philosophers claim this system will re-present or correspond to a unitary Being beyond history, particularity and change. This Being is not the product, artifact, or effect of particular historical or linguistic practices. It is an external or universal subject or substance, existing 'out there' independent of the knower. Philosophers' task is to 'mirror', register, mimic or make present the Real. Truth is correspondence to it.

For postmodernists an unacknowledged will to power lies concealed within and generates such claims to truth. The quest for the real conceals most Western philosophers' desire. They desire conclusive mastery over the world. Mastery can be achieved (and desire concealed) when philosophy encloses the world within an illusory but absolute system.

The philosopher also obscures another aspect of his desire: to claim a special relation and access to the True or Real. Only philosophy can be the thought of the Real itself. The presence of the Real for us depends on the philosopher – the clarity of his consciousness, the purity of his intention. Only the philosopher has the capacity for Reason, the love of wisdom (philo-sophia), the grasp of method, or the capacity to construct a logic adequate to the Real. As the privileged representative of the Real and interrogator of truth claims, philosophy must play a 'foundational' role in all 'positive knowledge' (Grunbaum, 1979).

Postmodernists attack Western philosophers' self-understanding in a number of ways (Bayes, Bohman and McCarthy, 1987; Cohen and Dascal, 1989). They question the ideas of mind, truth, language and the Real that underlie and ground any transcendental or foundational claims. They wish to remove discussions of knowledge from the terrain of truth. Instead, they seek to construct genealogies of the histories of our beliefs and to analyse their pragmatic consequences. Discourses should be evaluated according to the specific, historically situated projects and interests they generate, permit, marginalize and prohibit.

Postmodernists deny the possibility that an ahistorical or transcendental standpoint could exist. Lacking such a standpoint, even if the Real existed, we could never immediately apprehend or directly report it. Universal, transcendental, or *a priori* mental categories or ideas do not exist. Sense data, ideas, intentions or perceptions are already constituted. They only occur in and reflect linguistically and socially determined practices. The human mind is not homogeneous, lawful and internally consistent in or over time.

Postmodernists deny language can be a transparent, passive or neutral medium. Each of us is born into an ongoing set of language games. We must learn these games to be understood by and to understand others. As speaking animals, language partially constructs our personhood. Language speaks us as much as we speak it. Furthermore, language affects the *meanings* of our experiences and understandings of them. Thought depends upon and is articulated to ourselves and others through language. Therefore, thought and the mind itself are partially socially and historically (pre-)constituted.

Rather than mourn the inaccessibility of the Real, postmodernists investigate the sources of desire for it. They analyse how knowledge claims are generated within certain discourses. Western philosophers create an illusory appearance of unity and stability by reducing the flux and heterogeneity of the human and physical worlds into binary and supposedly natural oppositions. Within contemporary Western culture important binary oppositions include male/female, white/black, culture/nature, health/deviant, heterosexual/homosexual. We create order and maintain it by displacing chaos into the lesser of each binary pair. The desire for control and domination is expressed and revealed whenever such categories are constructed as and through oppositions. Such oppositions are necessary for the plausibility of a linear or orderly story; hence narrators tend to obscure their fictive and asymmetric qualities. Once we unveil these moves, a fundamental premise underlying all binary systems is apparent. To be other, to be different from the defining one is to be inferior and to have no independent character or worth of one's own. The philosopher hopes eventually to subsume all difference/disorder within the benign sovereignty of the One. In the Enlightenment self-understanding, this view is an optimistic, humane and progressive one.

Postmodernists regard all such wishes for unity with suspicion. Unity is an effect of domination, repression, and the temporary success of particular rhetorical strategies. They desire to open up possibilities and create spaces in which multiple differences can flourish. Postmodernists believe philosophers and other knowledge constructors should generate an infinite 'dissemination' of meanings. We should abjure any attempt to construct a closed system in which the other or the excess is pushed to the margins and made to disappear in the interest of coherence and unity. The task is to disrupt and subvert rather than (re-)construct totalities or grand theories.

Postmodernists do not claim there is no truth. Truth and our desire for it are discourse dependent. Postmodernism is not a form of relativism, because relativism only has meaning as the partner of its binary opposite – universalism. The relativist assumes that the lack of an absolute standard is significant. If there is no one thing against which to measure all claims, then 'everything is relative'. If the hankering for a universal standard disappears, 'relativism' would lose its meaning. We could turn our attention to the limits and possibilities of local productions of truth. The imperial, impersonal Cartesian ego will be deconstructed; its desires can play freely within and as language. The 'view from nowhere' will be displaced by admittedly partial and fragmentary multiples of one (Baynes, Bohman and McCarthy, 1987; Cohen and Dascal, 1989; Derrida, 1981; Foucault, 1988; Fraser, 1989; Rorty, 1982).

2(b) Feminism and the Instabilities of Gender

Feminists define gender as a changeable set of social relations that pervade many aspects of human experience from the constitution of the 'inner self' and family life to the 'public worlds' of the state, the economy and knowledge production. Gender is not a consequence or effect of 'natural sexual differences'. It cannot be explained by reference to anatomical or biological attributes, although the relations of gender to embodiment are an interesting and controversial question. Gender is an indispensable category in the analysis of current Western cultures (Butler and Scott, 1992; Jagger and Bordo, 1989; Mohanty, Russo and Torres, 1991; Pateman and Gross, 1986).

Within contemporary Western cultures, neither men nor women exist outside gender systems. One of their effects is the constitution of masculinity/ femininity as exclusionary and unequal opposites. Power and domination partially constitute and maintain these relations. In relations of domination, no subject can simply or voluntarily switch sides. We receive certain privileges or suffer certain injuries depending on our structural positions, no matter what our subjective intent or purposes may be. Men can no more easily resign from masculinity and its effects than I can from being a white woman.

Gender/race relations mark both men and women, although in different and unequal ways.

Feminists track the effects of gender in the structuring of individual experience, social relations and knowledge. The necessary connections between the marginalization of certain experiences and forms of knowledge and the persuasiveness and power of claims about the truth of dominant beliefs have become more evident. For example, feminist discourse allows us to reveal the gendered qualities of a central element in Enlightenment metanarrative: Reason. This metanarrative both constructs and depends upon a disembodied and asocial notion of Reason. Reason and hence the ideal knower appear to be ungendered. Since Enlightenment philosophers define Reason as the essential human quality, presumably any and every person possesses and can exercise it.

Yet is this so? The claim of universality has a gendered subtext (Cixous and Clement, 1986; Griffiths and Whitford, 1988; Irigaray, 1985; Landes, 1988; Okin, 1989; Pateman, 1989). The Enlightenment view of Reason depends upon antinomies between reason and body, reason and passion, thought and imagination, objectivity and subjectivity, truth and belief, fact and value. The very *appearance* of neutrality or universality of Reason depends upon an interdependent and simultaneous set of moves: naming women as different in relation to the true measure of humanity: men, devaluing difference (the different is always inferior to the same) and suppressing men's dependence on and complicity in this difference.

Our understanding of Reason depends on what it is not, on its difference from and superiority to other faculties such as the passions. Associating women with the body and the particular are two of the necessary conditions for the possibility of imagining that a disembodied and universal faculty (e.g., the Cartesian ego or Kant's pure reason) could exist. The effects of male embodiment and social experiences on Reason and its products are obscured or displaced. With the contaminating effects of difference located in women, suppressed or denied, Reason acquires its unitary and universal appearance.

By situating men as well as women within gender relations, we remove their purity/privilege. The social production of reason and knowledge production becomes more evident. Rather than insisting that women's reason can be as 'pure' as men's, it is more productive to question the purity of reason itself and the claim that no valuable or truthful knowledge can arise from the activities traditionally associated with women or the passions.

We can also investigate the motives for insisting on such splits and this hierarchal ordering of human qualities. The insights derived from feminist object relations psychoanalysis are especially helpful in this investigation (Chodorow, 1978; Dinnerstein, 1976; Fast, 1984).[1] Children develop in and through the context of relations with others. Given the current sexual division of labour, both men and women will first begin to develop a self in interactions with a woman – a mother and/or other female relations. To some extent, male identity emerges out of oppositional moves. He must become not-female, and in a culture where gender is an asymmetric binary relation, he must guard against the return of the repressed – his identification with his mother and those 'female' qualities within him. This provides a powerful unconscious motive for identifying with and overvaluing the abstract and the impersonal and for reinforcing gender segregation, including within intellectual work, to ensure that women will never again have power over men.

3. Implications for Psychoanalysis

3(a) Theory

Psychoanalysis' relation to recent intellectual and political developments in the postmodern West is profoundly ambivalent. Freud was powerfully attracted to Enlightenment notions of science and shared its belief in the emancipatory potential of rational thought. Nonetheless, he and subsequent analysts such as Winnicott and Klein contribute to the undermining of confidence in the character and powers of reason. Freud's post-1920s writings on the structure of the mind as intrinsically conflicted and simultaneously psychic and somatic are especially important. Winnicott's notions of the psyche-soma and the transitional space as the locus of culture also provide many suggestive possibilities as does Klein's concept of an epistemophiliac instinct (Freud, 1923; Klein, 1971; Winnicott, 1971; 1975).

Within psychoanalytic accounts, psychic structures and processes appear increasingly fragmented, multidetermined, fluid, and subject to complex and often unconscious alterations. Unlike many philosophers, analysts such as Freud (1915), Klein (1975) and Winnicott (1975) conceptualize the mind as fully embodied, inherently conflict-ridden, dynamic, heterogeneous, and constituted in and through processes that are intrinsically discordant. These processes cannot be synthesized or organized into a permanent, hierarchal organization of functions or control. The equation of mind and conscious thought or reason, or the psychical and consciousness, becomes untenable.

Their ideas subvert the dualisms such as mind/body, subject/object, thought/passion, rational/irrational that pervade some forms of modern philosophy and science and impede the success of their own projects. They challenge Enlightenment ontological premises by positing various forms of desire (for objects, drive satisfaction, mirroring or the Other) as the definitive and motivating core of our being.

Psychoanalytic theories of mind also contradict and challenge many contemporary epistemologies. Both the rationalist's faith in the powers of reason and the empiricist's belief in the reliability of sense perception and observation are grounded in and depend upon the mind's capacity to be at least partially undetermined by the effects of the body, passions, and social authority or convention. However, psychoanalysis throws into doubt all epistemologies that rely on the possibility of accurate self-observation and direct, reliable access to and control over the mind and its activities.

Psychoanalysis identifies forces whose effects and boundaries can never be transparent to us. These forces, which include bodily experience, libidinal wishes, authority relations and cultural conventions, perpetually affect thought. Insight into the mind's operations will remain incomplete and provisional, because even aspects of the observing ego are repressed.

We cannot not 'control for' bias if its source is in the dynamically unconscious repressed material to which the conscious mind lacks direct access. The agency of our knowing is contaminated by the influence of these unconscious forces, including desire and authority. Being able to give reasons for one's choice of action or definition of self-interest is not straightforward evidence of rationality or freedom from the unconscious. A 'rational reconstruction' of the reasons for a choice or belief may be an elaborate rationalization of or reparation for an irrational wish or fear.

This complicated view also challenges those who portray mental life as the epiphenomena of a relatively simple series of electrochemical processes and networks. The subjective meanings of, say, delusions will never be captured within the discourse of neural firing, yet the rich content of such phenomena is clearly important in understanding the intricacies of subjectivity.

While psychoanalysts have much to contribute to conversations about subjectivity, they are vulnerable to challenges to the validity of their truth claims. Analysts cannot solve this problem by claiming that psychoanalysis is or could (given certain specified conditions) be a science. In my view, this approach is profoundly erroneous for several reasons. It makes it difficult for others of all sorts, including philosophers and practitioners of the natural sciences, to take psychoanalysis seriously. It generates endless and unproductive debates about the scientific status of psychoanalysis. Instead, we should question the beliefs behind the assumption that this is a crucial matter. What could a status mean, and what would it add to the content or usefulness of psychoanalytic theory?

Obsession with this topic repeats rather than interprets Freud's own fixation on Enlightenment thinking in that it equates 'real' knowledge and science. Such arguments arise out of outmoded and inaccurate views of what science is and how it produces its own truth claims. Most importantly, it obscures, avoids and retards addressing a problem faced by all discursive formations – how to generate discourse-specific means and tests of the production of truth. For psychoanalysis, this project will require better accounts of the knowledge which clinical experience generates and of the qualities of clinical relations and treatment. Were it able to give a better account of this process, psychoanalysis could contribute much more to epistemology, philosophy of mind and to stories of human development, subjectivity and the importance of human relations within them.

3(b) Clinical Treatment

Psychoanalytic thinkers such as Freud and Lacan also undermine the Enlightenment belief in the intrinsic or necessary relationships between reason, self-determination, and freedom or emancipation. Contrary to the great hope of Enlightenment, use of one's own reason will not necessarily make us free. If the conscious/rational self is 'not even master in its own house, but must content itself with scanty information of what is going on unconsciously in its mind', (Freud, 1937: 353) the possibilities for autonomous action are quite constrained.

The ego does not necessarily express or ensure the possibility of an autonomous or rational will. Analysis may increase one's capacity for self-reflection. Decrease of the powers of rationalization and the influences of unconscious deference to authority will not necessarily follow. In its relations with the id, for example, the ego 'too often yields to the temptation to become sycophantic, opportunist and lying, like a politician who sees the truth but wants to keep his place in popular favour' (Freud, 1923: 46).

While analysts track the complicity between ego and superego forces, including political authority, they have often ignored the impact of such influences on the theories and practices of psychoanalysis. One of the important lessons of both postmodernism and feminism for psychoanalysis is that clinical treatment cannot be politically or socially neutral. The knowledge that informs its practices, like all knowledge, contains traces of the relations of power that circulate through it.

Psychoanalysis has played an important part in generating categories of identity and standards of normalcy and health, especially in practices of sexuality, childrearing and gender. The normalizing veils of scientific language and claims to the objective discovery of 'natural' forces, identities or drives disguise the existence of these standards. Yet, a closer examination reveals the congruence of these identities and standards, especially those of femininity/masculinity, good/bad mother, healthy/deviant and homosexuality/heterosexuality, with the practices and wishes of other dominant power/knowledge configurations.

In its normalizing and regulatory aspects, psychoanalysis is both empowered by and contributes to a modern form of power, 'biopower'. Biopower generates and is constituted by the production of new sorts of truth and by particular disciplinary and confessional practices. The concrete and precise character of its knowledge of and interest in human bodies is unusual. Biopower is based in and effects a 'real and effective "incorporation" of power. It circulates through and roots itself in the concrete lives of individuals and populations through multiple and variegated means' (Foucault, 1980a: 119; 1980b). This is one of the most pervasive and characteristic modes of power in the postmodern world.

The purpose of disciplinary power is to ensure a cohesive public body. The heterogeneous elements of a population can be made more coherent through practices of 'normalization'. These practices are supported and exercised both by the state and by new bodies of knowledge, especially medicine and the human sciences. Under the humanistic rubric of the state's interest in and obligations to the creation and protection of the 'well-being' of its inhabitants, global surveillance of its members is increasingly instituted. The state needs experts to amass the knowledge it requires and to execute the policies said to effect and maximize this well-being and protection. Instances of such knowledge and associated practices include medicine, education, public health, prisons and schools.

Concepts of deviancy, illness, maladjustment and so forth are products of the same discourses that create the normal. These concepts also name the dangers the normal must be protected against. They justify the need for new and better knowledge to control the problems and for the exercise of power. The knowledge is simultaneously individual and global. It entails the study of specific 'traits' possessed by individuals that cause their deviations and the search for methods that can be applied to all such individuals to effect the desired disciplinary results in the populations as a whole. 'Prevention' of disease or crime requires the at least potential extension of these knowledges and practices to everyone.

The state's interest is in ensuring regularity of behaviour, not only in punishing crimes after the fact. The more peaceful (e.g., controlled) the population, the more the state's power is legitimated and ensured. As the state becomes more powerful, it can dispense disciplinary legitimacy. It supports, regulates and enforces the monopoly of certain professions over specific domains and practices. Failure of disciplinary practices becomes the basis for 'experts' to ask for more resources and power to pursue and exercise their knowledge in the name of the public good.

Along with the processes of normalization and discipline, the individual subject is created through confessional practices. The primary exemplars of these practices are psychoanalysis and psychiatry. Psychoanalysts and others believe in the existence of a particular form of being, the 'individual'. This individual has certain 'natural', 'universal', or 'true' traits. However, the constitution of this individual and our belief in its existence is an effect of biopower. These discourses produce dangerous forces within us such as sexuality controllable only by the person exercising surveillance upon her- or himself. This surveillance is said to lead to both 'self-knowledge' and freedom from the effects of these forces. However, to attain such self-knowledge and self-control, the individual must consult an expert whose knowledge provides privileged access to this dangerous aspect of the person's 'self'.

These discourses create the idea that there is something 'deep inside' us, something bodily but at least partially knowable by consciousness, a source of both pleasure and danger. By transforming pleasure into 'sexuality', these confessional discourse/practices generate further practices/knowledge of self-control and self-knowledge. They teach us we have an individual 'self' about which knowledge is possible. We experience this self as true and foundational. However, such experience is not 'true' in some ontological or essentialist sense. It is an effect of a subjectivity constituted in and through certain discourses, including psychoanalysis. In other discourses such notions and experiences might not exist.

While psychoanalysis contributes to and benefits from biopower, it also subverts it. The norms it posits and the categories it produces are notoriously ambiguous.[2] Unlike many other discourses, excess and excluded material are readily accessible and available to disrupt conversation or move it in a different direction. This is a strength of psychoanalytic discourse. Analysts should exploit this ambiguity rather than trying to standardize the meanings of its concepts and occlude their productive ambivalence. Psychoanalysts claim that tolerance of ambiguity is a sign of psychological well-being. It should become a norm for the health of psychoanalytic discourse as well.

Clinical practice subverts biopower in other ways. It presents the possibility of a relationship that escapes such modern binary oppositions as subject/object, work/play, instrumental/affective, child/adult, inner/outer and public/private. Analysis is a form of relational work. It is an open-ended and mutually constituted field of activity in which multiple aspects of activity and experience come into play. Language, visual images, dreams, passion, reason, bodily experience, childlike wishes and adult responsibility are all components of analytic discourse. Analytic time is not linear. Analysis is not oriented to material production, nor is it governed by a precise definition of output. Cost/benefit analysis cannot capture the utility or qualities of its activities or effects. This complexity is one of the strengths of analysis. Analysts err and even risk destroying analysis when they try to exercise order or control by marking one aspect as the true, foundational or curative one.

The multiplicity of analysis and its emphasis on relationships help to account for the devaluation, identity crises and current social dislocations of psychoanalysis. Its relational qualities place it within the female side of gendered circuits of identity and power. The confounding of binary oppositions disrupts its potential place within discursive formations, for example some empirical sciences, whose knowledge and practices produce and depend upon their existence and stability.

3(c) Disciplinary Training and Practices

If psychoanalysts try to cling to the medical model and to establish analysis as clinical science, psychoanalysis will not survive in the postmodern West. The knowledge-producing practices of psychoanalysis cannot meet the regulatory standards of other discourses, such as medicine or biochemistry, nor should they. Without discourse-specific standards, questions such as who should be authorized to practise analysis cannot be resolved. Satisfactory answers will require more discursive consensus about which knowledge legitimates analytic practices.

If psychoanalysis is to survive in the postmodern world, it must broaden the topics considered legitimate within its discursive conversations. It should increase the number and kinds of partners with whom it converses and explore the implications of their knowledge for analysis. Analysts can have productive conversations among themselves and with others concerning the discourse-specific qualities of their own knowledge and practices and the implications of these for other discursive formations. Such conversations should address the politics of psychoanalytic knowledge and practices and the complex networks of discipline, confession and resistance within which psychoanalysis circulates. These networks are components of both the internal practices of psychoanalysis and its relations with other discourses.

The paradoxical existence of increasing fragmentation and concentration of disciplinary practices and powers pervades the postmodern world. Psychoanalysis cannot be immune from the consequences all citizens of such a world must face. We find ourselves sometimes in an inadvertent but unavoidable complicity with powers whose ethical and political practices are ambiguous at best. Simultaneously we experience both vulnerabilities and responsibilities to other discursive communities whose practices are (if we are lucky) only partially compatible with ours. Perhaps more than ever, psychoanalysts need to establish new colleges of psychoanalysis. In itself this will not be sufficient for psychoanalysis to survive, much less to flourish. However, intolerance of difference, disorder and complexity will doom the discourse of psychoanalysis to increasing marginality and obscurity in the postmodern world.

Notes

1. Many psychoanalysts, even those working within an intersubjective framework, ignore this work. For example, the recent survey by Mitchell (1988) mentions none of these authors. Object relations theory has many gender biases and is used against women as well (Flax, 1990: 120–6).
2. For example, Freud (1975) is an exemplar of ambiguity. It would be quite revealing to track the eruptions of tensions and multiple definitions of crucial terms throughout this text.

References

Baynes, K., Bohman, J. and McCarthy, T. (1987), *After Philosophy*, Cambridge, MA: MIT Press.

Brenner, C. (1955), *An Elementary Textbook of Psychoanalysis*, Garden City: Anchor.

Butler, J. and Scott, J.W. (1992), *Feminists Theorize the Political*, New York: Routledge.

Chodorow, N.J. (1978), *The Reproduction of Mothering*, Berkeley: University of California Press.

— (1989), *Feminism and Psychoanalytic Theory*, New Haven: Yale University Press.

Clement, C. (1983), *The Lives and Legends of Jacques Lacan*, New York: Columbia University Press.

Cixous, H. and Clement, C. (1986), *The Newly Born Woman*, Minneapolis: University of Minnesota Press.

Cohen, A. and Dascal, M. (1989), *The Institution of Philosophy*, LaSalle, IL: Open Court.

Derrida, J. (1978), 'Violence and metaphysics', in *Writing and Difference*, ed. A. Bass, Chicago: University of Chicago Press.

— (1981), *Positions*, Chicago: University of Chicago Press.

Dinnerstein, D. (1976), *The Mermaid and the Minotaur: Sexual Arrangements and the Human Malaise*, New York: Harper & Row.

Fairbairn, W.R.D. (1952), *Psychoanalytic Studies of the Personality*, London: Routledge, Kegan Paul.

Fast, I. (1984), *Gender Identity: A Differentiation Model*, Hillsdale, NJ: The Analytic Press.

Flax, J. (1990), *Thinking Fragments*, Berkeley: University of California Press.

Foucault, M. (1977), 'Revolutionary action: until now', in *Language, Countermemory, Practice*, ed. D.F. Bouchard, Ithaca: Cornell University Press.

— (1980a), 'Truth and power', in *Power/Knowledge*, ed. C. Gordon. New York: Pantheon.

— (1980b), *The History of Sexuality: An Introduction*, New York: Vintage.

— (1988), *Politics, Philosophy, Culture*, New York: Routledge.

Fraser, N. (1989), *Unruly Practices: Discourse and Gender in Contemporary Social Theory*, Minneapolis: University of Minnesota Press.

Freud, A. (1966), *The Ego and the Mechanism of Defense*, New York: International Universities Press.

Freud, S. (1915), 'The unconscious', in *Collected Papers*, Volume 4, ed. J. Strachey, New York: Basic Books, 1959.

— (1920), *Three Essays on the Theory of Sexuality*, New York: Basic Books, 1962.

— (1923), *The Ego and the Id*, New York: W.W. Norton, 1960.

— (1927), *The Question of Lay Analysis*, New York: W.W. Norton, 1950.

— (1937), 'Analysis terminable and interminable', in *Collected Papers*, Volume 5, ed. J. Strachey, New York: Basic Books, 1959.

Gay, P. (1988), *Freud: A Life For Our Time*, New York: W.W. Norton.

Goldberg, A. (1975), *The Prisonhouse of Psychoanalysis*, Hillsdale, NJ: The Analytic Press.

Griffiths, M. and Whitford, M. (1988), *Feminist Perspectives in Philosophy*, Bloomington, IN: Indiana University Press.

Grosskurth, P. (1986), *Melaine Klein: Her World and Her Work*, New York: Knopf.
Grunbaum, A. (1979), 'Epistemological liabilities of the cinical appraisal of psychoanalytic theory', *Psychoanalysis and Contemporary Thought*, 2: 451–526.
Hoover, K. (1988), *The Elements of Social Science Thinking*, New York: St Martins.
Irigaray, L. (1985), *Speculum of the Other Woman*, Ithaca: Cornell University Press.
Jagger, A. and Bordo, S. (1989), *Gender/Body/Knowledge*, New Brunswick, NJ: Rutgers University Press.
Kernberg, O. (1975), *Borderline Conditions and Pathological Narcissism*, New York: Jason Aron.
Klein, M. (1975), *Love, Guilt and Reparation*, New York: Delta.
Kohut, H. (1984), *How Does Analysis Cure?*, Chicago: University of Chicago Press.
Kuhn, T. (1962), *The Structure of Scientific Revolutions*, Chicago: University of Chicago Press.
Lacan, J. (1973), *The Four Fundamental Concepts of Psycho-analysis*, New York: W.W. Norton.
Landes, J.B. (1988), *Women and the Public Sphere*, Ithaca: Cornell University Press.
Langs, R. and Stone, L. (1980), *The Therapeutic Experience and Its Setting*, New York: Jason Aronson.
Lowenstein, R.M., *et al.* (1966), *Psychoanalysis – A General Psychology*, New York: International Universities Press.
Mitchell, S. (1988), *Relational Concepts in Psychoanalysis*, Cambridge, MA: Harvard University Press.
Mohanty, C.T., Russo, A. and Torres, L. (1991), *Third World Women and the Politics of Feminism,* Bloomington, IN: Indiana University Press.
Okin, S.M. (1989), *Justice, Gender and the Family*, New York: Basic Books.
Pateman, C. (1989), *The Disorder of Women*, Stanford: Stanford University Press.
Pateman, C. and Gross, E. (1986), *Feminist Challenges: Social and Political Theory*, Boston: Northeastern University Press.
Rorty, R. (1979), *Philosophy and the Mirror of Nature*, Princeton: Princeton University Press.
— (1982), *Consequences of Pragmatism*, Minneapolis: University of Minnesota Press.
Schafer, R. (1983), *The Analytic Attitude*, New York: Basic Books.
Spence, D.P. (1982), *Narrative Truth and Historical Truth*, New York: W.W. Norton.

Sullivan, H.S. (1953), *The Interpersonal Theory of Psychiatry*, New York: W.W. Norton.

Turkle, S. (1981), *Psychoanalytic Politics: Freud's French Revolution*, Cambridge, MA: MIT Press.

Winnicott, D.W. (1971), *Playing and Reality*, New York: Basic Books.

— (1975), 'Mind and its relation to psyche-soma', in D.W. Winnicott, *Through Paediatrics to Psycho-Analysis*, New York: Basic Books.

— (1989), *Psychoanalytic Explorations*, Cambridge, MA: Harvard University Press.

3 Postmodernism and the Adoption of Identity

Stephen Frosh

What does it mean to have an identity? Presumably reference is being made to location, to how one conceives of oneself, to an act of self-reflection or self-cognition which fixes one according to one's place in an order of things. The usual association to 'finding one's identity' is that it is something which comes from within, involving some 'recognition' of the actuality of the inner self. In this way of seeing things, growing into, or discovering, an identity, entails constructing a relationship to the world which is compatible with one's inner self – ideally, allowing what one is to reach fulfilment in what one can come to be. Even those who understand that the term, psychologically speaking, should be in the plural – 'identities' – can still fall into the trap of regarding it as something to be achieved in order to ally oneself to the truth of one's experience. 'My identity as a man', 'my identity as a psychologist', 'as an academic', 'as a father', 'as a white person': these are slogans often put forward unproblematically, as if what they mean is clear. But, in truth, they are formulae which cover over something more complex and uncertain. Not only do they tend to hide a process of struggle and incompleteness – my identity as a man is something which I can never feel to be completely and authentically achieved, only worked at every day in a range of contradictory situations – but they also obscure a more radical sense in which identities are constructed rather than found.

I want to work with a few ideas here, to explore the relationship between postmodernism, identity and – relatively briefly – psychotherapy. This may seem a strange concatenation, but I am going to argue that postmodernism makes all identities problematic, and that out of the ensuing chaos emerges a picture of identities as adopted in order to preserve the psyche against the threat of dissolution. Identities are, in the fashionable terminology, narrative fictions;

behind them lies an anxiety which can never be fully named, and which therefore acts as a source of disruption of all attempts to pin identity down. Contemporary psychotherapy is often concerned with the process of 'restorying', constructing new narratives to redefine relationships and hence forge new identities. However, it is in danger of misconstruing the task, of rearranging the deckchairs while the ship of meaning sinks. There is no 'identity' which is not adopted, and none which absolutely fits.

Psychic Flux

The most striking claim relating to the issue of identities to have come from the general postmodernist stable is the following: that identities do not refer to the inside but to the outside. That is, notions of identity, like notions of self or 'ego', are misleading because they suggest the existence of an inner essence with form and substance. Instead, the 'truth' of the human subject, such as it is, is one of incoherence, constituted either by emptiness and lack (the Lacanian view) or by contradiction and disorder. The apparent stability of self and identity is a way of fleeing from the affective impact of this inner chaos, of taking refuge in fantasies of containment suggested by external features of the social world. Lacan (1954–55), in his commentary on Freud's (1900) famous dream of 'Irma's injection', makes this point particularly eloquently and influentially:

> [The] ego is the sum of the identifications of the subject, with all that that implies as to its radical contingency. If you allow me to give an image of it, the ego is like the superimposition of various coats borrowed from what I will call the bric-à-brac of its props department (Lacan, 1954–55: 155).

This is the familiar Lacanian idea of the speciousness of the ego as a unified entity: what in ordinary life we take as the core component of selfhood is revealed under analysis to be 'bric-à-brac', bits and pieces placed together or on top of one another more or less by chance, covering up an emptiness beneath. Moreover, the ego is 'the sum of the identifications of the subject'. Identification is that process whereby the ego takes the object and makes it *subject*, incorporating each object as part of itself. For example, in Freud's developmental account, as the growing child has to give up desired sexual objects, so in fantasy does the ego take them in, internalizing them and changing as a result. The ego thus comes to be a home for lost desires and forsaken objects; its character is formed along the line of these objects, which are introjected and absorbed, accompanied by the id-originated psychic energy invested in them. In Freud's words, this 'makes it possible to suppose that the character of the ego is a precipitate of abandoned object cathexes and that it contains the history of these object choices' (Freud, 1923: 368).

Usually, the concepts 'ego', 'self' and 'identity' are differentiated from, but also allowed to blur into, one another. The self is the most problematic and obscure of these notions, sometimes considered to refer to the whole of the person ('The total person of an individual in reality, including one's body and psychic organization; one's 'own person' as contrasted with 'other persons' or objects outside one's self' – Moore and Fine, 1990: 174), at others just the symbolized, consciously reflective parts. The ego, taking a somewhat more precise psychoanalytic definition, is that part of the mental apparatus in which consciousness resides; but it is also home to unconscious defence mechanisms and hence is more extensive than just what is available to the subject's awareness. If one is to know who one is – a reasonable, if undoubtedly approximate, definition of possessing an 'identity' – then this can be achieved only by the process of more-or-less conscious reflection on the activities of the ego. However, given that identification, out of which the ego is formed, is itself a largely unconscious procedure, then the ego – the centre of the conscious subject – is ripped open by the subject's fantasized perceptions of others. The ego is formed out of 'abandoned object cathexes'; that is, identity comes from the outside.

In all this, it is clear that subjectivity is more than just what is symbolized or known, and that there is a process of construction going on to make one's identity or identities coincide with the demands of this subjectivity. This process involves the taking in of material from the outside; that is, it is a process of *adoption* undertaken by every human subject as part of the search for a structure through which the complex multifariousness of subjectivity can be made stable and grounded in something apparently safe and under control. One insight which has been stressed by many postmodernists, including some contemporary psychoanalysts, is just how much subjectivity is a contingent and fluid phenomenon. Here, the work of Cornelius Castoriadis (e.g. 1995) is exemplary. He argues that the Freudian unconscious is a site for constant production of imaginary representations of self and other: that is, for fantasy as a constructive and ever-transforming basis for all psychic activity. He claims two 'characteristic features of the human psychism' that mark human versatility (through symbolism and representation) as distinct from the instinctual regulations dominating animal behaviour. These two features are given by Castoriadis as:

> 1. The autonomization of the imagination, which is no longer enslaved to functionality ... There is unlimited, unmasterable representational flux, representational spontaneity without any assignable end ...
> 2. The domination, in man, of representational pleasure over organ pleasure. (Castoriadis, 1995: 28)

'There is, therefore,' writes Castoriadis, 'a bursting of man's animal psychism under pressure from the inordinate swelling of the imagination' (*ibid.*). Society, however, is instituted in a state of 'closure', offering structure and constraint to the radical wildness of the imagination. This constraint is experienced as necessary, but it works like a strainer through which travels the multiplicity of the human psychic flux, leaving behind the excess from which taste derives:

> [Through] this social fabrication of the individual, the institution subjugates the singular imagination of the subject and, as a general rule, lets it manifest itself only through dreaming, phantasying, transgression, illness. In particular, everything occurs as if the institution had succeeded in cutting off communication between the subject's radical imagination and its 'thought'. Whatever it might imagine (whether it knows it or not), the subject *will think* and will make/do only what it is socially obligated to think and make/do. We see here the social-historical side of the process that, psychoanalytically speaking, is called repression. (Castoriadis, 1995: 29)

Castoriadis's emphasis on the primary status of the imagination, the way representations are produced endlessly by the human subject, is an important marker of a view of the psyche as indefatigably active and creative. New forms are continually brought into existence, then displaced by newer ones, as the mind goes about its task. As each moment is met, so new associations are produced; moreover, the dizzying excess of fantasy is not just an accompaniment to perception – and still less a substitute for reality; rather, it is a primary nexus out of which perception and thought emerge.

However, the state of effervescence is necessarily unstable, perhaps at times unbearable. What Castoriadis refers to as 'the institution' or 'society' is here taken to refer to those external reference points which are turned to with relief by the subject, as they offer to pin down the otherwise uncontainable emergence of representations, of one impulse after and alongside another. When we struggle to find out what it might mean to be such-and-such a person, to have this or that identity, we are engaged in an act of self-labelling and self-construction that is essentially static, a 'prop' out of which an imaginary stability can be made. We do this by inserting ourselves in a social-symbolic order, by what might be thought of as 'seeking out a name'; when we have found it, we try to rest content, although frequently what we are faced with is a sense that there is something missing, something which our identities have not been able to express. This is because identities can never be whole, full expressions of the stream of subjectivity, whose flowing fantasies always push at the boundaries of what we allow them to be. There is no 'natural' identity, according to this way of reading the world; rather, all identities are adopted, none will ever satisfy. It is in the nature of things, because identities are not found, they are made.

Something at the Edge of the Mirror

In Lacan's (1949) famous exposition of the mirror stage in development, he captures something of the sense of being 'misrecognized' which is possibly characteristic of contemporary culture. In contrast to Winnicott (1967), who uses the idea of mirroring to convey the importance of a developmental process in which the child sees her- or himself accurately and thoughtfully reflected back by a concerned mother, Lacan emphasizes the impossibility of identity as related to a 'true' self. In his view, the ego is used to create an armour or shell supporting the psyche, which is otherwise experienced as in fragments. Lacan emphasizes the *exteriority* of this process – that which appears to us as our 'self' is in fact given from the outside as a refuge, an ideal ego, a narcissistically invested image.

> The fact is that the total form of the body by which the subject anticipates in a mirage the maturation of his power is given to him only as a *Gestalt*, that is to say, in an exteriority in which this form is certainly more constituent than constituted, but in which it appears to him above all in a contrasting size that fixes it and in a symmetry that inverts it, in contrast with the turbulent movements that the subject feels are animating him. (Lacan, 1949: 2)

Here, Lacan is arguing that the subject gains relief from the intensity of fragmenting internal impulses through the boundedness and apparent stability of the mirror image – something external but connected to the subject, holding a promise of future 'power'. Whereas Winnicott portrays the mirroring function as one which allows the child actually to grow into her or his self – to genuinely find the 'maturation of his power', one might say – for Lacan this is a specious process, in which the subject is hoodwinked, or hoodwinks her- or himself, into taking on the image as if it were real. The mirror suggests that the subject is integrated, but 'in fact' there is to be found a multiplicity of drives and desires. Moreover, as with the rather different understanding put forward by Castoriadis and described above, there is here an image of the external, social world as operating both reassuringly and antagonistically – in a sense, guilefully – to divert the subject away from its terror of dissolution. The message given to the infant 'in the mirror' is that the ego has integrity and wholeness; but this message is a socially constructed one, legible in the reflecting surfaces and faces of an order stressing the autonomy and psychological independence of individuals.

Identity fades away as an issue here. According to Lacan, the structure of human knowledge and ego functioning is a delusional one – the misleading promise of integrity to be found in the spectral image. This is read by Lacan as a paranoid sensation. The negativity and persecutory associations of the paranoiac are to do in part with the aggressivity of the drives, threatening to burst the image apart – a notion akin to those worked on by Klein (1946) in her description of paranoid-schizoid functioning. But it is also connected with the haunting of this satisfying image of the integrated self by the spectre or memory of something else; somewhere inside, each of us knows that we are not really whole, that this seeming-self is a bare cover for something disturbing. As we look in the mirror, we catch a glimpse of something in the corner, just moving out of sight, running away before we can see what it is. The mirror is a source of reassurance and threat, its seemingly smooth surface containing unexpected ripples caused by that which can be seen yet not quite named. In contrast to the generative and creative sense of the unconscious evoked by Castoriadis, Lacan emphasizes the threat to be glimpsed at the corner of the visual field. Using the ebullient disintegration to be found in the paintings of Hieronymous Bosch as an emblem, Lacan focuses on what happens when the veneer of integrity shatters:

> This fragmented body ... usually manifests itself in dreams when the movement of the analysis encounters a certain level of aggressive disintegration in the individual. It then appears in the form of disjointed limbs, or of those organs represented in exoscopy, growing wings and taking up arms for intestinal persecutions ... (Lacan, 1949: 4)

The mirror stage reflects the impossibility of becoming a self without taking on the meanings of the other – without becoming *identified* with another's gaze, with the pre-existing desire of the other that one should be some one thing and not anything else. In the mirror stage, the terrible struggle to hold the forces of dissolution at bay is repressed in the face of a manic optimism that 'identity' will solve the problem, fixing what is fluid in us as a meaning expressible in an easy sentence: 'I am this and not that.' Looking in the mirror, we see what we wish for: a home for our hopes and impulses, a surface to bind our inner fragments together. As an image of the adoption of identity, this is excruciatingly painful: we leap into the other's gaze, to escape the turmoil inside.

In Lacanian terminology, the imaginary wholeness promised by the mirror is shattered by another step of alienation, the move to the symbolic order of experience in which the structures of language interfere with the image-making process, revealing that it is already organized by a law indifferent to the emotions and desires of the individual subject. Lacan expresses this idea most economically at the end of his seminar on Edgar Allen Poe's story, *The Purloined Letter* (Lacan, 1954–55). Having traced in masterful detail the structural interconnections between the different characters in the Poe story as a consequence of the movement of the eponymous letter, Lacan comments as follows on what constructs the identities of the individuals concerned:

> Everything which could serve to define the characters as real – qualities, temperament, heredity, nobility – has nothing to do with the story. At every moment each of them, even their sexual attitude, is defined by the fact that a letter always reaches its destination. (Lacan, 1954–55: 205)

All is determined. The position of each one of us, our sensations, feelings and actions, are given by our place in the system; it gazes on us irrevocably, and we struggle against it at our peril. Lacan has no time for, or patience with, claims of the significance of character and selfhood; he consistently debunks the notions of affect and of mature relationships used by object relational theorists. Instead, he evokes an empty subject, constituted through lack and marked by the impossibility of fulfilment or of recognition of the actuality of the other. Desire is a difference, it is:

> neither the appetite for satisfaction, nor the demand for love, but the difference resulting from the subtraction of the first from the second, the very phenomenon of their splitting (Lacan, 1958: 81).

It resides in the gap, in what cannot be answered, in the lack of satisfaction that both fuels and undermines the search for an imaginary identity. For that is the register of 'identity' in the Lacanian scheme:

it is an aspect of the fantasy of fulfilment which is split apart by the discovery that the subject is produced by, rather than generative of, the signifying chain. When we find an identity we believe we have found something with substance; but the order of causality is the other way around, it finds us. That is, the symbolic order positions the subject in relation to other subjects, marking us as incomplete, only present through our relationship with what lies outside.

Already, the notion of identity is slipping away. Yet, if the Lacanian symbolic is deeply pessimistic, the third Lacanian order, the 'real', is troubling and also powerfully evocative. The finest extended meditation on the place of the real in ordinary life (specifically, in popular culture), can be found in Žižek's (1991) *Looking Awry*. Here, the real is portrayed as that which erupts from the borderline between inside and outside – in the terms used above, that which is just at the edge of the mirror, in the out-of-sight margin. It is catastrophic in its threat, in its impact as reminder or return ('it erupts in the form of a traumatic return, derailing the balance of our daily lives' – Žižek, 1991: 29); yet it also offers substance to life, represents that contingent element that makes life worthwhile:

> For things to have meaning, this meaning must be confirmed by some contingent piece of the real that can be read as a 'sign'. The very word *sign*, in opposition to the arbitrary mark, pertains to the 'answer of the real': the 'sign' is given by the thing itself, it indicates that at least at a certain point, the abyss separating the real from the symbolic order has been crossed, i.e. that the real itself has complied with the signifier's appeal. In moments of social crisis (wars, plagues), unusual celestial phenomena (comets, eclipses, etc.) are read as prophetic signs. (Žižek, 1991: 32)

The real resides outside the registers of imaginary and symbolic; it is the order of the left-over, that which is bubbling under the surface: rhythmic, uncertain, disruptive. But it is not a mystical order outside of the realm of experience; rather, it is what our psychological and social devices keep at bay. At certain times, it breaks through to link us with everything we have left out; this is what Žižek refers to as 'the answer of the real'. But much of the time it pulses away as a threat, as that which can demolish all our attempts at identity-construction. It is this threat of the real against which the imaginary bulwark of identities defends the subject. At times of radical change, when the social-symbolic order breaks down, when, for example, death is on the streets, when change is intense and uncontrollable, then the real stalks its prey. The ambivalence with which the subject confronts its destiny is then apparent. That which is left over, that which cannot be contained, is terrifying but also exhilarating; just as war disturbs and excites, so the breakdown of identities is devastating but also can be felt as an illumination, a kind of freedom. Hence, perhaps, the otherwise incomprehensible mythic attraction of madness: symbolizing (in contrast to its banal and miserable actuality) the ultimate state of de-individuation, of escape from formal identity, psychosis has frequently been romanticized as the way through or out, as that which might put the subject back in touch with her or his essence. Lacanian theory does not romanticize psychosis in this way (see Frosh, 1991), but it does tell us something about this urge towards self-destruction.

Julia Kristeva (1983) presents a moving image of the relationship between the real and symbolism in her notion of the 'abject'. After birth, claims Kristeva, the infant experiences the maternal object as encompassing and potentially annihilating. The 'abject' is the term she applies to this elementary, pre-subjective object; abject because it is marked by horror, because the subject, constituted as an experiential emptiness, always tends towards falling into a space of nothingness. In Kristeva's thought, the infant subject is preserved when the mother has an object of her own to turn towards, allowing a space for growth. But treating the whole thing symbolically, analogically, one might say that the world of symbols – which Lacanians presume comes into play only with the advent of the Oedipal Law, but which actually seems to have important functions well before this time – preserves the infant from disappearing into this black hole. Faced with the abyss, we build a bridge over it, usually but not necessarily a linguistic one. Our symbolic activity covers over the horror of falling into space, a space which will not give us any bearings, but instead faces us with the impossibility of self-location and identity.

Many postmodernists have taken up this interest in the dislocating power of contemporary space with considerable verve (e.g. Jameson, 1984). As with Žižek's account of the real, they have tended to stress the ambiguity in the experience – how, by removing the subject's bearings, postmodern space offers excitement as well as confusion, endless stimulation of the senses alongside panic-inducing dizziness. A permanent roller-coaster ride, reproduced inside a simulator, a source of fascination and desire and a producer of fear. In this setting, the whole notion of identity seems bizarre: leaving all identities behind is much more to the point.

But postmodernity is not a permanent roller-coaster ride. Most of the time it seems like ordinary life, in which people struggle to make sense of what is happening to them and try to form satisfying relationships with other people. What, however, is continually reiterated in the culture of postmodernity is something present in all the strands of postmodern thinking outlined so far, ranging from Castoriadis's idea of representational flux, through the Lacanian real and the psychology of lack, to the notion of abjection and disjunctive space. This is an idea, or perhaps just an image, of *rupture*, of something that breaks through, unsettling any set identities. Even multiplicity is not an answer to this: simply accepting the existence of more potential identities does not prevent them all from being rattled by rupture's force. Nevertheless, what is being argued here is that our multiple adoptive identities are taken on as a way of keeping that force at bay, of holding ourselves together in the face of the continuing and possibly escalating suspicion that something utterly unknowable might be just around the corner.

The Stranger Within

It is here that the notion of 'strangeness', of the 'foreign', becomes most vital:

> To discover our disturbing otherness, for that indeed is what bursts in to confront that 'demon', that threat, that apprehension generated by the projective apparition of the other at the heart of what we persist in maintaining as a proper, solid 'us'. By recognizing *our* uncanny strangeness we shall neither suffer from it nor enjoy it from the outside. The foreigner is within me, hence we are all foreigners. If I am a foreigner, there are no foreigners. (Kristeva, 1988: 192)

In postmodern times, the condition of strangeness is forced upon us, but this is no new thing, only a possible increase in intensity and scale. Psychoanalysis, indeed, places something strange and unknown at the centre of every human subject. This is the unconscious, whether theorized as affectivity, as lack, or as self-generating imagination. By definition, the unconscious is the not-known, the strange. In addition, it is disruptive: it sets one's teeth on edge, one never knows when and in what language it will speak. Writing about the biblical Book of Ruth, Kristeva (1988) points out how essential strangeness is to sovereignty – how King David's origins in the outsider, the Moabite Ruth, whilst endlessly problematic for him, grant him that edge that propels him towards greatness:

> If David is *also* Ruth, if the sovereign is *also* the Moabite, peace of mind will then never be his lot, but a constant quest for welcoming and going beyond the other in oneself. (Kristeva, 1988: 76)

The home-born, the settled one, the never-adopted, never strange; these are not the material for royalty. Denial and repression of the stranger within, the site of otherness from which creativity emerges, are signs of failure; for each one of us, encountering our own strangeness is the only way to go.

If the strangeness within is linked to the unconscious, and if the unconscious is linked to nameless dread and excitement, then each of us harbours a place of rupture to which we have constantly to return. Calling this 'the real' only marks out its area of activity; it does not sum it up or moderate it. Unlike the adoptive identities with which we console ourselves all the time, the place of rupture does not respond to a name; it simply keeps acting, surprising us, keeping us in contact with that from which we turn. Faced with the external stranger, we may be both curious and afraid; we may find the strangeness exotic and erotic, but also abrasive and shadowy. All these responses are appropriate, too, to the strangeness within. As we ponder the identities we adopt, we should remain aware that what exists in the margins is perhaps the most intense source of meaning in our lives.

Part of the irony of contemporary experience is that this strangeness is near the surface, face to face with consciousness, yet also, through its familiarity, so banal as to lose its sting. Other cultures are just a channel-switch away; extremities of visual and auditory experience, sexual excitement and variation, 'other' worlds are available for inspection and encounter all the time. In principle, this should face us with our own otherness so incontestably, that acceptance of the foreign and the strange should be a matter of course: with all that variation around, we should know that any assumption of truth and fixed identity must be fictitious. However, what actually happens is more like the opposite. The very availability of otherness denudes it of its exotic force; the fact that much of this otherness is 'virtual', displayed through media images, makes it all the more subject to colonization. Because everything is revealed on equal terms, using the same language and equivalent imagery, it is hard for anything to retain its power to shock or move, its exotic/erotic force. The other becomes 'same', cutting off its capacity to disturb and enlighten. Under postmodern conditions, strangeness becomes entertainment rather than an answer of the real.

Keeping the stranger alive within us is no easy task, therefore. Yet it is clear from the continued existence of nationalism and xenophobia, misogyny and racism around the world that the other still retains its power to shock. This produces a particularly depressing conundrum, suggesting that otherness can exist only if it is repudiated, otherwise it is made banal. Or can one hope that the strangeness within us is defined by its disruptive quality, and that as every previous form of otherness becomes familiar and loses its force, so new ones will appear? However disturbing it may be, the preservation of a place of rupture, immune to fixed identity, might be thought of as a moral task. If this place, seen by so many theorists as central to human subjectivity, is not kept open, then meaning itself risks being lost. To give the full form of the quotation from Žižek mentioned in passing above:

> The role of the Lacanian real is, however, radically ambiguous: true, it erupts in the form of a traumatic return, derailing the balance of our daily lives, but it serves at the same time as a support of this very balance. (Žižek, 1991: 29)

Once again it is worth repeating: access to the real in the place of rupture grounds the symbolic order in meaning, giving it emotional force and substance.

The Claims of Psychotherapy

There are important implications for psychotherapy in this. In both psychoanalysis and family systems therapy, there has been a very active response to the agitations of postmodernism. In both cases, this has taken the form of an increased interest in the contribution of the therapist to the therapeutic process (called 'countertransference' in psychoanalysis and 'co-construction' or 'second-order cybernetics' in family systems theory) and a focus on narrative and story-telling. As an example of the similarity of ideas here, take the following two quotations, the first from a psychoanalyst and the second from a family therapist.

> One of the central underlying objectives of clinical work is the joint construction of organized and interlocking narratives ... To the extent that the therapeutic process is successful – and we have to bracket the unsuccessful analyses – the analysand masters the pain and anxiety, overcomes the amnesias, and corrects the distortions, and thereby acquires a set of narratives that form a convincing and seemingly accurate biography. (Wax, 1995: 550)

> The therapeutic interview is a performative text, as the postmodernist jargon has it. This text will take its shape according to the emergent qualities of the conversations that have inspired it, and will hopefully create an emancipatory dialogue rather than reinforce the oppressive or monolithic one that so often comes in the

door ... In therapy, we listen to a story and then we collaborate with the persons we are seeing to invent other stories or other meanings for the stories that are told. (Hoffman, 1990: 11)

In both these examples, there is an active engagement of the therapist's subjectivity as part of the raw material out of which narratives are built. What is appreciated here is the constructive function of language, the way putting ideas into words transforms them in the therapeutic space and makes it possible to render new versions of them, versions which allow for more movement and new understandings of experience. To some extent, this is a relativistic procedure, suggesting that a therapeutic narrative can be substituted for a self-damaging one in a rather schematic way; but as Elliott and Spezzano demonstrate (see Chapter 1 of this book) this is an incomplete model of the possible contribution of a postmodernist psychotherapy.

This needs taking rather slowly. The idea that constructing a new narrative may be therapeutically beneficial derives from the realization that language has constructive possibilities which materialize in interpersonal situations, as meanings are forged through the negotiations between one subject and another. In this respect, the 'talking therapies' are potentially very good examples of a general postmodern idiom, in which alternative narratives – new identities, perhaps – are tried on for size, experimented with in the therapeutic situation, and developed or discarded as feels fit. As contact is made between one subject and another – here, therapist and client – meanings are forged and take shape, always contingent and flexible, available to replacement as the generative process proceeds.

What should be apparent from all that has gone before is that this is at best a very partial view of the therapeutic lessons to be learnt from postmodernism. Certainly, there is much to be said for an acknowledgement of the productivity of language and of the reflexivity of the therapist–patient relationship, understood as the emerging into mutual knowing of two sets of subjectivities. In addition, postmodernism's deconstruction of the position of the 'expert', in psychotherapy as in other arenas of the knowledge/power industry, is a matter of considerable importance for everyday work as well as for high theory. But it should be quite clear that postmodernism is not simply an encouragement to linguistic playfulness, to telling better stories. Rather, it works in the margins, with what happens in that space between what can be said and what cannot. Take, for example, the following famous definition:

The Postmodern is that which, in the modern, puts forward the unpresentable in presentation itself; that which denies itself the

> solace of good forms, the consensus of a taste which would make it possible to share the nostalgia for the unattainable; that which searches for new presentations, not in order to enjoy them but in order to impart a stronger sense of the unpresentable. (Lyotard, 1979: 81)

Lyotard suggests here that postmodernism, by focusing on the act of presentation whilst also removing the props of aesthetic coherence which underlie the modernist sensibility, directly evokes the 'unpresentable', that aspect of human experience which cannot be reduced to symbolic form, whether 'co-constructed' or not. The effect of this is to draw attention to the limitations of all narratives, their inability to get anywhere near what here has been called the place of rupture, the real. Postmodernism imparts 'a stronger sense of the unpresentable', it does not do away with it.

The best modernists, Freud amongst them, always saw reality as complex and organized their perceptions of it in line with this complexity – faced with ambiguity, they struggled with the difficulty of living in doubt. Postmodernism adds to this an appreciation of the ambiguous dynamics of the process of making sense itself – of how the activity of story-telling reflects confusion, emotional investment and desire, and cannot be reduced to rationality, including the implied rationality of freedom of choice. When postmodernism limits itself to leaving this appreciation spinning in the air, so that one story is allowed to replace another without rhyme or reason, without debate over values and power, then it is possible that it will turn into something cynical and nihilistic. The claim that everything is the same shifts quickly into the feeling that nothing matters. A nihilistic stance like this, which the 'narrative turn' in therapy is too prone to invite, misses what the postmodernist vision has to offer. In particular, it misses the urgency of the value-driven opposition to totalizing discourses of all kinds – fascist, authoritarian, fundamentalist – as they threaten to mop up people cast adrift in late modernity's assault on identity, and find them a home in the most blinkered and violent stories of 'truth'.

What all modes of therapy need to address is the process of rupture, whereby every adopted identity is made problematic and unstable. In this sense, therapy, which often seeks to make the irrational comprehensible and hence to allow people to arrive at a sense of safety with themselves, has to become more self-reflexive and disruptive. This does not imply that it should trade in irrationality itself, as some of the wilder counter-culture therapists have proposed at various times in the history of the psychotherapeutic movement. Once therapy forsakes its task of helping to make meaning out of what seems meaningless, it moves into precisely that field of nihilistic 'enjoyment' of the symptom which is warned against by modernists and responsible postmodernists alike. Escaping *into* madness is not an honest response to the mad-making pressures of postmodern society. But psychotherapy cannot rest content with a salvational narrative, as Freud recognized long ago when he pronounced himself incapable of offering 'consolation' ('for at bottom that is what they are all demanding – the wildest revolutionaries no less passionately than the most virtuous believers' – Freud, 1930: 339). The principle discovery of postmodernism, such as it is, is that all truths are provisional, all stories can be better told, because they all just miss the point.

What is this point? It is that the human subject is not designated by its identities: I am not fully present in my clothing 'as a man', 'as a writer', and so on. These identities, adopted as they are from the bric-à-brac lying all around, merely cover over and give approximate and temporary shape to something quite strange: an otherness inside, a foreignness which is constitutive, productive, endlessly changing. For some, like Lacan, this strangeness takes a negative form; for others it is ebullient and full. Psychotherapy needs to preserve this strangeness even as it makes each of us less fearful of it; finding 'the other in oneself' is an important counterweight to the tendency to slide into too cosy a relationship with the truth. If postmodernism can teach us this much then, despite its incessant undermining of identities, it can have a humanizing impact on us all.

References

Castoriadis, C. (1995), 'Logic, imagination, reflection', in A. Elliott and S. Frosh (eds), *Psychoanalysis in Contexts,* London: Routledge.

Freud, S. (1900), *The Interpretation of Dreams,* Harmondsworth: Penguin, 1976.

— (1923), *The Ego and the Id,* Harmondsworth: Penguin, 1984.

— (1930), *Civilization and its Discontents,* Harmondsworth: Penguin, 1985.

Frosh, S. (1991), *Identity Crisis: Modernity, Psychoanalysis and the Self,* London: Macmillan.

Hoffman, L. (1990), 'Constructing realities: an art of lenses', *Family Process,* 29: 1–12.

Jameson, F. (1984), 'Postmodernism, or the cultural logic of late capitalism', *New Left Review,* 146: 53–93.

Klein, M. (1946), 'Notes on some schizoid mechanisms', in M. Klein, *Envy and Gratitude and Other Works,* New York: Delta, 1975.

Kristeva, J. (1983), 'Freud and Love', in T. Moi (ed.), *The Kristeva Reader,* Oxford: Blackwell.

— (1988), *Strangers to Ourselves,* London: Harvester Wheatsheaf, 1991.

Lacan, J. (1949), 'The mirror stage as formative of the function of the I as revealed in the psychoanalytic experience', in J. Lacan, *Écrits: A Selection,* London: Tavistock, 1977.

— (1954–55), *The Seminars of Jacques Lacan, Book II: The Ego in Freud's Theory and in the Technique of Psychoanalysis,* Cambridge: Cambridge University Press.

— (1958), 'The meaning of the phallus', in J. Mitchell and J. Rose (eds), *Feminine Sexuality,* London: Macmillan, 1982.

Lyotard, J.-F. (1979), *The Postmodern Condition,* Manchester: Manchester University Press, 1984.

Moore, B. and Fine, B. (1990), *Psychoanalytic Terms and Concepts,* New Haven: Yale University Press.

Wax, M. (1995), 'How secure are Grunbaum's *foundations*?', *International Journal of Psycho-Analysis,* 76: 547–56.

Winnicott, D.W. (1967), 'The mirror-role of mother and family in child development', in D.W. Winnicott, *Playing and Reality,* Harmondsworth: Penguin, 1980.

Žižek, S. (1991), *Looking Awry,* Cambridge, MA: MIT Press.

4 The Shadow of the Other Subject: Intersubjectivity and Feminist Theory

Jessica Benjamin

> The result was not the normal one of a withdrawal of the libido from this object and a displacement of it on to a new one ... the free libido was not displaced on to another object; it was withdrawn into the ego. There, however, it was not employed in any unspecified way, but served to establish an identification of the ego with the abandoned object. Thus the shadow of the object fell upon the ego ...
>
> Freud, 1917

It is well understood that Freud's development of a theory of identification was a momentous step in understanding how the apparent boundaries of the self are actually permeable, how the apparently isolated subject constantly assimilates what is outside itself. The implications of this realization are manifold, but we might say this otherness casts a shadow on the ego from two directions: the ego is not really independent and self-constituting, but is actually made up of the objects it assimilates; the ego cannot leave the other to be an independent outside entity, separate from itself, because it is always incorporating the other, or demanding that the other be like the self. From these points follow two distinct interpretations of the idea that the self is nonidentical. First, the self is constituted by the identifications with the other that it deploys in an ongoing way, in particular to deny the loss and uncontrollability that otherness necessarily brings. Second, it is reciprocally constituted in relation to the other, depending on the other's recognition, which it cannot have without being negated, acted on by the other, in a way that changes the self, making it nonidentical. While both ideas reveal the self's dependency on the other, only the second takes the intersubjective view of the other as more than the self's object.

An intersubjective theory of the self is one that poses the question of how and whether the self can actually achieve a relationship to an outside other without, through identification, assimilating or being assimilated by it. This question – how is it possible to recognize an other? – may be taken as another aspect of the problem addressed by much feminist writing: from what position is it possible to respect difference, or rather multiple differences? That discussion of difference has been closely tied to the questioning of the subject (Smith, 1988), which has raised certain objections to the very notion of recognition that is central to intersubjective theorizing. These objections, I will suggest, ought to be addressed for they will serve to clarify a psychoanalytic theory of intersubjectivity. The need for this challenge is evident when we consider the tendency in psychoanalytic writing to label intersubjective all interaction involving two persons (Stolorow and Atwood, 1984), while ignoring the difference between the subject's relationship to others and objects (Benjamin, 1995).

The form of this challenge to the philosophical notion of subjectivity serves to differentiate poststructural thought from earlier critical theory (that associated with the Frankfurt school in particular), and seemingly led to a schism between them. Since I find that this schism, which in some respects parallels the division between Lacanian and relational feminists, results in an unproductive characterization of both sides, I shall try to bring these viewpoints into a productive confrontation, a negotiation of differences. I shall begin by referring to a debate among feminist philosophers (Benhabib *et al.*, 1995), putting it to use to clarify issues I believe vital to an intersubjectively conceived psychoanalysis. Before doing so, let me briefly orient my psychoanalytic readers who may be less familiar with the terms of this debate.

French philosophy and social theory, in particular the deconstruction and poststructural theory of the Sixties and Seventies, became so influential in North America by the Eighties that they arguably established the main discursive connections in feminist thought and cultural theory. Although it is not my intent here to make hash of the differences in these schools of thought (Butler, 1990), certain ideas emerged from that matrix which shaped many discussions within feminist theory and cultural studies in Britain and North America, leading to debates about postmodernism and feminism (Flax, 1990; Nicholson, 1990). A central theme in this matrix has been the critique of essentialism (Fuss, 1989), of any attempt to secure the normative foundations of political inclusion and individual autonomy by reference to the nature of the subject, history, etc. This challenge superseded and indeed faulted the neo-Marxist, Freudian critique of the autonomous individual thinking subject such as one finds in modernist critical theory like that of the Frankfurt School. It claimed that the neo-Marxist Freudian critique was content to reveal the material, social interdependency and unconscious *nature* that underlies the apparent discreteness of the bourgeois subject, but still retained nature as an ultimate locus of authority. For example, in the work of Marcuse, sexuality assumes the place of nature as that which is repressed by civilization, much like it does for Freud. But in that of the poststructuralist Foucault, nature and sexuality are not uncovered by psychoanalysis, they are rather produced by modern discourse (Martin, 1982; Rajchman, 1991). From this perspective, one could say that the modernist critiques also reasserted essentialism by allowing the 'social' or 'history' to occupy the same essential, universalizing place that had formerly been occupied by nature. In this sense, the Marxian idea of the working class as a universal subject of a universal history with a defined telos could now be seen as an attempt to invent 'second nature'. This centred subject of history or critical theory simply displaced, while preserving its formal position and attributes, the autonomous individual that liberal theory situated in the state of nature.

Particularly significant for feminist theory was Lacan's (1988) argument that the Cartesian consciousness was overthrown by Freud's notion of the unconscious but was reintroduced by ego psychology – a Copernican revolution followed by a North American counterrevolution. The pivotal step beyond modernist theory and away from this emancipatory, humanistic concept of the ego consisted of the structural, linguistic turn: establishing that the subject is a position produced in language, not a signifier that refers to the actual mind of a person. Through a process of mutual assimilation between psychoanalysis and modern French theory, the objection to a pregiven subject was grafted onto the phenomenology of the self or psyche as well. For Lacan, the linguistic turn made it possible both to situate the subject in language, indeed to see 'him' as subjected, and to reject the notion of identity or unity of the ego. Arguing that the division between conscious and unconscious in modernist psychoanalytic thought did not secure psychoanalysis against a notion of a unitary ego, Lacan's position defines the ego as created in alienation, irrevocably split (Lacan, 1977a).

While Lacan's attack on the idea of a unitary ego scarcely affected its target, North American ego psychology, it has deeply imbued feminist thought. Thus arose another point of intense disagreement between feminist object relations theory and a large body of feminist theory oriented to Lacan, deconstruction, and poststructuralism. But whereas that disagreement seemingly defined the feminist psychoanalytic debates in the 1980s, much has since changed. Despite the obvious divergences that separate relational psychoanalysis from Lacanian and poststructural thought, this challenge to the centred subject has found resonance among many relational psychoanalysts. Influenced by feminist thought (Rivera, 1989) and social constructivism (see Hoffman, 1991), relational analysts posed a related challenge to the idea of the unitary self and the objective, knowing subject of classical psychoanalysis (Aron, 1996; Bromberg, 1993; Dimen, 1995; Hoffman, 1991; Mitchell, 1993; Stern, 1992). It now seems particularly pertinent to query the usefulness of the old way of formulating the theoretical oppositions that arose from the postmodern challenge to the subject. I shall therefore take up some of the issues that have been raised by feminists influenced by Lacanian and poststructural thought, working from my own relational feminist position with roots in critical theory.

Perhaps what most distinguishes my viewpoint from the feminist fusion of French theorizing is that I have emphasized the question of recognizing the concrete other whereas they have focused on the deconstruction of the split subject as dispersed or decentred. But it seems, as I have said, that the two positions might fruitfully interact, questioning the subject while considering the problem of recognition. For this questioning has elaborated the intrinsic problem of identity or identification, that of assimilating difference. It is thus implicitly linked to the problem of recognizing the different other. I shall begin by recalling the debate between Benhabib and Butler (Benhabib, 1992; Benhabib *et al.*, 1995), which might appear to move along the lines of schism between critical theory and poststructuralism, and to a lesser degree object relations and Lacanian theory.

Benhabib (1992e), who is allied with the tradition of critical theory, the later works by Habermas in particular, takes aim at some of the postulates of 'the postmodern position', among which the challenge to the subject is central.[1] Benhabib objects to the 'strong version' of the formulation that the subject is an effect of discourse, suggesting instead a 'weak version' of the thesis, that would situate the subject in the context of various 'social, linguistic and discursive practices'. She hopes thereby to save the 'traditional attributes of the philosophical subject of the West, like self-reflexivity, the capacity for acting on principles ... in short, some form of autonomy and rationality' (1922 (a or b): 214). She wants to argue that 'the subject is not reducible to "yet another position in language"', but has the autonomy to 'rearrange the significations of language'. Otherwise, says Benhabib, it would not be possible to maintain as Butler does that the subject can be constituted by language and yet not be determined by it.

In arguing this, Benhabib raises the crucial objection to the post-structural position: does the structuring of the I by language and cultural codes not bypass the question 'what mechanisms and dynamics are involved ... *how* the human infant becomes the social self, regardless of the cultural and normative content which defines selfhood' (1992 (a): 217). This distinction between the subject and self is crucial. But in a more problematic vein, Benhabib outlines a notion of self that may not be sufficiently distinct from that of the philosophical subject, not sufficiently problematic. She asks if we are able to 'articulate a sense of self better than the model of autonomous individuality with fluid ego boundaries and not threatened by otherness?' And here Benhabib's reference to *The Bonds of Love* implies that this is my position as well. But, as I tried to emphasize there and subsequently, negation is an equally vital moment in the movement of recognition. Nor can any appeal to the acceptance of otherness afford to leave out the inevitable breakdown of recognition into domination.[2] Benhabib's formulation seems to avoid the well-known objection, raised not only by Butler, that recognition itself can go over the edge into knowledge as mastery (Hegelian synthesis). To articulate the conditions for recognizing the other, we must understand the deepest obstacles within the self, and acknowledge that this ideal of autonomous knowing reason has served to obscure those dynamics, if not, indeed, to foster them.

Butler (1992) replies to Benhabib that power is always implicated in both authorizing certain speakers as subjects and excluding others, that discourse already constructs the positions that the subject takes, even the ones opposed by the subject. The hypothetical 'I', and even Butler herself, 'would not be a thinking, speaking "I" if not for those positions ... [since even the positions] that claim that the subject must be given in advance, that discourse [must be] an instrument or reflection of that subject, are already part of what constitutes me'. Butler contends that her position does not eliminate agency but clarifies its conditions. The determination of the subject, the fact that it is constituted over and over again, is a way of recognizing the 'very precondition of its agency' and thus to deconstruct the subject is 'not to negate or to dismiss' it, only to expose the concealed authority and acts of exclusion behind the subject. The upshot of her argument is that 'no subject can be its own point of departure' (1992: 9–15). The autonomy and intact reflexivity that Benhabib wants to rescue have been revealed to be an illusion, based on the denial of the subject's social production, as well as on a break that conceals and represses what constitutes it. As feminist theory has shown, the subject, more precisely the historically masculine subject, has always been constituted by its disavowal of dependency on the maternal, the subordination and control of what it needs.

Fraser (1995), in her comments on the debate, rightly suggests that one does not have to choose between critical theory or postmodernism, that this opposition leads to false antinomies. Rather, each can help to clarify the problems in the other, even as Butler and Benhabib each expose the weaknesses of the other's argument. Butler collapses self and subject, as if political, epistemological positions, such as the 'identity' of women as a unified political subject, fully correspond to the psychological concept of the self. To the extent that she defines emancipation as liberation from identity she also finds the problem of the other less interesting than the problem of identity. This tendency, perhaps endemic to critiques of identity, may perpetuate an elision between the other whom we create through our own identifications and the concrete outside other. But Fraser poses the crucial problem in Benhabib's return to the idea of the autonomous subject, which in effect falls short of her own arguments elsewhere (Benhabib, 1992b) that autonomy is itself a discursive ideal, one based on exclusion and domination of the other, within and without.

But I think this challenge to the autonomous subject requires more than deconstruction of the old notion of a centred unified self. I agree with Benhabib that it requires a notion of an inclusive subjectivity that can assume multiple positions and encompass the Other within. In contrast to Benhabib, I emphasize the negative: that omnipotence is and has always been a central problem for the self, disavowed rather than worked through by its position as rational subject. In fact, if the other were not a problem for the subject, the subject would again be absolute – either absolutely separate or assimilating the other. Therefore, the negativity that the other sets up for the self has its own possibilities, a productive irritation, heretofore insufficiently explored.

A further danger of the rationalist appeal to the notion of the reasoning subject is that it excludes from itself the violence and horror of which we are capable. That is, it excludes unreason. As Bataille (1991) (not unlike Adorno, 1966) proposed in his remarks on a memoir of Auschwitz, the critique of the subject need not deny reason, but it must grasp its negative moment. Thus, in his reflections on the concentration camps, Bataille (1991) points to the problem of positioning the excluded other of reason as that which alone exposes the truth. He suggests rather that 'reason brings about in and of itself that which the irrational does from the outside: its own endless questioning ... the doubt that awakening is. Only what would this awakening be ... if it did not awake first to the possibility of Auschwitz, to the potential for stench and unalleviated fury?' Bataille expatiates on the use of moral rationalism to suppress the full extent of horror: 'There exists in a certain form of moral condemnation an escapist denial. One says, basically, this abjection would not have been, had there not been monsters ... one subtracts the monsters from the possible. One implicitly accuses them of exceeding the limit of the possible ... ' (1991: 15–19). This possible self, this monster, must be included in any conception of the self that intends to confront that violence to the other, the revulsion which motivates the appeal to respect, recognition of difference.

Psychoanalytically, we associate violence with the problem of omnipotence. By omnipotence, we mean not merely a wish, but a mental state, generally understood as one of undifferentiation. In this state we are unable to take in that the other person does not want what we want, do what we say. Paradoxically, however, the self may be invested in depositing its repudiated aspects in the other, using it to represent what is despised or intolerable – for instance weakness or aggression – and so necessarily casts the other in the role of opposite (see Altman, 1995). Violence is the outer perimeter of the less dramatic tendency of the subject to force the other to either be or want what it wants, to assimilate the other to itself or make it a threat. It is the extension of reducing difference to sameness, the inability to recognize the other without dissolving her or his otherness (Irigaray, 1985).

The query into the obligation or possibility of sustaining respect for difference without reducing the other to the same – 'the ethical question' – has emerged as a logical counterpart to the question of the subject (Cornell, 1992). Such a query obliges us to avoid the ultimate escapism of moralism, of denying the monster, the Other, within. This is the danger common not only to the defences of the rational subject but also theories of exclusion that make identification with the outside Other into an unquestioned position of the 'good'. Therefore, the difficulty I wish to address regarding the subject relates as much to the typical reversal it spawns as to itself. I believe such reversals are inevitable and unproductive unless we are aware of the psychic structure that underlies them.

If an emphasis on the production of the subject as a position in discourse overrides consideration of the psychological production of the self, it is not possible to ask the question of what allows the self to respect difference. Any number of theorists, not merely those like Benhabib who come from the direction of critical theory, have taken up the issue of eliminating social agency from the 'subject' (Flax, 1990; Smith, 1988), but my concern here is with the elimination of psychic agency (Mahoney and Yngvesson, 1992): the disregard of motivation, need, or desire, which are inextricable from the concrete other, who not only constructs but responds to need or desire.[3] To be sure, the psychological notion of the self has its limits just as the idea of the subject of discourse has: either notion will, if used to displace the other, become falsely totalizing.

But if the idea of 'the doer behind the deed', (see Butler, 1990) an agent or self that precedes the act, is rejected, the psychological relations that constitute the self collapse. They become indistinguishable from the epistemological and political positions that constitute the subject of knowledge or history. Take Butler's use of the objection that the 'I' is a grammatical fiction derived from the statement 'I think' – that instead things, thoughts, feelings 'come to me' (1990: 21). It aims at the self-originating philosophical ego but misses the psychoanalytic concept of self. A psychoanalytical conception of the self always includes what 'comes to me', even if felt to be alien. It is necessarily composed of such otherness, if only at the schizoid level, in which the self's experience appears as 'it' rather than as 'I' (Ogden, 1986). The self may or may not experience thoughts as coming from 'outside', or 'inside', and may in so doing own them and acknowledge its own division.

Butler's main assertion in *Gender Trouble*, that there is no gender identity 'behind' expressions of gender, is clarifying, reminding us that gendered positions are multiple, nonidentical. But identity is not self. Self is a category distinct from that of identity. We can say that a self can be nonidentical, and yet contain a state, express a feeling, identify with or assume a position. The critique of identity does not prevent us from postulating a psychic subjectivity that takes up various positions through identification, a kind of 'identifier behind the identification'. Consider Butler's (1993a) statement that 'the forming of a subject requires an identification with the normative phantasm of "sex", and this identification takes place through a repudiation which produces a domain of abjection'. We see it is possible to write of the subject in a wholly passive voice, as something that is formed, produced by an exclusionary matrix, whose sex will be materialized, and this will all be done through 'the regulation of identificatory practices'. There is no self that does the identifying in this text.

Oddly, Butler's (1990, 1995) use elsewhere of Freud's notion of melancholy in the formation of identifications seems to rely on a self that identifies, as in object relations theory. In this text, however, Butler postulates a discursively produced dichotomy between a world of subjects and abjects, the latter formed through exclusion. While this discourse analysis does not preclude a use of the concept of identification, it does seemingly ignore the fact that both groups require psychological selves, that both identify or disidentify with their place. Again, the political position of subject or abject must be understood as distinct from the notion of a self who may take up either or both positions. Otherwise one fails to ask how and why, dynamically, a self excludes something that is felt to be dangerous, makes it abject – an operation that Kristeva (1986), and in other terms, Theweleit (1987), have explored in the relation to woman and to the origins of abjection and horror.

The operative concept involved in understanding this process – the concept of splitting – works very differently in Lacanian thinking than in object relations theory. While any rigorous psychoanalytic notion of splitting challenges the post-Cartesian view of a unitary, self-enclosed consciousness (Whitebook, 1994), Lacan's (1977b) strategy was to locate that challenge in the fact that the subject can only operate through the division and alienation language institutes. We have no access to a self prior to, not formed through, language. The purpose of his argument was thus to break up the omnipotence of the subject through this notion of its subjection, its irrevocable split. The approach of object relations psychoanalysis, by contrast, is to link omnipotence with the act of splitting as the ego's defensive act, not to say that the subject split, rather that the self (or ego) *splits*, that is, engages in the activity of splitting. The notion of splitting as an active, ongoing process of psychic defence performed by the self sets up the question of the subject differently from the notion of a split subject or identity constituted by discourse, language, normative practices, or any other structures that render the subject an 'effect'.

The object relations viewpoint, with its roots in Kleinian theory, is that the self is constantly, dynamically engaged in acts of incorporation and projection in which parts of self and other are split off (Klein, 1946; Rosenfeld, 1971). This theory would seem to be the origin of Kristeva's (1982) idea of abjection, in which the self actively creates the abject within the dichotomy 'part-of-self' and 'repudiated not-part-of-self'.[4] The ability to split may be seen as endemic, innate, a pregiven property of the mind like the ability to use language. Indeed, splitting in that sense is not only defensive but organizing; by setting boundaries and discriminating, it allows the self to keep from being overwhelmed by bounding and discriminating what confronts it (Ogden, 1986; Aron, 1995). Unlike the 'split subject', a concept that is set up in opposition to 'unity' – relying on the falseness of its binary Other to generate its oppositional truth – the notion of splitting does not require that we posit a pre-existing unity, or an ideal of unity to which splitting gives the lie.

Butler (1992) works with the active form of splitting when she warns against any version of the 'subject' that 'disavows its constitutive relations by recasting them as the domain of countervailing externality'. Here she is referring to male disavowal of the mother. But I would maintain that such a postulate about the constitution of the autonomous subject through the disavowal of maternal dependency unavoidably leads to a further, unstated consequence: the notion of recasting presupposes that the maternal other could have been or could be something apart from and prior to the disavowal, that it was and is a partner. It was, in short, once a concrete other in a reciprocal relationship where each constitutes the other. Cornell (1995), in her comment on the debate between Benhabib and Butler, does explicate this consequence and does show how a notion of recognizing the externality of the other might follow from Butler's position, and I shall return to her argument later.[5] Unlike Lacanian theory, which locates this relationship in the unknowable, prelingual domain outside history, intersubjective theory begins with the possibility and necessity of this relationship in the (partially knowable) history of the self.

Such a historicized conception of the relationship to the original other prior to its psychic and social disavowal in the Oedipal repudiation of the mother has been formulated by psychoanalytic feminists as diverse as Irigaray (1991) and Chodorow (1980), in both Lacanian and object relations language. Only this presupposition of a prior erotic attachment/identification, as Butler (1990, 1995) indeed argues regarding homosexual relationships, explains that violent mental act through which a concrete other is transformed into a split-off, repudiated part-self. If we return the subject to the position of self confronting an external other, actively engaging this transformation, we may then see how the shadow of the other (in contrast to the internalized object) falls upon the subject. To do this requires a distinction between the intrapsychic and intersubjective dimensions of psychoanalytic theory, not an elimination of one in favour of another. It requires upholding the double-sidedness of the relation to the other.

Let us consider the distinction between intrapsychic and intersubjective. The difference between the conception of ego and its object and that of self with other roughly parallels Winnicott's (1971) distinction between relating through identifications to the subjectively conceived object and using the externally perceived object. While acknowledging the contribution of the object to the subject, intrapsychic theory did not fully confront the subject with the outside other, with anything external to its own projections and identifications. This left the subject with nothing other than introjective-projective 'web-spinning', as Eigen (1981) aptly put it.

Thus despite the recognition of the relation to the object and the insight into manic defences, intrapsychic theory did not produce a critique of the self-enclosed, independent self. In Kleinian theory, if the self can contain the tension between the positions of being good and bad, between envy and reparation, the relation to the 'whole object' will follow. Alterity is not in itself formulated as a problem.

The crucial move beyond this Kleinian position was Winnicott's (1971) realization that omnipotence cannot be broken up without a process of 'destruction', which may, if survived, lead to recognition of the existence of the other as external. Winnicott emphatically stated that he called it destruction because of the liability of the other not to survive. In this liability is contained the indeterminacy and irreducibility of the other for the subject. To survive is to withstand the self's act of negation – which might consist of an attack, a refusal to comply, a 'You do not exist for me' – and reflect the subject's impact without retaliation or submission. The other who survives can be seen in its alterity, as external – outside one's own control and yet able to have decisive impact on the self.

In the individual history of the self, we visualize the problem of destruction arising at the point where the significant others do not survive the child's acts, but rather through punitive retaliation or failure to react, through aggression or absence, do not facilitate the emergence of feeling for and with the other. The more acute failures of survival are usually enacted at the level of the early body ego, where projection of the bad, angry self is expressed in bodily metaphor, perhaps in concrete physical disgust or real violence. Ordinary failures often are reflected at the level of language when the ego excludes, silences, and devalues the externalized bad object. When destructiveness has not been survived but met with punishment by a 'moral force' it is commonly internalized in the moral agency – as in Freud's (1930) description of the superego feeding on the aggression toward the 'unattackable authority'. The self now has a choice of fleeing or being the superego: condemning the other's evocations of unameliorated destructiveness, or identifying with them. The self thus limited in its contact with externality remains in the thrall of idealization and repudiation, of identifications and projections. These then facilitate or even require submission to an authority or redeemer, or (to bring in the matter of identity) subjection to a 'moral' identity set up to oppose the externalized, bad object.

From the concept of survival follows a distinction crucial in psychoanalytic practice: that between transference–countertransference based on projective identification, in which the other is only felt to embody part of self, and (un)conscious communication based on mimetic resonance, in which two separate minds are felt to be present (Sandler, 1993). For Winnicott's final conclusion is that only the outside other can be loved. It is ultimately this pleasure in the discovery of somebody to love that compensates the breakup of identity. And, as Winnicott added, there is always the problem of waste disposal. For it is possible to remain in self-enclosed web-spinning, to rely on the superego to contain destructiveness (not without mentally attacking the self object, to be sure). But only the concrete outside other can break up the closed energy system, only the other who can be moved but not coerced by us can take on some of what is too much for the self to bear. There is no question that we need the other – the question is only, can we recognize her? And, has not the master–slave problematic made clear to us that her otherness becomes vitiated if we fail to do so? (Benjamin, 1988).

What about the objection to recognition, on the grounds that it falsifies the difficulties of difference? Contrary to those who find in this call for recognition of the concrete other/mother a myth of harmonious reconciliation (Scott, 1993), I will suggest how the intersubjective emphasis on the relation to the outside other expands the critique of identity as it has been developed in both critical theory and postmodern feminist thought. The critique of identity has often been reiterated in feminist thought as part of the rejection of essentialism (Smith, 1988). It has been formulated in Lacanian terms, for example, by Gallop: '... any identity will necessarily be alien and constraining. But I do not seek some liberation from identity. That would lead to another form of paralysis – the oceanic passivity of undifferentiation. Identity must be continually assumed and immediately called into question' (Gallop, 1982). This position recapitulates Adorno's critique of identification and identity, his excoriations of the absolute subject. Adorno was concerned to show how the act of knowing aimed to assimilate the other completely into itself. Thus he speaks of 'the totality of the concept, the absolute domination of the subject':

> The circle of identification, that finally only identifies with itself, is drawn by the thought that tolerates nothing outside; its imprisonment is its own handiwork ... Even the theory of alienation, ferment of the dialect, confuses the need to come close to the heteronomous and thereby irrational world ... with the archaic barbarism of the longing subject that is not capable of loving the alien, the other; with the greedy thirst for incorporation and persecution. (1966: 172)

Adorno's effort to unseat identity finally could only offer the continual negation through self-reflection. And this position, whether in its critical theory or later deconstructionist versions, has been most assiduous in exposing the absolutism of the thinking subject, the domination inherent in the process of identification. However, Adorno's critique of the subject remained constrained by his view of the object, which was never formulated intersubjectively (Benjamin, 1977). In the absence of intersubjectivity, the subject of reflection can only reflect upon itself, not account for the possible transformation made by the intervention of an other whose negativity is fully independent of the subject. Habermas, on the other hand, recognized this problem and formulated an idea of intersubjectivity close to that of Mead, based on self-reflection in the third person and situated in speech interaction. However, Habermas does not allow that intersubjectivity returns us to the liability of the other not to survive, the inevitable failure of recognition. His notion of internalizing the other's position does not distinguish externality from identificatory assimilation of the other (see Habermas, 1992). In fact, neither Adorno nor Habermas succeeded in elaborating a position of recognition or reflection that takes us 'beyond' the superego.

On balance, in considering the well-known line-up of Habermas vs. Adorno, we might say that whereas Adorno bequeathed us the critique of identity without intersubjectivity, Habermas provided an entry into intersubjectivity, but without sufficient attention to the subject's destructive omnipotence. In this case, a synthesis seems tempting. But it is not my intent to discuss their two theories in detail. Here I merely want to emphasize that the adumbration of intersubjectivity must continually retain the awareness of the other's liability not to survive. It therefore cannot dispense with the critique of identity, which addresses the self where survival fails, in the intrapsychic enclosure of identification and projection. The embrace of intersubjectivity does not constitute a transcendence (*Aufhebung*) of the intrapsychic, but rather a modification and addition to it (Benjamin, 1995a).

But this modification is crucial. The intersubjective idea of negation is especially relevant to those who, even as they embrace the critique of identity, seek a way out of the dilemma posed by it; who accept the premise of a nonunified, constructed subject but do not want to leave the subject merely decentred and dispersed. Attempting to get beyond the impasses proceeding from the deconstruction of the subject, such critics (de Lauretis, 1986; Smith, 1988) propose that the subject's agency and liberation derive from identity's very negativity the contradictions between its multifarious positions. The notion of agency can, in this view, be rescued by locating its source in the clash of culturally instituted subject positions – an argument Butler (1992) seems to make as well. But, even if this were so, agency is not the only thing to be rescued from our critique of the subject. And so I would argue that it still remains necessary to articulate the indispensable negativity provided by the other, alongside the negativity within. In order to go beyond a conception of a self-enclosed self, to recuperate difference and respect for otherness along with agency, we have to account for the impact of the other on the self. This impact provides a negation that is at once indeterminate and irreducible to the subject's own mental world, thus not the subject's own constructed, internal Other, even though related and interdependent with it.

The psychoanalytic formulation of the question of the other corresponds to the 'ethical question' to which poststructural and deconstructionist thought have returned (see Bernstein, 1992; Cornell, 1992). Cornell (1995) draws the link this way: 'The beginning of the other subject demands the recognition that Woman is Other to the fantasy structures of the masculine psyche. Thus there is an ethical and a political meaning for feminism in the recognition of the externality of the other.' This recognition by the subject of his reproduction which 'follows' the other/mother is 'not the death of the subject but the "birth" of a subject other for the ego' (1995: 154). Here again the necessity of conceiving a being external and given to the subject: only thus can we make a distinction between locating the other as a disowned part of the self (fantasy other) in a complementary opposition and recognizing the 'real' concrete other/mother who has preceded us, whom we require. (Indeed, necessarily mother and father precede us, so that mother's desire comes before our own.)

The question of recognition is also, as Cascardi (1992) suggests, always the question of whether there will be peace or war, a struggle to triumph and annihilate or a negotiation of difference. The question – Can a subject relate to the other without assimilating the other to the self through identification? – corresponds to the political question, Can a community admit the Other without her or him having to already be or become the same? What psychoanalysis considers the problem of overcoming omnipotence is thus always linked to the ethical problem of respect and the political problem of nonviolence.

It is worth considering what we mean by omnipotence, and whether it is necessary to posit it as a kind of primordial condition (see the discussion of Stern and Pine in Benjamin, 1988). If omnipotence is asserted only in the moment when the self recognizes the possible threat that the other poses, we see that otherness and omnipotence are always mutually constituting. Omnipotence is only known retroactively, when it no longer is such. Only in the moment of constituting a separate I (for myself) can the other threaten it –

even when, in fact, I am constituted for an other, and this constitution is called in question by a second other. The moment in which omnipotence is continually recharged is that of facing the fact of dependency on others outside our control. Of course, this confrontation extends beyond the need for loved others to the world at large. Merely by living in this world, we are exposed to others and subjected to unconscious, unwilling identification with others (on television, if not begging on the streets). Whether we will or no, the world exposes us to the *different* others who not only in their mere existence as separate beings reflect our lack of control, but who also threaten to evoke in us what we have repudiated in order to protect the self: weakness, vulnerability, decay, or perhaps sexual otherness, transgression, instability – the excluded abject in either Kristeva's or Butler's sense. It is not truly in our power not to identify; what we cannot bear to own, we can only repudiate.

In yet another sense we are captive to identification, for recognition inevitably takes the indirect and potentially alienating form of identification, in which self takes the other as ideal or as a part of self, thus abrogating difference and externality.[6] The object may be assimilated as like or opposite, taking the form of the split unity, in which self and other are assigned complementary parts that can be switched, but never held together. But the way out of these identificatory processes is not merely escape into the superego, whose moral condemnation may be used to counter idealization or repudiations; nor through simple identification with or revaluing of the despised half of the complementarity, the done to, which creates new moral imperatives, a new normativity. Identification can serve as a means for bridging difference without denying or abrogating it, but the condition of this form of identification is precisely the other's externality. The other's difference must exist outside; not be felt as a coercive command to 'become' the other, and therefore not be defended against by assimilating it to self. It is here that the notion of recognition as mediated not only through identification, but through direct confrontation with the other's externality, makes a difference.

Only the externality of the other that survives destruction allows a representation of the other as simultaneously outside control and nonthreatening – a form of negation that social relations of domination enforced by violence intrinsically prevent. The loss of externality plunges the self into unbearable aloneness, or escape into merger with like-self beings, creating an identity that demands the destructive denial of the different. I have suggested that the early developmental route out of projective-introjective assimilation turns out to be through recognition's opposing term, negation, which has to be revalued. Thus, I elaborated on Winnicott's notion of destruction – the mental refusal to recognize the other, the negation of the external – and contended that recognition practically, psychically depends upon symbolic processing of destruction.

This transposition of terms, such that recognition now depends upon negation, momentarily reverses the terms in favour of negation. But this move, in turn, makes the tension between negation and recognition dependent upon the recognition of the negation, of the other's impact or intent. For example, in the psychoanalytic framework, we understand the necessity of catching, receiving and holding the patient's negation. Thus, negation can only be revalued as a more equal term within the context of recognition itself as the superordinate value that enables negation to have impact. It is when negation, as destruction, is not survived that it explodes this superordinate function; it is when the other is not able to change or recognize the effect, but only deflects, attacks, or withdraws (the other is 'destroyed') that we can speak of the breakdown of recognition, which is not equivalent to mere negation.

The opposition recognition/negation is therefore not precisely the same opposition as mutual recognition/breakdown. The first tension can exist within the second. All negotiation of difference involves negation, often leading to partial breakdowns which we might call disruption. Breakdown, full rupture, is only catastrophic when the possibility of re-establishing the tension between negation and recognition is foreclosed, when the survival of the other for the self, of self for other, is definitely over. By the same token, recognition does not require a full reconciliation, least of all an 'extorted' one, as Adorno termed it, but rather something that is both 'tensed and unstable – never quite *aufgehoben* or reconciled' (Bernstein, 1992).

The complementary opposite to breakdown should not be seen as an original constancy or tension, a 'steady state'. It might, as has been done in the study of infant interaction, more properly be conceptualized as repair of disruption (Tronick, 1989). However, the danger of repair lies in creating false unity, which in turn will inevitably inspire breakdown, the unleashing of aggression against it. Conversely, fear of the aggression that is unleashed in breakdown may lead to the stabilization of complementarity, to 'false reconciliations' whose stuckness prevents a real dialectic of breakdown and repair. The experience of repair can retroactively light up destruction's creative, differentiating side, which has the effect of placing the other in a space outside coercive reconciliation. Without the recognition of negation, there is only the false closure of contradiction, the defensive assumption of identity that conceals the real strain of acknowledging the other. Acceptance of this strain is a condition of acknowledgement, not an invalidation of it. In fact, we have reason to believe that repeated experiences of breakdown and repair result in the subject's confidence in the possibility of reinstituting tension after breakdown (Beebe and Lachman, 1994). This confidence is what allows her or him to relinquish ossified forms of complementarity, to risk the negotiation of difference (see Pizer, 1992). In this light, splitting and breakdown can be seen as a necessary moment of destructiveness to break up what is calcified (Eigen, 1993).

Further, we might recognize that alienated forms of complementarity, based on the idealization and repudiation created by splitting, are inevitable. In the best of circumstances, these alternate with recognition. It follows that the ability to symbolically work and play with the fantasmatic relations produced by splitting will be a condition of reinstituting recognition.[7] Splitting itself is not the problem, but only its rigid congelation into indissoluble complementarity, which structures the subject and his or her other as mirror opposites (good/bad, excluded/included). Splitting, then, need not be conceived in opposition to some normative ideal of the whole self, but rather as the initial form adopted by the self with respect to contradictions in feelings or apprehensions; it can either be transformed in relation to the outside other or reduce the other to a locus of the self's disowned parts. The point of departure for this view of splitting is not the self-enclosed unity of the subject, but the contradictions that our need for the other's independent existence demands we bear.

In sum, respect for the different other requires that within the binary hierarchy of recognition–negation, negation receives its due. Recognition would be the 'superordinate' but not the 'superior' term. Nonetheless, without positing the capacity for reciprocal recognition as one side of subjectivity, the demand to respect the different Other (and its negative form, the objection to being silenced), has no basis other than a problematic form of guilt, a projection of one's own injured narcissism on to the other. Likewise, the demand to be recognized in one's difference, raised from the position of the Other, would have no basis other than narcissism. It reduces the ethical question to the competition of abstract, self-interested individuals.

One of the most subtle forms of breakdown of tension occurs when the Other is seen as exempt from the responsibilities of the subject to deal with his or her own narcissism. As when the abused Other makes a claim to absolute restitution by attacking the subject, and that subject tries to flee his own guilt and preserve his own narcissism by identifying with the victim and accepting that claim. The subject capitulates, rather than surviving with impact. This political countertransference is like that of the analyst, working with the abused patient, who finds herself in the role of the abused, unconsciously playing to the patient's sadistic identification with the aggressor. The analyst, in flight from her own identification with the aggressor, accepts this reversal, is driven to make restitution for all suffering, until she finally collapses or retaliates (Davies and Frawley, 1994). It therefore behoves the analyst to find a way to preserve her subjectivity without counterattack, not to relinquish it in an act of false reparation. This has been a key theme in current discussions of relational analysis. The analyst must find some avenue to communicate with the patient from one subject to another, despite the inevitable asymmetry of responsibility, for instance by controlled acknowledgement of the patient's emotional impact (Maroda, 1995). This implies an ongoing tension between asymmetry and mutuality (Aron, 1996).

An historic exemplification of the breakup of exclusion, of the self-enclosed world of the subject, might be the South African whites' relinquishment of apartheid. The strategy of the African National Congress exemplified the intervention of the Other as subject, achieving through their own solidarity and recognition a form of agency despite persecution and denial of recognition by their opponents. The ANC and Mandela assumed an ethical responsibility for the consequences before that responsibility had been honoured by the white government, before symmetrical power had been established. Much of what transpired in the initial transition offered an alternative to the reversal of power relations that silence the silencer. This is the difference the Other can make, precisely because the Other insists on being a subject, not simply attacking the other's subjectivity. We should not forget, however, that it was also De Klerk's ability to envision *surviving* the destruction of the Afrikaner way of life that allowed difference and externality to emerge.

The notion of intersubjectivity postulates that the barbarism of incorporating the Other into the same, the cycle of destructiveness, can only be modified when the Other intervenes. Therefore *any subject's primary responsibility to the other subject is to be her intervening or surviving other.* This perspective allows us to move beyond the critique of the thinking subject into the problem of identity as it presents itself in the psychopolitical world. It permits a differentiation between the simple reversal of complementary power relations and the concrete negation that breaks up fixed identity and allows survival – in effect, a negativity of nonviolence.

Here, indeed, is the reason it is necessary to distinguish the subject of discourse and the self as agent. Only such a self can *own* – assume responsibility for containing – destructiveness in self and other rather than projecting it into the not-I or turning it against the self. In political thinking the move to locate what is harmful in that which constructs the subject (discourse) tends not so much to foster awareness of subjection as to heighten the tendency to split, projecting outward what properly belongs to self.

Along with such capacity for ownership must go the capacity for recognition. The danger of split complementarity arises if we forgo the requirement of mutuality in recognition. Unless we accept the formal terms of reciprocity, even in the face of asymmetry, the critique of the subject becomes paradoxical. For then the subject is always critiqued from the standpoint of the other who is excluded, assimilated, unrecognized. But, I would emphasize, if this other, who must likewise be a subject, is as incapable as the first of such recognition, he or she is no other, but only a ruse of the subject's will to power. To refuse this consequence is simply to split, to reverse the complementarity, to speak from the position of the Other as 'good' and pronounce the subject 'bad', thus disowning the bad subject in ourselves. To postulate a self who can assume both 'goodness' and 'badness', both recognition and negation of the other, is the only ground for a critique of the subject's inability to recognize the other.

While my formulation of this position derives primarily from work within psychoanalytic theory, it turns out to correspond quite closely to the philosophical controversy between Derrida and Levinas regarding alterity (Derrida, 1978; Cornell, 1992). At issue here is whether the reduction of the other to the same is to be avoided by declaring the other to be absolutely other (Levinas), positing a radical alterity outside a knowledge which inherently strives to control it; or whether it is to be avoided by recognizing that the other must also be an alter ego, irreducible to my ego precisely because it is an ego. This issue is taken up by Derrida in his critique of Levinas's insistence on irreducible alterity: 'If the other was not recognized as ego, its entire alterity would collapse' (1978: 125). The condition for the other being recognized is that the other also be a subject, an ego, capable of negating. As Cornell puts it, 'The strangeness of the Other is that the Other is an 'I.' But, as an 'I,' the Other is the same as 'me.' Without this moment of universality, the otherness of the Other can be only too easily reduced to mythical projection' (1992: 57).

Reciprocity must therefore be preserved as a condition of conceiving the ethical relationship, in which, as Bernstein (1992) says, both self and other 'stand under the reciprocal obligation to seek to transcend their narcissistic egoism'. For 'without a *mutual* recognition of this *Aufgabe* [task/obligation] of searching for commonalities and precise points of difference, without a self-conscious sensitivity of the need always to do justice to "the other's" *singularity* ... we are in danger of obliterating the radical plurality of the human condition' (1992: 75). I have suggested how the concept of recognition can take account of both the intrapsychic negation 'within the subject' that has been elaborated against the logic of identity and the intersubjective negation of/by the other. This can be done without reconstructing a normative identity, without establishing a subject–object unity, without implying a transparent knowledge of the self or the other – these being the objections to recognition raised by feminists (Young, 1990).

It has been widely argued that, in the Hegelian concept of recognition, difference is sacrificed to recognition because both subjects are reconciled and absorbed in the higher determinations of another form of absolute subject: *Geist*, history, the state, or community. But Cornell (1992) argues that to uphold difference also requires the preservation of Hegel's concept of recognition, with its distinction from reflection, in which the other exists simply for the self: 'the protection and care of difference is not carried out to the detriment of the possibility of mutual self-recognition, if understood in the sense of the recognition of *phenomenological* symmetry' (1992: 57).

What does the protection of difference actually mean? Young (1990), in her critique of the ideal of community, argues that the notion of overcoming of otherness in mutual sympathy of reciprocal recognition upholds an ideal of homogenization in which significant differences could never be acknowledged. The other's alterity would no longer be irreducible, but fully knowable, assimilable, subject to our internalization. The notion of a transparent understanding of the other implies a transparent self, a self which does not allow the existence of its own negative, its unconscious otherness, what Kristeva called the Stranger within us. A notion of recognition as full knowing of the other, Young continues, would revive the norm of an autonomous, self-enclosed subject who always knows itself, its desires, a unity rather than heterogeneous and multiple being. It would also affirm identification with commonality as *the* basis for respecting the other. This would be less likely to produce respect for otherness than chauvinism and nationalism. Or it would produce a reverse identification with the other, a self-denial that installs the excluded other in the position of the ideal.

Politically, the possibility of mutual intersubjectivity is predicated on the very difference that also leads to continual misfiring of recognition, the very plurality that strains subjectivity. Psychologically, the struggle to try to know the other while still recognizing the other's radical alterity and unknowability has to be formulated not only as one between different identities, but as disagreement and contradiction within identities. For, indeed, ideological disagreements may well override identity – not all identities think alike. Such equations between identity and thought reduce thinking itself. (One has to ask whether the notion that differences stem from identities does not repeat the perversion of Marxism according to which Leninist parties attributed challenging ('deviationist') ideas to the ('objective') class position of their advocates.) This requires a notion of self that need not aim at a seamless unity of consciousness by exclusion, by mistaking a part for the whole. A self that allows different voices, asymmetry, and contradiction, that holds ambivalence.

In light of these arguments, I want to take another, critical look at the theme of exclusion as it has been continually asserted in feminist thought. Here let us consider Butler's argument that subjects are necessarily created in opposition to the abject. She says, 'Subjects are created through exclusion, through the creation of a domain of deauthorized subjects, presubjects, figures of abjection, populations erased from view', (Butler, 1992) or that 'subjects are formed through exclusionary operations' (Scott, cited in Butler, 1992). Butler seems to posit an exclusion that has no opposing term, no *inclusion* no formation of the subject through recognition. But if this were so, how could the 'contesting and rifting' she calls for occur, how could the demand to respect difference be posed? On what basis other than an ideal of inclusion, of recognition of the other's right to participate in the polity, on what grounds – besides the sheer self-interest or power of the excluded – is exclusion to be opposed? Surely this critique of exclusion implicitly functions to make inclusion of preserved differences a normative, universal demand? And why not, as long as it remains open to interrogation?

First, let us agree that, from the standpoint of psychoanalytic theory, exclusion is a term that can only mean to psychically 'relocate'. Remember that a split off part of self, the internal other, is not equivalent to an external, social other who may or may not be excluded. Excluded refers to that which is repudiated, cast out of self, abjected, in order to shore up the subject's identity, not to the truly outside other. As in our representation of the universe of energy, so in that of the psychic universe the principle of conservation applies: something that is pushed out of one psychic place ('inclusion') has to go elsewhere ('exclusion'); likewise, what one refuses to recognize outside re-emerges as a dangerously threatening internal object. This internal object may then reappear 'outside' as the dangerous other. It would seem, psychoanalytic theory once accepted, that we can formulate this as the essential 'law of inescapability': nothing leaves our psychic universe. To deconstruct the terms by which exclusion operates, or even the opposition inclusion/exclusion, reveals that we cannot reject exclusion without affirming inclusion, for that is a psychic impossibility.

In light of the fundamental givens of the psyche, exclusion is an illusion. The question is merely what type of inclusion we seek or flee, critique or promulgate, conceive or deny. Here our acknowledgement of the ongoing intrapsychic process of identification and projection is essential. The injunction to respect the other's external alterity, even unknowability, comes up against the problem that the *position* of the other is internal to the self (internal alterity). This position is 'already' represented in the mind, either as object or other subject. This representation of the other in the self depends, in turn, on certain psychic terms – love/hate, attachment/loss, life/death – which cannot be avoided, but at best can be reconfigured. As I see it, this is the position Butler (1990; 1995) takes in regard to gender identifications that become the melancholic residue of internalized prohibition: what cannot be mourned, cannot be let go, is held inside as abject, repudiated otherness. Thus, paradoxically, only inclusion, the reavowal of what was disavowed, in short *owning*, could allow that otherness a place outside the self in the realm of externality, could grant it recognition separate from self.

The challenge to the subject in terms of exclusion or identity unavoidably poses a demand for inclusion and yet that demand carries the risk of reinstituting identity, if only the identity of the Other. Indeed, it is difficult to see how a genealogy of the concept of exclusion would not find its roots in the very universal norms Butler sees as a ruse of power, as well as to the reaction spawned by those norms: the privileged position of otherness that wishes to establish a 'pure' ideal, outside power. Thus I would argue that the criterion of exclusion can itself become a regulatory counterideal, establishing the position of the excluded other as a reified, indissoluble position of identity from which to attack exclusion and unmask power, as if it were free of it. Likewise, the attack on universality can fuel itself through this counteridealizing zeal, drawing its power from the act of reversal.

The idea of inclusion may be parallel to the principle of recognition, which works only insofar as it continually apprehends its dependency on negation, the breakup of identity. Only by apprehending its own inevitable failure – the ongoing tendency toward splitting, toward negation of the other, toward exclusion – can recognition of the other function. The same could be said of inclusion. The dangers of normativity, including the creations of ideals of self and other that are potentially punitive and exclusive, are evident. But these dangers cannot be avoided by repressing the idealizing, normalizing tendencies of the mind: the self's inevitable involvement in identificatory processes that foster idealization and exclusion, splitting of good and bad. Butler's use of the idea of exclusion as a touchstone seems to imply that it can function unproblematically, as if it did not rest upon another ideal, susceptible to idealization and deployment as power. But why should it not be susceptible? We may agree that, as she herself suggests (Butler, 1993b) in her discussion of Cornell's *Philosophy of the Limit*, the point is not to dispense with the ideal, but to accept the failures and losses attendant upon any relationship to ideals, the necessary tension of the difference between the ideal and the real.

Butler asks how we are to distinguish the 'valorization of infinite striving' based on accepting that tension and those failures from the slave morality that uses this relation to the ideal to reinstitute a sense of failure and turn the will-to-power back on the self. What, in other words, is the difference between a philosophy of the limit and a philosophy of the superego, between a mourning that allows renewal and a melancholia that finds all political agency impossible. The main inconsistency I find in Butler's position is that she offers as worthy but unrealizable ideals Cornell's Good as a condition of the ethical relation, Laclau's emancipation as the condition of a political field mobilized by antagonisms, and her own idea of 'loss of the subject as the ground of meaning' as a condition of a 'discursive modality of agency'. If we are able to retain ideals of the good and of emancipation, why not an ideal of an inclusive self that is the condition of multiplicity, difference and incomplete knowledge of the other? Why, when it comes to ideals, no locus of self or subjectivity, only discursivity?

Granted that inclusion is an unrealizable ideal that is worthy of our striving, it remains to establish something about the nature of a self or a polity that gives content to this ideal. Here I would like to briefly sketch an idea of the self that might hold this demand for inclusion, and yet would not require a hold in identity, which is necessarily created through exclusion. The object relations concept of self has framed the possibility of an inclusiveness without identity, a self that sustains difference and contradiction. Necessarily, however, where identity once grounded the ego, the relation to the other must now ground a self that would live without identity. For, as I said before, self does not equal identity. To include without assimilating or reducing requires us to think beyond the binary alternatives of self-enclosed identity and fragmented dispersal to a notion of multiplicity. What kind of self can sustain multiplicity, indeed, the opposition to identity that the relation with the different other brings?

Here we may see the limits of the philosophical critique of integration as a false reconciliation, which pointed out the normative problem in the psychoanalytic language of unity, coherence, identity.

That critique does not speak to the concretes – fear, pain, loss – that generally drive disintegration and therefore make integration look like a good thing. The philosophical critique of the subject conflated the theoretical denial of multiplicity and discontinuity with the experience of self-continuity that Winnicott called 'going on being'; it made ordinary unhappiness and neurosis indistinguishable from the anguish of 'the slide into psychosis' (Flax, 1990: 219). When we move to the psychoanalytic register of the self, we change our vantage point in such a way as to focus on such experiences of anguish. To rethink integration and formulate a different notion of inclusion requires a rethinking of what the self is capable of, its catastrophes as well as its possibilities. In referring the self to its relationship with the concrete other, we locate the self in the fragile, unenclosed space of intersubjectivity, a possible reciprocity of difference and recognition, from which negativity, both creative and disastrous, cannot be excluded.

The psychoanalytic effort to replace splitting with the sustaining of psychic tension and the ability to tolerate opposing attitudes toward self and other could well stand to be freed of its legacy of normativity and advocacy for identity. But an object relations view of integrating split-off aspects of self need not imply a mythical unity, a harmonious identity. To think of the self only as discursively regulated and produced would eliminate the space that includes this negativity of the self, however vital such self-reflection on the effects of regulatory discourse within psychoanalysis itself. Tolerating ambivalence, being able to feel both love and hate toward the same object, does not mean that love and hate are synthesized so that love triumphs over hate. Rather, it means that hate can be borne. Difference, hate, failure of love can be surmounted not because the self is unified, but because it can tolerate being divided. Inclusion of split-off feelings or blocked aspirations is motivated not by a compulsion to restore unity but out of the wish to be less resentful and afraid of projected anger, less terrified of loss, less punitive toward what one desires.

Many contemporary relational analysts have begun to consider the importance of conceiving of a multiple rather than a unified self. Statements about the discontinuity, contradictions and multiplicity of self experience are legion in the writings of contemporary relational analysts (see Aron, Bollas, Bromberg, Davies, Eigen, Mitchell, Pizer, Rivera). But unlike the discussion in feminist theory, the psychoanalytic discussion is less preoccupied with the opposition between identity and multiplicity, for this does not adequately describe the problem of unlinked psychic states. The most interesting thinking about the use and abuse of the idea of unity has come from reflection on people who suffer from dissociated states. When experiences with the other are immediately or cumulatively traumatic, the anxiety and intolerable conflict between different reactions leads to dissociation (Bromberg, 1995; Davies and Frawley, 1994; Rivera, 1989; Schwartz, 1994; Stern, 1992). In dissociation, the awareness of transition or discrepancy between different self states is blocked. In this case we understand that the self has lost contact with its multiplicity because of dissociation – barriers to awareness erected in the face of severe pain or fear – and not because of a repression of conflict by a unified self (Rivera, 1989).

As Stephen Mitchell (1993) has contended, from a clinical standpoint both rigidity and fragmentation are equally symptomatic; the self characterized by high degrees of dissociation may appear either fragmented or rigid, chaotic or organized. To recognize high degrees of dissociation as illness is not tantamount to espousing an ideal of digestion and blending over 'the capacity to contain shifting and conflictual versions of self' (1993: 105). Or as Bromberg (1993) put it, 'there is no such thing as an integrated self, "a real you", ... [H]ealth is not integration ... [it] is the ability to stand in the spaces between realities without losing any of them', to replace dissociation with internal conflict (1993: 166). Thus fragmentation and multiplicity are quite different, if not to say opposed. Rivera (1989), in her discussion of dissociation and multiple personality, has argued that integration does not imply a fictional unity, but rather 'the erosion of dissociative barriers to a central consciousness that can handle the contradictions of the different voices and different desires within one person ... not the silencing of different voices with different points of view – but the growing ability to call all those voices "I", to disidentify with any one of them as the whole story' (1989: 28).

The ability to disidentify is decisive for the reflexive process that makes ideals and identities separable and fluid rather than compulsory and coercive. On what is such an intrapsychic ability based? The issue cannot be discussed simply in terms of the intrapsychic ability to bring together disparate representations of the other, but also in terms of the psychoanalytic interaction that makes such a synthesis bearable. The self's ability to disidentify with any one story as the whole may appear to us as intact reflexivity, but in fact it depends upon a specific kind of *relationship* between self and other. The crux of the matter for relational theory has been to understand the way that threatening experiences necessarily reappear and require resolution as action within the relation to the analytic other. Because such threats to the self are linked to unmanageable experience with the other, it is only the simulation of that experience within a differently organized dyad in which the other take responsibility for their part in the experience that is therapeutic. What we strive for is not only the recovery of the story of suffering, but also the breakup of the story, once a seamless narrative of doer and done-to, in the new, therapeutic relationship. This occurs through survival, understood as the incremental transposition of the experience of retaliation and abandonment (often felt as literal repetition, for long stretches, by one or both participants) into metaphor. This metaphorical (Kristeva, 1986) capacity allows us to hold onto the reality of thoughts and feelings and own them as part of the self without insisting that they be the whole story.

How does the transposition into metaphor occur? The capacity to disidentify with any one version as the whole story and suspend identity is the very premise of the analyst's work. It is what the analysand may identify with in the analyst. Ordinarily, the analyst leaving on vacation has to be able to identify with the patient's feeling of abandonment and affirm it – 'I know you feel left' – without really experiencing herself as a neglectful, abandoning bad object. Only by establishing this double position, which is of course unconsciously communicated to the analysand, can the latter feel the analyst to have survived her reproaches and truly tolerate her feeling of loss. This allows the other/analyst to become external, and to no longer be wholly identified with the persecuting, inside object. More generally, the surviving other is the one who entertains the double identification (see Benjamin 1998, Chapter 1), recognizing the position of the subject without wholly abandoning her own position, who is thus relieved of persecutory aspects. More and more it has become clear, however, that this double identification has to be materialized in directed communication that allows the patient to consciously reflect on the analyst's self-expression.

As I have suggested, the analytic relationship provides some experience with the kind of intersubjective space that allows us to use identification to bridge difference, to hold multiple positions, to tolerate nonidentity rather than wipe out the position of self or other. This notion of nonidentical or doubly identified selfhood might also serve to challenge the binary principle of exclusion and inclusion, as I suggested before. Exclusion, understood in this way, means that the subject repudiates or silences the outside others who then are assimilated to the internal, dangerous abject; inclusion, conversely, allows the other to become outside, to be an external being with whom identification is possible, without that identification bringing about total assimilation of self or other. Inclusion thus calls for difference, not synthesis. Politically, it cannot mean anything but the principle of sustaining continual contest and contradiction among differences, which Butler formulated, albeit from very different premises about the subject. As each different voice ascends to the position of subject of speech, however contested, it has the chance to attain the status of an outside other, rather than a repudiated abject that threatens to contaminate or reabsorb the self.

To accept this form of inclusion is a precondition of disrupting the totalizing demand to make any voice absolute, even that of the formerly excluded other, or to silence others, even the silencers. This can only mean that the self as subject can and will allow all its voices to speak, including the voice of the other within. Owning the other within diminishes the threat of the other without so that the stranger outside is no longer identical with the strange within us – not our shadow, not a shadow over us, but a separate other whose own shadow is distinguishable in the light.

Notes

1. Part of this debate centres around the question of whether one could, as Benhabib applying a scheme proposed by Flax (1990) does, legitimately sum up the postmodern position into a set of theses about 'the death of man, the death of history and the death of metaphysics'. Butler takes strong exception to this synthesis, on the ground that it reduces stark differences between theorists, e.g. the poststructuralism of Foucault, the deconstruction of Derrida, the feminist psychoanalytic work of Irigaray, the cultural theory of Lyotard. Originally published in the journal *Praxis*, the papers are now available separately (Benhabib (1992a and b), Butler (1992) and with comments by Fraser and Cornell in a volume *Feminist Contentions* (1995).
2. Actually, Benhabib and Butler seem to agree in their view of what the object relations feminist position entails, although they disagree on its value: a balance between 'autonomous justice thinking and empathetic care' (Benhabib) or an 'androgynous resolution' of a 'unified self' which integrates 'nurturance and dependency into the masculine sphere ... autonomy into the feminine' (Butler, 1990). This strikes me as a simplification in regard to my work, which aims to deconstruct autonomy and show that these oppositions are traceable to a split pursuant on the paradoxical condition that we are dependent for recognition of our independence, and to the repudiation of the original other/mother upon whom this dependence devolves.
3. By 'concrete other' I do not mean the opposite of the 'generalized other' in Benhabib's (1992b) sense, the particular, historical individual with needs, but rather the phenomenological, 'real' other in contradistinction to the abstract other. The abstract other is always constituted as the negation of the subject, as woman is Other to man; and this abstract other parallels the psychoanalytic

split-off other who represents an unwanted or disowned part of self. The distinction between the concrete and abstract other is the basis for the distinction I will emphasize between the outside other and the intrapsychic object, the Other within.

4. Kristeva's notion of the abjected as that which is propelled out of the self, ab-ject rather than ob-ject, refers both to a process of separation as well as that which is separated from – principally the maternal body and the self's remainders (e.g. faeces) that become repellent through separation. See 'Freud and Love' (1986) for its use as a process of separation, and *Powers of Horror* (1982) for the discussion of the abject as repudiated substance.
5. Using a Lacanian framework, Cornell reaches a position similar to the one that I see as essential to the critique of ego psychology (Benjamin, 1995e): that the act of internalization is that by which the ego denies the alterity of the other. Thus internalizing stands in an obverse relation to recognition; is that which occurs when the sequence of destruction, survival, and recognition of externality fail. However, to the extent that Lacan locates (or so he is read) the early maternal relationship outside the knowable, her point may not be internally consistent.
6. Identification may function as ratification of sameness (merger, or potentially chauvinism, as in identity politics), as incorporation of the other whom one has lost or can lose because she is outside (ego as the precipitate of abandoned object relations), and identification with difference in which the subject struggles to become 'like' what is different to be closer to it (relation to the ideal). Each of these blocks the acknowledgement of the externality of the other.
7. This alternation of recognition and subordination is beautifully described in Ogden's (1994) discussion of the analytic third.

References

Adorno, T.W. (1966), *Negative Dialektik,* Frankfurt: Suhrkamp.

Altman, N. (1995), *The Analyst in the Inner City: Race, Class, and Culture through a Psychoanalytic Lens,* Hillsdale NJ: Analytic Press.

Aron, L. (1995), 'The internalized primal scene', *Psychoanalytic Dialogues* 5 (2): 195–237.

— (1996), *A Meeting of Minds: Mutuality in Psychoanalysis,* Hillsdale NJ: Analytic Press.

Bataille, G. (1991), 'Reflections on the executioner and the victim', *Yale French Studies: Literature and the Ethical Question* 79: 15–19.

Beebe, B. and Lachmann, F. (1994), 'Representation and internalization in infancy: Three principles of salience', *Psychoanalytic Psychology* 11: 127–65.

Benhabib, S. (1992a), 'Feminism and the question of postmodernism', in *Situating the Self,* New York: Routledge.
— (1992b), 'The generalized and the concrete other', in *Situating the Self,* New York: Routledge.
Benhabib, S., J. Butler, D. Cornell and N. Fraser (1995), *Feminist Contentions,* New York & London: Routledge.
Benjamin, J. (1988), *The Bonds of Love,* New York: Pantheon.
— (1995), 'Recognition and destruction: an outline of intersubjectivity', in *Like Subjects, Love Objects,* New Haven: Yale University Press.
— (1998), *Shadow of the Other,* New York: Routledge.
Bernstein, R. (1992), *The New Constellation,* Cambridge: MIT Press.
Bromberg, P.M. (1993), 'Shadow and substance: a relational perspective on clinical process', *Psychoanalytic Psychology* 10 (2): 147–68.
— (1995), 'Psychoanalysis, dissociation, and personality organization', *Psychoanalytic Dialogues* 5: 511–28.
Butler, J. (1990), *Gender Trouble,* New York and London: Routledge.
— (1992), 'Contingent foundations: feminism and the question of "Postmodernism"' , in J. Butler and J. Scott (eds), *Feminists Theorize the Political,* New York: Routledge.
— (1993a), *Bodies That Matter,* New York: Routledge.
— (1993b), 'Poststructuralism and postmarxism', *Diacritics* 23: 3–11.
— (1995), 'Melancholy gender/refused identifications', *Psychoanalytic Dialogues* 5: 00.
Cascardi, A. (1992), *The Subject of Modernity,* Cambridge: Cambridge University Press.
Chodorow, N. (1980), 'Gender, relation and difference in psychoanalytic perspective', in *Feminism and Psychoanalytic Theory,* New Haven: Yale University Press, 1989.
Cornell, D. (1992), *Philosophy of the Limit,* New York: Routledge.
— (1995), 'Rethinking the time of feminism', in *Feminist Contentions,* New York: Routledge.
Davies, J. and Frawley, M. (1994), *Treating the Adult Survivor of Sexual Abuse,* New York: Basic Books.
de Laurentis, T. (1986), 'Issues, terms, and contexts', in *Feminist Studies/Critical Studies,* Bloomington: University of Indiana Press, pp. 1–19.
Derrida, J. (1978), 'Violence and metaphysics', in *Writing and Difference,* trans. A. Bass, Chicago: University of Chicago Press.
Dimen, M. (1995), 'The third step: Freud, the feminists, and postmodernism', *American Journal of Psychoanalysis* 55: 303–20.
Eigen, M. (1981), 'The area of faith in Winnicott, Lacan, and Bion', in *The Electrified Tightrope,* Northvale NJ: Aronson, 1993.

— (1993), *The Electrified Tightrope*, Northvale NJ: Aronson.
Flax, J. (1990), *Thinking Fragments: Psychoanalysis, Feminism, and Postmodernism in the Contemporary West,* Berkeley: University of California Press.
Fraser, N. (1995), 'False antithesis: a response to Seyla Benhabib and Judith Butler', in *Feminist Contentions,* New York: Routledge.
Freud, S. (1930), *Civilization and its Discontents, SE* XXI: 59–197.
Fuss, D. (1989), *Essentially Speaking: Feminism, Nature and Difference,* New York: Routledge.
Gallop, J. (1982), *The Daughter's Seduction: Feminism and Psychoanalysis,* Ithaca, NY: Cornell University Press.
Habermas, J. (1992), 'Individuation through socialization: George Herbert Mead's theory of subjectivity', in *Postmetaphysical Thinking,* trans. W. Hohengarten, Cambridge: MIT Press.
Hoffman, I. (1991), 'Reply to Benjamin', *Psychoanalytic Dialogues* 1 (4): 535–44.
Irigaray, L. (1991), 'The bodily encounter with the mother', in M. Whirford (ed.), *The Irigaray reader,* Oxford: Basil Blackwell, pp. 34–6.
Klein, M. (1946), 'Notes on some schizoid mechanisms', in *Contributions to Psychoanalysis,* New York: McGraw Hill, 1964.
Kristeva, J. (1982), *Powers of Horror: An Essay on Abjection,* New York: Columbia University Press.
— (1986), 'Freud and Love', in *Tales of Love,* New York: Columbia University Press.
Lacan, J. (1977a), 'The mirror stage as formative of the function of the I', in *Ecrits: A Selection,* trans. A. Sheridan, New York: Norton.
— (1977b), 'The signification of the phallus', in *Ecrits: A Selection,* trans. A. Sheridan, New York: Norton.
— (1988), *The Seminar of Jaques Lacan: Book I, Freud's Papers on Technique; Book II, The Ego in Freud's Theory,* New York: Norton.
Mahoney, M. and Yngvesson, B. (1992), 'The Construction of subjectivity and the paradox of resistance: Reintegrating feminist anthropology and psychology', *Signs* 18: 44–73.
Maroda, K. (1995), 'Projective identification and counter-transference interventions: since feeling is first', *Psychoanalytic Review* 82: 229–48.
Martin, B. (1982), 'Feminism, criticism, and Foucault', *New German Critique* 27: 3–30.
Mitchell, S. (1993), *Hope and Dread in Psychoanalysis,* New York: Basic Books.
Nicholson, L. (1990), *Feminism/Postmodernism,* New York: Routledge.
Ogden, T. (1986), *The Matrix of the Mind,* Northvale NJ: Aronson.

— (1994), *Subjects of Analysis,* Northvale NJ: Aronson.
Pizer, S. (1992), 'The negotiation of paradox in the analytic process', *Psychoanalytic Dialogues* 2: 215–40.
Rajchman, (1991), *Truth and Eros: Foucault, Lacan, and the Question of Ethics,* New York: Routledge.
Rivera, M. (1989), 'Linking the psychological and the social: feminism, post-structuralism and multiple personality', *Dissociation* 2: 24–31.
Rosenfeld, H. (1971), 'Contribution to the psychopathology of psychotic states: The importance of projective identification in the ego structure and the object relations of the psychotic patient', in *Melanie Klein Today,* Vol. 1, ed. E. Spillius. London: Routledge, 1988.
Sandler, J. (1993), 'On communication from patient to analyst: not everything is projective identification', *International Journal of Psychoanalysis* 74 (6): 1097–108.
Schwartz, H. (1994), 'From dissociation to negotiation: a relational psychoanalytic perspective on multiple personality disorder', *Psychoanalytic Psychology,* 11 (2): 189–233.
Scott, J. (1993), 'The tip of the volcano', *Society for Comparative Study of Society and History:* 438–51.
Smith, P. (1988), *Discerning the Subject,* Minneapolis: University of Minnesota Press.
Stern, D.B. (1992), 'Commentary on constructivism in clinical psychoanalysis', *Psychoanalytic Dialogues* 2: 331–63.
Stolorow, R. and Atwood, O. (1984), *Structures of Subjectivity: Explorations in psychoanalytic phenomenology,* Hillsdale, NJ: Analytic Press.
Theweleit, K. (1987), *Male Fantasies,* Vols 1 and 2, trans. Stephen Conway, Minneapolis: University of Minnesota Press.
Tronick, E. (1989), 'Emotions and Emotional Communication', *American Psychology* 44: 112–19.
Whitebook, J. (1994), 'Hypostatizing Thanatos: Lacan's analysis of the ego', *Constellations* 1 (2): 214–30.
Winnicott, D.W. (1971), 'The use of an object and relating through identifications', in *Playing and Reality,* London: Tavistock.
Young, I.M. (1990), 'The ideal of community and the politics of difference', in *Feminism/Postmodernism,* ed. L. Nicholson, New York: Routledge, pp. 300–23.

5 The Ambivalence of Identity: Psychoanalytic Theory in the Space Between Modernity and Postmodernity

Anthony Elliott

> Postmodernity is modernity coming of age: modernity looking at itself at a distance rather than from the inside, making a full inventory of its gains and its losses, psychoanalysing itself, discovering the intentions it never before spelled out, finding them mutually cancelling and incongruous. Postmodernity is modernity coming to terms with its own impossibility; a self-monitoring modernity, one that consciously discards what it was once unconsciously doing.
>
> Zygmunt Bauman

> Contradiction, conflict, spiraling, reconciliation, a dissolving of achieved reconciliations, new resolutions of dissonances – these are at the center of life and the mind's life.
>
> Hans Loewald

The central message of the past few decades in contemporary theory, the philosophy of science and the sociology of culture is that personal and political life is increasingly dislocated, dispersed, and fragmented. Such a view defines the core contours of our postmodern condition. Yet social-theoretic discourses about modernity and postmodernism raise important issues about the nature of psychic life and intersubjective experience which are rarely given adequate psychoanalytic scrutiny. A range of difficulties spring to mind here. How can one make sense, psychologically, of recent fragmentations and dislocations of subjectivity whilst also recognizing that people experience their 'identity' as something central to the texture of their day-to-day lives? What does selfhood and identity mean today? How are we connected and related to each other in contemporary culture? In this chapter, I consider the problems that emerge – the tensions and reconciliations – when selfhood is viewed against the conceptual backdrop of modernist and postmodernist theory. The chapter will thus draw out the significance of contemporary social transformations in relation to psychic structure and self-identity, and especially of what identity comes to mean. It will draw these issues out through an examination of modernity and postmodernity from the standpoint of developments in psychoanalysis – a theoretical hermeneutic which, parallel to much modernist and postmodernist thought, emphasizes the *ambivalence of identity*, the tension between self and other, desire and lack, life and death, consciousness and the unconscious. It will be argued that psychoanalysis uncovers aspects of contemporary experience as creations of the unconscious imagination. It will also be argued, against fashionable pronouncements about the disintegration of human subjectivity, that postmodernity ushers into existence a *radicalization of human imagination*. Focusing primarily upon the global restructuring of self/other boundaries, I argue that postmodernity deals in a wholly new way with psychic containment, turbulence and autonomy.

Brave New World: Modern and Postmodern Orders

Imagine a global pain map. In crude form, we might designate on this map pockets of collective rage, hate and negativity (describing polities from the Middle East to the Balkans); emotionally charged fields of gender domination and oppression (from the asymmetry of sexual difference to child sexual abuse); the uncertainty and fear that comes into play when considering our possible collective futures (including anxieties which focus upon ozone depletion, the greenhouse effect, and overpopulation); the personal and ethical problems about the present plight of sexual relationships and family life (such as the risk of AIDS); as well as the broader emotional dislocations of identity and selfhood in contemporary society (such as disturbances in creating personal meaning and self-continuity). Dread, fear, anxiety – it is easy enough to recognize such emotional states of pain on this map, even if the concerns listed are somewhat selective.

Nevertheless, I make this inventory of personal and cultural problems to underscore the deep strains of modern living. I emphasize discontinuities and negativities within the psychological roots of social, cultural and political life because it is precisely here that we confront the furthest extremities, or disturbances, of today's world. Under contemporary social conditions, our innermost hopes and longings are in ongoing dialogue with our most fearful anxieties and gripping terrors. Yet the ambivalences of modern living – expectant hopes and fearful anxieties – are certainly not closed in upon themselves, sealed off from the social-historical world. On the contrary, society enters fully into the construction of our most personal hopes and dreads. Social phenomena or trends are not just incidental to the forging of personal identity; they in some part constitute the inner texture of self-experience (as can be gleaned from the foregoing account of contemporary anxieties and fears). That is to say, there is a mutual penetration of inner and outer worlds, from which the criss-crossings of fantasy and culture are fabricated and sustained.

At a broader level still, this brings us to issues concerning the 'emotional agenda' of our times. What is truly contemporary about the links between selfhood and society, personality and culture? According to many, from newspaper commentators to academic theorists, our era is one of radical transition. Changes in social organization that have occurred in recent decades are said to be incomprehensible within existing general theories and conceptual frameworks. A dazzling variety of social, political and cultural transformations are highlighted in this regard. Globalization, transnational communication systems, new information technologies, the industrialization of war, the collapse of Soviet-style socialism, universal consumerism: these are the core dimensions of modern institutions and social affairs. Yet what are the connections between changes at the level of social institutions and those in everyday life, the domains of personal and aesthetic reflection? How do contemporary social processes affect the personal domain?

There are two very different ways of thinking about the relations between contemporary institutional transformations on the one hand and personal and cultural experience on the other in recent social theory. These discussions concern the ideas of modernity and postmodernity – as a diagnosis of the contemporary epoch – and both offer powerful and compelling frameworks for social and cultural analysis.

The modernist argument is that personal and cultural experience in the contemporary world involves various tensions and ambiguities, the distinctive characteristics of which involve contradiction, fluidity and fragmentation. These instabilities are directly connected to processes of modernization. Modernity is a post-traditional social order, involving the continual overturning of previous collective assumptions, traditions and customs. The globalized world of institutional interconnectedness in which we now live, marked as it is by rapid technological and industrial change, is experienced by people ambivalently – as exciting opportunity and threatening risk. An openness to the social world can mean the opportunity for experimentation and renewal, personal transformation and autonomy. Equally, however, it can mean the risk of personal and cultural turmoil, the disintegration of things thought solid and secure. Hence, the central modernist dilemma: to attempt to reach some kind of personal balance between security and risk, opportunity and danger.

Postmodernism, on the other hand, recognizes something different in contemporary cultural experience. It reacts against the tiredness of the modernist negotiation of risk and uncertainty by attempting to dissolve the problem altogether. Postmodernism suggests that cultural ambivalence cannot be overcome, that ambiguity and discontinuity cannot be straightened out, that social and cultural organization cannot be rationally ordered and controlled. Postmodernism denies that there is any repressed truth to the paths of modernity, and as such recasts society and history as *decentred*; there are only images of the past framed from different points of view. From this perspective, the multidimensional, chaotic world of global communication ushers in a plurality of local rationalities and identities – ethnic, religious, sexual, cultural and aesthetic. In a postmodern frame, this giddy proliferation of discourses opens individuals and collectivities to other possibilities and ways of experiencing the world. In short, postmodernity opens the way for a liberation of differences.

Modern Hopes, Modern Fears

Broadly speaking, the term 'modernity' refers to that set of social, political and economic institutions brought into existence in the West sometime during the eighteenth century, and which have become worldwide in influence in the twentieth century. Max Weber (1974: 155) characterized the emergence of modernity as a process of 'rationalization' and 'disenchantment'. Today at the turn of the twenty-first century, however, there is a marked and profound disenchantment with the emancipatory promise of modernity itself. The political theorist Claus Offe (1987: 2ff) says of this contemporary disenchantment:

> [it] is not so much that the gaze is turned away from either 'the others' or from history and toward one's own contemporary and structural conditions, but rather that the situation of 'modern' societies appears just as blocked, just as burdened with myths, rigidities, and developmental constraints, as modernization theory had once diagnosed to be the case for 'pre-modern' societies.

Current debates about modernity focus on the relation between the nature of social rationalization on the one hand, and aspects of cultural reproduction and identity on the other. In this connection, the following issues are raised. How have contemporary social processes of rationalization affected the personal and cultural spheres? What has been the impact of the institutionalization of rational calculation, mastery and control upon human subjectivity?

As a first approximation, it can be said that the social structures in which contemporary selves are constituted are profoundly different from cultural forms of the premodern world. In contrast to traditional types of social organization, in which tradition, custom and status held a legitimizing force, modernity radically transforms the intensity, dynamism and extensionality of social relations and processes. The development of modernity has involved a rejection of the sureties of tradition and custom – the worldview that there is an essential, internal order to culture. Against the sociological backdrop of capitalist economic development, industrial upheavals, urban expansions, the creation of parliamentary democracy, mass movements and the like, modernity has produced stunning technological transformations in the experience of space and time, the generation of information and knowledge, and the widening of human experience. The culture of modernity is a form of world-construction marked by the rejection of fixed, traditional boundaries.

This dissolution of traditional frameworks of meaning, however, has only been achieved at a substantial psychological cost. In the critical theory of the Frankfurt School, modernity is linked to the 'decline of the individual' (Horkheimer, 1974). Anticipating current debates about mass society and narcissistic pathology, the Frankfurt School regarded the logic of capitalist economic exploitation as penetrating the deepest recesses of human subjectivity. In this perspective, the psychic costs of modernity are the end of autonomous individuality and the emergence of passive, decentred consumerism. In Fromm's gloss, capitalist modernity generates 'individuals wanting to act as they have to act'.

The most influential recent view in social and cultural theory draws attention to the rise of large-scale bureaucratic institutions, and the associated impact of depolitization as it affects the personal domain. In this perspective, the rationalization of public life is said to weaken and drain the personal sphere, such that the individual subject recedes into the shadows. Selfhood and personal identity become increasingly precarious in conditions of modernity, as the individual loses all sense of cultural anchorage as well as inner reference points. Thus Christopher Lasch detects a 'culture of narcissism' at the heart of capitalist modernity, a culture in which selfhood contracts to a defensive core (Lasch, 1980, 1984). The result is that personal life turns inward upon itself: a narcissistic preoccupation with self becomes central to psychic survival, a preoccupation which reinforces capitalist consumption and manipulation. Another, more sophisticated, variant on this position is Jürgen Habermas's thesis of an 'inner colonization of the life-world' by technical systems (Habermas, 1987). Modern social life, according to Habermas, has become increasingly subject to administrative and bureaucratic control, and this has led to a crushing of individual creativity and autonomy.

For many theorists, however, such accounts of modernity appear too one-sided. The critique of social institutions and the public sphere as primarily invasive and destructive of personal life has been interpreted as a kind of conceptual closure in the face of the sheer intensity and scale of contemporary social processes. This closure, as Cornelius Castoriadis (1992) has argued, is an instance of the failure of social and political thought to address the imaginative opportunities ushered into existence by modern social institutions and their worldwide spread.

By contrast, Marshall Berman's (1982) treatise, *All That is Solid Melts into Air*, is representative of another line of thought concerning the cultural possibilities and limits of modernity. Berman's book is a provocative, polemical intervention into the debate concerning modernity and the consequences of modernization. Berman is little concerned with charting the sociological trajectories of Western modernity, and instead traces the divisions in intellectual thought regarding the nature of modern experience itself. The cultural ambivalence of modernity, he says, is echoed throughout social and political thought, with its schizoid splitting of contemporary social life into either pure affirmation and idealization or condemnation and denigration. 'Modernity', writes Berman (1982: 24), 'is either embraced with a blind and uncritical enthusiasm, or else condemned with a neo-Olympian remoteness and contempt.' In particular, the conceptual contrast between the iron cage of cultural conformism, from Max Weber to Herbert Marcuse, and the energetic vitality attributed to modern sensibility, from Walter Benjamin to Marshall McLuhan, parallels a division between constraint and empowerment which is intrinsic to modernity itself. The problem, as Berman sees it, is that contemporary social processes are increasingly portrayed from only one side of this divide. An either/or logic can thus be said to haunt the field of modernity.

In place of such 'rigid polarities and flat totalizations', Berman attempts to recover a sense of the ambivalence of modernity. To move beyond the barren binary impasse of theories of modernist theories, Berman considers the intrinsic ambiguities of modern city life. In this cultural field, he locates the simultaneous fragmented and liberated sense of contemporary urban living, its bizarre blending of personal isolation and loneliness on the one hand and intense social proximity and cultural interconnectedness on the other. Turning to the great modernists of the early twentieth century, in particular Goethe, Baudelaire and Marx, Berman argues that the very dislocations of the social process which modernity brings into existence, such as isolation and the loss of connection, paradoxically serve to create a new and instantaneous world of cultural possibilities and pleasures. That is to say, Berman theorizes the ambivalence of modernity *positively*. As he observes:

> To be modern is to find ourselves in an environment that promises us adventure, power, joy, growth, transformation of ourselves and the world – and, at the same time, that threatens to destroy everything we have, everything we know, everything we are. Modern environments and experiences cut across all boundaries of geography and ethnicity, of class and nationality, of religion and ideology: in this sense, modernity can be said to unite all mankind. But it is a paradoxical unity, a unity of disunity: it pours us all into a maelstrom of perpetual disintegration and renewal, of struggle and contradiction, of ambiguity and anguish. (Berman, 1982: 15)

Modernity, according to Berman, is a double-edged phenomenon. Instead of assigning persons to preordained social roles, as in premodern cultures, modernity succeeds in leading human subjects into a creative and dynamic making of self-identity and the fashioning of lifestyles according to personal preference. Such a transformation in the social fabric leads to vastly greater opportunities as concerns freedom and autonomy. But the modern way of life also has a darker side. Attempts to legislate rational order this century have regularly been at the cost of destroying individual particularity and human life. In the wake of Nazism, the Holocaust, Hiroshima, Stalinism and other social-historical catastrophes this century, the veil of illusions which underpins the moral and political practice of modernity has been lifted for all to see.

Central to modernity is the abandonment of any fixed social status and rigid hierarchy of power relations. This dissolution of communal traditions and customs, says Berman, carries major implications for the individual self, and especially the expression of personal identity. In brief, modernity opens up spaces for continuous individualization; it opens up positive possibilities for self-modification in regard to our emotions, desires, needs, and capabilities. In so doing, anxiety comes to replace the sureties of tradition and of habit. This is an anxiety that is at once deeply disturbing and exhilarating, an anxiety that frames the freedom of the self in its dealings with the social world. The premodern world, the ordered world of role-hierarchy and local tradition, has dissolved, leaving uncertainty and ambiguity. Self-definition begins anew, this time more in step with the hopes and dreads of emotional life.

Seen from this angle, modernity is about the celebration of dynamism, an ever-expanding acceleration of personal and cultural life. This acceleration is expressed as a multiplication of the possibilities of the self on the one hand, and of self-dislocation by global social processes on the other. Construction and deconstruction, assembly and disassembly: these processes interweave in contemporary societies in a manner which has become self-propelling.

The account of selfhood implicit in the work of Berman is one that suggests that individuals develop an emotional framework for handling the troubled waters of the culture of late modernity. In a post-traditional society, identity – as a forging of self-continuity – becomes something that has to be 'worked at', intersubjectively negotiated, reflected upon and thought about. This necessarily brings the self into an engagement with the wider world, and the ravages operating within modernity. But self-experience and interpersonal relations, in this reading, are nevertheless of meaning and value. Individuals are more or less involved in the recognition of the difficulty of creating meaningful experience, and of building relationships based on trust, intimacy and love, against the backdrop of the terrors and anxieties of modernity. The fashioning of self-identity is therefore intimately related to wider social processes that are worldwide in their impact. Person-planet/planet-person, as Theodore Roszak (1979) has argued. People handle risks, and the fears and anxieties associated with them, in terms of the expansion or compression of identity, the opening out or shutting down of the self to an enveloping outside world.

Self and Desire in Psychoanalysis

The ambiguities and contradictions of contemporary culture sketched in the foregoing section make the theory of modernity fertile ground for exploring the problem of identity and subjectivity. For implicit in the foregoing theories of modernity, there is the suggestion that individuals have within themselves an authentic capacity for self-definition and the subjective organization of meanings. In each person there is the struggle to negotiate the opportunities and dangers of modernity in terms of an ongoing, enduring sense of self;

to respond to the continuities and discontinuities of contemporary social processes in terms of one's own distinctive subjectivity. In psychoanalytic terms, this self-organization is refracted through unconscious processes of fantasy, drive and affect, an organization which provides core emotional linkages from one subjective state to the next. There is no experience of ourselves or others which is free of sexuality or the unconscious, as there is no cultural process untainted by the libidinal and aggressive drives in and through which society is fashioned. It is precisely at this juncture, between unconscious sexuality and social meaning, that the discourse of psychoanalysis recasts the relations between self and society, showing that fantasy and desire are deeply intertwined with the law and social order.

Freud's elaboration of the interplay between libidinal passion and self-control, outlined in his structural model of the psyche in *The Ego and the Id* (Freud, 1923), is the psychoanalytic blueprint which perhaps best prefigures the foregoing images of modernity as a world of contradiction and ambivalence. Freud pictures internal conflict as the psychic clash among libidinal drives (id), regulatory functions of self-control (ego), and moral injunctions (superego). To hold with Freud that the id is constitutively unconscious is to claim it as a realm of inner impulse, of drives, wishes, desires; an indestructible centre-point of radical imagination. The ego, by contrast, is a direct outcrop of these chaotic passions, a kind of defensive internal registration of the id's ceaseless demands for pleasure, but coupled with a painful awareness of the difficulties of human survival in the external world. The relation between id and ego is therefore one of tension and anxiety, as the latter seeks to contain the unstructured energy of the former by attempting to reconcile such passions with external cultural pressures for self-control. Yet if the outside world forcefully exerts its presence upon psychical life at the level of the ego, it does so to an even greater extent at the level of the superego. For Freud, the superego is the remainder of the human subject's attempt to master the Oedipus complex. A primary splitting of the ego, the superego is the internalization of Oedipal desires and taboos, wishes and prohibitions. Superego development is thus a taking in of the 'external world', and most particularly the moral prohibitions of culture as a whole, into parts of the self.

Ambivalence thus has its roots in the clash among unconscious drives, ego-anxiety and superego guilt in the individual. Personal continuity and discontinuity are envisioned in Freudian psychoanalysis as the struggle to maintain the tension between contrasting and conflictual desires and self-organizations. Psychoanalytically, the investment of desire in self–other relationships and cultural representations is a key part of self-identity, because it forms the emotional backcloth for any experience of a stable external world. In the object-relational terms to be explored more fully later, selfhood is a plural, shifting organization, patterned around constructive and reparative object relationships, and derived from different interpersonal contexts. In this vision, we are all negotiating a complex, contradictory subjective sense of self, and our experience of the world involves multiple perspectives of unity and fragmentation. But neither selfhood, nor the object relationships from which self-organization derives, is free from unconscious anxiety. For constructive and loving interpersonal relationships necessarily opens the self to anxieties concerning loss, pain and destructiveness. 'For tragedy to be possible', writes Stephen Frosh (1991: 19–20), 'for destructiveness to be meaningful and loss appreciated, there has to be something that can be identified with, something that can love as well as lose, hope as well as be betrayed. In this something, this self, there is enduringly the spark of an optimistic resistance, a potential to respond in a humanly worthwhile way to the mess that is all around.'

These emotional capacities, derived from multiple relational configurations, are deeply interwoven with the institutional settings of society and culture. That is to say, the human capacity to respond to 'the mess that is all around' is a response to the ambiguity of modernity, its mixture of opportunity and danger. Individuals develop a subjective sense of self designed to simultaneously handle the stunning opportunities and destructive terrors of the late modern age. In Freud's vision, such a negotiation demands a strong ego, an ego of rational self-control; a state of mind capable of struggling with anxieties generated internally and externally, and capable of repressing, displacing, or sublimating threatening unconscious drives and asocial desires. This is the classical Freudian image of modern culture as repressive, the global diagnosis that modernity denies the true expression of sexuality and personal desires. As Marcuse (1956) develops this point, the real turbulence of modernity is that of 'surplus-repression' – a repressive, political structuring of the psyche which produces intense personal misery and emotional suffering. Yet unconscious desire is not, as Marcuse and other Freudian radicals have argued, exclusively tied to the repressive anchoring constraints of culture. One of the most substantial insights of Freudian psychoanalysis is that desire, which splits and disperses the human subject, is always caught up in the process of symbolic representation. That is to say, the unconscious, through condensation and displacement, is a force always pressing for wish-fulfilment. It is this ceaseless pressure of the unconscious, represented in dreams and fantasy, which leads the late Freud to the view that the task of analysis is itself interminable.

It might be claimed, then, that there is a more full-blooded imaginary – a realm of fantasy and affect that is essentially creative – in Freudian psychoanalysis (Elliott, 1999). Fantasy, dream, identification, symbol, representation: these are not ordered, cognitive experiences of ourselves but rather aspects of unconscious mental life which are absolutely other and deliciously indeterminate. The unconscious, Freud comments, knows nothing of time, contradiction or closure. Beyond the structures of instituted logic, the unconscious 'does not think, does not calculate or judge in any way at all' (Freud, 1900). Moreover, it is from this crafty ambivalence – the fabrication of unconscious wishes which are intrinsically contradictory and mutually incompatible – that the multiple contradictions of subjectivity develop. Significantly, there is a potential subversiveness here as concerns the connections between self and society. There is for Freud another place, another mode of time, a mode of otherness which subverts and derails the impersonal decrees of the social order and law. Again, the temporal specificity of the primary libidinal process should be noted. 'The timelessness of the unconscious', Jacques Derrida (1972) writes, 'is no doubt determined only in opposition to a common concept of time, a traditional concept, the metaphysical concept: the time of mechanics or the time of consciousness.' Another way of putting this point is to claim that there is a subtle flaw at the heart of the social process, the negativity or perversity of unconscious sexuality and desire, an imaginary realm outside of time which thwarts and transforms the reality principle of daily life. Wishes that escape from time: this is for Freud the turbulence of the unconscious, as culture and desire continually displace one another.

It is thanks to unconscious ambivalence, to the polysemic richness of human passion, that Freud could elaborate a theory of human subjectivity as fragile, split, multiple, heterogeneous. One of the major contributions of psychoanalysis to reframing the concept of the autonomous individual, a central ideal of modern Western culture, lies in its vision of the subject as decentred. As Freud (1917: 143) puts this, 'the ego is not master in its own house'. The discovery and underlining of a hidden world of unconscious desires and fantasies was itself a dramatic challenge to the ideologies of rationality and objectivity of modernity. For Freud, examination of the hysterical and obsessional discourse of his patients revealed forbidden (sexual) wishes underneath the specious surface of consciousness. Significantly, this psychoanalytic rehabilitation of irrationality at the heart of rationality both captures and reflects the darker side of the project of Enlightenment – of the terror generated in and through modernist ideals of knowledge, economic growth, scientific and technological progress. It undercuts the perpetual condensation of autonomy as unfettered activity, showing the modern impulse of instrumentality to be the imagined product of an unbearable anxiety. By the same token, the psychoanalytic excavation of unconscious desire deconstructs contemporary ideological oppositions – between the cognitive and affective, reason and desire, order and chaos, masculinity and femininity – as a set of compromise formations designed to keep ambivalence and contingency at bay.

But let us comment that Freud's self-understanding of the subterranean forces of the unconscious was also deeply coloured by his scientific vision, in particular those elements of his thinking that privileged Enlightenment rationality and objectivity as the bearers of sure knowledge. The primary aim of exploring the unconscious for Freud was principally to overcome the dislocating effects of fantasy and primary process alterity. 'Where id was, there ego shall be': analysis aims to appropriate distorting unconscious fantasy in the interests of rationality and autonomy. In this sense, Freud's understanding of the ego in terms of rationality (secondary process) was a means of escaping the radical otherness of unconscious desire, and thus doing away with the discomfort of anxiety.

With respect to the social and cultural dimensions of modernity, the same orientation towards mastery and control can be found. Creation of a world free of ambivalence, the rationally structured life-world of uniformity and hierarchy, is central to the self-containment of modernity. Science, technology and bureaucratic expertise all play a fundamental role in this respect: imposing co-ordination upon otherwise plural, multidimensional aspects of human experience, crushing difference in the name of order and control, ordering reality into the structured space of social interaction. The idea that modernity is associated with instrumentality, an instrumental logic which denies difference, particularity and otherness, is familiar enough. What is being stressed here, however, is the impact of these cultural and social factors upon psychic structure and self-organization. Psychoanalysis suggests that modern selves are, in part, constituted through a repudiation of difference and heterogeneity; a denial which leads to the privileging of self-control over desire, actualization over reflection, reason over emotion. The most influential recent psychoanalytic account of the pathologies of self-mastery is be found in Jacques Lacan's theory of the creative and coercive effects of the phallus. Phallic mastery, says Lacan, involves narcissistic fantasies of oneness, of ecstatic plenitude, of unlimited power and authority. This is the imaginary component of phallic mastery; that non-gendered realm of primary narcissism which reunites the subject with that obscure object of desire, the lost maternal object, in immensely powerful ways. Here there is no division or gap between self and other, internal and external experience, desire and satisfaction. In Lacan's thought, however, the phallus also has a symbolic status; it is a signifier, a master signifier, which mediates the relation between human subject and object-world, that something beyond the self which Lacan designates as 'Law' or the 'Name-of-the-Father'. Hence, the phallus is a predetermined marker for the entry of sexualized subjects into the symbolic order, an order understood as a formal structure of language which represents and defines sexual difference. Imagined mastery, power and self-unity; symbolic decentring, difference and loss: these are two sides of the psychical effects of the phallus, and they are expressed in complex, contradictory ways in the reproduction of late modern society.

To summarize all this, the experience of modernity is double-edged, generating both progressive and defensive paths of self-discovery. The discovery of the self, in conditions of modernity, involves an opening out to internal and external forces of multiplicity, contradiction and division. Modernity displaces twice over: the radical otherness of the unconscious, a strangeness within, coupled with an awareness of the otherness of the Other, the globalized world of shared experience. The counterpart of displacement is self-mastery. The dislocations of modernity can be experienced as extremely threatening and overwhelming; in fact, so much so that individuals develop rigid defences against the intensity of human experience. Such a repudiation of experience is achieved through narcissistic fantasies of omnipotence, self-control, ordering, mastery.

Postmodernity: Theory, Identity, Society

The 'project of modernity', as has been seen in the preceding pages, is in part characterized by an institutionalization of unilinear history and meaning. Science, bureaucracy and technological expertise serve in the modern era as an orientating framework for the cultural ordering of meaning. A conception of history as having a single direction, the endeavour to develop a rational programme of collective emancipation, the grounding of all human experience and representation in reason: these are some of the key criteria of modernity. Paradoxically, though, it is precisely such modernist aims for self-mastery and control that fall victim to the very social processes they seek to colonize. Recent decades have powerfully shown that the ethos of modernity has come to haunt us. From the awesome destructive potential of nuclear arms to the massive risks of ecological catastrophe: the world in which we live today is fraught with dangers and risks, many of which arise directly as a consequence of the successes of science and the drive for progress. Such threats have powerfully served to highlight the gross limitations of modernist aims and perspectives, generating in turn the emergence of a new social and political agenda that seeks to counterbalance these oppressive features of modernity. This sphere of awareness is that of postmodernity.

Postmodernity confounds identity, theory and politics in a scandalous way, with its levelling of hierarchies, its dislocating subversion of ideological closure, its interpretative polyvalence, its self-reflexive pluralism. The world of postmodern culture is heterogeneous. On the one hand, postmodernism refers to certain currents of cultural and critical discourse which seek to deconstruct the ideological affinities of totalizing thought, the operations of power, the legitimating functions of knowledge and truth, and the discursive practices of self-constitution (Baudrillard, 1978; Derrida, 1976 and 1978; Foucault, 1973 and 1980; Lyotard, 1984 and 1988; Poster, 1988). On the other hand, however, postmodernism penetrates well beyond the boundaries of theory, at once inaugurating and designating new forms of personal and cultural experience. From a radical viewpoint, postmodern theories seek to demonstrate that the interconnections between self and society no longer depend upon the epistemological and ideological categories of modernity. Although it is admitted that we are still living in a time of extraordinary social and political transformation, there is no longer a blind faith in metadiscourses of scientific knowledge and technological legitimation. Our growing appreciation of the limits of rationality, it is argued, has led us to abandon the epistemological illusions of emancipatory declarations made in the name of Freedom, Truth, Equality, Liberty and so on. There has been, in short, a breakdown in the metanarrative of Enlightenment. For, as Lyotard puts this in *The Postmodern Condition*, postmodernity is defined as an 'incredulity toward metanarratives'. The grand narratives that unified and structured Western science and philosophy, grounding truth and meaning in the presumption of a universal subject and a predetermined goal of emancipation, no longer appear convincing or even plausible. Instead, the anti-totalizing, postmodern perspective reveals the generation of knowledge as singular, localized and perspectival. Knowledge is constructed, not discovered; it is contextual, not foundational. In this vision, truth-validation is itself explicitly recognized as entering into the pragmatics of intersubjective transmission.

Social transformations are understood to be of central importance in this erosion of the grand narratives of the modern era. The globalization of social institutions, and especially the proliferation of transnational communication systems, introduce a qualitative transformation in the experience of space and time, the result of which is a dramatic acceleration in the turmoil and flux of personal and cultural life. The overall effect is one of a blurring of the boundaries of cultural life itself; or, as Baudrillard argues, there is an implosion of all boundaries, an erasure of the distinctions of high and low culture, of appearance and reality, of past and present. The postmodern, in this view, is the abandonment of the modernist goal to find an inner truth behind surface appearances. Postmodernity is thus inherently decentred and dispersed: everything is of the same value, which means that nothing much counts in terms of meaning, distinction, hierarchy. On the contrary, postmodern culture, with its dislocation of structure and surface-obsessed profusion of style, supplants authenticity with copies, reality with images. Images and copies, 'simulation' in Baudrillard's terminology, in fact constitute postmodernity as hyperreal. 'The real', writes Baudrillard (1983: 146), 'becomes that of which it is possible to give an equivalent reproduction – the real is not only what can be reproduced, but that which is always already reproduced, the hyperreal'. From the aesthetically commodified images of pop art to the media spectacle of the Gulf War: the postmodern world is a circuit of transient signs.

This situation, however, is not only a purely cultural affair. With the development of globalization and mass communication technologies, the fragmentation of social space and dislocation of historical time presses in deeply upon self-organization. The world of mass media and brilliant technology in which we now live is captivating and mesmerizing, not only because it offers new textures of social experience, but because this global network of signification penetrates deeply into psychic structure itself. That is to say, the excess or overload of cultural meanings in postmodernity impacts upon the psychic space of the subject as disorientation, discontinuity and fragmentation. The drama of individual human life is increasingly bound up with the dislocation and dispersal of postmodern social space. Significantly, this dislocation is itself located in fairly specific, if somewhat elusive, social, economic and political contexts. The social and economic world in which the postmodern subject is constituted is, as Fredric Jameson has argued, the world of late, multinational capitalism. The immense communicational and computational networks of late capitalism, with its plurality of surplus-generating forms (from the stock market to the industrialization of war), derails the symbolic framing of reality, the grasping of psychic experience, the mapping of social space between self and other. As Jameson (1991: 25) comments:

> If, indeed, the subject has lost its capacity actively to extend its pro-tensions and re-tensions across the temporal manifold and to

> organize its past and future into coherent experience, it becomes difficult enough to see how the cultural productions of such a subject could result in anything but 'heaps of fragments' and in a practice of the randomly heterogeneous and fragmentary and the aleatory.

Anticipated by the Frankfurt School, the dissolution of the bourgeois ego is today a reality in postmodern society.

Yet it should not be thought that this collapse of the centred, self-determining ego leads to a disintegration of subjectivity itself. On the contrary, there is a dramatic intensification of libidinality, an intensification fully wrapped within the circuits and signs of the postmodern. The postmodernism which celebrates the random intensities of the subject, now drained of psychological depth and significance, highlights the exhilaration of forgetting, the addiction of mindlessness, and the pleasure derived from the surface, the immediate, the particular.

The combined effect of all these transformations in theory, identity and society is that postmodernity comes to be seen as a culture permeated by fragmentation and dislocation. It is this vision which is generally conveyed by the characterization of postmodernity as anti-historical, relativist and negative. In this view, postmodernity is defined entirely by absences, the dissolution of inner experience and received social meanings. It is possible to make sense out of this apparent disorientation, however, provided that we grasp the irreducibility of the plurality of human worlds. The recent theoretical work of Zygmunt Bauman is especially significant in this respect. On the basis of a thoroughgoing study of modern and postmodern social practices, strategies, worldviews, and orientations, Bauman argues that postmodernity represents a new dawning, rather than a twilight, for the generation of meaning. 'Postmodernity', Bauman (1991: 35) writes, 'is marked by a view of the human world as irreducibly and irrevocably pluralistic, split into a multitude of sovereign units and sites of authority, with no horizontal or vertical order, either in actuality or in potency.' This emphasis on plurality and multiplicity highlights that postmodernity involves a rejection of the typically modern search for foundations, absolutes and universals. Postmodernity is a self-constituting and self-propelling culture, a culture which is increasingly self-referential in direction. From cable TV to the information superhighway: postmodern culture is a culture turned back upon itself, generated in and through internal systems of technological knowledge. Pluralism, contingency, ambiguity, ambivalence, uncertainty: these features of social life were assigned a negative value – they were seen as pathologies to be eradicated – in the modern era. For Bauman, however, these are not distortions to be overcome, but are the distinctive features of a mode of social experience which has broken with the disabling hold of objectivity, necessity, law.

Bauman's discussion of the interconnections between modernity and postmodernity is extremely persuasive. He is critical of those who celebrate the postmodern as a mark beyond modernity. Any such reading of postmodernity as a cultural phase beyond modernity, he argues, is itself an exercise in self-contained ordering. Rather than attempting an historical periodization of the modern and post-modern eras, Bauman argues that contemporary culture, not without certain tensions and contradictions, deploys both orders simultaneously. Contemporary society revolves around a modernist impulse for creating order, boundaries and classifications as well as a post-modern tolerance for plurality, difference and uncertainty. Contemporary society, it might be said, embraces and avoids ambivalence in equal measure. There is something in all of this which is deeply disturbing and problematic: the more society generates pluralism and ambivalence, the more this rebounds as a loss of orientation and meaning. To become more aware of personal and cultural contingency is to break with the hold of social-historical fixation and to court vulnerability. But this seemingly contradictory, and often confused, state of affairs is, in fact, one of the supreme values of post-modernity. 'Postmodernity', says Bauman (1990: 98), 'is modernity that has admitted the non-feasibility of its original project. Postmodernity is modernity reconciled to its own impossibility – and determined, for better or worse, to live with it. Modern practice continues – now, however, devoid of the objective that once triggered it off.'

This leads directly to Bauman's central thesis: *postmodernity as modernity without illusions*. Postmodernity is an opening out to the complex, contradictory realm of human and social experience, in all its wonder and insecurity. The end of codes equals an encounter with experience, pure and unrestrained. The postmodern subject is preoccupied, among other things, with creative and pragmatic living, free of the distortion of unrealistic hopes and aspirations, of unrealizable goals and values. The ethical distinctiveness of the postmodern age is well expressed by Bauman (1993: 245):

> What the postmodern mind is aware of is that there are problems in human and social life with no good solutions, twisted trajectories that cannot be straightened up, ambivalences that are more than linguistic blunders yelling to be corrected, doubts which cannot be legislated out of existence, moral agonies which no

> reason-dictated recipes can soothe, let alone cure. The postmodern mind does not expect any more to find an all-embracing, total and ultimate formula of life without ambiguity, risk, danger and error, and is deeply suspicious of any voice that promises otherwise. The postmodern mind is aware that each local, specialized and focused treatment, effective or not when measured by its ostensive target, spoils as much as, if not more than, it repairs. The postmodern mind is reconciled to the idea that the messiness of the human predicament is here to stay. This is, in the broadest of outlines, what can be called postmodern wisdom.

Beyond the self-mastery of modernity there exists a postmodern, cultural space which calls for, and indeed celebrates, difference and otherness. Rejecting the supra-individual authority of blank technologism, rationality, economic progress, causality and system, postmodern culture transmutes the foundations of identity and society as fluid, ambivalent and radically contingent.

Contemporary Psychoanalysis, Postmodern Identities

The dislocation and dispersal which characterize the postmodern age seem radical and novel in social and cultural theory, but the psychic fissures which they serve to promote can be found in many approaches and in many forms throughout contemporary psychoanalytic literature. Melanie Klein, D.W. Winnicott, Wilfred Bion and Jacques Lacan, and in recent years, such psychoanalysts as Julia Kristeva, Cornelius Castoriadis, Christopher Bollas and Thomas Ogden have radically reconceptualized the creative and empathetic capacities of psychical life – especially rudimentary thought processes, primitive fantasy, and the interactional matrix which sustains the evocation of affect. Each of these psychoanalysts, in one form or another, have sought to undo the repressive stamp of modernist epistemology within psychoanalysis (particularly the polarization between primary and secondary process, fantasy and reality, nature and culture, and femininity and masculinity), and hence shift psychoanalysis to a more complex, post-Enlightenment understanding of psychical life and human subjectivity.

Classical Freudian psychoanalysis, exploring the affective sensibility of modernity, encouraged self-control, the renunciation of unconscious passion. Jürgen Habermas, in *Knowledge and Human Interests*, sees Freudian psychoanalysis as a self-reflective, reconstructive hermeneutic which, in uncovering the disabling effects of psychic censorship and repression, generates a capacity for the rational control of the self (Habermas, 1972: Chapters 10 and 11). In this modernist reading of Freud, psychoanalysis aims at making the unconscious conscious. But emancipation from unconscious repression is no longer the central issue in postmodern times. In recent years, psychoanalysis in Europe and the United States has increasingly defined contemporary personal and cultural experience, not only as an encoding of repression, but as shot through with depletion, lack and emptiness. Winnicott (1958), for example, points to the prevalence of patients who complain of 'not feeling real', of 'being unable to feel', and of 'never saying what they mean but rather just mouthing the words of others'. For these patients, the experience of subjectivity is fragmented or lacking; the self being disconnected from social experience and discourse. Personal meanings, which individuals need to experience as real and authentic, are felt to be non-existent. In an age of globalized media images, it seems as if everything is a copy of something else: the self simply mouths the words of others.

Some of the most provocative elements in recent discussions of postmodernity have been in those areas of social and cultural theory which have explored the splintering, surface facets of contemporary selfhood. The direction of this literature has been to link the cultural eclecticism of postmodernism to the demolition of psychic interiority and personal meanings. Postmodernity, in its displacement of discursive meaning with glittering surfaces and libidinal intensities, is seen as producing a fragmentation of the individual self. The most important psychoanalytic concept through which these ideas have been developed has been that of Lacan's 'mirror stage', with its claim that the ego is a 'fiction' because it is frozen as an image of something which does not exist. For Lacan, the ego represents an imaginary world of wholeness and plenitude; it is a psychic defence aimed at masking the painful contradictions of desire itself. Significantly, Lacan's theory provides an account of how something outside and other – a mirror-image – is taken inside subjectivity. Yet there is no interiority or depth in Lacan's conceptualization of the mirror. One cannot get behind the mirror because it is pure surface, a flattened image which has its roots in otherness. In this respect, the links to the surface manifestations of postmodern culture are compelling. Postmodernity transmutes the social world into a wilderness of mirrors. The Lacanian decentred self, now recast as fully representative of postmodernism, is simply a copy of another, and that subject of another and another. Hence, nothing of selfhood exists beyond the surface, the immediate, the spectacle.

But to portray matters in this way demands a particular sorting of the relations between subjectivity and knowledge. It is important in this context to highlight the modernist epistemological understructure of Lacan's 'mirror stage'. I have in mind here the realist assumptions which underpin Lacan's delineation of the subject of imaginary misrecognition. Misrecognition in relation to what? The force of reality, and particularly the reality that desire is overwhelming because it is inscribed in lack. Although Lacan seeks to problematize the theoretical value of reality, his own writings continually emphasize the fantasy/real dichotomy. Lacan elucidates the self as a copied distortion, a filter which is played off against disfiguring perspectives of reality. Reality, in the Lacanian perspective, is that which derails the self in imaginary and symbolic terms, generating in turn further distortion and misrecognition.

The polarities fantasy and reality, which psychoanalysts from Freud to Lacan have employed to reach an objective interpretation of unconscious processes, show a characteristic of thought which belongs to the ideology of the Enlightenment, with its emphasis on mimesis and dichotomy. In contemporary psychoanalysis, by contrast, there has been a radical shift away from such realist aspirations to scientific objectivity, coupled with a rejection of the view that the clearest form of understanding occurs when secondary-process thinking is divorced from the unconscious imagination. With post-traditional psychoanalysis, the creative power of human imagination is given explicit attention. Analysts today are increasingly interested in the process of meaning-construction and of the imaginary fantasies and symbolic representations in and through which a world of interconnecting signification is created. What is involved in contemporary psychoanalytic practice, at least in principle, is a gradual transition from reactive despair to the creation of personal meaning. In developing alternative and different experiences of subjectivity and intersubjectivity, psychoanalysis is concerned to (re)collect the terrors of the postmodern age and to recast experience within a shared, affective space. This is a matter of neither denying nor celebrating the chaotic dislocations of postmodern society, but of developing and nurturing a sense of creative meaning and value within symbolic representations of the self, of others, and of the social world. Yet whereas modernist psychoanalysis strived for clarification, renunciation and sublimation, post-traditional psychoanalysis founds itself upon the paradoxes of postmodernism by fully considering the nature of psychic ambiguity, ambivalence and contingency. Confusion and contradiction are thus no longer cast as ideological obstructions to creative living. On the contrary, in contemporary psychoanalysis, through 'mirroring', 'containing', and 'holding', subjects are encouraged to explore disturbing and painful unconscious fantasy as the basis for a revised narrative of their torn selves.

In traditional Freudian psychoanalysis, the recovery of unconscious desire is primarily traced along cognitive and developmental lines, through the reconstruction of subjective narratives of the past. But, in contemporary psychoanalytic theorizing, the core capacity for encountering unconscious knowledge is located in the transmission of affect, and especially of primitive affective states that underly the process of meaning-construction. Consider Winnicott's account of maternal mirroring, which he designates as the basis for the split between true and false selves. Winnicott proposes that the image through which the infant first begins to gain a sense of itself as a human being is its mother's face. He suggests that the mother acts as an emotional mirror for the child; through responding to the infant's needs and wishes, she communicates feelings of love and connectedness; through tolerating and containing the infant's destructiveness, she communicates an acceptance of feelings of fear and hatred. For Winnicott, and this is where he parts company with Lacan, there is both creative identification and dislocating division in the process of mirroring. The mother, as mirror, when good enough, assists the infant in the development of its capacities for feeling, understanding and connection with others. The infant's own needs and wishes are recognized and responded to by the mother, from which feelings of spontaneity and aliveness develop. Where the mother fails to establish an emotional sensitivity to the infant's needs, however, the infant will withdraw into itself, learning to want only what the mother provides. Such experience of compliance Winnicott terms the 'false self', an inauthentic sense of self which compulsively anticipates the expectations and reactions of others. Significantly, both authentic and inauthentic experience take place within an interpersonal field of interactions.[1] Yet it is the degree of immersion in the other person, particularly a mindfulness for the feelings and emotions which are being experienced, which distinguishes the authentic from the inauthentic.

Winnicott points to the crucial importance of a sense of mutual understanding and shared feeling in the achievement of both identity and differentiation in psychical life. In 'Transitional Objects and Transitional Phenomena', Winnicott (1965) argues that psychic growth and development unfold through the creation of a transitional zone, a certain blending of fantasy and reality, of internal and external worlds. The child's construction of a transitional or 'not-me' object – a teddy bear or blanket, for example – is experienced as an extension of the mother but also as a separate part of the child's mind. Such transitional objects facilitate transactions between internal and external worlds in terms of playfulness and creativity. Significantly, transitional space is also the fundamental means for a mature, reflective involvement in social and cultural life, since it allows for the exploration of fantasy and affect in symbolic terms. Thus, in Winnicott's theory, human subjectivity is forged, not through a polarization of opposites, but through a creative, transitional zone which links self and other, internal and external experience, fantasy and reality.

What knits self and other together, therefore, is a responsiveness to experience, which is a matter more of affect than of reason. There is something in the primitive processes, the intense passions and anxieties of the unconscious, which at once defines and delimits the self–other boundary. The importance of primitive processes in the development of intersubjectivity is that the unconscious announces itself in feeling before it can be thought about or reflected upon. The experience and meaning of our subjective needs, sensations, affects, representations and fantasies are forged through a linking with the Other. The theoretical consequence of this is that immersion in other people, in psychological terms, lies at the root of self-reflective consciousness and understanding. This is especially clear in Melanie Klein's theory of the paranoid-schizoid position, in which the infant entertains fantasies of tearing the maternal body to bits as well as incurring delusions that this body will in turn devour it. Notwithstanding that such fantasies represent a kind of self-disintegration, the Kleinian argument is that the paranoid-schizoid mode of generating experience, with all its destructive elements, can be emotionally modified by maternal containment in the early months of the infant's life. Through the elaboration of projective and introjective identification, the channelling of fantasized parts of self into the other or the incorporation of aspects of the other into self, the infant establishes connection with the mother's mind. As such, by functioning as a container for the infant's projections of destructive fantasy, the mother helps the infant to tolerate and manage those projections. The mother takes these negative, destructive fantasies into her own, internal world, dealing with them in terms of her own characteristic patterns of organizing emotional experience; and, by continuing to be emotionally available and receptive, communicates an acceptance of the turbulence of human relatedness.

In the terms of the post-Kleinian analyst Wilfred Bion, maternal receptivity is achieved in and through a state of 'reverie'. 'Reverie', writes Bion (1962; 36), 'is that state of mind which is open to the reception of any "objects" from the loved object and is therefore capable of the reception of the infant's projective identifications whether they are felt by the infant to be good or bad.' In the earliest preverbal relations between infant and mother, the child rids itself of feelings that cannot be tolerated by projecting them into the mother.

In states of maternal reverie, the mother, by accepting these projections, contains (and thus remains related to) her infant in a way that makes emotional pain and anxiety more manageable and acceptable. Particular emphasis is given here to the emotional capabilities of the mother to tolerate and reflect upon the infant's unwanted feelings. Through intersubjective, unconscious transactions, the mother can offer these feelings back to the infant, after a period of containment, in a form which is more meaningful and less threatening to the infant. This state of emotional receptivity to the other is also considered central in post-Kleinian psychoanalytic treatment; in particular, the idea that the analyst should use, and reflect upon, their own feelings as information about the unconscious content's of the other's mind. Here the patient communicates unconscious fantasies to the analyst through projective identification, the placing of sectors of unconscious experience into the analyst's mind. If the analyst can take in and remain open to these unwanted fantasy communications, holding the patient through containment, and reflecting upon these unconscious representations as meaningful, new experiences of insight, awareness and creativity are likely to emerge. Where containment is not achieved, either because the individual cannot accept aspects of his or her unconscious experience or because the mother/analyst is not sufficiently capable of reverie, the subject will increasingly ward off pain and anxiety through projective identification. Significantly, where psychical pain and frustration become too great, the subject may rid itself, not only of bad feelings and experiences, but also of that part of the mind which registers thinking itself. The inability to tolerate any form of confusion is what Bion terms 'anti-thought', a process in which significatory elements are 'stripped of their meaning and only the worthless residue retained' (Bion, 1962: 98). Such an emptying out of the mind of terrifying, persecutory objects, when coupled to the expulsion of thinking and reflectiveness, can lead to extreme psychological disturbance, such as psychosis.

There is something broader, relating to the cultural conditions of postmodernity, which should also be considered at this point. The contemporary self, as we have seen, has been characterized by some commentators as narcissistic, illusory and brittle, and by others as decentred, disorientated and fragmented. Kleinian and post-Kleinian theory profoundly questions these descriptions of the prevailing sense of self. The unconscious process of meaning-construction, in Kleinian and post-Kleinian accounts, is one characterized by an inmixing of self and other; the migration of subjective meaning into the other, tangled and confused, through the mechanisms of projective and introjective identification. The idea of emotional receptivity

– of 'holding' and 'containing' the other – is recognized as central to discovering and understanding self-experience; struggling with something other, tolerating it and reflecting upon it, is fundamental to attaining an authentic sense of personal relatedness. Similarly, it might be suggested, there is a remarkably fluid and reflexive encounter with otherness generated under the cultural conditions of postmodernity. The Western world of postmodern culture – with its circuits of technology, networks of interlinking computational systems, and media simulation – restructures the local/global intersection, and hence our experience of otherness. Through the communicational conveyor belt of mass media, from news coverage of regional wars and famines to information concerning ecological and nuclear crisis, the local becomes global and/or the global becomes local. In this context, interpersonal communication is projected into larger national and global spaces. Postmodern culture creates new possibilities as regards the extensional links between self and other: immersion in the other, and particularly fantasized aspects of the other, is continually invoked and negotiated through the key role of media simulation.

Once again, however, it must be stressed that this kind of communicational linkage between self and other, refracted through transnational media systems, would appear resistant to clear and ordered articulation. In post-Kleinian terms, the articulation of such mediated experience of the other only becomes possible through an immersion, an incorporation and working through, of the imagined fantasies and symbolic representations created. A toleration of confusion and disorder, as the globalized screening of otherness impacts upon the self, is necessary in order to discover new ways of thinking and new domains of personal experience. Indeed, in the light of Jameson's thesis regarding the disintegration of the 'cognitive maps' of individual and collective identities in postmodern culture, it seems likely that it is increasingly necessary to tolerate and reflect upon emotional states of uncertainty generated by the cultural conditions of the late modern age.

What is important about this reflectiveness upon self-organization and unconscious experience is not only a containment and toleration of the other, but the searching of fantasy life itself. It is here, tracking psychic identifications with self and others, that the idea of new imaginary structures of subjectivity has most importance. What seems to be involved is that which concerns coming to terms with the self-legislating power of fantasy itself. How much can subjective experience take in of imaginative perception? Or, to put the issue slightly differently, how much is left of identity once the subject turns back upon its own mental activity? This idea of reflexive fantasy connects with Cornelius Castoriadis's claim that psychoanalysis is the discovery of psychical imagination, of psychical creation *ex nihilo*: the constitution and reproduction of imaginary forms in and through which men and women image themselves, and each other, in daily life (Castoriadis, 1995). Significantly, inquiry into the process of fantasy production involves what I have previously called 'rolling identification', an unconscious interchange across the self/other boundary (Elliott, 1995). Rolling identifications, which entail a 'representational wrapping of self and other', permit the constitution of identity as a relation to the self-as-object and pre-object relations, both of which are central to pre-Oedipal development.

Much of this recent emphasis on the power of fantasy and imagination has been developed within feminist psychoanalytic thinking. For Julia Kristeva, to take a particularly powerful integration of psychoanalysis and feminist social theory, the human subject's capacity for creativity and autonomy is deeply intertwined with the repressed maternal, a 'semiotic' connection to the maternal body. By the semiotic Kristeva means a heterogeneous play of unconscious forces – of drives, affects and representations – which exert a pulsional pressure within language itself, and which can be discerned within the rhythm, tone and disruption of speech. Kristeva argues that the primordial jouissance of the child/mother dyad is smashed apart by, and is repressed through reference to, the Law of the Father, the symbolic cultural structure. Semiotic connection with repressed maternal drives remain however; symbolized in the rhythms, fractures and dislocations of social significations. Kristeva argues that contemporary psychoanalysis has become increasingly concerned with the complexities of semiotic disruptions, the overflow of unconscious representation into the confined, patriarchal space of the symbolic order. This pre-Oedipal, semiotic experience of the maternal body functions as a point of Otherness – an Otherness which is experienced, in fantasy spaces such as dreams and day-dreams, as a remembering of the imaginary bliss of the maternal sphere itself. The semiotic is the scene of something other, an otherness central to the fluidity of the 'subject-in-process'; an otherness which underlies the multiplication of fantasy as it intersects with received social meanings.

One way of understanding this continual remembering of the maternal body is in terms of the alterity, the strangeness and uncanniness, of human subjectivity. For Kristeva, the trauma of primitive psychic separation from the maternal body renders us subjectively divided, internally strange. This is a strangeness which is at once alluring and threatening. It is alluring insofar as it acts to neutralize otherness, rendering self and world pseudo-rational through fantasies of narcissistic completeness. Yet it is threatening because of the fragility of psychic repression, a fragility which returns the sense of strangeness to conscious experience. In fact Kristeva, developing upon Freud's work on uncanny strangeness, portrays subjective experience of otherness as central to the development of human creativity and autonomy. 'The sense of strangeness', writes Kristeva (1991: 189), 'is a mainspring for identification with the other, by working out its depersonalizing impact by means of astonishment.' This astonishment, linked to unconscious anguish, leads to a destructuration of self: as the fragile boundaries between self and other break down, psychic identity is put into question and there is a dissolution (and regeneration) of imaginary structures. Strangeness, for Kristeva, is essential in the very production and formation of psychic space and imagination. As she develops this point:

> Also strange is the experience of the abyss separating me from the other who shocks me – I do not even perceive him, perhaps he crushes me because I negate him. Confronting the foreigner whom I reject and with whom at the same time I identify, I lose my boundaries, I no longer have a container, the memory of experiences when I had been abandoned overwhelm me, I lose my composure. I feel 'lost', 'indistinct', 'hazy'. The uncanny strangeness allows for many variations: they all repeat the difficulty I have in situating myself with respect to the other and keep going over the course of identification-projection that lies at the foundation of my reaching autonomy. (Kristeva, 1991: 187)

Postmodernity and Otherness, or Re-spacing Self and World

How do these trends in psychoanalytic theorizing relate to postmodernity? Let me approach this question from the inside, the domain of imagination, and then move out, to consider the ways in which contemporary psychoanalysis sheds new light on society at large. Contemporary psychoanalysis, notwithstanding its heterogeneity, is profoundly occupied with the complexity of fantasy itself, as a process of self-construction and other-directedness. 'The bridge supporting connection with others', writes Stephen Mitchell (1993: 21), 'is not built out of a rationality superseding fantasy and the imagination, but out of feelings experienced as real, authentic, generated from the inside, rather than imposed externally, in close relationship with fantasy and the imagination.' Fantasy zones of transitional space, reverie, containment, semiotic forces, rolling identifications: imagination constitutes human subjectivity and the unconscious to its core. The realm of unconscious imagination, I claim, is a generative space. It is a space in and through which the subject creates meaning in the moment of differentiation of self to other. It is an affective, representational space in which to think the limit of subjectivity: the struggle of placing the 'subject' in question.

What, though, of the boundaries of personal, unconscious meaning? Are we talking here of a communicational immediacy between self and other; or of a world of multiple meaning and codes; or perhaps of a schizoid dissolution of identification and signification into an imaginary hall of mirrors? Again, the current state of psychoanalytic thinking is instructive. The contemporary subject, as experienced in therapy and represented in theory, continually moves along emotional paths of not-knowing on the one hand, and the generation of symbolic meanings, demands and representations on the other. A disconnection from symbolic representation is viewed as a precondition for the generation and reconstruction of meanings. The suspension of preconceived thoughts, coupled with an immersion in the unfolding of ambiguity, is a central means for the transformation of unconscious experience into interpersonal communication. This is a subjectivity, then, of multiplicity and fluidity; a narrative reconstruction of identity without beginning or end; a conception of the imaginary and the imagination which, following Kristeva, can be called a 'subject-in-process'. It is important to note once again the reflexive form granted to the intersubjective space of analysis – particularly transference and counter-transference – as concerns the exploration of unconscious fantasy. The experience of containment and holding in the analytic situation – the receptivity of the psychoanalyst to all of the patient's feeling states, from anxiety to the projection of destructiveness and hate – is crucial for any reclaiming of those torn or split-off dimensions of subjectivity, and for their potential reintegration into self-experience. In Bion's terms, the reverie of the therapist or analyst acts as a container for an exploration of psychic processes prior to and underlying self-organization. Taking in, holding, making sense of fragmented experience, and returning unconscious communications as meaningful: this is a creative, intersubjective process of containment, a process which underscores the affective, reflexive resources of subjectivity in a powerful and provocative manner.[2]

Of course, none of this is straightforward as regards self-experience. The reflexivity of selfhood, as elaborated in intersubjective settings, is filtered through that crisis in representations and legitimations which postmodern culture ushers into existence. Simply put, the self-experience of intersubjective meaning and containment is continually rendered problematic in postmodern contexts of cultural fragmentation, political dislocation and the economic interchangeability of commodities, objects and persons. But if creative and reflexive psychic organization underpins the construction of subject-positions and identity, then alternative avenues for personal and cultural development must exist. The problematizing of psychic boundaries of subjectivity, as both Kristeva and Castoriadis point out, is always carried on within the tangled frame of the repressed unconscious – the heterogeneity of radical imagination, the disruption of semiotic functioning.

The nature of postmodernity, or so I want to propose, promotes a reflexive involvement with human imagination: through an 'opening out' of the cultural sphere there are also many points of personal engagement which offer the possibilities for revised imaginary space. Recognizing the irreducible character of fantasy means living with uncertainty, ambivalence, otherness and difference. Our day-to-day activities – insofar as they are increasingly influenced by instantaneous global communication – have become focused around otherness. Today the centrality of the Other, whether in terms of sexuality, race or nationalism, refocuses relations between identity and difference, subjectivity and politics. Thus, for example, the refashioning of sexuality and intimacy in the light of AIDS is directly bound up with research that has been conducted on a global scale, and which has influenced perceptions of security and danger in the sphere of gender relations. In an era of ambivalence and uncertainty, the social imaginary has become less and less encumbered with the rigid hierarchies and flat rationalizations of the modern era. In certain respects, this has led the postmodern subject into a void, as the self is now left to feel the full force of its inner pain, loneliness and anxiety. Postmodern selfhood we might thus describe, following Baudrillard, as anchored in nostalgia – 'Playing with the pieces – that is post-modern' (Baudrillard, 1984: 24). But, crucially, this is only one side of the story of postmodernity. One of the most distinctive aspects of the interconnections between postmodernity and the personal domain, though certainly one of the most neglected in recent discussions, is the capacity of human subjectivity for imaginative elaboration, symbolized by new representations of self and world. The global spread of cultural production in the mass media, the pluralization of local histories and cultures, the transformation of sexuality: we witness in this pluralistic world an intensification of symbolic, intersubjective linkages, as well as an increasing awareness of the creativity of fantasy itself. At such times, we are exposed to a reordering of the symbolic codes of society, not as Law or the Name-of-the-Father, but rather as a form of openness to ourselves.

Various institutional developments, in the era of postmodernity, mark this multiplication of fantasy and imagination as regards human subjectivity. As we have seen in the preceding pages, postmodernity is characterized by institutionalized ambivalence, pluralism and contingency – all of which modernity uncovered and disowned in equal measure. Postmodernity, in this sense, refers to the dissolution of centralized perspectives and authorized identities; the end of 'grand narratives', to recall Lyotard. However, postmodern identity is not simply a phase of development beyond modernity. Rather, as identities without illusions (in Bauman's sense), postmodern subjectivity is a subjectivity seeking to come to terms, to accommodate, its inhabiting selves of cultural and political identification. Contemporary identities, and this plural form is basic to the framework of postmodern experience, create reflexively organized 'narratives' (or case histories) in respect of the cultural diversity of self and other; representations fabricated out of sexual, cultural, ethnic, religious, political and aesthetic influences. Postmodern identities trade in complex, contradictory networks of intersubjective meanings; questioning fantasy, or perhaps more accurately seeking to turn fantasy back upon itself, in order to glimpse the creative workings of unconscious desire.

The links between this new cultural experience and psychic reorganization, briefly sketched in the foregoing paragraphs, are premised upon a confrontation with the decentredness of the subject. As the contextual supports for fantasy become increasingly self-referential in postmodern times, human subjects become more and more aware of the constructedness of selfhood, relationships, and society itself. 'Decentring' here is understood, not as a separation of the ego from the subject in Lacan's sense, but rather in terms of representational contingency, by which I mean the filtering of self and other through the flux of unconscious imagination. In conditions of postmodernity, people become profoundly aware of the contingency of meaning and of the sign; they see that meaning is not fixed once and for all, but rather that signification is creatively fabricated and negotiated. In this sense, fantasy is located at the root of our traffic with meaning.

Yet this contingency of fantasy, as mediated through symbolic representation, often resists being brought over into reflexive awareness and thinking, the result being instead an immersion in unconscious denials, disavowals and negations. Personal confusion and dislocation – the feeling that nothing makes sense – is reflective of the immense emotional difficulties of sustaining any form of meaningful experience in the late modern age. One way of interpreting the existence of such dislocation is in terms of the disturbance and pathology of postmodern society itself. Under postmodern conditions, the fragmentation of social processes penetrates fully into the psychic world, deconstructing and fracturing subjectivity in one stroke. 'Postmodernism', writes Jameson (1991: 15), 'is not merely a liberation from anxiety but a liberation from every other kind of feeling as well, since there is no longer a self present to do the feeling.' The human subject, in this reading, suffers from a kind of psychic burnout. This burnout signals an end to the ideological mirage of unified subjectivity, as well as the depersonalization of affect. Self-experience as integral and continuous is displaced in favour of schizoid desire and random libidinal intensities. Hence, the cynical erasure of subjectivity in certain currents of post-structuralist and postmodern social theory, an erasure which involves a wholesale transmutation of the subject into a subjectless world of images and surfaces, abstract signifiers and disembodied communications.[3]

Yet while the oscillation and fragmentation of selfhood is certainly a phenomenon of increasing significance in the postmodern age, there are good reasons for supposing that this disintegration of the subject in contemporary theory is substantially inadequate. To begin with, much contemporary theory displays a lack of interest in the internal dimensions of psychological fragmentation, reducing issues of emotional abandonment and psychotic unhinging to the cultural and ideological imperatives of power as such. As a result, the pain and terror of psychotic disconnection are completely sidestepped.[4] Significantly, the euphoric celebration of psychotic fragmentation and libidinal intensification in some currents of critical theory betrays, I think, a strong affinity with those older, modernist conceptions of subjectivity it claims to overcome. That is to say, the poststructuralist deconstruction of subjectivity into fragmentation takes the form it does because it is principally a reaction to – an intellectual defence against – modernist pressures for self-control and mastery.

What happens if this dominant conception of postmodern dislocation and dispersal is rejected? What happens if we reject the linkage of fragmentation and subjectivity in postmodernity, and replace it with a conception of our psychic capacity for imaginative elaboration of self and world, a conception which suggests the possibility of some more facilitating agency in the reproduction of postmodern cultural forms? In the view I wish to develop, postmodern selfhood signifies open-endedness, not irrevocable fragmentation. Postmodernity, it might be said, breaks down the symbolic order of society as Law or Reason, and reconstitutes it as a form of openness, a space for radical imagination. In such circumstances, an awareness of fantasy processes as self-constituting becomes central, not only in the reproduction of social institutions, but also in framing the fluid and ambiguous field of self/other relations. Inside and out, at the level of psychic interiority as well as that of the outside world, living in postmodernity means living with an awareness of the over-determination of personal and cultural worlds by fantasy. Fantasy, as a creative flux of the unconscious, is bound up in a direct way with both knowledge and experience of the world; it cannot be avoided or overcome. Such postmodern awareness of the no exit from fantasy, however, opens the possibility for challenging the terms of intersection between human imagination and social processes. The passage from the modern symbolic, as a mode of ordering and mastering fantasy eruptions of otherness, to the postmodern symbolic, an awareness of the tension and anxiety embedded in the sites of fantasy, produces new possibilities for personal and cultural life.

Radical imagination, the destructuration and reconstruction of fantasy positions, becomes a central psychological and political issue with the development of postmodernity. Applied to society and culture, the exploration of fantasy as a means of intrapsychic and intersubjective communication, as a deconstruction of the fixed positions of the past, is especially important. Postmodernity, as we have seen, is marked by ambiguity, contingency and ambivalence, all of which fuse to produce an openness as regards contemporary social processes. For many, this situation is something to be welcomed; it generates excitement and hope. At the same time, however, the uncertainty of postmodernity promotes anxiety and fear as well. This is, perhaps, the central postmodern challenge for personal and cultural life: the creation of subject-positions in which unconscious flux and fluidity and symbolic representations and meanings are directly related to each other. The meaning and potentialities arising from an awareness of uncertainty and contingency, however, need also to account for the anxiety which such a state of mind produces. It is, above all, personal meaning, knowledge and creativity which are at stake here. Psychic transgression can produce with equal ease, or equal difficulty, an opening or closure of imaginary possibilities. A radical encounter with uncertainty, in my view, must extend to an engagement with the 'catastrophic' – the subject-in-process experiencing itself as 'coming apart at the seams'. In Kleinian terms, such an encounter with the disturbing demands a shift from the paranoid-schizoid phase to the depressive phase, with despair being properly owned and explored. Or, in the post-Kleinian terms of Bion and Meltzer, personal authenticity and creativity require a capacity to tolerate inner disorder, a catastrophe within.[5] It is out of this confusion and turbulence of passion that creative living can occur.

This brings the discussion back to issues raised by Kristeva. An exploration of the representations, affects and meanings invested in fantasy sites, says Kristeva, necessarily involves a dimension of uncanniness, of strangeness, of otherness. 'The sense of strangeness', writes Kristeva (1991: 189), 'is a mainspring for identification with the other, by working out its depersonalizing impact by means of astonishment.' This sense of astonishment, as previously noted, revolves around a confrontation with the unknown. Each time unknown experience is confronted, notes Kristeva, there is a deconstruction and reconstruction of self, and especially of infantile desires and fears of otherness. Constructed positions of self and other, and their organization in the symbolic order itself, are explored and, by implication, questioned. But there is something more significant at work in these unconscious interpretative procedures, both as concerns fantasy and postmodernity, and of their mutual implication in each other. The sense of depersonalization activated by strangeness of which Kristeva speaks is, I suggest, structured by the social and political dislocations of postmodernity. Experience of otherness and uncanny strangeness becomes more and more apparent in conditions of postmodernity. In a globalized world of political, economic and military relations, the encounter with otherness is continually evoked in and through mass media and generalized communication. Newspaper headlines of mass death and torture, snippets of the plurality of cultures on television, sexual imagery deployed in advertisements: these may all activate a sense of otherness within – of desire and fear, oppression and power, sexuality and dissolution.

Such otherness is problematic. In the face of our deep-seated psychological longing for the familiar, consciousness of internal otherness – destructive, fearful, empty, desiring, lacking – cannot be guaranteed. As regards traditional boundaries of displacement and repression, self and world can appear so fixed that it seems impossible to think, feel or act differently. Indeed, the rejection of otherness, as Bion has shown, can often lead to an elimination of the psychic capacity for thinking itself. Anti-thought, the blocking out and elimination of experience and affect, opens the way for a translation into action of fearful and destructive psychical states. Excessive projection, paranoia and psychotic splitting can be unleashed when symbolic space is violently excluded; and, under contemporary ideological authorizations of the expenditure of hatred, this often leads to the dehumanization, and actual murder, of others.

Individually and collectively, however, it is at the strange borders of otherness that the fixed positions of the past can be questioned and reshaped. Contemporary psychoanalysts such as Kristeva and Castoriadis (but also post-Kleinians like Bion, Meltzer and Ogden), in showing that the unconscious experience of subjectivity is deeply interwoven with otherness, ambivalence and imagination, help us to see that the postmodern world opens new zones of engagement for being with ourselves and others. In the postmodern society of transnational communication and the plurality of cultures, imagination makes personal and cultural reflexivity possible, and underlies this ceaseless psychic construction and deconstruction of self and world. Thus, in contrast to the prevailing characterization of the 'death of imagination' in contemporary theory, postmodernity is better characterized, I argue, as a culture of imagination without illusions, a cultural space which admits the provisional and contingent form of imaginary structures. Postmodernity is a reflexive world, a world in which we are increasingly subject to ourselves.

Notes

1. It should be underlined that Winnicott's notion of the 'true self' is an ideal type, relied upon to track disturbances in relating to self, to others, and culture. As Winnicott puts this, 'there is but little point in formulating the concept of a True Self, because it does no more than collect together the details of the experience of aliveness' (Winnicott, 1965: 148).
2. The best recent discussion on the role of affects is Charles Spezzano (1993). See also A.F. Davies (1980).
3. See in particular Deleuze and Guattari (1977) and Lyotard (1974). I discuss the limitations of the theories of schizo-analysis and libidinal economy in Elliott 1994 (144–61).
4. On this point see Glass (1993).
5. Thomas Ogden, in his contribution to this book (Chapter 8), suggests that psychic creativity arises in and through a dialectical relation between the paranoid-schizoid position and the depressive position. Paranoid-schizoid turbulence breaks up the structuration of integration and ambivalence reached in the depressive position, as depression serves to balance the psychic turbulence of pure loving and pure hating. I discuss this interplay more fully in Elliott 1996 (Chapters 3 and 5).

References

Baudrillard, J. (1975), *The Mirror of Production*, trans. M. Poster, St Louis: Telos.
— (1983), *Simulations*, New York: Semiotext(e).
— (1984), 'On Nihilism', *On the Beach*, 5, Winter.
Bauman, Z. (1990), *Modernity and Ambivalence*, Cambridge: Polity.
— (1991), *Intimations of Postmodernity*, London: Routledge.
— (1993), *Postmodern Ethics*, Oxford: Blackwell.

Berman, M. (1982), *All That is Solid Melts into Air*, London: Verso.

Bion, W. (1962), *Learning From Experience*, London: Maresfield.

Castoriadis, C. (1992), 'The retreat from autonomy: post-modernism as generalized conformism', *Thesis 11*, 31, pp. 14–23.

— (1995), 'Logic, imagination, reflection', in A. Elliott and S. Frosh (eds), *Psychoanalysis in Contexts: Paths Between Theory and Modern Culture*, London and New York: Routledge, pp. 17–49.

Davies, A.F. (1980), *Skills, Outlooks and Passions*, Cambridge: Cambridge University Press.

Deleuze, G. and F. Guattari (1977), *Anti-Oedipus: Capitalism and Schizophrenia*, New York: Viking.

Derrida, J. (1972), 'Freud and the scene of writing', *Yale French Studies*, 48.

— (1976), *Of Grammatology*, trans. G. Spivak, Baltimore: Johns Hopkins University Press.

— (1978), *Writing and Difference*, trans. A. Bass, Chicago: University of Chicago Press.

Elliott, A. (1994), *Psychoanalytic Theory: An Introduction*, Oxford and Cambridge, MA: Blackwell.

— (1995), 'The affirmation of primary repression rethought', in A. Elliott and S. Frosh (eds), *Psychoanalysis in Contexts: Paths Between Theory and Modern Culture*, London and New York: Routledge.

— (1999), *Social Theory and Psychoanalysis in Transition: Self and Society from Freud to Kristeva*, 2nd Edition, London: Free Association Books.

Foucault, M. (1973), *The Order of Things*, New York: Vintage.

— (1980), *Power/Knowledge: Selected Interviews and Other Writings 1972–77*, New York: Pantheon.

Freud, S. (1900), *The Interpretation of Dreams*, *SE* V.

— (1917), 'A difficulty in the path of psycho-analysis', *SE* XVII: 135–44.

— (1923), *The Ego and the Id*, *SE* XIX: 3–66.

Frosh, S. (1991), *Identity Crisis: Modernity, Psychoanalysis and the Self*, London: Macmillan.

Glass, J.M. (1993), *Shattered Selves: Multiple Personality in a Postmodern World*, Ithaca: Cornell University Press.

Habermas, J. (1972), *Knowledge and Human Interests*, London: Heinemann.

— (1987), *The Theory of Communicative Action*, Cambridge: Polity.

Horkheimer, M. (1974), 'Rise and decline of the individual', in *The Eclipse of Reason*, New York: Seabury Press, pp. 128–61.

Jameson, F. (1991), *Postmodernism, or The Cultural Logic of Late Capitalism*, Durham: Duke University Press.

Kristeva, J. (1991), *Strangers to Ourselves*, London: Harvester.

Lasch, C. (1980), *The Culture of Narcissism*, London: Abacus.
— (1984), *The Minimal Self*, New York: Norton.
Lyotard, J.-F. (1974), *Economie libidinale*, Paris: Minuit.
— (1984), *The Postmodern Condition: A Report on Knowledge*, Minneapolis: University of Minnesota Press.
— (1988), *The Differend: Phrases in Dispute*, Minneapolis: University of Minnesota Press.
Marcuse, H. (1956), *Eros and Civilization: A Philosophical Inquiry into Freud*, London: Ark.
Meltzer, D. (1973), *Sexual States of Mind*, Perthshire: Clunie.
— (1986), *Studies in Extended Metapsychology: Clinical Applications of Bion's Ideas*, Perthshire: Clunie.
Mitchell, S. (1993), *Hope and Dread in Psychoanalysis*, New York: Basic Books.
Offe, C. (1987), 'Modernity and modernization as normative political principles', *Praxis International*, 7: 1, April.
Poster, M. (ed.) (1988), *Jean Baudrillard: Selected Writings*, Cambridge: Polity.
Roszak, T. (1979), *Person-Planet: The Creative Destruction of Industrial Society*, London: Gollancz.
Spezzano, C. (1993), *Affect in Psychoanalysis: A Clinical Synthesis*, Hillsdale, NJ: Analytic Press.
Weber, W. (1974), 'Science as a vocation', in H.H Gerth and C.W. Mills (eds), *From Max Weber: Essays in Sociology*, New York: Free Press.
Winnicott, D.W. (1958), *Collected Papers: Through Paediatrics to Psychoanalysis*, London: Tavistock.
— (1965), *The Maturational Process and the Facilitating Environment*, New York: International Universities Press.

6 Lacanian Psychoanalysis and Postmodernism

Mark Bracher

Competing Models of Subjectivity

When one thinks of Lacan in the context of postmodernism, the tendency is often to try to identify Lacan as either an exemplar or an opponent of postmodernism. In textbooks on theory, for example, Lacan is often included in sections on poststructuralism, itself one of the most significant theoretical instantiations of postmodernism. In such cases emphasis is given to Lacanian concepts – such as the split subject, the radically linguistic nature of the human subject, and the incessant slippage of the signifier – that are congruent with post-structuralist and postmodernist views of the subject. Other theorists, citing other Lacanian notions – such as that of the phallic signifier and the analyst's function as the subject supposed to know – argue that Lacanian theory is still a creature of the Enlightenment or of modernism. In fact, however, the Lacanian subject cannot be reduced either to the Enlightenment or to the postmodernist model of subjectivity. Rather, it incorporates both of these modes, offering a comprehensive model of the subject that can provide us with unique understanding of the psychological challenges posed by the postmodern condition and of the relative efficacies of the various social, cultural and personal strategies that have emerged for meeting these psychological challenges.

We can identify three basic models of subjectivity, and the Lacanian understanding of subjectivity incorporates the partial validity of each of these. At its simplest level, each model can be characterized according to the number it assigns to subjectivity: one, two, or more than two. These models are, respectively, the liberal humanist, the romantic or modernist, and the postmodernist. Each model corresponds to an observable aspect of subjectivity. The liberal humanist view sees the subject as one, or unity. This model is grounded in the fact that every subject is based in a single body governed by a single brain, and in the sense of identity, including unity through time, that most subjects have, insofar as we speak of what 'I' do, what 'I' did moments, days, or even years ago, and of what 'I' will do in moments or years hence. The romantic-modernist model – which received its classic formulation in Faust's cry, 'Two souls, alas, dwell within my breast' – and other perspectives that see the subject as basically two, focus on experiences of self-division: between body and mind, conscious and unconscious, reason and passion, and so on. The postmodernist view of the subject as fragmented emphasizes the multiplicity of motives, roles, identifications and identities that characterize every subjectivity and give the appearance of fragmentation.

Most theories and theorists tend to emphasize one of these aspects of subjectivity over the other two, and as a result we have a situation analogous to that of the blind men arguing over the nature of the elephant: each position grasps part of the subject and takes it for the entire animal. The liberal humanist model of the unified subject is alive and well, particularly in much education and social practice (such as the 'Just say no' approach to drugs, sex and gangs). The major problem with the notion of a unified subject is that it cannot adequately account for multiple and often conflicting impulses. The romantic-modernist model does a better job of accounting for intrapsychic conflict, but it still fails adequately to account for the self-contradictory impulses and intentions that constitute human subjectivity. Many more souls than two, alas, dwell within our breasts.

The postmodernist model of the subject does account for this self-contradictory multiplicity. As Lester Faigley (1992: 226–7) explains:

> Postmodern theory decisively rejects the primacy of consciousness and instead has consciousness originating in language, thus arguing that the subject is an effect rather than a cause of discourse. Because the subject is the locus of overlapping and competing discourses, it is a temporary stitching together of a series of often contradictory subject positions ... Human action does not rise out of a unified consciousness but rather from a momentary identity that is always multiple and in some respects incoherent ... Postmodern theory ... would situate the subject among many competing discourses that precede the subject ... Postmodern theory understands subjectivity as heterogeneous and constantly in flux.

In Derek Owens's (1993: 167) words:

> We all contain a transient maze of personalities, a fact quickly ascertained when we think of the numerous voices we adopt and discard in speaking to various audiences. ... Further complicating

> the issue are the host of moods that affect my voice – when I'm irritable, dead tired, complacent, hungry, or insecure and defensive. If we add to all these voices the intensely private ways lovers speak to each other, the peculiar ways people talk to animals, and the style one adopts when talking to oneself, then the complex quilt we call personality is discovered to be utterly unfixed. Add in the even greater range of voices floating around us within the media ... and it becomes amazing that any of us can keep track of who we are among this relentlessly noisy crowd.

But keep track most of us do, more or less, and this fact is something that the postmodernist model of subjectivity has trouble explaining. In fact, the postmodernist characterization of the experience of fragmentation, which presents itself as a corrective to the liberal humanist and the romantic-modernist illusions of the unified or the bifurcated subject, is itself profoundly illusory, for it defines subjectivity as such in terms that accurately represent only dysfunctional and tormented subjects suffering from multiple personality disorder, and it totally ignores the horrible suffering often endured by subjects that are truly fragmented. As the political psychologist James Glass has shown, subjects who are truly fragmented feel anything but the freedom and flexibility that some advocates of the postmodernist view believe multiplicity and fragmentation bring. As Glass (1993: 260) observes, 'Postmodernism calls for multiple selves, without taking into account the psychological effects of literally living with multiple (discrete) selves within the same body.' Glass documents the 'terrifying journey through the lived experience of multiplicity, fragmentation, and death' (1993: 259) of patients with multiple personality disorder – 90 per cent of whom are women whose disorder is the result of sexual abuse suffered during childhood at the hands of men – and he concludes: 'The most striking examples or illustrations of multiplicity are to be found in human beings, specifically female human beings, who are the tragic victims of patriarchal domination. ... It makes no sense to idealize a form of human experience whose most dramatic etiology lies in some of the most perverse representations of human desire' (1993: 277).

Thus although the postmodernist model of subjectivity offers important correctives to the liberal humanist and the romantic-modernist models, it also results in problems. In addition to its gross misrepresentation of the experience of fragmentation, the postmodernist model, because it accords the subject 'no grounding outside contingent discourses' (Faigley, 1992: 227), cannot explain how a subject can escape the chaos of absolute relativism and ever come to choose one 'contingent discourse' over another, or how a subject is able to resist any of the contingent discourses into which the subject is interpellated. Nor is the postmodernist model able to explain how a subject is able to manifest a more or less consistent and stable style or focus from one sentence to another, much less from one piece of discourse to another. As Marshall Alcorn (1994: 38–9) observes:

> Clearly, selves are not mere radio receptors for social discourse. They are not passive vehicles constantly animated in different patterns by the passing through of ceaselessly changing social discourse. Selves do not become each and every socially constructed discourse formation they encounter; something within its own inner organization prompts the self to identify with certain social forms and to reject others. ... A particular self is not, as in poststructuralist terms, a simple, random, and constantly changing collection of texts shaped by historical forces. A particular self is not an infinitely changing collection of voices housed within a biological organism. It is a relatively stable organization of voices.

There is thus a pressing need for, as Faigley (1992: 239) puts it, 'ways of theorizing subjectivity ... that neither hold out for liberal humanism, collapse subjectivity into vague notions of community, nor reject the idea of the subject altogether'. Simply put, we are faced with the urgent question of 'how subjectivity might be conceived in terms other than the coherent, unified subject of modernity or the fragmented, dissolved subject of postmodernity' (1992: 79).

The Lacanian Psychoanalytic Model of Subjectivity

In contrast to these two models, the Lacanian model accounts for all three aspects of subjectivity: unity, multiplicity and division. The Lacanian model of the subject, like the postmodernist model, recognizes the subject's multiplicity, in the numerous and conflicting identifications, desires and enjoyments that are constituents of every subject. But in Lacanian theory, unlike postmodernism, this multiplicity is not the whole picture. Lacanian theory also recognizes, as does liberal humanism, aspects of unity in subjectivity. The unity is present from the perspective both of the ego, which functions precisely to create a sense of unity and identity through time, and of the fundamental fantasy and the fundamental modes of enjoyment that the subject seeks consistently through all events and relationships. And Lacanian theory also recognizes division as an important quality of the subject. This division is a function of the fact that each of the multiple psychological forces operating in the subject is, at any given moment, either allied with or opposed to the ego. That is, the finding of psychoanalysis is that each of the multiple, fragmented impulses recognized by the postmodernist model derives from one of two camps, which we can designate as the 'me' and the 'not-me' – i.e., either the ego, which Lacan sometimes calls the statue, or the internal otherness of unconscious identifications, desires and enjoyments. Beneath the surface multiplicity and fragmentation lies the divided subject, split between the intentions and qualities that it recognizes as 'me' and around which a semblance of unity is formed, and those impulses and qualities that the ego misrecognizes or refuses to recognize at all, dismissing as 'other'.

In the postmodern condition, however, the fragmented dimension of subjectivity has become more prominent. Lacan's model of subjectivity can help us understand more fully how and why this change has occurred, what its consequences are, and what possibilities of response are available to us. More specifically, the postmodern condition has produced significant changes in the three basic registers, which, according to Lacan, constitute the human subject: the Symbolic, the Imaginary, and the Real. Stated very succinctly, the Symbolic is the order of language; the Imaginary is the order of visual, spatial and kinesic experience (related in various ways to Piaget's sensori-motor stage) and hence of the body image and body ego; and the Real is that dimension both of one's own body and of the rest of the world that is neither captured nor controlled by the Symbolic or the Imaginary register. For Lacan, each of these registers is crucial to the establishment and functioning of identity. A human subject will not be fully constituted, or will be unable to function optimally, (a) if there is significant impairment to any of the three registers, or (b) if the interconnection of any of these registers with the other two is damaged.

In what follows, I want first to explain how each register functions as a bearer of human identity. Following this, I will indicate how the postmodern condition constitutes a threat (a) to identity in each register and (b) to the interconnection of the three registers. I will then sketch out and evaluate various ways in which people as individuals and as members of societies are responding to and trying to counter these postmodern threats to identity, and I will conclude by proposing a psychoanalytic alternative.

The Symbolic Order

Master Signifiers

Consider first the Symbolic Order, the central instance of which is language. Lacan emphasizes two fundamental aspects of the Symbolic order as sources of identity. The first is the value of particular signifiers within a given code, or positions within a given system. Any code or system – whether it be a general cultural code, a professional code, a familial code, the code of a particular group, or the group itself as an articulated system of positions – valorizes certain signifiers or positions above others, and it is these valorized positions, these signifiers, that we desire (often desperately) to embody. Such signifiers constitute our ego ideal, and the extent to which we convince ourselves that we embody these signifiers determines to a significant extent our sense of identity and self-worth. The ego ideal is constituted through our identification with certain key signifiers, or 'master signifiers', including words such as 'man', 'woman', 'athlete', 'scholar', 'fair', 'honest', 'powerful', 'independent', 'sensitive', 'shrewd', 'brilliant', 'daring', 'innovative', and 'competitive'. Such signifiers define us, give us identity, for ourselves and for others. This aspect of our identity-construction begins when we begin to learn language. In learning language, we come to recognize ourselves as either male or female and as being of a certain race, ethnic group, class, religion and nationality, as well as being 'good' or 'bad', 'smart' or 'dumb', 'strong' or 'weak', 'big' or 'small', and so on.

These signifiers of our identity are very precious to us, for they are quite literally essential elements of our being. Our embodiment of signifiers valorized within a code can provide us with a profound sense of well-being and enjoyment, and, conversely, our failure to embody such a signifier, or our embodiment of signifiers denigrated within a given code, can cause us severe anxiety or depression or evoke powerful feelings of aggression in us. Thus a fundamental and continuous aim, present to some degree (although not necessarily consciously) in virtually every utterance and action, is to consolidate and enhance our ego and its sense of identity by allowing the ego to recognize itself as embodying the signifiers constituting its ego ideal. We can see the significance of this identification with signifiers by observing the extent to which people will go to defend both the integrity of their identity-bearing 'master' signifiers, as well as their own claim to these signifiers: most people become upset when someone denigrates one of their master signifiers – as, for example, in the statement, 'Men are pigs!' or when someone threatens to deprive them of one of their master signifiers, as with a statement like, 'You're not a real man!' or 'You're not a true American!'

Systems, Codes and Knowledge

The second aspect of the Symbolic order that profoundly affects our identity is its systemic aspect: the relationships, especially relations of alliance and opposition, that obtain among all the different signifiers or positions that make up a code or system. In addition to its practical value, serving as means to all sorts of ends, awareness of systems – i.e., knowledge – often also functions as an end in itself: possessing knowledge of even the most impractical or trivial sort, not to mention knowledge in which our own being is directly implicated, can be profoundly orienting and stabilizing for us, and establishing, maintaining, preserving, or displaying this knowledge can provide us with intense feelings of well-being and enjoyment. This is the case because identity itself is a function of relationships, which give identity its definition, its boundaries. Knowledge provides such definition and boundary, and thus knowledge of even the most trivial or impractical sort can support our identity by giving us a sense of orientation and stability through connecting us to something other, the object of knowledge. At some level we all use knowledge – both profound and valuable knowledge and trivial and impractical knowledge – in the way it is used by the autistic Raymond, Dustin Hoffman's character in *The Rainman*, who possesses detailed, encyclopedic knowledge of the most insignificant sort (for example, baseball statistics and the television schedule) and resorts to it whenever he feels anxious or disoriented. Virtually everyone derives significant security and enjoyment from possessing, rehearsing and displaying a certain body of knowledge, regardless of any practical value the knowledge may have. Most kinds of historical knowledge fall into this category for most people: we value and enjoy trading in knowledge of the history of sports, fashion, technology, politics, music, literature, art, and so on, without putting this knowledge to any use, other than consolidating our sense of identity through positioning ourselves in relation to others.

The Postmodern Condition of Symbolic-Order Identity

Master Signifiers

The postmodern condition has radically altered the status of both the master signifiers and the knowledge systems that we rely on for the Symbolic-order dimension of our identities. More specifically, the postmodern condition has destabilized both signifiers and systems of knowledge, and as a result, these two pillars no longer offer the support to identity that they once did. The destabilization of master signifiers is a consequence of our being inundated with a multitude of competing and mutually contradictory master signifiers (i.e., values and ideals), and as a result, it is much harder – and perhaps also less necessary – for us than it is for subjects in traditional societies to settle on a stable and coherent set of master signifiers to constitute our ego ideal in which to ground ourselves from one situation to the next. As Walter Truett Anderson (1990: 257) observes, 'For most of us, one-dimensional social identities are not what they used to be. ... They are simply not adequate to our self-concepts or to the situations in which we function. ... More and more, we find it suitable to identify ourselves with more than one term. Multiple identity becomes a common feature of postmodern life.'

The primary reason for the destabilization is our massive exposure to others, which saturates us with competing and even mutually contradictory master signifiers, in the form of values, goals and ideals. Kenneth Gergen (1991: xi, 61) describes this social saturation as follows:

> In the process of social saturation, the numbers, varieties, and intensities of relationship increasingly crowd the days. ... An array of technological innovations has led to an enormous proliferation of relationships. ... As a result of advances in radio, telephone, transportation, television, satellite transmission, computers, and more, we are exposed to an enormous barrage of social stimulation. Small and enduring communities, with a limited cast of significant others, are being replaced by a vast and ever-expanding array of relationships. ... A century ago, social relationships were largely confined to the distance of an easy walk. Most were conducted in person, within small communities: family, neighbors, townspeople. ... From birth to death one could depend on relatively even-textured social surroundings. Words, faces, gestures, and possibilities were relatively consistent, coherent, and slow to change. ... But as a result of the technological developments just described, contemporary life is a swirling sea of social relations.

This saturation of social relationships destabilizes our master signifiers in two ways. First, as Gergen (1991: 74) notes, we internalize master signifiers embodied in many of the people we come into contact with: 'As others are incorporated into the self, their tastes, goals, and values also insinuate themselves into one's being':

> As we incorporate others into ourselves, so does the range of proprieties expand – that is, the range of what we feel a 'good,' 'proper,' or 'exemplary' person should be. Many of us carry with us the 'ghost of a father,' reminding us of the values of honesty and hard work, or a mother challenging us to be nurturing and understanding. We may also absorb from a friend the values of maintaining a healthy body, from a lover the goal of self-sacrifice, from a teacher the ideal of worldly knowledge, and so on. (1991: 76)

But even if we don't internalize master signifiers embodied in people we are in contact with, the positions we occupy in our contact with others constitute in themselves certain identities or master signifiers:

> As relationships develop, their participants acquire local definitions – friend, lover, teacher, supporter, and so on. To sustain the relationship requires an honoring of the definitions – both of self and other. If two persons become close friends, for example, each acquires certain rights, duties, and privileges. Most relationships of any significance carry with them a range of obligations – for communication, joint activities, preparing for the other's pleasure, rendering appropriate congratulations, and so on. (Gergen, 1991: 75)

And such master signifiers or values are inherently competitive, as Gergen (1991: 77) explains:

> The problem with values is that they are sufficient unto themselves. To value justice, for example, is to say nothing of the value of love; investing in duty will blind one to the value of spontaneity. No one value in itself recognizes the importance of any alternative value. And so it is with the chorus of social ghosts. For each voice of value stands to discredit all that does not meet its standard. All the voices at odds with one's current conduct thus stand as internal critics, scolding, ridiculing, and robbing action of its potential for fulfillment. One settles in front of the television for enjoyment, and the chorus begins: 'twelve-year-old,' 'couch potato,' 'lazy,' 'irresponsible' ... One sits down with a good book, and again, 'sedentary,' 'antisocial,' 'inefficient,' 'fantasist' ... Join friends for a game of tennis and 'skin cancer,' 'shirker of household duties,' 'underexercised,' 'overly competitive' come up. Work late and it is 'workaholic,' 'heart attack-prone,' 'overly ambitious,' 'irresponsible family member.'

Many people respond to this postmodern proliferation of competing and conflicting master signifiers by scrambling to procure and embody as many such signifiers as they can. As David Harvey (1990: 288) notes, 'The acquisition of an image [or signifier, in our terms] (by the purchase of a sign system such as designer clothes and the right car) becomes ... integral to the quest for individual identity, self-realization, and meaning. Amusing yet sad signals of this sort of quest abound.'

Postmodern Systems

The destabilizing/liberating effects of multiple master signifiers is reinforced by a similar proliferation of mutually disjunctive or contradictory systems – especially systems of knowledge and belief, in which these master signifiers and other identity-orienting signifiers give us our bearings. As Anderson (1994: 3) notes, 'If there is anything we have plenty of, it is belief systems.' Moreover, Anderson (1994: 3) goes on to observe, 'we also have something else: a growing suspicion that all belief systems ... are social constructions'. This 'breakdown of old ways of belief', together with globalization, which 'provides a new arena (or theater) in which all belief systems look around and become aware of all other belief systems', has resulted in 'a kind of unregulated marketplace of realities in which all manners of belief systems are offered for public consumption' (1994: 6). 'In the collapse of beliefs, a thousand subcultures bloom, and new belief systems arrive as regularly as the daily mail' (1994: 10). This situation, Anderson (1994: 27) explains, can have a profoundly destabilizing effect on identity: 'The collapse of a belief system can be like the end of the world. It can bring down not only the powerful, but whole systems of social roles and the concepts of personal identity that go with them. Even those who are most oppressed by a belief system often fear the loss of it. People can literally cease to know who they are.' Gergen (1991: xi, 6–7) makes much the same point:

> With social saturation, the coherent circles of accord are demolished, and all beliefs thrown into question by one's exposure to multiple points of view. ... Social saturation furnishes us with a multiplicity of incoherent and unrelated languages of the self. For everything we 'know to be true' about ourselves, other voices within respond with doubt and even derision. This fragmentation of self-conceptions corresponds to a multiplicity of incoherent and disconnected relationships. These relationships pull us in myriad directions, inviting us to play such a variety of roles that the very concept of an 'authentic self' with knowable characteristics recedes from view. The fully saturated self becomes no self at all.

Harvey (1990: 46), drawing on the work of Jean François Lyotard, articulates the same point in more specifically linguistic terms:

> While 'the social bond is linguistic,' [Lyotard] argues, it 'is not woven with a single thread' but by an 'indeterminate number' of 'language games.' Each of us lives 'at the intersection of many of

> these' and we do not necessarily establish 'stable language combinations and the properties of the ones we do establish are not necessarily communicable.' As a consequence, 'the social subject itself seems to dissolve in this dissemination of language games.'

Other types of Symbolic systems proliferate as well, including systems of relationships embodied in organizations and systems of skills. People today typically belong to many more organizations than they did previously, and their membership in organizations is much more transient than used to be the case. The same multiplicity and flux characterize the systems of skills or professions we inhabit. As Harvey (1990: 229–30) notes, 'Workers, instead of acquiring a skill for life, can now look forward to one if not multiple bouts of deskilling and re-skilling in a lifetime. The accelerated destruction and reconstruction of workers' skills have been ... a central feature in the turn from Fordist to flexible modes of accumulation.'

As a result of this proliferation of both master signifiers and Symbolic systems, the Symbolic order in the postmodern condition no longer provides the same secure sense of identity that it once did. This would not be a problem if people no longer felt a need to embody master signifiers or to possess ultimate or comprehensive knowledge of their world. But people clearly do have this need. The need to embody dominant master signifiers can be seen in the incessant and often frantic attempt to acquire master signifiers, and the need for systems is evident in the intransigent and often vicious defences that are thrown up against the incursion of any competing systems of knowledge and belief. The first attitude manifests itself in the purchasing of signifiers – in the forms of particular brands of clothes, cars, food, drink and so on – while the second is most prominent in fundamentalism of various types – including (ironically), in some quarters, Lacanian and poststructuralist forms of fundamentalism.

The Imaginary Order

The postmodern condition involves disruptions in the Imaginary register of similar scope and consequence as those in the Symbolic order. The Imaginary order is the register of the body ego, the sense (always threatened and never fully adequate) that we have of ourselves as unified, coherent, co-ordinated bodies. Our body ego derives its sense of either security or threat from our visual and kinesic experiences of our physical, spatial, visual surroundings (e.g., landscape and weather), and also from other bodies, animal and inanimate as well as human. In order for us to feel a secure sense of identity, our body ego must be secured both in its relation to other embodied individuals and in its relation to our physical, visual and spatial surroundings. Our central desire in the Imaginary register is to maintain our sense of bodily integrity and unity in face of otherness, particularly in relation to the other person, and often at the other person's expense. Any perception or situation that threatens our sense of bodily integrity or that evokes a sense of disunity is opposed by the ego in one way or another. When the physical environment is non-threatening, other human bodies constitute the most significant threat and solace, and we respond to these bodies with display, rivalry, competition and aggressivity, as well as with identification, in order to promote and defend our visual and spatial sense of bodily integrity.

Surrogate Bodies

We are thus continually scanning our environment both in order to find nourishment for our sense of bodily unity and coherence and to defend this unity and coherence against threats. The search for such nourishment and defence is one of the fundamental motives of spectatorship. One of the basic reasons we enjoy watching athletes perform is that viewing feats of strength, agility, co-ordination and grace gives us, through identification, a heightened sense (largely, but not totally, illusory) of the unity and coherence of our own bodies. And a significant part of this heightened sense derives from the success of the athletes in defending against threats (from their opponents or from the situation) to their bodily integrity. Animal bodies often serve a similar function, as is indicated not only by people's attraction to events such as dog and livestock shows, but also by advertising's use of the technique of dissolving or 'morphing' a graceful or powerful human body into an animal body, or vice versa.

Even inanimate bodies and shapes function as surrogate bodies for us to identify with in order to fortify our sense of self. An example is William Wordsworth's identification with the image of a castle during a time in his life when he had been shaken by the deaths of a brother and a child. 'This huge Castle, standing here sublime,' Wordsworth writes in response to a painting of Peele Castle, 'I love to see the look with which it braves,/ Cased in the unfeeling armour of old time/ The lightning, the fierce wind, and trampling waves' (Wordsworth, 1993: 29–32). Houses, and especially cars, are obvious examples of inanimate objects that serve for many people as a kind of surrogate body and/or prosthetic device. Tools also function as prosthetic devices to enhance the body ego, as the TV sitcom *Home Improvement* demonstrates (while simultaneously celebrating and satirizing the fact).

Visual-Spatial Environments

We also seek to fortify our body ego through inhabiting, literally or imaginarily, physical-visual-spatial environments that stimulate experiences of bodily coherence and unity. Different landscapes, buildings and urban spaces can produce very different effects on body egos. Soothing, balmy warmth can provide a profound sense of bodily security, as can bracing cold, both of which enhance the sensual awareness of the continuous surface – i.e., the image – of our body. But oppressive heat and bitter cold can constitute a threat to our body ego. A forest can fortify a body ego through the enclosed, protected spaces that it provides, or it can constitute a maze in which the body ego is disoriented and vulnerable to physical danger at every step. Similarly, a plain can nourish the body ego through the sense of unrestricted, unencumbered freedom of movement that its space offers, or it can threaten the body ego with its absence of structures that would serve as refuges, points of orientation, or sites of activity. Our body ego can be sustained and enhanced by the high energy movement of a crowded Fifth Avenue as well as by the serene, pastoral spaces of a Central Park. Or it can be threatened by the highly energized alien bodies of the avenue and left depressed by the relatively static and passive spaces of the park.

Buildings, too, constitute spaces that are always at least slightly reassuring or alienating. Sometimes a clean, well-lighted, modern, functionalist place is the optimum environment for the body ego, while in other instances such a place is experienced as lifeless and alienating, and spaces that offer the body ego more intricate, textured, colourful, dynamic or monumental spaces to inhabit are preferred. The abstract spaces of sculpture, painting and graphic design can also reinforce or threaten our body ego's sense of unity and coherence, albeit usually in a subtle way. The smooth, rounded forms of Henry Moore's sculptures, for example, constitute a space and a body image in which body and environment are continuous with each other rather than separate, and such a continuity is comforting to some viewers and unsettling to others. Cubism seems to offer some viewers a sense of transcendence of, or escape from, the confines of a rigid body image, while for others its fragmented and discontinuous spaces constitute a threat to the body ego.

Desire for Prestige

While threats to our body ego can come from images of fragmented bodies as well as from fragmenting or otherwise hostile environments, our body ego can also be threatened by another person who is unified either literally, in a bodily sense, or figuratively. This is because in the physical, spatial logic of the Imaginary register, no two bodies can occupy the same place at the same time. In the Imaginary register, other bodies are always rivals for the preferred place. The basic structure of Imaginary-order desire is thus rivalry or competition, and desire for recognition takes the form of desire for prestige, pride of place.

Key elements of rivalry and competition are aggressivity and display, including boasting and showing off. Such aggressivity manifests itself most clearly in brutal physical competitions such as boxing and various team sports involving physical contact. Aggressivity serves to protect the body ego's integrity, including its privileged position in the eyes of the Other. Display aims more directly at winning the Other's highest esteem, the fullest recognition, as can be seen clearly in various instances of 'showing off' the body image, including beauty pageants, bodybuilding competitions and fashion shows. But people also engage in display through various types of surrogate bodies. In fashion shows, clothing provides a kind of surrogate body to show off. Animal bodies and inanimate bodies can also serve as a surrogate body image, as is the case, for example, in dog and livestock shows, and even in automobile shows.

The Postmodern Imaginary

The Literal Body

The body ego figures in postmodernism in a number of very basic ways. First, the literal situations, positions and movements of bodies in the postmodern world are significantly different from those of previous times. Postmodern existence obviates or precludes significant bodily activity for a significant number of people: for many people, communication and transportation technologies have drastically reduced the need for physical exertion, and as a result, many people have assumed a quite sedentary lifestyle and thus a more passive and amorphous body ego. This new situation can either support or threaten people's body egos. Lack of activity makes postmodern subjects more passive and lethargic, even depressed. It can make people more aggressive, searching for an alternative mode for expressing aggression that might otherwise be gratified through bodily activity in work. A sedentary condition, by failing to provide affirmation of bodily unity and integrity, can render one narcissistically vulnerable and thus elicit bodily or interpersonal activities that provide narcissistic reaffirmation.

The degree of threat posed to the body ego by the sedentary lifestyle may be inferred from the dramatic reaction against this lifestyle that has occurred during the past two decades. During this time there has been an explosion of physical conditioning and body-sculpting activities, together with the knowledge, techniques and strategies to achieve these ends. Twenty-five years ago only a small percentage of the population engaged in jogging, aerobic dancing or walking, swimming, or weight training, whereas today most middle-class people under fifty have probably pursued one or more of these activities at some time in their lives. Postmodern technologies have provided a certain segment of the population with not only surgical techniques but also the leisure and exercise technologies and facilities so that they can now structure and strengthen their bodies – and hence their body egos – in ways never before possible. This development can be seen as a response to the threat that the postmodern condition poses to the body ego and an attempt to reinforce that pillar of identity constituted by the body ego.

Literal Spaces

Postmodern spaces have also had a significant impact on the body ego. In the first place, many of the spaces that high technology has allowed us to construct and to explore are spaces of non-human, and even dehumanizing, scale. The proliferation of spaces and places constructed on the scale of machines, including cars, trains, and planes, both alienate and physically threaten the human body. Many places today are unlivable for pedestrians; in order to be able to procure food, lodging, and employment, it is often necessary to have access to, or even to own, some form of motorized transportation. Air travel, the exploration of outer space, and, to a lesser extent, the exploration of the oceans also contribute mightily to the rescaling of space and the trivialization of the human body. The exploration of outer space (and also the oceans), moreover, has made us more aware of just how vulnerable and dependent our bodies are on particular environmental factors (e.g., temperature, atmospheric pressure and composition and gravity).

Also disorienting are the rapid construction, destruction and reconstruction of built environments, often to make more efficient operation of machines possible. Virtually no adult in the US has not experienced a significant disruption of his or her lived space by this construction/destruction/reconstruction, and anyone who returns after a few years to a city or neighbourhood that one had previously inhabited will be struck by significant changes in the built environment, changes that often make the place seem more alien than familiar.

In addition to the ephemerality, instability and escalation of scale of lived space, the postmodern condition also confronts the body ego with what Fredric Jameson (1991: 38) refers to as 'something like a mutation in built space itself'. Jameson (1991: 38–9; 44) explains:

> We ourselves, the human subjects who happen into this new space, have not kept pace with that evolution; there has been a mutation in the object unaccompanied as yet by an equivalent mutation in the subject. We do not yet possess the perceptual equipment to match this new hyperspace, as I will call it, in part because our perceptual habits were formed in that older kind of space I have called the space of high modernism. The newer architecture therefore ... stands as something like an imperative to grow new organs, to expand our sensorium and our body to some new, yet unimaginable, perhaps ultimately impossible, dimensions. ... This latest mutation in space – postmodern hyperspace – has finally succeeded in transcending the capacities of the individual human body to locate itself, to organize its immediate surroundings perceptually, and cognitively to map its position in a mappable external world.

Virtual Spaces

Perhaps the proliferation of virtual spaces and bodies in postmodernism is an attempt to escape from postmodern spaces and also an attempt to develop the new capacities necessary for inhabiting it comfortably. Beginning in the nineteenth century with photography and then film, and culminating in our own century with television and video, the past century has increasingly provided subjects with the opportunity to inhabit virtual spaces that fulfil psychological needs not met by the actual spaces at their disposal. Whether it be through the photographic images of an Ansel Adams or the filmic panoramas of a D.W. Griffiths, the intimate spaces of television shows or the more agonistic spaces of video games, the proliferation of virtual spaces in postmodernism has served as an antidote to the alienating and threatening actual spaces of the postmodern condition.

As Harvey (1990: 293) notes, 'Mass television ownership coupled with satellite communication makes it possible to experience a rush of images from different spaces almost simultaneously, collapsing the world's spaces into a series of images on a television screen.' This proliferation can be profoundly disorienting for subjects, insofar as it reduces their sense of a homogeneous, continuous space to which our bodies are conformed or adapted. At the same time, however, these multiple images offer a much greater variety and hence greater likelihood that a subject can encounter more satisfying body images to identify with and spatial images to inhabit virtually. Harvey (1990: 300) points out that

> in entertainment palaces like Epcot and Disneyworld, ... it becomes possible, as the US commercials put it, 'to experience the Old World for a day without actually having to go there.' The general implication is that through the experience of everything from food, to culinary habits, music, television, entertainment, and cinema, it is now possible to experience the world's geography vicariously, as a simulacrum. The interweaving of simulacra in daily life brings together different worlds (of commodities) in the same space and time.

These virtual places can be used by the body ego to counter the threats of actual postmodern spatial instability and fragmentation. In fact, the primary reason for the existence of such virtual spaces may be to reinforce vulnerable body egos.

Virtual and Surrogate Bodies

The proliferation of virtual and surrogate bodies in the postmodern world can also have important effects, both positive and negative, on the body ego. As with virtual spaces, here, too, the proliferation of surrogate bodies – including cars, appliances, tools, houses and other commodities – compensates for threats to the body ego and other elements of identity posed by the postmodern condition. People who feel physically vulnerable can compensate for this vulnerability, or at least gain temporary respite from it, by driving a high-performance automobile, dwelling in their own private, inviolable house, or using powerful tools or appliances.

Other forms of compensation for, or defence against, body ego vulnerability are offered by films, television and video games. Some video games and slasher films, for example, allow one to confront and desensitize oneself to primal fears of bodily dismemberment (one of our most primal fears, according to Lacan), sometimes by identifying with the aggressor and becoming the victimizer rather than the victim. Television broadcasts of sports events, particularly contact sports, place the gratifications of identification with virtual bodies on the screen literally at one's fingertips, while video games allow one to confront and survive all sorts of bodily threats in virtual space.

The Real Order

The postmodern condition has also had a destabilizing effect on the Lacanian Real. The Real refers to the most profound dimension of enjoyment, desire, anxiety and identity. This register originates in our earliest experiences of the primal, maternal object, which Lacan, following Freud, refers to as *das Ding*, the Thing. Our experience of this primal object is the prototype both of all subsequent enjoyment that we seek and of all that we fear and seek to avoid throughout the rest of our lives. The Real thus involves those aspects of our bodily experience that precede and/or exceed both conceptualization by the Symbolic order and organization by the Imaginary order. As such, the Real promises profound bliss beyond all gratifications of the Symbolic and Imaginary orders. Part of the Real is congruent with our Imaginary- and Symbolic-order identity, or ego. This ego-syntonic part of the Real includes those drives and fantasies that involve enjoyments and desires that are legitimate in the terms of the ego-ideal and non-disruptive of the body ego. The most common examples would be sexual drives and fantasies that are compatible with one's conscious gender identity. Another part of the Real, however – those unconscious desires and enjoyments that are antithetical to our ego ideal and body ego – threatens disruption and even annihilation of our Symbolic- and Imaginary-order identity.

According to Lacan, we associate the lost bliss of the Real with particular parts of the maternal-infant symbiotic body that provided us as infants with profound enjoyment that is no longer available to us because it has been socialized out of us. Socialization, or 'Symbolic castration', involves identification with certain master signifiers like 'man' or 'woman', which in effect cut off certain parts of our bodies from the desire and enjoyment that we experienced as polymorphously perverse infants, and concentrates the remaining enjoyment in certain precisely defined and delimited parts and activities. This socialization is most pronounced in the area of gender identity. We come silently and unconsciously to assume, for example, that if one is really a 'boy', there are certain things that one must *be* (strong, aggressive), *do* (act, assert oneself), *feel* (pride, aggression), and *desire* (to excel, to win, to do rather than to be done to). And we come to assume that there are certain things that one must not be (soft, passive, 'like a girl'), do (cry, play with dolls), feel (fear, tenderness), and desire (to have done to). Girls are subject to a similar and arguably even more debilitating socialization.

Drives

The primary result of this identification with master signifiers is the colonization of the human organism in such as way as to evacuate enjoyment from most of its regions and restrict it to certain specific, finite zones, which function much like wildlife refuges or game preserves. These zones where enjoyment is still able to occur after socialization of the body include the oral, anal, urethral, genital, scopic, and auditory functions, which constitute the basis of the subject's drives. The form of each drive is derived from its foundation in what Lacan calls the object *a*, the prototypes of which are delimitable, detachable parts of one's own and/or the maternal body (such as breast, faeces, urinary flow, phallus, gaze, voice and phoneme). In adulthood, we attain what enjoyment remains accessible to us through the stimulation of these particular bodily zones or the activation of modes of interaction with otherness or particular types of objects that characterize the enjoyment we derive from these zones. Drive gratification, that is, involves the enactment of a particular type of relation with a particular type of object or Other, and the role of the Other or object of the drive can be filled by a virtually unlimited number of entities, including not only physical objects and real people but also intangible objects and imaginary personages. This means that a particular type of action can involve a particular type of drive gratification even if the action bears no significant relation at all to the originary bodily locus of the drive. The oral drive, for example, can obtain gratification through biting, chewing, sucking, swallowing and spitting: the satisfactions people get from eating, drinking, chewing (gum, tobacco, or food) and sucking (a drink, a cigarette, candy or part of another person's body) are all clear instances of oral drive gratification. But oral drive gratification can also be obtained through more figurative (i.e., sublimated) instances of these actions (e.g., through 'biting' sarcasm) and in more general instances of devouring and incorporation (e.g., in learning), which do not directly involve the mouth, oesophagus or stomach at all.

One can get drive gratification either by possessing an object *a* or by being the object *a* for an Other. There are numerous ways people can *be* the object *a*. Whenever one performs an action, assumes a function, or occupies a position that is to a significant degree outside a system or Symbolic order, resisting assimilation by the system, one is functioning as an object *a* in relation to the system. The object *a* can function in relation to the system either as something positive – i.e., as a special something that complements, supplements and completes the system – or as something negative, something that frustrates, challenges, or thwarts the system. Either way, the person or group embodying the object *a* experiences a heightened sense of being. Since we have all suffered symbolic castration as a result of being socialized by the various systems to which we are subject, we find a dual gratification in positions outside the system. First, as an object that frustrates the system, we (a) gain a sort of revenge on our aggressor (the system) and (b) have a basis of existence or being that is not subject to or dependent on the system. Second, as an object that the system needs or lacks, we gain recognition from the system and a certain value *within* the system precisely by being *outside* the system.

We can occupy the position of the positive object a by virtue of products that we produce, services that we provide, or other functions that we have in relation to the system or Symbolic Other. For example, insofar as a person feels that he or she is producing a uniquely valuable product or providing an indispensable service, he or she is assuming the position of object *a* in relation to society as a whole.

The negative instance of the object *a* is found in various kinds of rebels, outlaws and counterculture members. Any kind of activity that is radically disjunctive from the Symbolic order or official system of the organization can provide an individual or group with the status of a negative object *a*. Subversive or nonconformist individuals, as well as gangs and various countercultural groups, including subgroups such as Marxist teachers, Legal Services attorneys, and so on, can occupy the position of a negative object *a* for society as a whole insofar as they function as gadflies, obstructionists, subversives or revolutionaries. Such a position can be quite gratifying.

In addition to being the object *a* that the Symbolic Other lacks but needs in order to be itself or to be whole, groups and individuals can also themselves seek the object *a* that promises to make them whole, fully themselves. Obvious examples would include drugs, food, drink, tobacco and sometimes also houses, cars, tools, appliances and so on. Money, perks (such as company cars and expense accounts), certain types of offices, particular pieces of equipment – any of these, despite its Symbolic dimensions, can also function as an object *a* for both organizations and individuals.

Fantasy

While the drives provide the enjoyment that remains available to the socialized subject, fantasy constitutes a scenario for recovering the enjoyment that has been lost to the subject through the process of bodily socialization. This lost enjoyment is represented by the object *a* in the fundamental fantasy, which is unconscious. The fundamental fantasy gives form to the subject's desire to reclaim its (mythical) lost enjoyment, or to become whole and complete, by locating that enjoyment or wholeness in a magical, mythical object or special substance, the object *a*, which represents for the subject all the enjoyment and being that has been lost by virtue of the internalization of the Symbolic order and its prescriptions and proscriptions pertaining to enjoyment. Anything that promises to overcome Symbolic castration and restore lost enjoyment – i.e., to render the subject whole and fulfilled – functions as an instance of the object *a*. Women frequently function as the object *a* for men who believe that sexual possession of the right woman – one who represents Woman for them – will provide the missing enjoyment or full being. Heterosexual women sometimes experience a similar fantasy concerning men, as do homosexuals of both sexes in relation to their partners. Any item that one longs for or feels that one can't do without can function as an object *a* for fantasy: drugs, jewellery, perfume and various other commodities such as cars, power tools or articles of clothing.

In addition, the fundamental fantasy involves not only the desire to possess an object *a*, but also the passive desire to be an object *a* that provides ultimate enjoyment or completion for the Other. This passive fantasy can involve one's body as a whole or a specific part (phallus, vagina, breast, voice, gaze, scent, air, etc.) functioning as the object that mesmerizes the Other or drives the Other crazy with passion. People who cultivate one of these aspects of their bodies are often pursuing the fantasy of being the object *a* for the Other.

The object *a* in Postmodern Culture

Postmodern culture offers a plethora of objects *a* for both drives (which actually provide gratification) and fantasy (which promises to provide ultimate bliss or absolute fulfilment). In fact, one of the main functions of postmodern consumer culture is to make available to consumers (commodity fetishists) multiple and abundant semblances of various forms of the object *a*: breast, faeces, phallus, voice and gaze.

The plethora of different foods, cuisines, drinks and smoking products is an excellent example of the proliferation of oral objects made available in the postmodern world. Harvey (1990: 299–300) observes:

> The food market, just to take one example, now looks very different from what it was twenty years ago. Kenyan haricot beans, Californian celery and avocados, North African potatoes, Canadian apples, and Chilean grapes all sit side by side in a British supermarket. ... Innumerable local food systems have been reorganized through their incorporation into global commodity exchange. French cheeses, for example, virtually unavailable except in a few gourmet stores in large cities in 1970, are now widely sold across the United States. ... Baltimore was essentially a one-beer town (locally brewed) in 1970, but first the regional beers from places like Milwaukee and Denver, and then Canadian

> and Mexican beers followed by European, Australian, Chinese, Polish, etc. beers became cheaper. Formerly exotic foods became commonplace. ... This variety also makes for a proliferation of culinary styles, even among the relatively poor.

There is a similar proliferation of anal objects in the postmodern world. Baudrillard has dubbed postmodern culture 'excremental culture' (1990: 102), and as Harvey (1990: 286) notes, one of the primary characteristics of postmodern culture is disposability:

> The dynamics of a 'throwaway' society, as writers like Alvin Toffler (1970) dubbed it, began to become evident during the 1960s. It meant more than just throwing away produced goods (creating a monumental waste disposal problem), but also being able to throw away values, life-styles, stable relationships, and attachments to things, buildings, places, people, and received ways of doing and being.

Harvey (1990: 331–2) points out that 'the biggest physical export from New York City is now waste paper. The city's economy in fact rests on the production of fictitious capital to lend to the real estate agents who cut deals for the highly paid professionals who manufacture fictitious capital.' Harvey (1990: 102) also notes that for Freud, Baudrillard, and to some extent Marx, 'money=excrement'. Not only through the production of capital, but also through the production of disposable products and of products with planned obsolescence, as well as through rapidly changing fashion systems (clothes, cars, books, music), postmodern culture functions as a giant machine for 'making trash', a phrase which is itself a euphemism in some parts of the US for defecation.

Phallic objects – objects conferring on their possessors an aggressive, dominating, penetrating power or prominence – are also quite prominent in postmodern culture. Cars, planes, trains, boats and rockets are well-recognized examples, as are guns and missiles, and power tools and appliances of all sorts. But there is also a proliferation of somewhat less obvious, more high-tech versions of the phallic object, such as remote controls for televisions, VCRs and CD players (many women have observed that men always want the remote control in their hand), and pagers and cellular phones (where smaller means bigger).

Much high-tech research and production have been devoted to producing and distributing the voice and the gaze as well. The telephone, the radio, records, audio tapes, and now CDs all offer postmodern subjects the voice detached from its human source and its social context, commodified into a consumable object *a*. In fact, the multibillion dollar recording industry is nothing more than a factory of the voice as object *a*. The multiplicity and variety of musical styles puts all forms and aspects of the voice at the disposal of postmodern subjects. Harvey (1990: 301) notes that the abundance of musical styles rivals that of foods and cuisines, described above:

> Much the same can be said of popular music styles. Commenting on how collage and eclecticism have recently come to dominate, Chambers (1987) goes on to show how oppositional and subcultural musics like reggae, Afro-American and Afro-Hispanic have taken their place 'in the museum of fixed symbolic structures' to form a flexible collage of the already heard.' A strong sense of 'the Other' is replaced, he suggests, by a weak sense of 'the others.'

Photographic portraits, film, television, VCRs and CD ROMs function in the same way for the gaze. The TV is on for an average of over seven hours per day in US households, and the gaze of the Other is prominent among the images on the screen. In fact, the TV itself functions as a kind of one-eyed monster whose blind gaze mesmerizes and interpellates those who encounter it.

This proliferation of objects *a* in all forms promises to provide postmodern subjects with surplus enjoyment of the object *a*. At the same time, however, it also has significant negative consequences for identity, because the alien objects *a* threaten our core, identity-bearing jouissance, in several ways. The commodification of objects *a* makes the gratification we get from these objects vulnerable to theft, either outright, as when the prime wines and cheeses, etc., are exported, or implicitly, when others appropriate and transform our objects *a* for their own use and enjoyment. Making our own particular (national, ethnic, etc.) enjoyment available to everyone results in what Slavoj Žižek has called the theft of our enjoyment, depriving us of the sense of distinction and profound security that this enjoyment has provided for us.

In addition, by commodifying the unique enjoyments of other groups – their music, food, dance, religious rituals, sexual practices and so on – postmodernism makes these alien modes of enjoyment available to us, and this availability of alien enjoyment is itself doubly threatening. First, by tacitly demonstrating the arbitrary and socially constructed nature of our own core enjoyments, it destabilizes that enjoyment and the identity it grounds. And second, because we are inevitably attracted to these alien enjoyments, fascinated by them, it undermines our sense of identity by demonstrating to us that we are not thoroughly and integrally what we thought we were and, more importantly, by threatening to deprive us of our familiar lived core of enjoyment, should we succumb to the temptation to embrace an alien enjoyment and its alternative lifestyle.

Responses to the Postmodern Condition

In addition to destabilizing identity in each of the three Lacanian registers by inundating subjects with multiple and conflicting elements of these registers, the postmodern condition, by commodifying these elements – master signifiers, systems, body images, spaces and objects *a* – also disjoins each of the registers from the other two. These disjunctions constitute a fundamental problem for subjectivity, because without mutual anchoring points and interweavings among the Symbolic, Imaginary and Real, stability and continuity of identity, as well as solidarity with others, are impossible. In order for individual subjects and groups to prosper or even survive, subjectivity must be constituted as what Lacan referred to as a Borromean knot of all three registers: if one of the three cords is cut, the entire knot falls apart. The most significant linking, according to Lacan, is that between the Symbolic and the Real. When this link is deficient, the result is psychosis.

Now one of the fundamental features that distinguishes postmodern sensibility from other cultural dispositions, such as modernism, romanticism and (neo)classicism, is its recognition that the relation between the Symbolic and the Real is not only a problem but a problem that is ultimately unsolvable. (Neo)classicism sees the relation between Symbolic and Real as quite clear and unproblematic in principle, however vexed it may be in practice: the Real is adequate to human needs ('whatever is, is right'), and the role of the Symbolic is to be subservient to the Real by representing it adequately (art should imitate life). Romanticism, too, finds the Real (Hegelian matter or substance, Wordsworthian Nature) to be adequate in the final analysis, because it includes within itself the Symbolic (Hegelian mind or spirit, Wordsworthian Imagination) as its supplement or consummation. Modernism, in contrast to (neo)classicism and romanticism, sees the Real as deficient, but assumes that the Symbolic can compensate for it or replace it: whether in the form of totalitarian schemes of architecture, industry or government, or through art for art's sake, the modernist assumption is that the Symbolic can form, re-form, or replace the Real – that the Real (life) can be made to imitate the Symbolic (art).

Postmodernism recognizes with modernism that the Real is deficient in the face of human needs, and that consequently the (neo)classical and romanticist strategies of making the Symbolic serve the Real (either by representing it faithfully or by enhancing it) are of no avail. But postmodernism also recognizes, contrary to the modernist hope, that the Symbolic is impotent to adequately reform or compensate for the Real, because the two are mutually incommensurable. Hence the postmodernist rejection, in what many scholars identify as the original emergence of postmodernism, of functionalism in architecture (the idea that architecture and urban planning could control social relations by defining and ordering space) in favour of non-functionalist modes such as pastiche and collage. The recognition of the incommensurability of Symbolic and Real is also clearly at the heart of the problematizing of representation that characterizes postmodern literature and painting, as well as in other phenomena, such as atonal music, non-linear and non-mimetic narrative, and neopragmatic philosophy.

But although the postmodernism sensibility embodies the recognition of the incommensurability between Symbolic and Real, it does not sustain this recognition and work through it. Rather, in response to the profound anxiety that this recognition generates, postmodernism defends against this threat to identity by, as we have seen, attempting to fill the deficiencies of identity in each of the registers separately: it commodifies master signifiers, systems, body images, spaces and objects *a*, and offers these to subjects as identity supplements that one can consume to beef up one's identity in each register. But even if a subject should succeed in incorporating a single element (or a coherent group of elements) in each register and thus overcome the fragmenting effect produced in each register by consumption of the multiplicity of its commodified elements, the subject would still lack co-ordination among the three registers, with the resultant negative consequences of debilitating intra-psychic conflict, lack of commitment, perseverance and reliability, and minimal capacity to empathize and identify with others who are significantly different from oneself. Social consequences of these psychological qualities include increased egoism, narcissism, consumerism, scapegoating, fundamentalism, intolerance (racism, sexism, anti-semitism and homophobia) and even violence.

Two more specific coping mechanisms are involved in the commodification of elements of the three registers. These are fetishistic and phobic mechanisms, which can be seen in the opposing attitudes to issues like abortion, doctor-assisted suicide, gun control and drug use: one side views the object (foetus, human organ, gun or drug) – which is always an object *a*, but can also embody a master signifier and/or a body image – as having inestimable value and as capable of compensating for or completing the deficient Real (like a fetish), while the opposing attitude views the same object as the source of great evil or danger and the cause of the Symbolic order's deficiency (like a phobic object) (see Bracher, 1993 and 1995). This same logic is behind identity politics and the resurgence of racism, anti-semitism and other forms of intolerance.

An alternative response to the incommensurability of Symbolic and Real is an engagement of the psychoanalytic process, which involves an exploration of one's personal (individual and collective) lived conflict between the Symbolic and the Real (and also Imaginary) aspects of one's subjectivity (as in the conflict between one's ideals and one's drives or impulses). Such exploration focuses precisely on the conflicts among the three registers and forces one to find ways for each register to accommodate the other two, rather than encouraging one to simply try to solidify each register in separation from (and even opposition to) the other two, as the predominant strategies of postmodernism do. Through this process, people experience the fact that while the Symbolic and Real are ultimately incommensurable, the two can interact in ways that are mutually transformative and that benefit the subjects in whom this interaction occurs. The psychoanalytic insistence on continuous and interminable interaction between the Symbolic and the Real (and Imaginary) in terms of one's own (individual and collective) subjectivity is a very different strategy from the attempt to escape one or the other (as in immersion in video experiences (Imaginary escape) or in drugs (escape into the Real) or to conflate the two (as in the Baudrillardian hyperreal), and it promises to produce much more desirable social as well as personal consequences.

Such a process could be promoted by helping individuals and groups to become conscious of, verbally articulate, and work through their own impulses, anxieties, and conflicts elicited by the various features of the postmodern condition. This would involve, for example, offering more opportunities in schools, in universities and in public discourse for people to describe, examine and reflect on how it feels for them to be confronted with 'loss of family values' and other features of the postmodern condition, and what the consequences of their loss are, rather than simply listening to public figures lament or condemn the postmodern condition and insist that people reaffirm family values.[1]

In addition, we could offer (through schools, universities, community organizations, social services agencies, etc.) alternative ways of consolidating identity in each of the three registers. Consolidation of identity in the Symbolic order could be pursued through writing and talking about one's own feelings and experiences in a rigorous and systematic way in order to develop values, ideals and knowledge that are grounded in one's lived experience (rather than simply accepted from the System) and are thus less vulnerable to competing values and systems of knowledge or belief. Such a practice could counter the destructive effects of the proliferation of competing values and systems of knowledge and belief, and it would also help to integrate the Symbolic and Real dimensions of the people involved.

This same process of self-exploration would promote another crucial aspect of the psychoanalytic process described by Lacan: namely, helping people become conscious of their own particular mode of core enjoyment, recognize both its arbitrariness and its inevitability for them, and find ways of indulging in this enjoyment that do not conflict with their values and knowledge or harm other people. For example, a core enjoyment that involved combining aggression against the Other with being the negative object of the Other's desire can be indulged in not only through a violent crime but also by outrageous non-violent acts. This process would help to counter the destructive effects of the commodification of objects and images that characterize postmodernism.

To counter the negative effects of the postmodern condition on the body ego, one might offer people more opportunities to design, construct, or decorate the spaces in which they live, and to design, construct, and reconstruct their own bodies – as, indeed, postmodern culture is already doing. Such activities could mitigate the effects of homogenization, fragmentation, dehumanization, and compression of space characteristic of the postmodern condition.

This is just a sketch, in broad strokes, of some possible modes of intervention. My aim here, as in the previous parts of this chapter, is to be suggestive rather than exhaustive or definitive. Above all, I hope to have suggested that psychoanalysis has resources that can be used not only to understand the psychological consequences of postmodernism, but also to intervene in them in a positive way.

Note

1. For indications of how such processes might be promoted, see Berman, 1995; Bucci, 1997 and Pennebaker, 1991.

References

Alcorn, M.W., Jr (1994), *Narcissism and the Literary Libido: Rhetoric, Text, and Subjectivity*, New York: New York University Press.

Anderson, W.T. (1990), *Reality Isn't What It Used to Be*, San Francisco: Harper.

Bauman, Z. (1992), *Intimations of Postmodernity*, New York: Routledge.

Berman, J. (1994), *Diaries to an English Professor: Pain and Growth in the Classroom*, Amherst, MA: University of Massachusetts Press.

Bracher, M. (1993), 'Antiabortionist discourse', in *Lacan, Discourse, and Social Change: A Psychoanalytic Cultural Criticism*, Ithaca: Cornell University Press, pp. 103–18.

— (1995), 'Doctor-assisted suicide: psychoanalysis of mass anxiety', *Psychoanalytic Review*.

Bucci, W. (1997), *Psychoanalysis and Cognitive Science: A Multiple Code Theory*, New York: Guilford.

Chambers, I. (1987), 'Maps for the metropolis: a possible guide to the present', *Cultural studies* 1: 1–22.

Faigley, L. (1992), *Fragments of Rationality: Postmodernity and the Subject of Composition*, Pittsburgh: University of Pittsburgh Press.

Gergen, K. (1991), *The Saturated Self: Dilemmas of Identity in Contemporary Life*, N.P.: Basic Books.

Glass, J. (1993), 'Multiplicity, identity and the horrors of selfhood: failures in the postmodern position', *Political Psychology* 14: 255–78.

Harvey, D. (1991), *The Condition of Postmodernity*, Cambridge, MA: Blackwell.

Jameson, F. (1991), *Postmodernism, Or, the Cultural Logic of Late Capitalism*, Durham, NC: Duke University Press.

Lacan, J. (1991), *Le séminaire, livre XVII: L'envers de la psychanalyse*, Paris: Seuil.

Owens, D. (1993), 'Composition as the voicing of multiple fictions', in A.R. Gere (ed.), *Into the Field: Sites of Composition Studies*, New York: Modern Language Association, pp. 133–46.

Pennebaker, J. (1997), *Opening Up: The Healing Power of Expressing Emotions*, Revised Edition, New York: Guilford.

Toffler, A. (1970), *Future Shock*, New York: Random House.

Wordsworth, W. (1993), 'Elegaic stanzas', in M.H. Abrams (ed.), *The Norton Anthology of English Literature, Vol. 2*, Sixth Edition, New York: Norton, pp. 196–8.

7 From Ghosts to Ancestors: The Psychoanalytic Vision of Hans Loewald

Stephen Mitchell

Cosmologists tell us that our universe began in a primal density in which all the structures and differentiations we take for granted were collapsed in on one another. The constituents of future atoms and molecules were all there, but they were packed together tightly. Our world, the world as we know it, has evolved into atoms and molecules, stars and galaxies, and planets, animals and people, and spaces, vast spaces. The explosive force that powered all that development into differentiated and bounded entities is called the 'Big Bang'. But perhaps the greatest mystery of modern astronomy is that the extraordinary centrifugal rush into differentiated structures and boundaries and spaces seems to be balanced by an opposite, centripetal force that keeps all those structures from flying apart, that brakes the force of the Big Bang, that connects the seemingly separate and autonomous elements of our universe, and that may eventually draw them all back together again into yet another cataclysmic rebirth. There is something else, 'hidden matter' in the seeming vacancy of all that space, that generates enough gravity to tie together even galaxies rushing apart across mind-numbing distances into a single force field.

Perhaps it is not too fanciful to think of psychoanalysts as astronomers and cosmologists of the mind. Patients begin treatment with fragments, pieces of a life that seem bounded and separate from one another: symptoms, current 'reality' problems, memories, dreams and fantasies. Psychoanalysts have learned to think of these seemingly bounded fragments in psychic space as constituents of a single force field. And psychoanalysts, together with their patients, narrate not cosmologies, but developmental histories, in which they speculate about the way that the force field of the patient's life came to be.

Hans Loewald developed a psychoanalytic vision of the nature and origins of mind, a vision that has extraordinary richness and explanatory power. Like contemporary cosmology, it begins with a primal density in which all of the features of our everyday world which we take to be separate, bounded elements, are collapsed in on one another. We begin, Loewald suggests, with experience in which there is no differentiation between inside and outside, self and other, actuality and fantasy, past and present. All these dichotomies, which we come to think of as givens, as basic features of the way the world simply is, are for Loewald complex constructions. They arise slowly over the course of our early years and operate as an overlay, a parallel mode of organizing experience that accompanies and coexists with experiences generated by the original, primal unity. That earliest form of experience, Loewald suggests, never disappears. It underlies the later differentiations and bounded structures that make adult life possible. That original and continuing primal density, in Loewald's vision of mind, operates as 'hidden matter', tying together dimensions of experience that only appear to be fully separate, bounded and disconnected. In fact, in Loewald's view, psychopathology most broadly conceived represents an imbalance between the centrifugal and centripetal forces of mind. In psychosis, the primal density undermines the capacity to make adaptive, normative distinctions between inside and outside, self and other, actuality and fantasy, past and present. In neurosis or, Loewald occasionally suggests, the normative adaptation to our scientistic, hyper-technologized world, the constituents of mind have drifted too far apart from their original dense unity: inside and outside become separate, impermeable domains; self and other are experienced in isolation from each other; actuality is disconnected from fantasy; and the past has become remote from a shallow, passionless present.

The story of Loewald's own earliest years may serve as the best introduction to his vision of the original dense unity into which we are all born. Hans Loewald was born into his mother's grief. His father had died when Hans's mother was pregnant with him, and thus he drew his first breaths in a world suffused with his mother's mourning and the powerful presence of his father's absence. She was a pianist of considerable skill and, as she told him later, consoled herself in the months following the death of her husband by playing Beethoven's piano sonatas, often with Hans in his crib placed carefully beside the piano stool. Think of the transformative affective power of the 'Moonlight' and 'Appasionata' sonatas, and then try to imagine the experience of that baby. How could he possibly separate his own feelings from his mother's? His father from Beethoven? An inner world of his own generation from an outer world filled with loss and passion?

A past when his father was present from a present from which his father had passed? Perhaps the emotional intensity and drama of Hans Loewald's early months had something to do with the importance he placed on a primal, dense unity as the starting point for the psychic universe that constitutes each individual human mind.

Loewald's work is difficult for most readers, not immediately accessible. In some respects, it operates in the same sort of dialectical tensions that were so central to his vision. On the one hand, his work consists of individual papers, fragments, written over the course of more than twenty years and never really knit together into a book or comprehensive theory; on the other hand, there is an extraordinary consistency to Loewald's work, recurrent themes that surface again and again in all his writings. In one respect, the language Loewald uses to introduce his thinking is the language of classical psychoanalysis in all its archaic, metapsychological density; in another respect, Loewald radically changes the meanings of all of the classical terms, so they come to mean something quite different from what Freud and his contemporaries had in mind. In one sense, Loewald is an extremely systematic thinker and writer, working his way through dense conceptual problems with intense attention to details; in another sense, there is a visionary quality to Loewald's thought, at times approaching a kind of mysticism, that breaks through in occasional passages of lyrical power.

All this has made it difficult to locate Loewald either in the history of psychoanalytic ideas or within the contemporary landscape of diverse psychoanalytic perspectives. He is one of the most frequently cited authors within the current Freudian mainstream literature, but those who cite him rarely seem to appreciate the extent to which the radical nature of Loewald's thought challenges the very channel through which that mainstream flows. (Arnold Cooper has suggested that Loewald's use of traditional terms whose meanings he has subtly changed has resulted in a broad acceptance of his work by people who do not really understand him.) Loewald is cited only occasionally by post-classical or relational authors, who, misled by his use of traditional terminology, fail to notice that Loewald was struggling with many of the same issues that now dominate the writings of our most innovative contemporary authors, for whom his work might serve as a rich treasure trove of new ideas and inspiration.

The only way to fully grasp the power and breadth of Loewald's work is to read it slowly, carefully, and in its entirety. This chapter is offered as an aid to that project, a kind of reader's guide. Although I met Loewald only once and participated with him in a brief correspondence, this chapter is offered in the spirit of gratitude for an author who, I have come slowly to realize, has become my favourite psychoanalytic writer. I have found Loewald's papers, in repeated readings and teachings of them, to be an endless source of new ideas and elegant, conceptual refinement. My hope is that this chapter might help make his work more available to others. I also hope to demonstrate that Loewald was struggling, way ahead of his contemporaries, with issues that remain some of the thorniest problems facing psychoanalytic theorizing today. Tracing Loewald's thought and the reasons for the choices he made, helps to sharpen the issues and inform the choices confronting us now, both in theory and in clinical practice.

Language

Because Loewald understood every dimension of experience as proceeding from the original primal density, any of the major topics Loewald concerned himself with – drives and objects; fantasy and reality; time, memory and mourning; internalization and sublimation – can be traced back to its entanglements with the others. One *could* begin anywhere. Yet, somehow it seems most appropriate to ground an initial approach to Loewald's thought in a consideration of his understanding of language, because he was so mindful (for reasons that I make clear below) of the language in which he chose to present his ideas.

Most philosophers and psychologists of language regard early human development as bifurcated by a fundamental and perhaps unbridgeable divide between the preverbal and the verbal. Increasingly over the course of the twentieth century, language has become understood as the material out of which adult mentation is generated, the very stuff of mind. Following Wittgenstein and Ryle, thinking is often discussed as interiorized speech; following Lacan, many understand the unconscious itself in terms of linguistic structures. A divide has opened up between the early months of life, before the child is inducted into the linguistic/semiotic system through which he will become a person, and his later psychological self.

Theorists of language, depending on their own sensibilities, have different attitudes toward life on either side of the chasm (Marcia Cavell, (1993) following Wittgenstein, calls it the 'veil of language') between the preverbal and the verbal. For Harry Stack Sullivan (1950: 210–11) who valued the precision of language above all else, the movement from the preverbal to the verbal represents the emergence of the distinctively human from the animal:

> Don't permit yourself to think that the animal can be discovered after it has been modified by the incorporation of culture: it is no

> longer there. It is not a business of a social personality being pinned on or spread over a human animal. It is an initially animal human developing into what the term human properly applies to – a person ... While the many aspects of the physiochemical world are necessary environment for every animal – oxygen being one – culture, social organization, such things as language, formulated ideas, and so on, are an indispensable and equally absolutely necessary part of the environment of the human being, of the person.

On the other hand, for Daniel Stern, who is fascinated with the cross-modal sensory textures and affective richness of early experience, the advent of language is a mixed blessing. In its communicative function, language makes possible the generation of what Stern (1985: 162) terms 'the sense of a verbal self' making many features of our experience now knowable and shareable, opening up 'a new domain of relatedness'. Yet, whereas Sullivan sheds no tears over what is lost when the 'veil of language' renders inaccessible what has gone before, Stern (1985: 162–3) regards the advent of language as a

> double-edged sword. It also makes some parts of our experience less shareable with ourselves and with others. It drives a wedge between two simultaneous forms of interpersonal experience: as it is lived and as it is verbally represented.[1] Experience in the domains of emergent, core- and intersubjective relatedness, which continue irrespective of language, can be embraced only very partially in the domain of verbal relatedness. And to the extent that events in the domain of verbal relatedness are held to be what has really happened, experiences in these other domains suffer an alienation. (They can become the nether domains of experience.) Language, then, causes a split in the experience of the self. It also moves relatedness onto the impersonal, abstract level intrinsic to language and away from the personal, immediate level intrinsic to the other domains of relatedness.

Stern and Sullivan have quite opposite sensibilities. When words first appear, Sullivan suggests, they embody the particularities of their original context. Thus, when the baby says 'ma-ma', everyone gets very excited. But these 'parataxic' features, Sullivan believes, are usefully lost as language use takes on 'consensual validity' and moves into what Sullivan termed the 'syntaxic'. The abstract nature of language strips words of the idiosyncratic features of their first appearance, and this is all to the good. Language can now be used in a way that other speakers can understand precisely, and the residues of the original parataxic contexts remain as autistic pockets that detract from and compromise potentials. Humanity, Sullivan believes, takes place in interpersonal interaction. For Stern, on the other hand, the richest forms of experience emerge in the preverbal realm with its densely sensual, cross-model textures. This sensual intensity is lost with the advent of language. Like Sullivan, Stern seems to regard the loss as inevitable; unlike Sullivan, Stern regards the loss as tragic, a poignant compromise that inevitably accompanies development into social interaction.

Freud also made a sharp distinction between the preverbal and verbal realms. Language is associated with secondary process, the reality principle, the 'word-presentation', the present-day, adult world and is at considerable remove from the 'thing-presentation', the preverbal, fantasy-driven workings of primary process. In fact, consciousness itself is linguistically coded. In order for the unconscious, infantile impulse that generates the motive force of a dream to enter awareness, it has to piggy-back onto words provided by the residue of the present day's experience. Thus Freud too saw a gulf between the preverbal and verbal domains.

The key feature of Loewald's understanding of language is his challenge of that separation.[2] For Loewald, language transcends the distinction between preverbal and verbal; language begins to play an important role in the earliest days of life. The most important distinction is not between preverbal and verbal, or between primary and secondary process but between the *ways* in which language operates in these two developmental eras and levels of mental organization.

In the beginning, Loewald (1977: 186) suggests, language is a key feature of an original 'primordial density' in which feelings, perceptions, others, self are all part of a seamless unity:

> She [the mother] speaks with or to the infant, not with the expectation that he will grasp the words, but as if speaking to herself with the infant included ... he is immersed, embedded in a flow of speech that is part and parcel of a global experience within the mother–child field. (1977: 185)

> While the mother utters words, the infant does not perceive words but is bathed in sound, rhythm, etc., as accentuating ingredients of a uniform experience. (1977: 187)

Loewald is suggesting that the very distinction between preverbal and verbal developmental epochs is misleading, that there is no preverbal domain as such. Language is an intrinsic dimension of human experience from birth onward. The meaningful distinction is between a developmental era when language, as sound, is embedded in a global, dense, undifferentiated experience, and a later era, when the semantic features of language have taken precedence over its sensual, affective features. In his retooling of Freud's own language, Loewald characterizes the significant divide as a distinction between language *in* primary process and language *in* secondary process.

Some recent findings of infant researchers (DeCasper and Fifer, 1980) illustrate Loewald's point. Pregnant women, during the last trimester, read aloud the Dr Seuss classic, *The Cat in the Hat*, to their foetuses. Shortly after birth, the babies preferred a tape-recording of their mother's voice reading that story to hearing her read another Dr Seuss story. As Beebe, Lachmann, and Jaffe (1997: 137) note, these babies are clearly able to 'distinguish slight differences in rhythmicity, intonation, frequency variation, and phonetic components of speech'. Consider this astounding finding for a moment. Language is a salient feature of babies' experience not only *after* birth, but in utero. Babies distinguish remarkably subtle features of spoken words (after all, they tested two different Dr Seuss stories, not Dr Seuss and Hegel). And, perhaps most important for Loewald, the earliest experience of language is deeply embedded and embodied in the child's undifferentiated union with the mother inside of whom he slowly grows into awareness.[3] In the beginning, the word, the body, affect, relational connection – these are all indistinguishable components of a unified experience.

Gradually, over the first several years of life, language takes on a very, very different quality. The child slowly comes to understand the abstract, semantic significance of words; words have meanings, apart from the immediate sensory, affective context in which they appear. Language takes on an increasingly denotative significance, and language skills entail the ability to use words in a way that anyone, not just mother, can understand; words that have, in Sullivan's terms, a syntaxic, consensual validity. Thus, Loewald suggests, over the course of early development, language comes to function in a secondary process mode rather than in a primary process mode, facilitating an adaptive competence in dealing rationally with everyday reality.

What happens to the primary process experience of language after language has become harnessed for secondary process purposes? This question of the fate of earlier modes of organization is always the central issue for Loewald, in every major psychodynamic dimension, in assessing the quality of psychic life. And, for Loewald, balance is always the crucial concern. On the one hand, if language does not become abstracted, sufficiently broadened from its original primary process context, the child remains entangled in a dysfunctional, incompletely differentiated autistic state. On the other hand, if language has been drawn too completely into secondary process functions, if the original affective density of language has been almost completely severed, the result is a functionally competent but affectively dead and empty life.

There is a deep link between the same words in their primary process and secondary process forms. The key question for Loewald is: how alive is that link? does language in its adaptive, everyday (secondary process) form resonate with its earlier sensory, affective, undifferentiated (primary process) origins? Or, has a severing split the two realms from each other? Such a delinking becomes definitive of Loewald's reworking of Freud's concept of 'repression', no longer the denial of access to awareness for an impulse, fantasy, or memory, but a severing of developmentally earlier from later forms of experience and psychic organization.

An experience with my younger daughter brought this home to me in a powerful way. She was one when she began to use words in an enthusiastic fashion, which was very exciting to me. We would sit at the breakfast table, and she would hold her little cup up to me, saying emphatically something like: 'Numa numa numa numa joooooose.' I would respond by looking her intently in the eye and saying back, pronouncing the words slowly and very distinctly, something like: 'Samantha, would you like some more juice?'

Now it just so happened that I was reading Loewald's paper, 'Primary Process, Secondary Process and Language' around this time, and I began to reflect on how I was responding to my daughter. I seemed to have the idea that I was doing her a favour by helping her shape her babyish, playful way of asking for more juice (or at least that is what I assumed she was doing) into words that any English-speaking interlocutor could recognize and respond to. But reading Loewald made me notice how much more fun her way of using language was than mine, how much was lost in this lesson in linguistic competence I was offering her. I began to fear that I might, in fact, be ruining her life. She might become very competent at requesting drinks but lose the vitality and sensuous playfulness that helped make her so delightful. So, rather than teaching her to talk the way I did, I began to mimic her way of talking. The experience was much more fun, more engaging, sensuously rich. I did have occasional moments when I pictured her in a college cafeteria line, humiliating herself by asking for a drink in the same way. Over time, of course, she managed to learn to speak in a normative fashion. But Loewald's hope would be that there would remain a vital link between her adult experience of drinking and asking for more and her earlier affectively and sensuously laden experiences. It is language that provides that life-enriching link between past and present, body and world, fantasy and reality, and language is deeply embedded in its original relational context: 'The emotional relationship to the person from whom the word is learned plays a significant, in fact, crucial part in how alive the link between thing and word turns out to be' (Loewald, 1977: 197).

In the following passage, embedded in the middle of dense metapsychological language, Loewald (1977: 188–9) gives us a glimpse of his vision of life, with the richest, most vital forms of experience halfway on a continuum with psychotic chaos on one end and schizoid hyperrationality on the other:

> In everyday mental functioning repression is always more or less at work; there is a relative isolation of word(s) ... indirect ... or weak links usually remain, sustaining an average level of mental functioning that represents a viable compromise between too intimate and intense closeness to the unconscious with its threatening creative-destructive potentialities, and deadening insulation from the unconscious where human life and language are no longer vibrant and warmed by its fire. This relative deficiency or weakness of links between verbal thought and its primordial referents makes it feasible for language to function as a vehicle for everyday rational thought and action, comparatively unaffected by or sheltered from the powers of the unconscious that tend to consume rationality.

Note the subtle but crucial shift in metaphors regarding the unconscious here, from Freud's 'seething cauldron' to a hearth. The salient feature of the unconscious for Loewald is not explosive energy or propulsive drives but rather its dedifferentiating impact. Alongside differentiated, adaptive, secondary process experience is perpetuated another, earlier, primordial organization of experience of dedifferentiation, affective density, and fusion. The key determinant of the quality of experience is the relation between these two realms (sometimes Loewald talks of them as 'levels of organization'). Repression severs the connections or links between them; language has the capacity to bridge them. Language, Loewald (1977: 204) suggests, 'in its most genuine and autonomous function is a binding power. It ties together human beings and self and object world, and it binds abstract thought with the bodily concreteness and power of life. In the word primary and secondary process are reconciled.'

Loewald studied philosophy with Martin Heidegger for three years in Freiberg before he took up medicine. In many respects, Loewald's life's work might be regarded as a kind of Heideggerian reworking of Freud's basic concepts. Nowhere is Heidegger's influence more palpably felt than in the centrality Loewald placed on language. 'Language', Heidegger suggested, 'is the house of Being. Man dwells in this house' (Steiner, 1978: 127). Heidegger regarded modern, technologically-based living as shallow and empty. Much of his writings entail the struggle to return to original Greek terms, as a kind of ur-language, in which being once fully resided and that still contains being hidden therein. Loewald similarly regarded contemporary, conventional life as shallow and empty. And Loewald regards the uses to which language is put as embodying and creating different forms of psychic life. The centrality of language in the psychoanalytic experience makes possible a reanimation of psychic life through the excavation and revitalization of words in their original dense, sensory context in the early years of the patient's life.

The Language of Psychoanalysis

What language should psychoanalysis be written and spoken in? This has become something of a political issue. Quite a few other theorists no more boldly innovative than Loewald have felt that, with the shift from drive theory to more interpersonal, relational theorizing, Freud's language, the original language of psychoanalysis, has become anachronistic.[4] Sullivan is an instructive example here. In order to find words to convey his meanings, he decided that traditional psychoanalytic terminology was of no use, because it carried too much baggage. So, he made up lots of new words. Similarly, Kohut, in slowly introducing self psychology as a radically different analytic model, introduced new terms ('mirroring', 'empathy', 'selfobject'), and intersubjectivity theory has introduced more new terminology ('organizing principles', 'developmental strivings') while eschewing traditional words like 'drive' and, especially, 'projective identification'.

Loewald introduced no new terminology of which I am aware. He liked the old words. There are many passages from Loewald that, taken out of context, could easily be mistaken for psychoanalytic writing of the 1930s. Yet, the old words he uses all have distinctly different meanings for Loewald. It is precisely his use of old, traditional terminology that has made Loewald's innovations so easy to miss for so many readers. So, why this choice?

There is a passage in a paper Loewald wrote in 1977, the year after the publication of Schafer's (1976) book *A New Language for Psychoanalysis* that hints at the reasons. Schafer's work provides a fascinating counterpoint to Loewald's in this regard. Schafer, who had been supervised by Loewald and whose thinking greatly reflects the impact of Loewald's revision of Freudian theory, had worked under the shadow of Rapaport and the latter's project for organizing Freudian theory and making it systematic. Schafer's (1968) previous book was an extraordinary effort to clean up classical terminology, to make it more precise, to shed its anachronistic features. By the early 1970s, Schafer clearly had given up. He decided that the language of classical psychoanalysis was too saturated with misleading and erroneous meanings, and, in *A New Language for Psychoanalysis*, he developed a devastating critique of classical metapsychology accompanied by a new language, 'action language', which, he argued, was better suited for our purposes, both theoretical and clinical.

Loewald acknowledges the problems with traditional psychoanalytic theorizing and the usual way in which it is read, but argues against the abandonment of classical terminology. In a clear reference to Schafer, Loewald (1977: 191–3) asserts that:

> What psychoanalysis needs might not be a 'new language' but a less inhibited, less pedantic and narrow understanding and interpretation of its current language leading to elaborations and transformations of the meanings of concepts, theoretical formulations, or definitions that may or may not have been envisaged by Freud.

Loewald does not elaborate on the advantages of more imaginative usages of traditional terms, but his understanding of the nature of language and its place in development makes it likely that his reasoning went something like this. Freud's language, the language of drive theory, is the archaic language (like ancient Greek for Heidegger[5]) of psychoanalysis. It contains within itself and evokes powerful affective resonances with both the early infantile, bodily experience it was designed to describe and the revolutionary breakthroughs of Freud's genius. At the end of the 'Preface' to his collected papers, Loewald (1980: ix) writes, 'Freud is close enough to my generation to have been a commanding living force as I grew up and became a psychiatrist, although I never met him in person. He has remained for me, through his writings, that living presence.' Freud's living presence, for Loewald, was evoked in the language of his writings (much as his father, whom he also never met, must have, I would imagine, been evoked in the music through which his *mother* remembered and mourned him).

So, rather than finding new words to convey new insights, Loewald nestles his innovations carefully within the old words, giving birth to new meanings while attempting to preserve resonances with a deep past. There is one powerful lyrical passage in a paper entitled

'Motivation and Instinct Theory', dense with metapsychological struggles, in which Loewald gives us a sense of the enormous power for him of Freud's instinct theory. I quote it at some length because it is so unusual within Loewald's oeuvre and because it provides such a startling glimpse into Loewald's (1980: 125) own passion for Freud's profoundly revolutionary breakthrough:

> *Triebe*, instincts, were – much more than scientists, doctors, ministers, judges ('the educated circles') wanted to admit or know – what made the human world go around, what drove people to act and think and feel the way they do, in excess as well as in self-constriction, inhibition, and fear, in their daily lives in the family and with others, and in their civilized and professional occupations and preoccupations as well. They dominated their love life and influenced their behavior with children and authorities. They made people sick and made them mad. They drove people to perversion and crimes, made them into hypocrites and liars as well as into fanatics for truth and other virtues, or into prissy, bigoted, prejudiced, or anxious creatures. And their sexual needs, preoccupations, and inhibitions turned out to be at the root of much of all of this. Rational, civilized, measured, 'good' behavior, the noble and kind deeds and thoughts and feelings so highly valued were much of the time postures and gestures, self-denials, rationalizations, distortions, and hideouts – a thin surface mask covering and embellishing the true life and the real power of the instincts. The life of the body, of bodily needs and habits and functions, kisses and excrements and intercourse, tastes and smells and sights, body noises and sensations, caresses and punishments, tics and gait and movements, facial expression, the penis and the vagina and the tongue and arms and hands and feet and legs and hair, pain and pleasure, physical excitement and lassitude, violence and bliss – all this is the body in the context of human life.

The breakthrough quality of this passage, embedded in a very complex, abstract discussion of metapsychological issues, conveys something of the power (language in its 'magical-evocative function', Loewald, 1980: 200) Loewald found in a more poetic use of language in psychoanalysis, both in theorizing and in the clinical situation. He noted that poetry (and obscenity) are modes of speaking in which the meanings of the words and the sounds of the words as spoken create an interplay that generates experiences that are *both* cognitive and sensory – embodied understandings.[6]

How should the analyst speak to the patient? Loewald provided virtually no actual clinical examples of his own work, but it is clear that he regarded language in the analytic setting as serving a very different function from that of language used by traditional classical analysts (or by Sullivan, to choose another point of comparison). Traditional classical interpretations were regarded purely in semiotic terms, as a decoding, a translation of the manifest meanings of the patient's associations into latent unconscious meanings. Sullivan, in contrast, regarded the analyst's language in the analytic setting as an investigative tool for getting an increasingly clearer understanding of what actually happened in a particular interpersonal situation. Loewald's concern with regard to language is quite different from both of these approaches. He suggests that we use language not only to convey meanings and to clarify situations but to evoke states of mind, to generate and link domains of experience.[7] A brief clinical vignette of my own might make these differences clearer.

A patient begins analysis because of sleep disturbances with an extremely sceptical view of the whole concept of the unconscious which he regards as 'psychobabble'. The first two dreams he reports over the first several months are of frightening underground tunnels into which people disappear and might be lost forever. In his associations to the dreams, he tells me about the backyard of the house in which his family lived during his childhood. There was a septic system under the ground. The tank needed to be drained every so often in a process involving a big truck, at considerable expense and unpleasant smells. The patient's father was an extremely frugal man who defined the family purpose as saving money for the children's educational expenses. Reducing how often the tank needed to be drained would save the family money, and there was a way to make the system more efficient so that the truck was not needed as often. That entailed digging trenches adjacent to the tank and installing 'laterals' in the trenches so that there would be more flow out of the tank into the soil. Each summer, the father would lead a family project of digging trenches for more laterals. My patient, starting as a fairly young boy, would be enlisted. His memory of these activities, as virtually all his early childhood memories, was of happy, joyful participation. But there was one memory of his digging at the bottom of one of the trenches, dislodging a rock, and tapping into an underground spring, which began to fill the trench. As he was shorter than the trench was deep, it was with some alarm that he was pulled out as the hole was filling with water.

After several months of working on various facets of his current life, filling me in on his history, and discussing his evocative dreams, we hit a lull, and he reported a reluctance to come to his sessions. As I asked him about his reluctance and his feelings about what had been going on, he suggested that he was afraid that I would soon become disappointed in him. 'I am just afraid that you will feel I am not working hard enough, not digging deeply enough', he said.

His wording was, of course, quite striking, and I have subsequently come to think of that moment as the emergence of a major feature of the transference. The analytic project in which he and I were engaged had become a symbolic equivalent of his father's 'laterals'. It was supposed to be good for him, but he had begun to feel the strain of the demands placed upon him. My approval was terribly important to him, and his own self-esteem seemed to have become contingent upon it. The image of the backyard under which all sorts of shit was seeping seemed to resonate with recesses in his own mind, to which he was reluctant to allow himself access.

How should the analyst speak about this analysand's 'digging'? In a classical frame, a timely interpretation would be called for, establishing the analysis as a blank screen upon which the childhood experiences with the father were being played out. The purpose of the interpretation would be to translate the present into the past. Sullivan would have been interested in some digging himself, asking lots of questions about the patient's digging, both in the past and in the present. I imagine Loewald might have been interested in the sound of the word itself and in the physical experience of generating it. I found myself saying the word silently and noting the way in which the sounds of 'digging' have an aggressive, penetrating quality that matches the meaning. To say the word, one has to isolate the tip of the tongue against the palate and pull the lips back slightly from one's teeth. The more I thought about it, the more it seemed to me that the meaning, the sound, and the physical activity required to say the word all participated in creating a state of mind and a form of relatedness (first to the father and then to me) that conveyed a constrained, almost harnessed aggressiveness, a homoerotic sensuality (in digging together), and a submission. Rather than stripping the word of the accidents of its original context, it seemed to me that it would be most useful for us to try to resurrect the complex resonances of the word, both past and present, its relational significance, its sexual and aggressive connotations, its capacity to evoke both a state of mind and a subjective world.

Realities and Fantasy

That Loewald was grappling from the beginning with a profound rethinking of the nature of human reality is apparent in a close reading of his earliest papers. In 1949, he read before the Baltimore Psychoanalytic Society a paper entitled 'Ego and Reality', in which he teases apart two very different views in Freud's theorizing. In a fashion that was to become the signature feature of his own methodology, Loewald establishes a conventional reading of Freud on the relationship between the ego and reality, and then pieces together an alternative reading that becomes Loewald's own perspective and that is much more interesting.

The conventional understanding of Freud's view of the relationship between ego and reality (or, in a broader sense, the individual psyche and reality) is that they are fundamentally at odds with each other. The id demands instant relief from the tensions of its drives; external reality, particularly in the social constraints of civilized life, is a dangerous place to seek instant gratification for sexual and aggressive drives. Freud (1923: Chapter 2) suggests that the ego grows like a membrane on the surface of the id because the id and its pleasure principle clash irreconcilably with external reality. Thus the ego serves what is primarily a compromising, defensive function, protecting the mind from a reality separate and inhospitable to it; the ego finds largely surreptitious, disguised gratifications for the id's drives as best it can. 'This conception of the relationship between ego and reality', Loewald (1980: 3) suggests, 'presupposes a fundamental antagonism that has to be bridged or overcome otherwise in order to make life in this reality possible.'

Freud's vision of mind and the relationship between instinctual fantasy and perceptions of reality is sharply hierarchical. Fantasy is a lower form of psychic organization, closer to primary process, and subjectivity is saturated with fantasy-based wishes. Accurate perceptions of reality are associated with a higher form of psychic organization, secondary process; objectivity, of which Freud's beloved science is the apogee, has been decontaminated of fantasy-based wishes. There is in this hierarchical ordering (an analogue of the verbal/preverbal distinction explored in the previous section) an embedded Darwinian metaphor. Ontogeny recapitulates phylogeny; the individual psyche begins with lower life forms (the id) and, mirroring the evolution of species, generates higher life forms (the ego and the superego). Of course, Freud emphasizes repeatedly that human beings cannot simply cut themselves off (through repression) from their primitive motivational underpinnings without the inevitability of neurotic symptoms signalling the 'return of the repressed'. This is why sublimation, for those Freud thought were blessed with the constitutional talent for it, is such a gift, making possible the gratification of aim-inhibited versions of lower motivations within higher pursuits. The Freudian ego psychology of Loewald's day extended this hierarchicalization of value by adding the concept of drive 'neutralization', through which lower sexual and aggressive drives could be cleansed of their instinctual qualities by the ego, which would then use their now decontaminated energies for higher ego functions.[8]

But, Loewald suggests, there is a second thread, a subtext to Freud's theorizing on these issues, in which ego and reality are not two clashing realms but rather, in the beginning, an original unity. Drawing on one of Freud's passages to which he returns again and again, Loewald (1980) calls our attention to Freud's (1930) discussion of what he called the 'oceanic feeling' at the beginning of *Civilization and its Discontents*, and argues that:

> The relatedness between ego and reality, or objects, does not develop from an originally unrelated coexistence of two separate entities that come into contact with each other, but on the contrary form a unitary whole that differentiates into distinct parts. Mother and baby do not get together and develop a relationship, but the baby is born, becomes detached from the mother, and thus a relatedness between two parts that originally were one becomes possible. (Loewald, 1949: 11)

Loewald goes on to suggest not only that there is a developmentally early phase of unity between mother and baby (similar to Mahler's notion of a symbiotic phase), but that there is a mode of organizing experience that continues throughout life and in which later distinctions between self and other, internal and external, fantasy and perception are dissolved.[9]

It is crucial to grasp that Loewald does not regard the experience of undifferentiation as illusory or less 'real'. It is just as real as the differentiating distinctions essential to living adaptively in conventional reality. These are not just developmental phases; they are coterminous modes of experience.

In his last writings, Loewald challenged Winnicott's theorizing precisely on this point. Loewald had been aware that Winnicott's rich notions of transitional space and transitional experience addressed many of the same issues with which Loewald himself was struggling. Goldman (1996) captured well the way in which Winnicott, like Loewald, attempted to reclaim fantasy as a source of vitality and meaning:

> In potential space … we come alive as creators or interpreters of our own experience; reality is interpreted in terms of fantasy, and fantasy in terms of reality. Perception renders fantasy relatively safe; fantasy renders perception relatively meaningful. (1996: 341)

But Winnicott throughout grants greater epistemological and ontological status to conventional reality. The good-enough mother does not challenge the illusory status the child grants to the transitional object. The good-enough mother meets the child's 'spontaneous gesture' making possible the 'moment of illusion' in which the child believes she has created the breast herself. Not so, Loewald argues; there is no illusion whatsoever. Winnicott characterizes experiences in these moments as illusions, unreal in reference to an objective, conventional reality in which he himself is anchored. Both children and patients need these illusions to grow with a sense of security (and artists need these illusions to give free rein to their creativity), but, for Winnicott, they are illusions nonetheless. For Loewald, and this was very important to his whole vision of mind and experience, they are not.

Consider Loewald's (1988: 76) description of the interpersonal event Winnicott characterizes as the 'moment of illusion'. 'Mother and infant may be said to invent each other in the mouth–breast encounter: they come upon something and, out of need or desire, invent-jointly-its utilization.' And, at another point, Loewald challenges Winnicott's claim that the transitional realm, the 'intermediate area' takes place *between* inner and outer reality, which Winnicott designates as the province of illusion. 'But it is the separation into outer and inner reality', Loewald (1988: 71) points out, 'that makes for the possibility of "reality" and "illusion." Prior to sorting out inner and outer reality there is no "room" for an intermediate third area, no space in which to distinguish or oppose illusion and reality.'

There are two closely related but distinct concepts that Loewald is illustrating here. First, minds are very closely and complexly interrelated. In the nursing couple, the baby's need for the nursing experience is impossible to separate from the mother's need for the nursing experience. The baby's cry produces a 'letting down' response in the mother's breasts; to claim that the baby has, in some sense, created the readied breast is no illusion. The baby's rhythms of hunger and satiety almost immediately following birth are a product partially of the mother's own rhythms of interaction. In the language of recent infant research, mother and infant actually *do* co-create each other through subtle but powerful processes of reciprocal influence.

But Loewald is also making another, in some sense even more provocative point. In the baby's experience, and perhaps in some mothers', there is no differentiation between the cry and the response, the mouth and the breast. The nursing experience is one in which self and other are not clearly differentiated. This is difficult to grasp as anything but an illusion, as unreal, because we are so accustomed to thinking of our everyday differentiation of self from other, internal from external, as the sole, incontrovertible reality. But consider some phenomena that are difficult to explain based on this premise.

A woman[10] who has recently given birth finds herself holding her baby away from her body, with her arms outstretched, literally at arm's length. She *can* hold the baby in the customary fashion, up against her body with her arms bent at the elbow, but, for some reason that she cannot begin to explain, the arm's-length posture seems more natural, more comfortable, more 'right'. She later finds out that when her own mother was pregnant with her, she was in an automobile accident that broke both her arms. Both arms were in casts, constantly outstretched, for several months after giving birth.

The primatologist Steven Suomi (1995) provides data that seem to bear on this story. Suomi has explored and extended the implications of Bowlby's concept of 'attachment' in many different areas. One set of studies considered the question of mothering style in monkeys, attempting to sort out genetic from experiential factors. In precisely the kind of study impossible to do with humans, the researchers separated baby monkeys from their biological mothers and placed them with adopted mothers. They later evaluated the mothering styles of those babies once grown and having babies of their own. The researchers discovered that it was experience, not genes, that was determinative; what emerged was stylistically similar not to the genetic mother but the adoptive mother. Monkeys mother as they themselves were mothered.

In one sense, these kinds of data should not be surprising to psychoanalysts. Since early in this century Freud used the term 'repetition compulsion' to describe the forms through which early traumatic experiences emerge again and again throughout life, often with the roles reversed. The abused become the abusers. And most of us have had the extremely disconcerting experience of finding the same angry phrases that were hurled at us by our own parents when we were children erupting from our own mouths, as if from a demon that had taken up residence inside of us, in frustrating moments with our own children.

The challenge of these kinds of data is not in the phenomenon of the repetition in adult life of early childhood experiences, good and bad, but in the explanations customarily employed by psychoanalysts to account for them. Something outside of us has been stored inside of us. How did it get there? Analytic theorists have come up with a wide array of terms to account precisely for this phenomenon: internalization, internal objects, introjection, incorporation, identification and so on. I like these terms, and they accompany lots of clinically useful explanations for thinking about the ways in which external becomes internal, the ways in which what was done to people, or in the presence of people, becomes part of the person himself.

But these explanations seem strained when it comes to accounting for stories like the woman with the outstretched arms and monkey mothering. Do we really believe that the baby whose mother's arms were in casts or the monkey babies clearly perceived the relevant features of their mothers as objects outside of them and then, through a fairly sophisticated defensive process, established that image as an internal presence, later identifying with that image of a separate other?

It seems much more persuasive to me to assume that early experiences like these are stored not as images of a clearly delineated external other but as kinaesthetic memories of experiences in which self and other are undifferentiated. It seems likely to me that what is recorded and stored is a global sense of 'mothering' in which the mother and the infant are merged into a singular event that envelops both of them. It may be that many intense emotional experiences, not just in infancy, but in later life as well, are organized not only in terms of secondary process, in which internal and external, self and other are clearly delineated, but also in terms of a primary process, in which the participants are experienced as co-creating each other. Recent depictions of the analytic situation in terms of the reciprocal co-creation of the analysand and analyst in the transference and the countertransference are describing precisely such a process. In Ogden's depiction of the 'analytic third', for example, there is no way to cleanly separate what the analyst and the analysand are each bringing to the interaction, because each requires the emotional participation of the other (although through different roles) in order to become actualized in the analytic context.

Consider the difference between an extension of Loewald's approach to these issues and the closely related concept of an 'internal object world' as developed by Melanie Klein. Klein believed that the infant has elaborate introjective and projective phantasies of movements of substances and body parts back and forth across the boundary between inside and outside. So, when I find myself speaking in irritation to my daughter in precisely the words with which my father spoke to me, I am identifying with a paternal introject that was established inside me for purposes of omnipotent control.

In Loewald's vision, by way of contrast, my father's irritated words were not taken *into* me, they *are* me. I could probably tell you what was my father and what was me on a multiple-choice test designed to evaluate secondary process thought. Yet, in those affectively laden moments, when they originally happened and when they reappear decades later, the irritating child and the irritated parent are, on a primary process level, parts of a singular, undifferentiated experience. Thus, one could use Loewald's suggestions on these issues to redefine the phantasies constituting Klein's 'internal object world' as not at all illusory and unreal, but as tapping into a developmental phase and an on-going mode of experience in which the customary distinctions between internal and external, self and other, do not apply.

Consider a woman who seeks treatment in her early forties because she feels haunted by a sadness she has lived with her whole life related to the sudden death of her mother in a car accident when she was five years old. She lost more than her mother in that catastrophic event. Her father felt himself unable to take care of her and her older brother and sent both of them to boarding schools. She attended a school/orphanage run by nuns, returning home at weekends to be with a father she experienced as so bereft and overburdened, that she needed to eliminate any needs of her own in order to care for him. She became precociously mature and survived very successfully, although at great psychic cost. Thus, she had lost her entire world. To make matters worse, the father decided that the pain of talking about the mother would be too great for his children to bear, so all mention of her was forbidden. She had been lucky enough to find a picture of her mother in a closet, and her only experiences of even approaching mourning were closeted, solitary moments of searching the picture for memories of her mother. An experience in therapy in her thirties focused on the massive inhibition in her opportunities to mourn. The therapy helped a great deal, but she was able to call up only very faint memories of her mother, and the sadness remained.

Since that time, she married and gave birth to a child of her own, who was now five years old. He had begun school and was experiencing enormous difficulties separating from her. It was not long into our work that we realized that she had returned for treatment partially out of a dread that her own experience of devastation at the age of five would be recreated somehow in his life. In the course of our work, many facets of her own experience, her son's experience, and their interactions emerged. I want to pick up one thread relevant to this discussion.

She began to describe, somewhat shamefully, her sense that her son was 'part of me'. This, of course, is not what enlightened parents are supposed to think, but we explored some ways in which this was, in fact, her reality. She described her experience of watching him play with his classmates. She couldn't take her eyes off him. It was as if he were endlessly fascinating. I knew something about what she was describing from experiences with my own children, but this seemed to be something more intense and pervasive. So I asked her to see if she could get at the feelings connected with the sense that 'he is part of me'.

She remembered her absorption in her pregnancy when, in a quite literal sense, her son was part of her. She remembered the strangeness of the separation that constituted his birth; he still felt part of her though no longer literally part of her. She then associated to her memories that in losing her mother, she had lost a 'part of her'. In fact, she'd felt an absence, a kind of hole, in herself ever since that time, as if a part of her had disappeared and never returned. She'd felt that perhaps in becoming a mother, she could refind her own mother, although it had never really felt quite like that. I suggested to her that when she lost her mother she also lost a version of herself and that her fascination with her son was partly a fascination with a childhood of which she herself had been robbed. In watching him, she was also watching for lost parts of herself and for her lost mother, who had never seen them.

How would we want to characterize this woman's experience of her son as 'part of me'? Is this an illusion? Is it a primitive fantasy? Or, is it a reality of a sort different from the conventional one we generally inhabit? I find it compelling to think that this woman's early catastrophic loss was experienced not only as the loss of an other but as the loss of an other, a self, a world, all jumbled up together. I think that her pregnancy filled, temporarily, the hole left by that loss and that her son came to signify for her parts of herself that were there and parts of herself she experienced only as absences. He, in turn, must have come to experience her losses and terror of separation as his own.

Her experience of the analytic situation was very sensible. I was a professional and we had a professional relationship. She kept her feelings about me, and mine about her, neat and tidy. She had dreams with clear associations to me and our work in settings that evoked a room at the edge of the world, at vast distances from the rest of her life. It was only when these categories began to break down, as the not-so-sensible feelings about herself, her son, and me emerged and were more fully experienced and talked about, that she began to feel a fuller, less hauntingly sad sense about herself.

In early childhood, Loewald suggested, fantasy and reality are not experienced as antithetical to, or even separable from, each other. Rather, they interpenetrate each other.[11] There is a sense of enchantment in early experience, and an inevitable disenchantment accompanies the child's growing adaptation to the consensual world of objective reality. Loewald argued repeatedly that it is a fateful error, which has become a cultural norm, to mistake the world of objectivity for the true, sole reality. And psychoanalysis, following the idolization of science at the end of the nineteenth century and in the first half of the twentieth century, 'has unwittingly taken over much of the obsessive neurotic's experience and conception of reality and has taken it for granted as "the objective reality"' (p. 30).[12] For Loewald, in contrast, an adult reality that has been wholly separated from infantile fantasy is a desiccated, meaningless, passionless world. The traditional Freudian ego psychology of Loewald's day regarded the progressive neutralization of drives and the triumph of the reality principle over the pleasure principle as the acme of mental health. Loewald regarded such a state as a culturally valued, normative pathology. Health for Loewald is a state in which fantasy enchants objectivity, and the past enriches the present.

Consider the everyday clinical question of the relationship between infantile love and adult love. Are Oedipal love objects best renounced forever, as suggested by Freud (1924) in 'The Dissolution of the Oedipus Complex', or does Oedipal love perpetually shadow adult passion, threatening to draw adult love into inevitably conflictual incest, as Freud (1930) suggested in *Civilization and its Discontents*? Fromm (1956) following Freud's earlier notion, argued in *The Art of Loving* that any vestiges of Oedipal, childhood passion in adult love suggest neurosis and a failure to fully engage the present. In contrast to Fromm, Loewald, in his most famous lines, detailed the difference between a present that is haunted by the past and a present that is enriched by the past.

The psychoanalytic transference, Loewald (1960: 249) suggests, comes alive as the patient's unconscious tastes 'the blood of recognition' in feelings toward the analyst, 'so that the old ghosts may reawaken to life'. In the neurotic, the past has been improperly buried:

> those who know ghosts tell us that they long to be released from their ghost life and led to rest as ancestors. As ancestors they live forth in the present generation, while as ghosts they are compelled to haunt the present generation with their shadow life. ... ghosts of the unconscious, imprisoned by defenses but haunting the patient in the dark of his defenses and symptoms, are allowed to taste blood, are let loose. In the daylight of analysis the ghosts of the unconscious are laid and led to rest as ancestors whose power is taken over and transformed into the newer intensity of present life, of the secondary process and contemporary objects.

For Freud, transference operated as a resistance to the 'memory work' that was the heart of psychoanalysis, the sorting out and decontamination of the past from the present. For Loewald, transference serves as a revitalization, a relinking of the past and the present, fantasy and reality, primary process and secondary process. In Loewald's (1980) vision, the fantasy-saturated primary process of the unconscious and the secondary process of everyday reality need each other. 'The unconscious needs present-day external reality (objects) and present-day psychic reality (the preconscious) for its own continuity, lest it be condemned to live the shadow life of ghosts or to destroy life' (Leowald, 1980: 250). On the other hand, consciousness and its contemporary objects need links to the affective density of the unconscious, without which 'human life becomes sterile and an empty shell' (1980: 250). 'Our present, current experiences', Loewald suggests, 'have intensity and depth to the extent to which they are in communication (interplay) with the unconscious, infantile, experiences representing the indestructible matrix of all subsequent experiences' (1980: 251).

In his quiet, undramatic fashion, Loewald has transformed the basic values guiding the analytic process, substituting meaning for rationality, imagination for objectivity, vitalization for control.[13] The central ameliorative impact lies in relinking:

> In the analytic process the infantile fantasies and memories, by being linked up with the present actuality of the analytic situation and the analyst, regain meaning and may be reinserted within the stream of the total mental life ... At the same time, as the present actuality of the analytic situation is being linked up with infantile fantasies, this present gains or regains meaning, i.e., that depth of experience which comes about by its live communication with the infantile roots of experience. (Loewald, 1974: 362–3)

Consider Kate, a young woman in her mid-thirties who entered psychoanalysis because of a history of frustrating, abortive relationships with men. She suffered from the not uncommon tendency to choose men who seem strikingly unavailable for relationships. As we began to sort out some of Kate's experiences, it became apparent that there was something about being in a situation of possible intimacy with a man who might actually be available that made her very anxious; she tended to act extremely self-consciously and find a quick exit. Over the course of the first several months of sessions, as she became more aware of these patterns, Kate became a bit more able to bear her anxiety so that social and romantic experiences of a somewhat better quality became possible.

Interspersed with our focus on her current experiences were accounts of Kate's complicated relationships with members of her family and her early life. She grew up quite poor in a working-class area of a small, industrial town. Her father was alcoholic and reclusive, and her overburdened, depressed mother was generally unavailable to her and her several siblings. Both the mother's mother and brother lived with the family. At first, the uncle seemed to be an insignificant figure in Kate's development, but little by little I realized how important he was. Unlike the parents, he was somewhat worldly and successful. He owned a car and seemed skilled at enjoying life. He would take other family members out for drives on the weekends, knew about movies and other forms of entertainment, and was a much more exciting figure than Kate's father, who paid very little attention to her. The uncle was a great favourite of the mother, and in many ways filled the vacuum created by the father's withdrawal.

When Kate was several years old, the uncle was arrested for a serious crime. Kate remembered going with her mother to the trial and the enormous grief that enveloped the whole family. The uncle was sent to prison for five years. When he rejoined the family, he was a different man, angry, embittered, burned out. He became tyrannical and frightening. He bullied the children, unopposed by the parents, and Anna grew to hate him.

I slowly developed the hypothesis that this uncle had been very important to her, not just through fear in her later childhood, but through positive feelings in her early years. Kate did not like my suggestions along these lines. As far as she was concerned, she hated her uncle and did not even want to talk or think about him.

At about six months into the work, as Kate began to develop a relationship with a man that promised sustained intimacy, she had a series of dreams about the uncle. All she could remember was that they were violent, with yelling and screaming battles like the ones that actually took place during her adolescence. Toward the end of one session, I tried to get her interested in the possible connections between her new, deeper experiences with men and her old experiences with her uncle, reappearing in her dreams. She seemed quite uninterested. I offered an interpretation that went something like this: her uncle had been passionately important to her in her early childhood; she loved him deeply. His sudden exile was very painful, but her longings for him were kept alive in anticipation of his return. The dramatic changes in him were crushing, extremely painful to her. It became very important never to allow herself to connect with her former loving feelings, because the pain of their loss would have been unbearable. In fact, the fear of the pain connected with her love of her uncle had made all intimacy with men dangerous. Tolerating loving feelings toward men now, I suggested, would become possible only as she became able to allow herself to reconnect with her abruptly renounced love of her uncle. She allowed that my speculations were interesting, and she left.

At the beginning of the next session, she reported similar dreams about her uncle and said that she been thinking about my interpretation. Then she fell silent. I asked her what she was thinking about, and she said, with a bit of a twinkle in her eye, not uncommon for her, 'I am trying to figure out how to convince you that you are all wrong about my feelings about my uncle.'

I found myself responding jocularly, '*All* wrong! What do you mean *all* wrong? I figured I wasn't *all* right, but I was pretty sure I got *some* of it right. *All wrong*, boy.' She laughed. I think there was a little more kidding around between us. Then she went on to talk about other things, and we did not return to speaking about the uncle for several months. But Kate's relationships with men continued to deepen.

I have no idea about the impact of that particular interaction; it is so difficult to know. But I find it compelling to think about it in terms of Loewald's way of thinking about the relationship between past and present. Kate's uncle was a ghost, a piece of the past filled with passionate intensity, that was split off, through repression, from her present experience. We might well say that her current relationships with men were haunted by her lost, dangerous feelings toward her uncle. I believe something of that relationship came alive in our interaction. My interpretation was a lot more complicated and spoken in a more authoritative voice than is my custom. I think there was a kind of teasing in what I took to be the twinkle in her eye and her ambition to prove me 'all wrong'. I realized afterward that the tone of mock argumentation with which I responded actually derived from my own early relationship with my favourite, very admired, and also very argumentative and opinionated uncle, who could also be playful. I believe Kate and I were working out something about power, negotiation and play. None of this was self-conscious at the time; the meanings were constructed retrospectively. But I think Kate was experimenting with whether I could wield power differently from the way her uncle did, whether she could back me down. I had become her uncle, but this time we had worked out a different outcome.

In Loewald's terms, a delinking had separated Kate's past from her present, and both suffered. Her past, along with her capacity to play and fantasize in the presence of a man she was excited about, was lost to her. Her present became emptied of depth and vitality. The emergence of ghosts from the past in the transference and in the countertransference made it possible for new links to be opened up.

I conclude by noting Loewald's definition of reality-testing, which dramatically highlights the difference between Loewald's understanding of the relationship between fantasy and reality and the more conventional psychoanalytic understanding. 'Reality testing', Loewald (1974: 368) states,

> is far more than an intellectual or cognitive function. It may be understood more comprehensively as the experiential testing of fantasy – its potential and suitability for actualization – and the testing of actuality – its potential for encompassing it in, and penetrating it with, one's fantasy life. We deal with the task of a reciprocal transposition.

This statement is worth dwelling on a bit. Customarily, fantasy and reality are understood as incompatible. Fantasy distorts reality; reality undistorts fantasy. Reality-testing is conventionally understood to entail an evaluation of ideas for their veridicality: do they correspond directly to what actually exists? Are they contaminated by the skewing presence of fantasy?

For Loewald, it works quite differently. As with other major dichotomies like primary versus secondary process, internal versus external and self versus other, the distinction between fantasy and reality is important to adaptive functioning. But separating fantasy and reality is only one way to construct and organize experience. For life to be meaningful, vital and robust, fantasy and reality cannot be too divorced from each other. Fantasy, cut adrift from reality, becomes irrelevant and threatening. Realty, cut adrift from fantasy, becomes vapid and empty. Meaning in human experience is generated in the mutual, dialectically enriching tension between fantasy and reality; each requires the other to come alive. In the psychic universe of the individual mind, vitality and meaning require open channels between the developmentally earlier, but perpetually regenerated primal density and the clearly demarcated boundaries that make possible adaptive living. For Loewald, only the enchanted life is a life worth living.

Notes

1. It should be noted that many contemporary philosophers of language, following Wittgenstein, would have problems with Stern's distinction between experience 'as it is lived and as it is verbally represented' because lived experience is understood to take place only in semiotic, linguistic terms.

2. Loewald grounds his own views, as he generally does, in a subtext of Freud's, in this case an undeveloped hint of an earlier correspondence between the 'thing' and the 'word' that, puzzlingly, seems to predate the distinction between unconscious and preconscious (1977: 181–3).
3. Some features of Loewald's view of language in primary process experience (and Stern's view of early preverbal experience) were anticipated by Ernst Schactel (1959) in his remarkable book, *Metamorphosis*. Schactel argued that infantile amnesia for early childhood experience is caused not, as Freud believed, by a repression of infantile sexuality, but by a sharp discontinuity in the organizing patterns through which early and later modes of experience are processed. Early theorizing about psychedelic drugs (e.g., Aldous Huxley's (1970) *The Doors of Perception*, for whom the rock group 'The Doors' was named) thought that powerful hallucinogens like mescalin and LSD undercut developmentally later forms of organizing experience and revitalize experience as it appears in the earliest months of life.
4. The deadening of language is probably an inevitable feature of its overuse, in which the original freshness of a formulation or understanding is dulled in its repetition. But the deadening of psychoanalyatic language has also been partly a function of active editorial policies on the part of its journals. Innovative thinking is regularly shoehorned into a format in which new ideas are presented as already discoverable in Freud, either explicitly or implicitly. By the time the reader has reached the ideas themselves, her senses have been dulled into a disbelief in the very possibility of fresh thought.
5. Steiner (1978: 8) characterizes Heidegger's methodology, what he terms 'the cardinal move in Heideggerian philosophy' as follows:

> One takes a common locution, or a passage in Heraclitus, in Kant, in Nietzsche. One excavates from individual syllables, words, or phrases their original, long-buried, or eroded wealth of meaning. One demonstrates that the occlusion of this meaning has altered and damaged the destiny of Western thought, and how its rediscovery, its literal restoration to active radiance, can bring on a renascence of intellectual and moral possibility.

By substituting Freud for the other authors, this could stand as a very apt characterization of Loewald's methodology.

6. The capacity of language, in poetry and in psychoanalysis, to generate and transform states of mind is a major theme of Ogden's (1977) remarkable recent book, *Reverie and Interpretation.*
7. Recent studies of bilingualism (Perez-Foster, 1996) in analytic treatment have highlighted the ways in which the sounds of particular words in a particular language evoke total states of mind (and, often, accompanying memories) that do not lend themselves to translation.
8. Thus, in Hartmann's distinction in the ego's realms between a conflictual and a conflict-free (primary autonomous) sphere, the ego was divided into one portion still representing the id, primarily defensive and at odds with reality, and another portion, wired to be adapted to, and to join forces with, reality. It should be noted that many European Freudians (particularly the French) regard this ego-psychological extension of the powers of the ego *vis-à-vis* the id as a betrayal of Freud's vision. For them the id/ego and social reality are no less intrinsically at odds, but their sympathies lie more on the side of the instincts (defined in terms of the more appealing *desire* rather than the American term *impulse*) over and against conventional social reality.
9. Again, it is possible to trace the influence of Heidegger's depictions of being as inseparable from 'Being-in-the-world' on Loewald's understanding of the relationship of the psyche to social reality:

   > ... it is not the case that man 'is' and then has, by way of an extra, a relationship-of-being toward the 'world' – a world with which he provides himself occasionally. *Dasein* is never 'proximally' an entity which is, so to speak, free from Being-in, but which sometimes has the inclination to take up a 'relationship' toward the world. (Steiner, 1978: 84)

10. I am indebted to Judith Brisman, who told me about this case.
11. The surrealist Colombian author Gabriel Garcia Marquez has always insisted that the magical flights that take place in ... *One Hundred Years of Solitude* came not from his imagination but from the running stories told him by his grandparents during his childhood, at an age when he could make no distinction between fact and legend, or between rumour and reality (Reid, 1997).
12. Scattered throughout Loewald's writings, from his earliest papers to his final book *Sublimation*, are suggestions, always

undeveloped, of his deep critique of traditional psychoanalytic epistemology. 'I believe it to be necessary and timely to question that assumption, handed to us from the nineteenth century, that the scientific approach to the world and the self represents a higher and more mature evolutionary stage of man than the religious way of life. But I cannot pursue this question here' (Loewald, 1980: 228).

13. Cornelius Castoriadis has criticized both Freud and American Freudian ego psychology along very similar lines. He suggests that Freud's use of the reclamation of the Zuyder Zee to illustrate the progressive analytic conquest of the id by the ego is fundamentally misconceived:

> The unconscious is implicitly presented there as a sort of dirty, stagnant water which you have to reclaim, to dry up and to cultivate. Well, I think this is both unrealistic, utopian and wrong ... the traditional idea seems to be to clear up the unconscious, to close this chapter and to have the subject, the patient, living happily ever after with a strong ego. This has been the classical American tendency and the American meaning of 'autonomy.' I think this is wrong because the true nucleus of the individual's radical imagination is rooted in the unconscious ... we never reclaim the contents of the id. You change the relationship between the two agencies, that's all. (Castoriadis, 1991: 489)

References

Beebe, B., Lachmann, F. and Jaffe, J. (1997), 'Mother–infant interaction structures and presymbolic self and object representations', *Psychoanalytic Dialogues* 7: 133–82.

Cavell, M. (1993), *The Psychoanalytic Theory of Mind*, Cambridge, MA: Harvard University Press.

Castoriadis, C. (1991), 'Interview with Paul Gordon', *Free Associations* 2: 483–506.

Decasper, A.L. and Fifer, W. (1980), 'Of human bonding: newborns prefer their mothers' voices', *Science* 2208: 1174–6.

Freud, S. (1923), *The Ego and the Id*, *SE* XIX.

— (1924), 'The dissolution of the Oedipus complex', *SE* XIX: 173–9.

— (1930), *Civilization and its Discontents*, *SE* XXI: 64–145.

Fromm, E. (1956), *The Art of Loving*, New York: Harper.

Goldman, D. (1996), *In Search of the Real: The Origins and Originality of D.W. Winnicott*, Northvale, NJ: Aronson.

Huxley, A. (1970), *The Doors of Perception*, New York: Harper & Row.

Loewald, H. (1949), 'The ego and reality', in *Papers on Psychoanalysis*, pp. 3–20.

— (1960), 'The therapeutic action of psychoanalysis', in *Papers*, pp. 221–56.

— (1971), 'On motivation and instinct theory', in *Papers*, pp. 102–37.

— (1974), 'Psychoanalysis as an art and the fantasy nature of the psychoanalytic situation', in *Papers*, pp. 352–71.

— (1977), 'Primary process, secondary process and language', in *Papers*, pp. 178–206.

— (1980), *Papers on Psychoanalysis*, New Haven, CT: Yale University Press.

— (1988), *Sublimation*, New Haven, CT: Yale University Press.

Ogden, T. (1997), *Reverie and Interpretation*, Northvale, NJ: Aronson.

Perez-Foster, R. (1996), 'The bilingual self', *Psychoanalytic Dialogues* 6: 99–122.

Reid, A. (1997) 'Report from an undeclared war', in *The New York Review of Books*, 9 October, pp. 19–22.

Schachtel, E. (1959), *Metamorphosis*, New York: Basic Books.

Schafer, R. (1968), *Aspects of Internalization*, New York: International Universities Press.

— (1976), *A New Language for Psychoanalysis*, New Haven, CT: Yale University Press.

Steiner, J. (1978), *Martin Heidegger*, Chicago: University of Chicago Press.

Stern, D. (1985), *The Interpersonal World of the Infant*, New York: Basic Books.

Sullivan, H.S. (1950), 'The illusion of personal individuality', in *The Fusion of Psychiatry and the Social Sciences*, New York: Norton, 1964.

Suomi, S. (1995), 'Influence of attachment theory on ethological studies of biobehavioral development in nonhuman primates', in S. Goldberg, R. Muir and J. Kerr (eds), *Attachment Theory*, Hillsdale, NJ: The Analytic Press, pp. 185–202.

8 The Dialectically Constituted/Decentred Subject of Psychoanalysis

Thomas Ogden

In the first moments of the opening scene of Hamlet, a sound is heard coming from the darkness outside the palace walls. The guards demand, 'Who's there?' Like an opening dystonic chord of a piece of music, the question, 'Who's there?' reverberates in an unresolved way throughout the play. The same question could be said to be the opening theme that continues unresolved through the history of psychoanalysis. Beginning with Freud and Breuer's (1893–95) observations in *Studies on Hysteria*, the theme of the 'splitting of consciousness' (1893–95: 12) and the question of the location of the subject within this 'dual consciousness', has reverberated through the succeeding century of analytic thought.

It might be surmised that Freud's limited use of the terms *self* and *subject* is a matter of semantics since Freud used the term *Das Ich* (poorly translated as *the ego*) to refer in part to the experiencing subject, 'the I'. However, as will be discussed, *Das Ich* is not coincident with the subject and in fact it is precisely in the difference between the two that one begins to be able to discern the creation of a new conceptual entity: the psychoanalytic subject.

It is my belief that central among the irreducible elements that define a psychoanalytic understanding of man is Freud's conception of the subject. Despite the central importance of this theme, it remained a largely implicit one in Freud's writing. As will be discussed, the implicit Freudian conception of the process by which the subject is constituted is fundamentally dialectical (Hegel, 1807; Kojève, 1934–35) in nature and involves the notion that the subject is created, sustained (and at the same time decentred) through the dialectical interplay of consciousness and unconsciousness.

Dialectic is a process in which opposing elements each create, preserve and negate the other; each stands in a dynamic, ever-changing relationship to the other. Dialectical movement tends towards integrations that are never achieved. Each potential integration creates a new form of opposition characterized by its own distinct form of dialectical tension. That which is generated dialectically is continuously in motion, perpetually in the process of being created and negated, perpetually in the process of being decentred from static self-evidence. In addition, dialectical thinking involves a conception of the interdependence of subject and object: 'Dialectical thought ... [is] a process in which subject and object are so joined that truth can be determined only within the subject–object totality' (Marcuse, 1960: viii). One cannot begin to comprehend either subject or object in isolation from one another.

When I speak of the subject of psychoanalysis, I am referring to the individual in his capacity to generate a sense of experiencing 'I-ness' (subjectivity), however rudimentary and non-verbally symbolized that sense of I-ness might be. It is beyond the scope of this chapter to review the vast literature bearing on the concept of the psychoanalytic subject which includes much of the analytic discourse addressing the concepts of the ego, the self, identity, narcissism and so on. In addition to the works that are discussed and referred to in this chapter, the following represents a very partial listing of pivotal contributions to the development of an analytic conception of the subject: Bollas, 1987; Erikson, 1950; Fairbairn, 1952; Federn, 1952; Grossman, 1982; Grotstein, 1981; Grunberger, 1971; Guntrip, 1969; Jacobson, 1964; Khan, 1974; Kohut, 1971; Lichtenstein, 1963; Loewald, 1980; Mitchell, 1991; Sandler, 1987; Spence, 1987; Stern, 1985.

Throughout his work, one can sense Freud's struggle with the limitations of the linearity of thought demanded by positivistic notions of causality. Nowhere is this more evident than in his effort to grapple with the problem of the conceptualization of the experiencing subject. Examples of Freud's attempts to formulate his ideas in linear, diachronic terms are legion and span his entire opus (see for example Freud's formulation of his ideas concerning the progression from unconsciousness to consciousness (1893–95, 1900, 1923, 1925a, 1927, 1933), from the pleasure principle to the reality principle (1915a, 1930), from id to ego (1923, 1926a, 1940), from primary process to secondary process thinking (1911, 1915b).

Such linearity of thought obscures what I believe to be the radical nature of the psychoanalytic project, i.e. the notion that the experiencing subject can be conceptualized as the outcome of an ongoing process in which the subject is simultaneously constituted and decentred from itself by means of the negating and preserving dialectical interplay of consciousness and unconsciousness.[1]

In this chapter, I shall discuss aspects of the concept of the dialectically constituted and decentred subject of psychoanalysis that have their origins in the work of Freud and which were developed by Klein and Winnicott. In this effort, I shall define what I consider to be some of the central dialectics bearing on the constitution of the subject introduced by Freud, Klein and Winnicott. In addressing the work of Klein and Winnicott in the second part of this chapter I shall focus in particular on the development of a conception of an intersubjective context for the creation of individual subjectivity.

The Freudian Subject

Freud's Decentring of Man from Consciousness

Freud (1917) believed that psychoanalysis presented a reconceptualization of man's relationship to himself that involved a fundamental decentring of man from himself. Man, according to Freud (1916–17), has been decentred in three different ways in the course of modern history. First, the Copernican revolution effected the displacement of man from his position at 'the stationary centre of the universe, with the sun, moon and planets circling round it' (1917: 139). Second, the Darwinian restructuring of our conception of the biological world resulted in man's dislocation from the position that he had created for himself as 'different from animals' (1917: 141) and holding a divinely ordained position above and separate from them. The third and by far the most disturbing form of decentring of man was effected by psychoanalysis which decentred man from himself by undermining the illusion of the identity of consciousness and mind.

From a psychoanalytic perspective, man can no longer experience himself as 'absolute ruler' of his own mind: *'the ego is not master in its own house'* (1917: 143). 'Come, let yourself be taught something on this one point! What is in your mind does not coincide with what you are conscious of?' (1917: 143). The ego (the I), especially in its claim to sovereignty through its capacity for self-consciousness, perception, speech, motility, etc. believes that it knows itself: 'You [the ego] feel sure that you are informed of all that goes on in your mind ... Indeed, you go so far as to regard what is "mental" as identical with what is "conscious"' (1917: 142–3). The thinking, feeling, behaving, speaking subject is decentred from the self-evidence of his experience of consciousness. 'Thoughts emerge suddenly without one's knowing where they come from, nor can one do anything to drive them away. These alien guests even seem to be more powerful than those which are at the ego's command' (1917: 141).

The subject in the historical era of psychoanalysis is no longer to be considered coincident with conscious awareness, no longer equated with the conscious, speaking, behaving, 'I' (ego).

The Freudian decentring of the subject from consciousness by no means represents a simple transposition of the subject to a position behind the repression barrier. The psychoanalytic subject is not relocated from consciousness to the unconscious mind (in the topographic model), or to the id (in the structural model). Rather, Freud emphasized that consciousness and unconsciousness must be conceived as '[coexisting] qualities of what is psychical' (1940: 161). Neither consciousness nor unconsciousness in themselves represents the subject of psychoanalysis. The subject for Freud is to be sought in the phenomenology corresponding to that which lies in the relations *between* consciousness and unconsciousness.

The Dialectic of Consciousness and Unconsciousness

Freud by no means conceived of the unconscious mind as the seat of truth or as the locus of man's soul. He recognized that the claims of the unconscious to know and to constitute the totality of the subject are as ill-founded as those of the conscious, speaking subject. He neither romanticized the unconscious as the residue of 'natural man' (untainted by civilization), nor did he villainize the unconscious by viewing it as the source of sin, the wellspring of depraved lust and viciousness. Consciousness and unconsciousness are conceived of as mutually dependent, each defining, negating and preserving the other. Neither exists nor has any conceptual or phenomenological meaning except in relation to the other. The two 'cointend' (Ricoeur, 1970: 378) in a relationship of relative difference as opposed to absolute difference: the two coexist in a mutually defining relationship of difference.

It is critical to Freud's argument that conscious and unconscious experience be conceived of as qualities of experience that are created in a discourse (a 'communication' (Freud, 1915b: 190) between the two. By means of the discourse between conscious and unconscious qualities of experience, the illusion (or virtual image (Freud, 1940: 145) of unity of experience is created. The discourse of consciousness and unconsciousness is guaranteed by the principle of continuity and difference between the two coexisting modes of generating experience. The attribute of 'being conscious [*Bewusstheit*] ... forms the point of departure for all our investigations' (Freud, 1915b: 172) and, as will be seen, is also the point to which all of our investigations return.

Not only is discourse possible between unconsciousness and consciousness, the very existence of each depends upon the other: 'In themselves [unconscious processes] cannot be cognized, indeed are even incapable of carrying on their existence [independent of the System Preconscious-Conscious]' (Freud, 1915b: 187). The relationship between the two systems is that of a specific form of discourse, a discourse of a dialectical nature in which the components are comparable to empty sets each filled by the other (Ogden, 1986, 1989a). Each constitutes a presence affirmed by its absence in the other. The System Unconscious is the Other to the System Preconscious–Conscious and the System Preconscious–Conscious is the negating, preserving Other to the System Unconscious. In Freud's schema, neither consciousness nor (dynamic) unconsciousness holds a privileged position in relation to the other: the two systems are 'complementary' (Freud, 1940: 159) to one another, thus constituting a single, but divided discourse.

Freud felt that the term *subconscious* is 'incorrect and misleading' (1915b: 170) in that the Unconscious does not exist 'under' consciousness: there is only one mental life comprised of the product of the interplay of (dynamically) unconscious and conscious psychical qualities. In other words, we do not live two lives (a conscious and an unconscious one) concurrently; we live a single life constituted by the interplay of the conscious and (dynamically) unconscious aspects of experience.

The System Unconscious is not only incapable of carrying on life without access to perception, speech, motility, etc., all of which are linked to the System Preconscious–Conscious. Far more fundamental to an understanding of the psyche is the idea that unconsciousness is without meaning except in relation to the concept of consciousness, and vice versa. Unconsciousness cannot be described except by means of a series of statements of negations of qualities of consciousness, beginning with the very name given to each. Each of the qualities of the System Unconscious (for example, exemption from mutual contradiction, timelessness, replacement of external by psychic reality, lack of fixity of cathexis), is delineated as a concept by virtue of its relationship of negation to a concept defining the System Preconscious–Conscious.

Freud's (1923) structural model represents a system of dialectics built upon (and by no means replacing) the topographic model. In the structural model, the mind is conceived of in terms of mutually defining dialectics constituted by the ego (the I), the id (it that is not me and yet within me) and the superego (that part of me that lords over me threateningly and protectively). The decentring of the subject in the structural model is not different in kind from that which has been discussed in relation to the topographic model. The subject is no more coincident with the ego of the structural model than with consciousness in the topographic model. The subject of the structural model is located in the dialectically constituted stereoscopic illusion of unity of experience constituted by the negating and preserving discourse of the id, ego and superego.

The Dialectic of Presence and Absence

I shall now focus more closely on the principle of presence in absence and absence in presence, a concept that lies at the heart of the Freudian conception of the dialectically constituted/decentred subject. This principle subtends the dialectical movement between mutually negating and preserving dimensions of experience. Presence is continually negated by that which it is not, while all the time alluding to what is lacking in itself. That which is absent is always present in the lack which it presents.

Freud's 'Negation' paper presents a subtle, highly condensed statement of the dialectical relationship of presence and absence, affirmation and negation:

> the content of a repressed image or idea can make its way into consciousness, on condition that it is *negated*. Negation is a way of taking cognizance of what is repressed [what cannot be given cognizance consciously]; indeed, it is already a lifting [*Aufhebung*] of the repression, though not, of course, an acceptance of what is repressed. (1925b: 235–6)

Thus, in negation, the repression is 'lifted' and yet what is repressed is not accepted.

Hyppolite has pointed out that *Aufhebung* 'is Hegel's dialectical word, which means simultaneously to deny, to suppress and to conserve, and fundamentally to raise up' (1956: 291). The use of the word *Aufhebung* underscores that repression must not be understood as a linear movement from consciousness to unconsciousness. Freud's concept of negation represents a distinctive psychoanalytic conception of the constitution of the subject. The idea of a dialectic of affirmed and disavowed meaning played out phenomenologically in the form of the simultaneity of conscious and unconscious meaning is perhaps the most fundamental analytic proposition concerning the concept of mind. 'Presenting one's being in the mode of not being it, that is truly what is at issue in this *Aufhebung* of the repression, which is not an acceptance of what is repressed. The person speaking says: "This is what I am not"' (Hyppolite, 1956: 291).

Clinical Illustration

The following brief clinical vignette may serve to illustrate something of the phenomenology of the dialectic of consciousness and unconsciousness, of presence and absence, of affirmation and negation upon which the analytic enterprise rests:

> An analysand, Mr M, began an analytic hour with a ten-minute silence which was followed by a series of highly articulate, but affectless self-reflections. I said to him that I wondered whether something might have occurred during yesterday's meeting that was leading him to talk in such a detached way.[2] The patient replied that while in the waiting room he had been trying to remember what we had been talking about at the end of yesterday's meeting and was feeling stupid and clumsy for not being able to remember. It felt as if something had been left unfinished. I said that it had been important enough for him to forget. Mr M said that his not being able to remember felt like a hole in him; it wasn't only frustrating, it was frightening to know that something had happened and not to be able to know what it was.
>
> This feeling of the present absence reflected not only the existence of dynamically unconscious experience, but also reflected the specific nature of that unconscious experience. At the end of the previous meeting, the patient had been talking about the way in which as a child he had tenaciously insisted on wearing clothes that reflected his own taste, for example, wearing green-brown loafers as opposed to the plain brown ones that were prescribed by the school dress code. Mr M had begun to understand this as a response to a feeling that his mother (a schizoid woman) was unable to recognize that he had a personality of his own that was characterized by his own specific likes, dislikes, fears, hatreds, jealousies, competitiveness and so on. (The patient had previously mentioned that his mother each year bought the same Christmas present for all four of her children.) Enacted in the patient's forgetting in the current analytic hour was an effort to determine if I would be able to remember what it was that had occurred in the previous meeting, thereby reflecting my own capacity to distinguish him from everyone else in my life.
>
> I said to Mr M that I thought he was worried that I would not be able to remember our previous meeting. He was surprised by this comment and said that remembering seemed too personal a thing to expect of me. He had had a vague sense that I wrote things down and that I referred to them when I needed to.
>
> The patient's fear that I would not remember him, his wish for recognition, his anxiety about asking me directly for such recogni-

tion, and his anger connected with the feeling that in the past I had failed to recognize him and would certainly do so again today, were all present in the absence of affect and memory (and in the experience of there being something missing). What was present was an affirmation of all that was absent. Thus, that which was missing was experientially present (the conscious experience of the hole in himself) and that which was present was absent (the fantasy of me as mechanical that the patient became aware of after I interpreted his anxiety).

The psychoanalytic method as developed by Freud is built upon the process of constituting meaning through this type of dialectic of presence in absence and absence in presence. It would be inaccurate to say that Mr M was not feeling anger, loneliness, the wish to be recognized, and the fear of not being recognized. It would be equally inaccurate to say that he was 'really' experiencing such thoughts and feelings 'in his unconscious mind'. Both statements in themselves reflect forms of reductionism that fail to capture the phenomenology of dialectically constituted experience. The psychoanalytic conception of the nature of experience requires that any full statement of the patient's experience be framed dialectically in a way that acknowledges the mutually negating and preserving contextualization of presence by absence and of absence by presence. The concept of transference itself represents a dialectical conception of a past that is present and a present that is past.

Similarly, the analytic understanding of dream experience is built upon this dialectic of presence and absence: the latent dream content is not the solution to the riddle of the manifest dream. The phenomenology of dreaming is one that hovers between the visible and the invisible, the presented and the unpresented, the narrative text and the silent text. Presence and absence stand in an unending process of mutual affirmation and negation that prevents dream experience from ever lighting in any given locale. When one has 'figured out' the meaning of a dream, one has lost touch with the aliveness and elusiveness of the experience of dreaming; in its place one has created a flat, bloodless decoded message.

The Language of the Subject

From the perspective of the foregoing discussion, I would like to comment briefly on an aspect of psychoanalytic language. I believe that a psychoanalytic theory of experiencing 'I-ness' must incorporate into its own structure and language a recognition of the ineffable, constantly moving and evolving nature of subjectivity (described by Kundera (1984) as 'the unbearable lightness of being'). I have elected to use the term *subject* in this chapter to refer to the individual in his ever changing dialectically negating and negated experience of 'I-ness' instead of either the term *self* or the term *ego*.

Although the term *self* is indispensable in the description of aspects of the phenomenology of subjectivity (for instance, in describing the individual's sense of who he is or the experience 'me-ness' as the sense of self-as-object), I feel that the term *self* as a theoretical construct has become weighted down with static, reifying meanings. The concept of self is often used in a way that seems to designate a localizable entity 'inside' the person. This is particularly true when the self is conceived of as a 'psychic structure', 'a content of the mental apparatus' with a 'psychic location' (Kohut, 1971: xv). When used in this way, the term *self* is poorly suited to convey a sense of 'I-ness' emerging from a continually decentring dialectical process.

Spruiell (1981) has elegantly argued that the term *ego* when used in the sense that Freud employed *Das Ich* (i.e. to refer to the person as well as to a psychological system) is sufficiently flexible and ambiguous to encompass both the experiential and the metapsychological 'I'. However, the term *ego* is significantly different from Freud's far more personal term *Das Ich* (the 'I'). Freud specifically cautioned against the use of 'orotund Greek names' for *Das Ich* in order to 'keep [psychoanalytic concepts] in contact with the popular mode of thinking' (1926b: 195). Particularly when used to refer to a group of psychic functions, the term *ego* loses virtually all connexion with the phenomenology of the experience of 'I-ness' and becomes almost entirely a metapsychological abstraction (see, for example, Hartmann, 1950; Hartmann *et al.*, 1946; and Loewenstein, 1967).

Moreover, even Freud's term, *Das Ich*, chosen with the intention of keeping analytic discourse regarding the mind close to the everyday 'I', refers to only one aspect of the psyche. In the topographical model, Freud was clear that *Das Ich* (the ego) is not 'master in its own house' and therefore must not be equated with the psychoanalytic conception of the mind as a whole which necessarily includes that which is not the ego, i.e., the Unconscious, that which stands in tension with, in 'communication' with, the thinking, feeling, conscious, speaking 'I'.

As I have discussed above, in the structural model, *Das Ich* is no more coincident with the psyche than is consciousness in the topographic model. *Das Ich* in the structural model stands in a mutually preserving and negating relationship to *Das Es* (the it). The 'it' is not 'I' and yet in health is inextricably part of what is in the process of becoming 'I' and a part of what I am becoming *('Wo Es war, soll Ich werden*': 'Where id [it] was, there ego [I] shall be' (Freud, 1933: 80). To equate *Das Ich* (the ego of the structural model) with the experiencing 'I' is to obscure the generative process of mutual negation and preservation involving ego, id and superego upon which the structural model is based. To make such an equation is to mistake the part (the ego) for the dialectical (negating and negated) whole.

Although no single word can carry the requisite multiplicity, ambiguity and specificity of meaning, the term *subject* seems particularly well suited to convey the psychoanalytic conception of the experiencing 'I' in both a phenomenological and a metapsychological sense. The term is etymologically linked with the word 'subjectivity' and carries an inherent semantic reflexivity, i.e. it simultaneously denotes subject and object, I and it, I and me. The word *subject* refers to both the 'I' as speaker, thinker, writer, reader, perceiver and so on, and to the object of subjectivity, i.e. to the topic (the subject) being discussed, the idea being contemplated, the percept being viewed, etc. As a result, the subject can never be fully separated from the object and therefore can never be completely centred in itself. As will be discussed in the second part of this chapter, the reflexivity of the dialectic of subject and object is a fundamental component of the evolving psychoanalytic conception of the decentred experiencing 'I'.

Summary Comments

Freud proposed a model of the mind in which there is no privileged position in which to locate the subject either in consciousness or in the realm of the dynamically unconscious. Instead the subject is constituted by psychical acts that have qualities of consciousness and the absence of consciousness. Each is reflected through the other; each is negated by the other. Every way of being conscious is undercut by the unconscious with which it is 'co-implicit' or 'co-intended' (Ricoeur, 1970: 378); every way of being unconscious is experienced through its effects on consciousness, i.e. on the way in which perceptible, consciously registered experience is shaped, interrupted, intensified, lacunized, contextualized and so on. Although the Freudian decentring of the subject begins with the overcoming of the ego's presumption of mastery of its own house, we must always begin with and return to consciousness in some form 'in our investigations' since it is only through that which we can perceive that we feel the effects of that which lacks the quality of consciousness. However alien the unconscious may seem, the continuity between the System Unconscious and the System Preconscious–Conscious is maintained in that both pertain to the same system of human meaning (although not necessarily in the same symbolic form).

A Note on Lacan

A full discussion of the Lacanian conception of the subject is not possible within the space of the present chapter. However, before addressing the Kleinian and Winnicottian elaborations of Freud's conception of the subject in the second part of this chapter, I would like to note briefly that despite the fact that there are large areas of convergence of thought in the work of Freud, Klein, Winnicott and Lacan, I view the Lacanian project as differing in fundamental ways from the lines of thought being traced through the work of Freud, Klein and Winnicott. The latter three analysts worked entirely within a dialectical, hermeneutic framework wherein the analytic dialogue (as well as the intrapersonal dialogue) is based on a mutually interpretive discourse in which meanings are clarified and elaborated and in which enhanced understandings of the experience of oneself and the other are generated (Habermas, 1968). For Lacan also, the understanding of the analytic process and of the constitution and decentring of the subject is informed by dialectical thought, e.g. Lacan's (1957) conception of the nature of the interplay of the registers of the Imaginary, the Symbolic and the Real and his understanding of the nature of the interdependence of subject and object in the analytic transference–countertransference relationship (Lacan, 1951).

However, there is, alongside and in tension with the dialectical components of Lacan's work, a significant deconstructionist element in the Lacanian project that is not present in the work of Freud, Klein and Winnicott. For Lacan (1966a), there is a radical splitting between signifier and signified such that the chain of signifiers (the set of sound elements of language) is perpetually 'sliding' over the signified (the set of concepts generated by language). This disjunction makes the 'interval' (the break) the most fundamental structure of the signifying chain (Lacan, 1966b). Thus, the meanings we create through language are inevitably built upon misnamings, misrecognitions that we rely upon to create the illusion of understanding. These meanings do not have the same status as the Freudian manifest content from which chains of associations are generated and which allow increasingly rich contextualization and enhanced understandings of 'co-implicit' conscious and unconscious meanings. In Lacanian thinking, the manifest text must to a large degree be deconstructed in order to avoid endlessly circling in its misrecognitions. Slips, errors, witticisms, word plays, symptomatic acts and so on provide 'intervals' (Lacan, 1966b) (as opposed to the interplay of creatively negating contexts) through which to glimpse that which is unintended by the speaking subject.

The Lacanian project can be likened to an effort to see through the intervals or chips in the surface presentation of a painting over a painting. In contrast, the Freudian project can be conceived of in terms of the hermeneutic circle in which foreground is contextualized by background and vice versa: the Freudian text is assumed to have an integrity in which every part is related to, informs, and is informed by every other part of the text. There is no radical discontinuity among portions of the fabric of meaning whether conscious or unconscious, manifest or latent, intended or 'unintended'. In fact, the notion of the unintended is without meaning from the perspective of Freud's view of the relationship of the parts to the whole. The 'unintended' is more accurately termed the 'co-intended' (Ricoeur, 1970). The fundamental logic underlying the discordant elements of the text is the logic of the dialectical interplay of presence and absence discussed above.

A major outcome of the Lacanian notion of the radical disjunction of signifier and signified is the conception of the deconstructed subject that emerges from his work. The unconscious is constituted by the chain of signifiers, the Other. The subject is spoken by the Other and is in that sense 'without a head' (*'acéphale'*, Lacan, 1954–55). A radical disjunction separates the subject of the unconscious (that which is spoken by the Other, the chain of signifiers) from the self-conscious (misrecognizing and misnaming) speaking subject. The two orders of meaning and subjectivity do not constitute a dialectical whole. Rather, the Lacanian subject is not simply decentred, but is radically disconnected from itself leaving a central 'lack' or void resulting from the fact that the speaking subject and the subject of the unconscious are irrevocably divided by the unbridgeable gap separating signifier and signified.

The Contributions of Klein and Winnicott

Psychoanalytic thought emerging from the British School has contributed in significant ways to the elaboration of the concept of the dialectically constituted (and decentred) subject. Having discussed the Freudian conception of the subject in the first part of this chapter, the second part will be devoted to an exploration of the Kleinian and Winnicottian contributions to this project.

The Kleinian Subject

Three of the most important of Melanie Klein's theoretical contributions to the development of an analytic formulation of subjectivity are (1) the dialectical conception of psychic structure and psychological development underlying her concept of 'positions', (2) the dialectical decentring of the subject in psychic space, and (3) the notion of the dialectic of intersubjectivity that is implicit in the concept of projective identification. Klein's attention was not focused on the theoretical question of the nature of subjectivity and as a result, we, as interpreters of her work, may be in a better position than Klein herself to understand the place of her thinking in the development of the psychoanalytic conception of the subject.

The Dialectical Interplay of Psychic Organizations

Klein's (1935) notion of *positions* is fundamentally different from the concepts of developmental stages and developmental phases. The latter concepts are linear in nature with one phase or stage following, building upon, and integrating those that preceded. Klein's 'positions' do not refer to periods of development through which one passes on the way to psychological maturity: 'I chose the term "position" because these groupings of anxieties and defences, although arising first during the earliest stages [of life], are not restricted to them ...' (Klein, 1952: 93).

Positions neither follow nor precede one another; rather, each coexists with the others in a dialectical relationship (Ogden, 1988). Just as the concept of the conscious mind is without meaning except in relation to the concept of the unconscious mind, each of the Kleinian positions is without meaning except in relation to one another. The Kleinian subject exists not in any given position or hierarchical layering of positions, but in the dialectical tension created *between* positions.

The forms of experience associated with the paranoid-schizoid position (Klein, 1946, 1952) and the depressive position (Klein, 1935, 1948, 1952) can only be named by referring to the ways in which each represents a pole of the dialectical process in which each creates, negates and preserves the other. I understand the Kleinian 'positions' as psychological organizations that determine the ways in which meaning is attributed to experience (see Ogden, 1986, 1989a). Associated with each of the positions is a particular quality of anxiety, forms of defence and object relatedness, type of symbolization and quality of subjectivity. Together these qualities of experience constitute a state of being that characterizes each of the positions.

From the perspective of a conceptualization of the Kleinian idea of positions as poles of a dialectical process through which the subject is constituted, each of the positions is understood as a fiction, a non-existent ideal that is never encountered in pure form. Nonetheless, for purposes of clarity of discussion, I shall present a highly schematized view of each of the positions as if each could be isolated from the others.

The paranoid-schizoid position represents a psychological organization generating a state of being that is ahistorical, relatively devoid of the experience of an interpreting subject mediating between the sense of I-ness and one's lived sensory experience, part-object related, and heavily reliant on splitting, idealization, denial, projective identification and omnipotent thinking as modes of defence and ways of organizing experience. This paranoid-schizoid mode contributes to the sense of immediacy and intensity of experience.

The depressive pole of the dialectic of modes of generating experience (i.e. the depressive position) is characterized by (1) an experience of interpreting 'I-ness' mediating between oneself and one's lived sensory experience, (2) the presence of an historically rooted sense of self that is continuous over time and over shifts in affective states, (3) relatedness to other people who are experienced as whole and separate subjects with an internal life similar to one's own; moreover, one is able to feel concern for the Other, guilt, and the wish to make non-magical reparation for the real and imagined damage that one has done to others, and (4) forms of defence (e.g. repression and mature identification) that allow the individual to sustain psychological strain over time (as opposed to relying upon somatization, fragmentation, or evacuative phantasies and enactments as means of dissipating and foreclosing psychic pain). In sum, the depressive mode generates a quality of experience endowed with a richness of layered symbolic meanings.

I have elsewhere (1988, 1989a, b, 1991a, b) introduced my own conception of a third pole of the dialectic constituting human experience: the autistic-contiguous position. The autistic-contiguous position is conceived of as a psychological organization that is more primitive than the positions delineated by Klein. Such a conception represents an elaboration and extension of the work of Bick (1968, 1986), Meltzer (1975; Meltzer *et al.*, 1975) and Tustin (1972, 1980, 1984, 1990). The autistic-contiguous position is associated with a mode of generating experience that is of a sensation-dominated sort and is characterized by protosymbolic impressions of sensory experience that together help constitute an experience of bounded surfaces. Rhythmicity and experiences of sensory contiguity (especially at the skin surface) contribute to an elemental sense of continuity of being over time. Such experiences are generated within the invisible matrix of the environmental mother. Relationships with objects (that are not experienced as objects) occur in the form of experiences of autosensuous shapes' (Tustin, 1984) and 'auto-sensuous objects' (Tustin, 1990). These idiosyncratic, but organized and organizing uses of sensory experiences of softness and hardness, represent facets of the process by which the sensory floor of all experience is generated.

It must be emphasized that the negating and preserving interplay of positions evolves along a diachronic (temporally sequential) axis as well as a synchronic one. The interplay of diachronicity and synchronicity represents an inextricable component of the dialectical nature of the concept of positions. A psychological theory becomes untenable if it does not incorporate a recognition of the directionality of time and of life. It would be absurd to adopt an exclusively synchronic perspective that fails to recognize the progression of states of maturity that take place in the course of the life of the individual. To undervalue the importance of the diachronic axis in Kleinian theory would be to obscure the developmental significance (both in the course of maturation and during analysis) of critical moments or periods of psychic reorganization such as those involved in the achievement of a more fully elaborated depressive position, for example, as reflected in the development of the individual's capacity for guilt, mourning, empathy, gratitude and so on. On the other hand, a psychological theory that overvalues the diachronic (e.g. an over-reliance on the concept of the developmental line) at the expense of the synchronic, tends to ignore the importance of the primitive dimension of all experience including those forms of experience considered to be the most mature and fully evolved.

There are many instances in Klein's writing where the concept of position seems to shift from a dialectical conception (recognizing the coexistence and mutual contextualization of positions) to a linear one. For example, Klein (1948, 1952) regularly described the paranoid-schizoid position as being associated with the first quarter of the first year of life while portraying the depressive position as having its origins in the second quarter of the first year of life. There is a telling passage in which Klein (1952) states that the paranoid-schizoid and depressive positions arise very early in development and '*recur* during the first years of childhood and *under certain circumstances* in later life' (1952: 93, my italics). The idea that these fundamental positions 'recur' in childhood and then 'under certain circumstances' throughout life represents a reversion to a linear model of development in which positions are conceived of as early stages with fixation points to which the individual regresses in states of psychological illness or strain. Such a view is entirely inconsistent with Klein's larger view of positions as ever-present psychological organizations whose relationship shifts not by means of succession or progression from one to another, but by means of shifts in the way in which each contextualizes the others.

Klein's dialectical conception of psychic structure and its development fully incorporates an appreciation of Freud's notion of the timelessness of the unconscious. Freud's (1911, 1915b) conception of the timelessness of the unconscious dimension of experience established the notion of the individual existing simultaneously within two forms of time-diachronic (linear, sequential) time and synchronic 'time'. Each form of time has its own validity in the context of its own psychic system (the System Preconscious–Conscious and the System Unconscious). The psychoanalytic subject is therefore dialectically constituted (simultaneously) within and outside of diachronic, consensually measured time.

The Kleinian dialectical conception of psychic structure and psychological development effects a decentring of the subject from his position at the 'front' of a developmental line. Instead, the subject is conceived of as existing in psychoanalytic time (as opposed to linear, sequential time), thus partaking of all facets of subjectivity, all forms of primitivity and maturity, simultaneously and in shifting inter-relatedness. Psychoanalytic infancy is not restricted to the earliest months of life; instead, the notion of the timelessness of the unconscious requires that we view the autistic-contiguous, the paranoid-schizoid and the depressive positions as together constituting facets of time present in every period of life. The depressive position is not to be understood as a reflection of the successful negotiation of the conflicts and anxieties of the autistic-contiguous and paranoid-schizoid positions; rather, the depressive position is a component of psychological life from the very beginning (for example, in the infant's confrontation with otherness in his distress at the moment of birth).

Even before Klein introduced the concept of position, she (1932) had begun to challenge the idea of the individual's rootedness in developmental, linear time. She suggested that genital excitation, desire and phantasy (including oedipal phantasies) coexist with the 'earlier' (i.e. oral, anal and urethral) libidinal tendencies. 'Displacement' (Klein, 1932) or 'spreading' (Bibring, 1947: 73) of libidinal excitation and its attendant unconscious desires and object-related phantasies call into play 'all [aspects of libidinal development] at the same time' (Klein, 1932: 272).

It might be said that Klein has contributed to the compounding of man's third historical decentring, the psychological decentring of man from his own consciousness. A dialectical conception of psychic structure and its development displaces man from his position at the leading edge of what he believes to be his 'progression' through the stages of his life: 'The past is not dead: it is not even past' (Faulkner). The depressive position, despite its attributes of historicity and the capacity to create and interpret symbols, is no more the locus of the subject in Kleinian theory than is consciousness or the ego in Freudian theory.

The Dialectic of Splitting and Integration of the Subject

Having discussed the Kleinian dialectic of psychological organizations, I would now like to focus on a second contribution of Kleinian theory to the development of the concept of the dialectically constituted and decentred subject. For Klein, the psyche (after an initial hypothetical moment of unity) enters into an ongoing process of splitting of the ego and a corresponding division of the (internal) object. The ego and object are split into components that hold meaning for (are 'cathected by') one another. For example, the hating and hated component of the object is the facet of the (internal) object that (for defensive purposes) holds meaning for and is recognized by the hating and hated component of the ego. In this way, the individual can safely hate the bad object without fear of destroying the object that is loving and beloved.

The Kleinian subject is decentred from itself in that none of the multiplicity of components of the ego and internal objects is coextensive with the subject. Such a conception of the subject as constituted in large part by a multiplicity of phantasized internal object relationships represents an elaboration of the Freudian dispersal (decentring) of the subject over consciousness and unconsciousness (in the topographic model) and later among the psychic agencies (in the structural model). Thus, the Kleinian dispersal of the subject over the full field of phantasized internal object relations can be viewed as an extension of the decentred Freudian subject:

> The [Freudian] intrasubjective field [as conceptualized in the structural model] tends to be conceived of after the fashion of intersubjective relations, and the systems are pictured as relatively autonomous persons-within-the-person (the superego, for instance, is said to behave in a sadistic way towards the ego) (Laplanche and Pontalis, 1967: 452)

The Kleinian subject is not only split (dispersed) among the phantasized internal object relations constituting it; the splitting process itself represents part of a dialectic of dispersal and unity of the subject, a dialectic of fragmentation and integration, of de-linkage and closure, of part-object relations and whole-object relations. This dialectic of dispersal and unity represents another facet of the relationship of the paranoid-schizoid and depressive positions (represented by Bion (1963) by the notation Ps↔D).

The dialectic of splitting and integration in psychological space can be thought of as having both an intrapersonal and an interpersonal facet. Intrapsychically, the splitting processes associated with the paranoid-schizoid position lead to the construction of an internal object world continuously subjected to pressures of de-integration. There exists (as a facet of the paranoid-schizoid component of the dialectic constituting experience) a movement towards the breakdown of experience into part-object relations existing in an ahistorical context wherein thoughts and feelings are experienced as forces and objects. In the extreme, such disintegrative pressures lead to intense phantasies of the explosion of the subject (thus, dispersing the internal object world throughout the entirety of unbounded space) or to phantasies of the implosion of the subject (resulting from feelings of the fragmentation of internal objects in so thorough a fashion that the subject disappears into its own internal vacuum).

It is important that one not pathologize the negating, de-integrative, decentring pressures associated with the paranoid-schizoid component of the Ps↔D dialectic. The intrapsychic pressure for de-integration represents an essential negation of the integrative qualities associated with the depressive pole of the dialectic. In the absence of the de-integrative pressure of the paranoid-schizoid pole of the dialectic generating experience, the integration associated with the depressive position would reach closure, stagnation and 'arrogance' (Bion, 1967). The negation of closure the 'attacks on linking' (Bion, 1959) represented by the paranoid-schizoid pole of the dialectic has the effect of destabilizing that which would otherwise become static. In this way, the negating, de-integrative effects of the paranoid-schizoid position continually generate the potential for new psychological possibilities (i.e. the possibility for psychic change).

The experience of dreaming itself is a reflection of the dialectical tension between the paranoid-schizoid and depressive positions. Dreaming is not simply a process of speaking to oneself about unconscious thoughts and feelings in coded form during sleep; far more importantly, it is an experience of de-integrating one's experience and re-presenting it to oneself in a new form and in a new context (the context of the dream space). The act of re-presenting one's experience in the form of a dream constitutes the creation of a new experience, a new integration which is immediately undergoing de-integration (as reflected in the experience of the dream as a fading, ephemeral, barely knowable psychic event). At times, the dialectic of integration and de-integration underlying the experience of dreaming collapses into the terror of disintegration when one despairs about the adequacy of the containing (integrative) dimension of one's internal world. This may result in an intense fear of *falling* asleep, a fear that reflects the phantasy that one will not be 'held' in sleep and will be dropped into endless, shapeless space ('when the bough breaks').

Projective Identification

Having briefly discussed the intrapsychic component of the dialectic of integration and de-integration underlying the constitution and decentring of the Kleinian subject, I shall now turn to an exploration of the interpersonal component of this dialectic. The idea of projective identification (particularly as elaborated by Bion (1952, 1962a, 1962b, 1963 and Rosenfeld (1965, 1971, 1987) is the concept that most powerfully addresses the interpersonal component of the dialectic of dispersal and integration, of negation and creation of the subject in Kleinian theory.

The intersubjective dimension of the process of projective identification is suggested by Klein (1946) in her statement that in projective identification 'split-off parts of the ego are also projected on to the mother, or as I would rather call it, *into* the mother ... [in an effort] to control and to take possession of the object' (1946: 8). 'In so far as the mother comes to contain the bad parts of the self, she is not felt to be a separate individual but is felt to be *the* bad self' (1946: 8). Thus, Klein proposes that there exists from the earliest stages of life a psychic process by which aspects of the self are not simply projected onto the psychic representation of the object (as in projection), but *'into'* the object in a way that is felt to control the object from within and leads to the projector's experiencing the object as a part of himself.

The experiential level of projective identification is presented by Klein (1955) in the form of a discussion of a novella by Julian Green, *If I Were You*. In Green's story, the protagonist, driven by envy, makes a deal with the devil wherein he trades his soul for the power to leave his own body and take possession of the body and life of anyone he chooses. Klein describes the anxiety associated with the (phantasized) experience of inhabiting the Other while at the same time attempting not to completely lose one's sense of self. (It is essential not to entirely lose oneself in the Other since the complete loss of a sense of one's rootedness in oneself is equivalent to one's disappearance and psychic death.) Projective identification, according to Klein, is psychically depleting in that an immense expenditure of energy is involved in the effort to control the Other so thoroughly that he is experienced as having taken on an aspect of one's own identity.[3]

Bion (1952, 1962a, 1963) made a number of important contributions to the development of the concept of an interpersonal component of projective identification and to the beginnings of an articulation of the notion of an interpersonal space in which subjectivity and the capacity for thinking are created (and at times attacked). In describing the phenomenology of projective identification, Bion stated:'The analyst feels he is being manipulated so as to be playing a part, no matter how difficult to recognize, in somebody else's phantasy' (1952: 149). Thus, projective identification for Bion is not simply an unconscious phantasy of projecting an aspect of oneself into the Other and controlling him from within; it represents a psychological-interpersonal event in which the projector, through actual interpersonal interaction with the recipient of the projective identification, exerts pressure on the Other to experience himself and behave in congruence with the omnipotent projective phantasy.

From this starting point, Bion goes on to describe the way in which the infant paradoxically develops the capacity to experience his own thoughts and feelings by means of an experience with the mother wherein the mother experiences the infant's unthinkable thoughts, and not yet tolerable feelings, as her own. Projective identification is viewed as a process by which the infant's thoughts that cannot be thought and feelings that cannot be felt are elicited in the mother when the mother is able to make herself psychologically available to be used in this way:

> Projective identification makes it possible for him [the infant] to investigate his own feelings in a personality powerful enough to contain them. Denial of the use of this mechanism, either by the refusal of the mother to serve as a repository for the infant's feelings, or by the hatred and envy of the patient who cannot allow the mother to exercise this function, leads to a destruction of the link between infant and breast and consequently, to a severe disorder of the impulse to be curious on which all learning depends. (Bion, 1959: 314)

Bion (1962a) used the term *reverie* to refer to the psychological state in which the (m)Other is able successfully to serve a 'containing function' for the infant's/analysand's projection of unthought thoughts and unfelt feelings. The relationship of container and contained is non-linear and must not be reduced to a linear, sequential schematization of the following sort: an aspect of the projector in phantasy and through actual interpersonal interaction is induced in the Other; after being altered in the process of being experienced by a 'personality powerful enough to contain them', these 'metabolized' aspects of self are made available to the projector who by means of identification becomes more fully able to experience his thoughts and feelings as his own. Such a conception of projective identification obscures the question of the nature of the interplay of subjectivities involved in projective identification by treating the projector and recipient as distinct psychological entities. It is here that the dialectical nature of Bion's concept of the container and the contained affords the possibility of conceptually moving beyond the mechanical nature of the linear understanding of projective identification just described. (See Ogden, 1979, 1982, for clinical illustrations of the dialectical interplay of the intrapsychic and the interpersonal dimensions of projective identification in the analytic setting.)

From the point of view of the container/contained dialectic, projective identification becomes a conceptualization of the creation of subjectivity through the dialectic of interpenetration of subjectivities. In this dialectical relationship, projector and 'recipient' enter into a relationship of simultaneous at-one-ment and separateness in which the infant's experience is given shape by the mother, and yet (in the normative case) the shape that the mother gives the infant has already been determined by the infant. The mother allows herself to be inhabited by the infant in her 'counter-identification' (Grinberg, 1962) with the infant and in this sense is created by the infant at the same time as she is creating (giving shape to) him. The shape that the mother gives to the infant is a shape that is uniquely informed by her own experience of herself and of him. (The mother's experience of this intersubjective process is only alluded to by Bion. Moreover, there is almost no discussion in Bion's work of the specific contribution of the unique psychological make-up of the mother to the mother–infant relationship.)

A mother who cannot allow herself to be inhabited and taken over from within (and thereby created) by the infant cannot give the infant psychological shape. Under these circumstances, there is 'a destruction of the link between infant and breast' (Bion, 1959: 314). The destruction of this link results in the collapse of the mutually creating intersubjectivity underlying healthy projective identification and leaves the infant without a shape with which to contain his psychological and sensory experience of himself. The terror of this experience is described by Bion as 'nameless dread' (1962b: 116). It is nameless, because it lacks the shape and definition afforded by the mother's containing/creative response to the infant's projective identifications including those provided by her conscious and unconscious symbolizing functions.

When the mother is capable of reverie, she names (gives shape to) the infant's experience through her interpretation of the infant's internal states. For instance, the infant, in the beginning, does not experience hunger; he experiences a form of physiological tension that is not yet a psychological event that can be contained by the psyche of the infant alone. The mother's act of sensing the infant's tension, her holding him, looking at him, feeding him, talking and singing to him, all represent facets of an 'interpretation' of the infant's experience. In these ways, hunger is created and the infant is created as an individual (i.e. the infant's raw sensory data are transformed into a psychologically meaningful event) through the mother's recognition of his hunger.

I view the analytic process as one in which the analysand is created through an intersubjective process similar to that involved in projective identification. Analysis is not simply a method of uncovering the hidden; it is more importantly a process of creating an analytic subject who had not previously existed. For example, the analysand's history is not 'uncovered', it is created in the transference-countertransference and is perpetually in a state of flux as the intersubjectivity of the analytic process evolves and is interpreted by analyst and analysand (see Schafer, 1976, 1978). In this way, the analytic subject is created by, and exists in an ever-evolving state in the dynamic intersubjectivity of the analytic process: the subject of psychoanalysis takes shape in the interpretive space *between* analyst and analysand. The 'termination' of a psychoanalytic experience is not the end of the subject of psychoanalysis. The intersubjectivity of the analytic pair is appropriated by the analysand and is transformed into an internal dialogue (a process of 'mutual interpretation' taking place within the context of a single personality system).

In the light of the foregoing discussion, it can be seen that Klein's concept of projective identification as elaborated by Bion, Rosenfeld and others, presents a conceptualization of the subject interpersonally decentred from its exclusive locus within the individual; instead, the subject is conceived of as arising in a dialectic (a dialogue) of self and Other. Paradoxically, the subjectivity of the individual presupposes the existence of two subjects who together create an intersubjectivity through which the infant is created as an individual subject. The infant as subject is present from the beginning although the subjectivity exists largely within the context of the psychological-interpersonal (containing/contained) dimension of the relationship of the infant and mother.

In summary, I have focused on three aspects of Kleinian thinking that contribute to the development of the psychoanalytic concept of the dialectically constituted/decentred subject. First, Klein's idea of 'positions' represents a conception of the subject constituted in the creative and negating dialectical interplay of fundamentally different modes of generating experience. Development is no longer conceived of as a predominantly linear process involving the progression of the subject along developmental lines with pathological regressions to fixation points (see for example, Arlow and Brenner, 1964) and healthy regression (in the service of the ego (Kris, 1950). Instead, Kleinian thinking involves a temporally decentred subject generated between coexisting psychological organizations each reflecting different modes of attributing meaning to experience. The positions do not represent stages of maturity that are outgrown; instead, they represent permanent (and yet evolving) psychological organizations each providing a preserving and negating context for the others. The subject is not located in any given position, but in a space (tension) created by the dialectical interplay of the different dimensions of experience.

Secondly, the Kleinian conception of the splitting of ego and (internal) object extends the Freudian theme of the decentred subject by envisioning the subject as existing in a multiplicity of loci dispersed and united in psychic space. Thirdly, the idea of projective identification (particularly as elaborated by Bion and Rosenfeld) provides essential elements for a theory of the creation of the subject in the psychological space between the infant and mother (and between the analyst and analysand).

The Winnicottian Subject

Winnicott's work represents a major advance in the development of the psychoanalytic conception of the subject. The implicit dialectics of Freud and Klein became the foundation of Winnicott's effort to conceptualize in analytic terms the experience of being alive as a subject. At the heart of Winnicott's (1951, 1971a) thinking is the notion that the living, experiencing subject exists neither in reality nor in fantasy, but in a potential space between the two. The Winnicottian subject is not at the beginning (and never entirely becomes) coincident with the psyche of the individual. Winnicott's conception of the creation of the subject in the space between the infant and mother involves several types of dialectical tension of unity and separateness, of internality and externality, through which the subject is simultaneously constituted and decentred from itself. I shall focus on four forms of these overlapping dialectics: (1) the dialectic of at-one-ment/separateness of mother and infant in 'primary maternal preoccupation', (2) the dialectic of recognition/negation of the infant in the mirroring role of the mother, (3) the dialectic of creation/discovery of the object in transitional object relatedness, and (4) the dialectic of the creative destruction of the mother in 'object usage'. Each of these dialectics represents a different facet of the interdependence of subjectivity and intersubjectivity.

The Dialectic of At-one-ment/Separateness in Primary Maternal Preoccupation

The mother–infant relationship referred to by Winnicott (1956) as 'primary maternal preoccupation' involves a form of maternal identification with the infant that is so extreme that it is 'almost an illness' (1956: 302). The mother must 'feel herself into her infant's place and so meet the infant's needs' (1956: 304). In so doing, she takes the risk of losing a sense of groundedness in herself as a separate individual as well as the risk of suffering the loss of a part of herself if her infant were to die. The mother engages simultaneously in the psychological process of allowing her subjectivity to give way to that of the infant (in her experiencing his needs as her own) and at the same time maintaining sufficient sense of her own distinct subjectivity to allow herself to serve as interpreter of the infant's experience, thereby making her otherness felt, but not noticed. The intersubjectivity underlying primary maternal preoccupation involves an early form of dialectic of oneness and two-ness: the mother is an invisible presence (invisible and yet a felt presence).

Through this form of relatedness, a state of 'going on being' (Winnicott, 1956: 303) is generated. The term 'going on being' is an apt one in that it conveys the notion of a form of subjectivity almost, but not entirely, devoid of the particularity of a sense of 'I-ness'. In this way, Winnicott captures something of the experience of the paradoxical simultaneity of at-one-ment and separateness. (A related conception of intersubjectivity was suggested by Bion's (1962a) notion of the container–contained dialectic. However Winnicott was the first to place the psychological state of the mother on an equal footing with that of the infant in the constitution of the mother-infant. This is fully articulated in Winnicott's statement, that 'There is no such thing as an infant [apart from the maternal provision]' (Winnicott, 1960: 39 fn.).)

A brief clinical example may serve to illustrate the Winnicottian dialectic under discussion in which at-one-ment is a necessary condition for two-ness, and vice versa.

> A rather healthy adolescent patient in the final phase of his analysis told me that he had had a dream about two tropical islands that were very close to one another. 'Actually, it was just one island … no, there were two. I'm having a hard time explaining this … If you looked at the islands from above the water, there were two or them, but if you looked at them from under the water, there was really only one mass coming up from the floor of the ocean with two peaks coming out of the water that looked like, well they were, two islands.

I don't know. It wasn't confusing in the dream, it just sounds confusing when I try to explain it.'

I understand the two islands (that sounded very much like breasts in the patient's description) as a representation of this boy's experience of his simultaneous experience of being one 'thing' with his mother (and with me in the transference) and at the same time, being distinct from her/me. The dream occurred just prior to a summer vacation break in the analysis that was serving as a symbol for the termination of the analysis. In discussing the dream, the patient came to understand the way in which it represented his feeling that he and I 'could never really be apart, no matter what', and that this feeling made it possible for us to 'actually be apart without losing touch with one another'. In other words, oneness is the necessary context for two-ness, and two-ness safeguards the experience of oneness (by providing an essential negation of it). This dialectic that has its origins in the infant's experience of primary maternal preoccupation continues throughout life as a facet of all subsequent forms of subjectivity.

The 'I–me' Dialectic of the Mirroring Relationship

The experience of the infant in relation to the mirroring mother (Winnicott, 1967) generates a second form of dialectical tension necessary for the creation of the subject in the space between mother and infant. 'What does the baby see when he or she looks at the mother's face? I am suggesting that, ordinarily, what the baby sees is himself or herself. In other words, the mother is looking at the baby and *what she looks like is related to what she sees there*' (1967: 112).

As in the case of primary maternal preoccupation, Winnicott's description of the mother's mirroring role at first seems to represent a study in sameness, that is, a description of the way in which the mother disappears as a separate object and simply serves as a narcissistic extension of the infant. However, on closer examination, Winnicott's conception of the mirror-relationship of mother and infant is far more complex than that. Winnicott states that what the mother looks like to the infant '*is related to*', not the same as, what the mother sees in the infant. Mirroring then is not a relationship of identity; it is a relationship of relative sameness and therefore of relative difference. In her mirroring role, the mother (through her recognition of and identification with the infant's internal state) allows the infant to see himself as an Other (that is, to see himself at a distance from his observing, experiencing self).

Through the experience of seeing himself outside of himself (in the mirroring (m)Other), this facet of the infant's awareness of difference is not predominantly an awareness of the difference between me and not-me (i.e. the difference between self and object), but an experiencing of the difference between I and me (that is, the difference between self-as-subject and self-as-object). The infant's observations of himself (as Other to himself) in the mother's reflection of him generates the rudiments of the experience of self-consciousness ('self-reflection'), i.e. the awareness of observable me-ness. In other words, the mother, in her role as mirror, provides thirdness (Green, 1975) that allows for the division of the infant into an observing subject and a subject-as-object with a reflective space between the two.

The experience of I-as-subject cannot exist except insofar as 'I' also exist as, but am different from, me (I-as-object). The existence of I-as-subject requires the existence of me (I-as-object), otherwise, one's existence is without shape. Similarly, the self-as-object (me) presupposes the observing I-as-subject that recognizes me.

Thus, 'I' and 'me' have no meaning except in relation to one another: each form of experience of subjectivity creates the other and is fully dependent on the other. Moreover, 'I' and 'me' cannot be created by an infant in isolation from the mother. The infant requires the mirroring relationship with the mother in order to see himself as other to himself. In this way a reflective space between the poles of the dialectic of I and me is created in which the experiencing self-reflective subject is simultaneously constituted and decentred from itself.

Transitional Object-Relatedness: The Dialectic of the Creation/Discovery of the Object

Perhaps the most important of Winnicott's contributions to the psychoanalytic conceptualization of the subject is his concept of transitional object relatedness (1951, 1971a). Here, Winnicott describes a form of object relationship in which the object is experienced simultaneously as created by the infant and discovered by him: the question as to which is the case simply never arises. The transitional object is an extension of the infant's internal world and at the same time has a palpable, inescapable, immutable existence outside of, and independent of, the infant. It is simultaneously a subjective object (an omnipotent creation of the infant) and the infant's 'first "not me" possession' (Winnicott, 1951: 1): 'The essential feature ... is *the paradox and the acceptance of the paradox*: the baby creates the object, but the object was there waiting to be created' (Winnicott, 1968: 89). '[The paradox must not be] solved by a restatement that by its cleverness seems to eliminate the paradox' (Winnicott, 1963: 181).

Transitional phenomena are created in the space between mother and infant, a space 'that exists (but cannot exist) between the baby and the object' (Winnicott, 1971b: 107), a space that connects and separates. The form of mother–infant relatedness in which experience of this sort is generated is a relationship that evolves from the types of intersubjectivity involved in primary maternal preoccupation and the mirroring relationship of mother and infant. The latter two forms of dialectic of oneness and separateness are more primitive in nature than transitional relatedness in that the externality of the mother is not as fully developed in them. The transitional object *is always part of the real* (as opposed to the purely psychical). It would be a contradiction in terms to speak of the 'internalization' of a transitional object. An internalized object is an idea, a mental representation and has lost its physical connexion with the world outside of the infant's mind; an idea lacks actual sensory qualities, for example of hardness, warmth, texture and so on. Transitional object relatedness represents the first full confrontation of the infant with the irreducible alterity of the realness of the world outside of himself; and yet, paradoxically, this 'full' confrontation with the real is made possible because the transitional object never ceases to be the creation of the infant, a reflection of himself in the world. 'In the rules of the game we all know that we will never challenge the baby to elicit an answer to the question: did you create that or did you find it?' (Winnicott, 1968: 89).

By means of the dialectical tension of internality and externality involved in transitional object relatedness, a third area of experiencing is generated that lies between me and not-me, between reality and fantasy, while fully partaking of both poles of these dialectics. It is in the space created between these poles that symbols are created and imaginative psychological activity takes place.

In the absence of the role played by the mother, it would be impossible for the infant to generate the conditions necessary for his coming to life as a subject in the sense addressed by the concept of the creation of transitional phenomena. The infant requires the experience of a particular form of intersubjectivity in which the mother's *being* is experienced simultaneously as an extension of himself and as other to himself. Only later is this intersubjectivity appropriated by the infant as he develops the capacity to be alone (Winnicott, 1958a), i.e. the capacity to be a subject independent of the actual participation of the mother's subjectivity.

The Dialectic of the Creative Destruction of the Object

The final form of the dialectic of internality and externality that I shall discuss in Winnicott's work is that of the creative destruction of the mother in the process of the development of the infant's capacity to 'use' (Winnicott, 1968) the mother as an external object and to feel concern for her as a subject (Winnicott, 1954, 1958b). The experience of 'ruth' (concern) and the capacity for object usage are inter-related achievements in that both involve forms of recognition of the alterity of the object that is related to, but different from that involved in transitional object relatedness. In the latter, the full externality of the mother-as-object is confronted, while in the experience of 'ruth' (Winnicott, 1954, 1958b) (and object 'usage'), it is the mother-as-subject that is fully confronted for the first time. When the object becomes a subject, the recognition of oneself by the Other creates the conditions for a new way of being aware of one's own subjectivity, and subjectivity itself is thereby altered. In other words, the experience of the recognition of one's own 'I-ness' by an Other (who is recognized as an experiencing 'I') creates an intersubjective dialectic through which one becomes aware of one's own subjectivity in a new way, i.e. one becomes 'self-conscious' (Hegel, 1807) in a way that the individual had not previously experienced.

Winnicott's (1958b, 1968) understanding of the development of this aspect of subjectivity is rooted in his view of the psychological-interpersonal processes that mediate the infant's escape from the confines of the solipsism of his own omnipotent thinking and object relatedness. There is a quality of the infant's earliest relationship to the mother that Winnicott describes as 'ruthless' (1958b: 22), that is, without ruth. The mother who is treated ruthlessly is a 'subjective object', an externalization of an omnipotent internal object mother who is inexhaustible and indestructible ('a bundle of projections' (Winnicott, 1968: 88)). Because of the mother's fantasized inexhaustibility and indestructibility there is no need for ruth; in fact, the feeling of concern does not exist in the emotional vocabulary of the infant living in a world of omnipotent object relations. (One can highly value objects, but one can only feel concern for subjects.)

Paradoxically, the process of recognition of the mother as a person for whom the infant feels concern (and a person he can 'use' because of his recognition of her groundedness in the world outside of himself) involves the destruction of the mother by the infant while the mother survives (Winnicott, 1954, 1968). My understanding of this paradoxical notion (which I hope is not a resolution of the paradox of the creative destruction of the mother) is that the infant makes room for the possibility of the mother as a subject, a person other-to-himself, by destroying an aspect of himself (his own omnipotence as projected onto the omnipotent internal object mother).

As long as the infant holds on to his defensive omnipotence in the form of his relatedness to the omnipotent internal object mother, the mother, both as a subject and as an external object, is eclipsed by the infant's projections of his omnipotent self and internal objects. The fantasized destruction of the (internal) object mother is a reflection of the infant's relinquishing of his reliance on omnipotent defences in the form of dependence on the omnipotent internal object mother. The loosening of this tie to the omnipotent mother is an ongoing psychological task: 'I am all the time destroying you [the mother] in (unconscious) fantasy' (Winnicott, 1968: 90). By continually (in fantasy) destroying the internal object mother, the infant becomes capable of discovering the external object mother (both as object and as subject) if the mother is able to survive the infant's fantasized destruction of her (and his ruthless treatment of her) by remaining emotionally present over time.

The very fact of the infant's fantasized destruction of the omnipotent internal object mother reflects his readiness to move beyond the solipsism of his own omnipotence and to take the risks involved in the as yet unknown experience of relatedness to objects that he has not created and that he does not own, objects that have an internal life of their own. The infant has experienced something of the otherness of the object in his relationships with transitional objects, but he has not yet fully recognized the 'I-ness' of the object. As importantly, his own sense of I-ness has not yet been recognized by an Other who is also a subject.

For Winnicott, this psychological-interpersonal shift is mediated by forms of mother–infant relatedness in which the infant is experiencing the full intensity of omnipotent fantasies of destruction of the mother while the mother (as living subject) not only survives over time, but is there to catch the infant when he takes the risk of falling out of the arms of the omnipotent internal object mother into the arms of an only dimly perceived mother-in-the-world (Ogden, 1985). Moreover, the mother-in-the-world is a subject who recognizes the infant's concern for her as well as the beginnings of his capacity to feel guilt about his ruthless treatment of her. The mother's subjectivity and her recognition of the subjectivity of the infant are reflected in her recognition of the infant's reparative gift (e.g. a bowel movement) after a ruthless feed (Winnicott, 1954) and her acceptance of it.

In this creatively destructive process, the I-as-subject and mother-as-subject simultaneously come into being in relation to one another. (Buber (1970)) uses the term 'I–Thou' to refer to the relationship between oneself as subject and the Other who is experienced as being alive as a separate subject and who recognizes oneself as a subject.) A new type of intersubjective experience (a form of self-conscious subjectivity) is generated through the I–Thou dialectic, a dialectic of subjects creating one another through their recognition of one another as subjects. This conception of the space between I-as-subject and Other-as-subject represents still another way of describing the Winnicottian notion of the locus of subjectivity, a subjectivity that is always decentred from itself and always to some degree arising in the context of intersubjectivity. In this last instance, the emphasis is on the way in which it is necessary for the omnipotence of the infant (as well as that of the adult) to be continually negated, superseded ('destroyed' in unconsciously fantasized object relations), in the process of creating a more fully generative dialectic of self and Other. In this process subjectivity becomes aware of itself. I as self-conscious subject am created through the process of recognizing and being recognized by the Other-as-subject.

In summary, the forms of mother–infant relatedness that have been described all reflect a central theme that underlies the Winnicottian conception of the creation of the subject: the subjectivity of the infant takes shape in the potential space between mother and infant. This space is defined by a series of paradoxes that must be maintained and not resolved, paradoxes of simultaneous internality and externality, paradoxes that generate a third area of experiencing, 'the place where we live' (Winnicott, 1971b). Winnicott's use of the notion of paradox to describe the space in which subjectivity is created represents a quiet revolution in analytic thinking in that for the first time a dialectical conception of the intersubjective constitution of the decentred human subject is fully articulated.

Concluding Comments

The analytic conception of the subject represents a cornerstone of the psychoanalytic project and is at the same time one of the least well-articulated psychoanalytic concepts. In the first part of this chapter, I discussed the way in which the concept of the psychoanalytic subject involves a conception of experiencing 'I-ness' in which consciousness and unconsciousness coexist in a continual process of creative negation of one another. Consciousness and unconsciousness stand in a relation of relative difference. The unconscious represents an order of experience that is continuous with consciousness in the sense that it participates in the same system of meanings, but differs from consciousness in the way that meanings are represented, transformed, interrelated and so on.

Central among the contributions of psychoanalysis to a theory of subjectivity is the formulation of a concept of the subject in which neither consciousness nor unconsciousness holds a privileged position in relation to the other. Emanating from a continuous process of dialectical negation, the subject is forever decentred from static self-equivalence. That is, the psychoanalytic subject never simply is; the subject is always *becoming* through a process of the creative negation of itself.

The analytic conception of the subject has increasingly become a theory of the interdependence of subjectivity and intersubjectivity. The subject cannot create itself; the development of subjectivity requires experiences of specific forms of intersubjectivity. In the beginning, subjectivity and the individual psyche are not coincident: 'There is no such thing as an infant.' The constitution of the subject in the space between mother and infant is mediated by such psychological-interpersonal events as projective identification, primary maternal preoccupation, the mirroring relationship, relatedness to transitional objects, and the experiences of object usage and ruth. The appropriation by the infant of the intersubjective space represents a critical step in the establishment of the individual's capacity to generate and maintain psychological dialectics (e.g. of consciousness and unconsciousness, of me and not me, of I and me, of I and Thou) through which he is simultaneously constituted and decentred as a subject.

Notes

1. When I use the term consciousness, I am referring to Freud's System Preconscious-Conscious, and when I use the term unconsciousness, I am referring to an order of experience referred to by Freud as the dynamic unconscious or the System Unconscious. The latter order of experience is not only devoid of the quality of self-awareness, but is comprised of a set of meanings that are felt to be incompatible with, unacceptable to, and threatening to the system of meanings constituted in consciousness. In addition, the two orders of experience (the System Unconscious and the System Preconscious-Conscious) are characterized by different 'principles of mental functioning' (Freud, 1911), i.e. different forms of psychic representation, different rules of psychic transformation, different types of temporality, and so on.
2. Boyer (1988) has discussed the way in which the principal unresolved transference–countertransference anxiety of a given analytic hour constitutes a primary unconscious context for the subsequent meeting.
3. The notion of an interpersonal dimension of projective identification remained ambiguous and undeveloped in Klein's work. Bion (1952) and Rosenfeld (1971) pioneered the clinical exploration and theoretical formulation of projective identification as a psychological-interpersonal process.

References

Arlow, J. and Brenner, C. (1964), *Psychoanalytic Concepts and the Structural Theory*, New York: International University Press.
Bibring, E. (1947), 'The so-called English school of psychoanalysis', *Psychoanalytic Quarterly* 16: 69–93.
Bick, E. (1968), 'The experience of the skin in early object relations', *International Journal of Psychoanalysis* 49: 484–6.
— (1986), 'Further considerations on the function of the skin in early object relations', *British Journal of Psychotherapy* 2: 292–9.
Bion, W.R. (1952), 'Group dynamics: a review', in *Experiences in Groups*, New York: Basic Books, 1959, pp. 141–92.
— (1959), 'Attacks on linking', *International Journal of Psychoanalysis* 40: 308–15.
— (1962a), *Learning from Experience*, in *Seven Servants*, New York: Aronson, 1977.
— (1962b), 'A theory of thinking', in *Second Thoughts*, New York: Aronson, 1967, pp. 110–19.
— (1963), *Elements of Psycho-Analysis*, in *Seven Servants*, New York: Aronson, 1977.
— (1967), 'On arrogance', in *Second Thoughts*, New York: Aronson, 1967, pp. 86–92.
Bollas, C. (1987), *The Shadow of the Object: Psycho-analysis of the Unthought Known*, New York: Columbia University Press.
Boyer, L.B. (1988), 'Thinking of the interview as if it were a dream', *Contemporary Psychoanalysis* 24: 275–81.
Buber, M. (1970), *I and Thou*, trans. W. Kaufmann, New York: Scribners.
Erikson, E. (1950), *Childhood and Society*, New York: Norton.
Fairbairn, W.R.D. (1952), *An Object Relations Theory of the Personality*, New York: Basic Books.
Federn, N. (1952), *Ego Psychology and the Psychoses*, New York: Basic Books.
Freud, S. (1893–95), *Studies on Hysteria*, *SE* II.
— (1900), *The Interpretation of Dreams*, *SE* IV/V.
— (1909), 'Notes upon a case of obsessional neurosis', *SE* X.
— (1911), 'Formulations on the two principles of mental functioning', *SE* XII.
— (1915a), 'Instincts and their vicissitudes', *SE* XIV.
— (1915b), 'The unconscious', *SE* XIV.
— (1916–17), *Introductory Lectures on Psychoanalysis. XVIII*: 'Fixation to traumas – the unconscious', *SE* XVI.
— (1917), 'A difficulty in the path of psychoanalysis', *SE* XVII.
— (1923), *The Ego and the Id*, *SE* XIX.
— (1925a), 'A note upon the "mystic writing-pad"', *SE* XIX.

— (1925b), 'Negation', *SE* XIX.
— (1926a), *Inhibitions, Symptoms and Anxiety, SE* XX.
— (1926b), *The Question of Lay Analysis, SE* XX.
— (1927), 'Fetishism', *SE* XXI.
— (1930), *Civilization and its Discontents, SE* XXI.
— (1933), *New introductory Lectures on Psychoanalysis. XXXI*: 'The dissection of the psychical personality', *SE* XXII.
— (1940), *An Outline of Psycho-Analysis, SE* XXIII.
Green, A. (1975), 'The analyst, symbolization, and absence in the analytic setting. (On changes in analytic practice and analytic experience.)', *International Journal of Psychoanalysis* 56: 1–22.
Grinberg, L. (1962), 'On a specific aspect of countertransference due to the patient's projective identification', *International Journal of Psychoanalysis* 43: 436–40.
Grossman, W. (1982), 'The self as fantasy: fantasy as theory', *Journal of the American Psychoanalytic Association* 30: 919–38.
Grotstein, J. (1981), *Splitting and Projective Identification*, New York: Jason Aronson.
Grunberger, B. (1971), *Narcissism: Psychoanalytic Essays*, trans. J.S. Diamanti, Madison, CT: International Universities Press.
Guntrip, H. (1969), *Schizoid Phenomena, Object-Relations, and the Self*, New York: International Universities Press.
Habermas, J. (1968), *Knowledge and Human Interests*, trans. J. Shapiro, Boston: Beacon Press, 1971.
Hartmann, H. (1950), 'Comments on the psychoanalytic theory of the ego', *Psychoanalytic Study of the Child* 5: 74–96.
— Kris, E. and Loewenstein, R. (1946), 'Comments on the formation of psychic structure', *Psychoanalytic Study of the Child* 2: 11–38.
Hegel, G.W.F. (1807), *Phenomenology of Spirit*, trans. A.V. Miller, London: Oxford Universities Press, 1977.
Hyppolite, J. (1956), 'A spoken commentary on Freud's *Verneinung*', in *The Seminar of Jacques Lacan, Book 1. Freud's Papers on Technique, 1953–54,* trans. J. Forrester, New York: Norton, 1988, pp. 289–97.
Jacobson, E. (1964), *The Self and the Object World*, New York: International Universities Press.
Khan, M.M.R. (1974), *The Privacy of the Self*, New York: International Universities Press.
Klein, M. (1932), 'The effect of early anxiety situations on the sexual development of the girl', in *The Psycho-Analysis of Children,* New York: Humanities Press, 1969, pp. 268–325.
— (1935), 'A contribution to the psychogenesis of manic-depressive states', in *Contributions to Psycho-Analysis, 1921–1945,* London: Hogarth Press, 1968, pp. 282–311.

— (1946), 'Notes on some schizoid mechanisms', in *Envy and Gratitude and Other Works, 1946–1963*, New York: Delacorte, 1975, pp. 1–24.
— (1948), 'On the theory of anxiety and guilt', in *Envy and Gratitude and Other Works, 1946–1963*, New York: Delacorte, 1975, pp. 25–42.
— (1952), 'Some theoretical conclusions regarding the emotional life of the infant', in *Envy and Gratitude and Other Works, 1946–1963*, New York: Delacorte, 1975, pp. 61–93.
— (1955), 'On identification', in *Envy and Gratitude and Other Works, 1946–1963*, New York: Delacorte, 1975, pp. 141–75.
Kohut, H. (1971), *The Analysis of the Self*, New York: International Universities Press.
Kojève, A. (1934–35), *Introduction to the Reading of Hegel*, trans. J.H. Nichols, Jr, Ithaca: Cornell University Press, 1969.
Kris, E. (1950), *Psychoanalytic Explorations in Art*, New York: International Universities Press.
Kundera, M. (1984), *The Unbearable Lightness of Being*, trans. M.H. Hein, New York: Harper & Row.
Lacan, J. (1951), 'Intervention sur le transfert', in *Écrits*, Paris: Seuil, 1966, pp. 215–26.
— (1954–55), *The Seminar of Jacques Lacan. Book II: The Ego in Freud's Theory and in the Technique of Psychoanalysis, 1954–1955*, trans. S. Tomascelli, New York: Norton, 1988.
— (1957), 'On a question preliminary to any possible treatment of psychosis', in *Écrits: A Selection*, trans. A. Sheridan, New York: Norton, 1977, pp. 179–225.
— (1966a), 'The agency of the letter in the unconscious or reason since Freud', in *Écrits: A Selection*, New York: Norton, 1977, pp. 146–78.
— (1966b), 'Position de l'inconscient', in *Écrits*, Paris: Seuil, 1966, pp. 829–50.
Laplanche, J. and Pontalis, J.-B. (1967), *The Language of Psycho-Analysis*, trans. D. Nicholson-Smith, New York: Norton, 1973.
Lichtenstein, H. (1963), 'The dilemma of human identity: notes on self-transformation, self-objectivation, and metamorphosis', *Journal of the American Psychoanalytic Association* 11: 173–223.
Loewald, H. (1980), *Papers on Psychoanalysis*, New Haven: Yale University Press.
Loewenstein, R. (1967), 'Defensive organization and adaptive ego functions', *Journal of the American Psychoanalytic Association* 15: 795–809.
Marcuse, H. (1960), 'Preface: a note on dialectic', in *Reason and Revolution: Hegel and the Rise of Social Theory*, Boston: Beacon Press, pp. vii–xiv.

Meltzer, D. (1975), 'Adhesive identification', *Contemporary Psychoanalysis* 11: 289–310.
Meltzer, D. *et al.* (1975), *Explorations in Autism*, Perthshire: Clunie Press.
Mitchell, S. (1991), 'Contemporary perspectives on self: toward an integration', *Psychoanalytic Dialogues: A Journal of Relational Perspectives* 1: 121–47.
Ogden, T. (1979), 'On projective identification', *International Journal of Psychoanalysis* 60: 357–73.
— (1982), *Projective Identification and Psycho-therapeutic Technique*, Northvale, NJ: Aronson.
— (1985), 'The mother, the infant and the matrix: interpretations of aspects of the work of Donald Winnicott', *Contemporary Psychoanalysis* 21: 346–71.
— (1986), *The Matrix of the Mind: Object Relations and the Psychoanalytic Dialogue*, Northvale, NJ: Aronson.
— (1988), 'On the dialectical structure of experience: some clinical and theoretical implications', *Contemporary Psychoanalysis* 24: 17–45.
— (1989a), *The Primitive Edge of Experience*, Northvale, NJ: Aronson.
— (1989b), 'On the concept of an autistic-contiguous position', *International Journal of Psychoanalysis* 70: 127–40.
— (1991a), 'Some theoretical comments on personal isolation', *Psychoanalytic Dialogues: A Journal of Relational Perspectives* 1: 377–90.
— (1991b), 'Analysing the matrix of transference', *International Journal of Psychoanalysis* 72: 593–606.
Ricoeur, P. (1970), *Freud and Philosophy: An Essay on Interpretation*, trans. D. Savage, New Haven: Yale University Press.
Rosenfeld, H. (1965), *Psychotic States*, New York: International Universities Press.
— (1971), 'Contributions to the psychopathology of psychotic states: the importance of projective identification in the ego structure and the object relations of the psychotic patient', in P. Doucet and C. Laurin (eds), *Problems of Psychosis*, Amsterdam: Excerpta Medica, pp. 115–28.
— (1987), *Impasse and Interpretation*, London and New York: Tavistock.
Sandler, J. (1987), *From Safety to Superego*, New York: Guilford.
Schafer, R. (1976), *A New Language for Psychoanalysis*, New Haven: Yale University Press.
— (1978), *Language and Insight*, New Haven: Yale University Press.
Spence, D. (1987), 'Turning happenings into meanings: the central role of the self', in P. Young-Eisendrath and J. Hall (eds), *The*

Book of the Self: Person, Pretext and Process, New York: New York University Press, 1987, pp. 131–50.

Spruiell, V. (1981), 'The self and the ego', *Psychoanalytic Quarterly* 50: 319–44.

Stern, D. (1985), *The Interpersonal World of the Infant*, New York: Basic Books.

Tustin, F. (1972), *Autism and Childhood Psychosis*, London: Hogarth Press.

— (1980), 'Autistic objects', *International Review of Psychoanalysis* 7: 27–40.

— (1984), 'Autistic shapes', *International Review of Psychoanalysis* 11: 279–90.

— (1990), *The Protective Shell in Children and Adults*, London: Karnac Books.

Winnicott, D.W. (1951), 'Transitional objects and transitional phenomena', in *Playing and Reality*, New York: Basic Books, 1971, pp. 1–25.

— (1954), 'The depressive position in normal development', in *Through Paediatrics to Psycho-Analysis*, New York: Basic Books, 1975, pp. 262–77.

— (1956), 'Primary maternal preoccupation', in *Through Paediatrics to Psycho-Analysis*, New York: Basic Books, 1975, pp. 300–5.

— (1958a), 'The capacity to be alone', in *The Maturational Processes and the Facilitating Environment*, New York: International University Press, 1965, pp. 29–36.

— (1958b), 'Psycho-analysis and the sense of guilt', in *The Maturational Processes and the Facilitating Environment*, New York: International Universities Press, 1965, pp. 15–28.

— (1960), 'The theory of the parent–infant relationship', in *The Maturational Processes and the Facilitating Environment*, New York: International Universities Press, 1965, pp. 37–55.

— (1963), 'Communicating and not communicating leading to a study of certain opposites', in *The Maturational Processes and the Facilitating Environment*, New York: International Universities Press, 1965, pp. 179–92.

— (1967), 'Mirror role of mother and family in child development', in *Playing and Reality*, New York: Basic Books, 1971, pp. 111–18.

— (1968), 'The use of an object and relating through cross identifications', in *Playing and Reality*, New York: Basic Books, 1971, pp. 86–94.

— (1971a), *Playing and Reality*, New York: Basic Books.

— (1971b), 'The place where we live', in *Playing and Reality*, New York: Basic Books, 1971, pp. 104–10.

9 Why the Self Is, and Is Not, Empty: Trauma and Transcendence in the Postmodern Psyche

Karen Peoples

Psychoanalysis, like other disciplines, has been undergoing turbulent sea changes in its understanding of the ways in which reality, meaning and psychic structure take shape. Dismantled under the searching gaze of hermeneutic analysis are long-standing assumptions about stages, phases and fundamental truths of psychological development. Trenchant criticisms have emerged of late on the entire enterprise of psychodynamic therapies, specifically aimed at the theories of self upon which they rest. The title of this chapter is in part a response to such a critique in the *American Psychologist* by Phillip Cushman (1990) entitled, 'Why the Self Is Empty'. While it is only one of many voices in the so-called 'postmodern' dialogue, Cushman's articulate work stands out for its worthy challenge to therapeutic trends that are oblivious to their potentially adverse social and political implications. But, in addition, Cushman's work bears commentary because it reflects especially well a subtle and, perhaps, reactionary trend toward relativism and nihilism in certain constructionist accounts.

In 'Why the Self is Empty', Cushman seeks to demonstrate that a romantic conception of a true, or core, or unitary self threads through Western historical texts and ideas. This romanticized unitary self presumed hidden in the psyche's interior, demanding to be unearthed, falls asunder under the hermeneutic lens to reveal a shifting and inconstant identity. Cushman not only suggests that this self is illusory, but that it is manufactured and reinforced by depth psychotherapies and, in particular, by psychoanalytic ones. Through their exclusively interiorized focus, analytic therapies perpetuate an historic (and futile) quest for the grail of self-wholeness, a quest that ironically empties and depletes both individual and culture in its very search for restoration. The resulting, disturbing emptiness for which so many pursue analytic cures stems primarily, in Cushman's view, from a psychoanalytic reification, and cultural idealization, of a singular self that is not there.

This view hits only partially on the mark, and misses a great deal. To fully understand the relationship between the *sense* of self and its continuities and discontinuities, the evolution of *theories* of self with their consistencies and inconsistencies, and the striking range of experiences called 'emptiness', requires a broader view. While I agree with many of the cogent constructionist arguments which favour a discontinuous view of self, in this chapter I explore psychic unity, fragmentation, and ways of knowing emptiness through a different lens, with contrasting assumptions and speculations about the interrelationship of these states. Further, I examine these issues in the context of the rapidly expanding dialogue surrounding postmodern relativism and constructionist points of view on the self, a dialogue to which psychoanalysis has contributed richly, rather than ignored, been blinded to or subverted, as some contend.

It would appear useful to frame the parameters of debate along the following lines of questioning: if emptiness is a widespread cultural and clinical phenomenon, how is it experienced? Is it problematic? Is emptiness related to vacillations in self-state? If so, to what extent do cultural forces that dislocate meaning and engender vacuousness contribute to it? What is the relationship between the subjective sense of self-unity or self-coherence, and the awareness of psychic emptiness that may puncture, contain, expand from or engulf it? More simply put, what is the relationship between identity and psychic space? Are most experiences of space accompanied by dread and reflective of the pathological break-up of necessary identity structures, of self- and object-representations, or – alternatively – of cultural meaning? In contrast, does the notion of psychic emptiness contain the potential for a different relationship to identity than is typically assumed by Western culture and its depth psychotherapies?

Self and Identity: Changing Notions

A proliferation of recent writings has challenged the appropriateness of unitary notions of self-identity in psychology and in psychoanalysis, and is sculpting the shape of the postmodern debate in these fields. Elliott and Spezzano, surveying the debate in Chapter 1 of this book, provide a cautionary note on 'the messy truth of postmodern thinking' (p. 16): it is itself not a unitary whole, but rather a continuum of voices that intersect as well as diverge from each other. They write, '"Modernism" and "postmodernism" are not homogeneous or unambiguous facts, but only partially successful attempts to locate and define intellectual centres of gravity. Psychoanalysts looking to this epistemological debate, in their effort to assess their attitudes toward their own interpretations, must tolerate greater heterogeneity than they might have hoped to find' (p. 18).

Nonetheless, an argument common to these writings is that multiplicity, or at least, multifacetedness better characterizes self-identity and self-experience than previously held modernist notions of the consolidated self presumed to obtain from successful individuation. Theories of unitary identity that have dominated psychoanalytic thinking until recently, critics argue, contain veiled ideologies promoting particular American cultural values (Cushman, 1991). They are variously seen by postmodern writers as reinforcing a capitalistic agenda (Cushman, 1990, 1991), supporting patriarchal preferences for linearity, hierarchy and unity over multiplicity and diversity (Rivera, 1989), and generally entrenching a belief in the superiority of the individual over the society.

In this chapter I suggest that recent attempts to deconstruct the self go too far to dismantle, even deride, the conceptual possibility of 'universal' commonalities and syntheses operative in human consciousness. On the other hand, I suggest that they do not go far enough to challenge Western 'precritical assumptions and values' (Schafer, in Elliott and Spezzano, this book:, p. 25) about the unity of psychic structure. For example, contemporary discussions within psychoanalysis that take up the dialectic of unity and multiplicity of self, including the attempt at a 'comprehensive hermeneutic' (Cushman, 1995) of the political and historical context in which the unitary self-concept has arisen, tend to rest on modernistic Western presumptions that take psychic *structure* as bedrock. Whether fixed and unitary, or fluid and multiple, the premise of foundational psychic structure is an embedded assumption. Neither historical accounts, nor contemporary ones (for the most part) successfully explore or describe what the nature of this structure actually is. As a mostly tacit or implicit assumption, self as structure (or selves as structure) obscures awareness of the quality of the psychic *space* or consciousness in which aspects of mental structure arise.

For this reason, even the deconstruction of a unitive theory of self that makes universal claims into a situational theory that emphasizes local contexts fails to question fundamental Western assumptions about the nature of consciousness itself. Few Western theories sufficiently define the complex variations in states of emptiness known to human consciousness that are considered non-pathological – for example, those in which clarity and luminosity permeate. Nor, until recently (cf. Bromberg, 1994; Epstein, 1986; Mitchell, 1993), have

Western theories carefully distinguished between different levels of self, such as self-experiencing, self-agency, self-structure, self as superordinate organizing principle, and the capacity for self-reflection that is typically considered to be the hallmark of successful analytic therapies (Deikman, 1982; Suler, 1993). Little attention has been paid in psychoanalysis to what may be referred to as the 'backdrop' upon which psychic structures and processes play, such as states of consciousness in which the awareness of self becomes relatively transparent to the spatial qualities of mind, to awareness of emptiness without dread. An investigation of these states and of the meta-awareness that attends them may well yield useful information on the function of psychic space as a fundamental creative ground of consciousness.

By contrast, dread-filled experiences of emptiness appear to represent a type of 'freezing' of this creative capacity of psychic space that may indeed reflect emptying forces within the individual and/or culture. Yet such extreme states may merely highlight by their starkness a more normative freezing of psychic space, one that is inherent in the developmental process of psychic structuralization itself, and to which Western psychology is relatively blind. One given of psychic structure, for example, is self-image. Can the Western mind conceive of healthy functioning devoid of self-image? One writer reflecting such a radical possibility is Almaas (1986), who notes, '… [o]ntologically, self-image is simply frozen boundaries in space, frozen by their cathexis with libidinal energy. When the cathexis is undone, the boundaries dissolve into empty space, which is what actually exists as the nature of the mind' (Almaas, 1986: 55).

Constructionist Critiques

Before examining this notion further, it is necessary to address in greater detail some of the potentials and perils (Gergen, 1994) of postmodern critiques of contemporary theoretical conceptions of self, identity and emptiness. In 'Why the Self Is Empty' Cushman decisively claims, '[t]here is no universal, transhistorical self, only local selves; no universal theory about the self, only local theories', (1990: 599), indicating that theories of self 'are cultural artifacts, elements of the cultural text'. He contends that significant absences in the social sphere of community, tradition and shared meaning have been interpreted by Western psychotherapies, especially self psychology and object relations theory, as individual internal or self-structural deficiencies. Such theories of self have reified and perpetuated a myth of the masterful, cohesive, bounded self, the authentic or 'true' self, that can be 'uncovered' at core; this ideological premise supports, according to Cushman, the misdirected interiorization of strivings for meaning in the therapy patient and thus fosters the very sense of emptiness that analytic therapies are meant to dispel.

Cushman criticizes object relations theories of self for this 'hidden ideology' and for their failure to identify the economic and political purposes these theories purportedly serve; namely, necessitating a protracted internal – that is, depth psychotherapeutic – solution. Cushman suggests such theories have only described a very particular 'Western' self, one dislocated from community and deficient in social rituals that sustain a context of meaning to life.

In a more recent commentary, Cushman (1995: 21) describes this 'enchanted American interior', presenting the reader with an amalgam of the European romantic idea of the true self, carried forward in the analytic writings of Winnicott and in the Emersonian-transcendentalist 'ideology of self-liberation'. Both of these, Cushman feels, have contributed to the shaping of a self-entitled character associated with American individualism, reinforcing the quest into the psychic interior in search of the independent 'artist-hero', an individual liberated from the constraints of moral and political ethos. The gist of this argument is that a covert ideology of self-sufficient avarice has been promoted by contemporary analytic theories of the self. Dangers inhere in failing to recognize the way such ideologies have been used historically to justify unbridled assertions of the right of the 'natural' self to claims of land, kinship and resources (Cushman, 1995).

Certainly, one of the constructs rooted in Western models of self historically has been what Stolorow and Atwood (1992: 7) rather belatedly recognize as 'the myth of the isolated mind'. Why, they muse, has this myth of 'the autonomous ego, the omnipotent agent, the inviolable pristine self ... [been such a] difficult demon to exorcise?' (1992: 22). Tracing the self's isolation from nature, from social life, and from subjectivity, the authors wonder at the difficulty Westerners face in acknowledging the 'unbearable embeddedness of being'. Cushman views this state of alienation, with its attendant malaise of emptiness, to result from a search for meaning in the wrong direction – inward rather than outward.

A more moderated view of constructionist critiques on the self comes from Kenneth Gergen (1994), who suggests that modern mythologies of self are undergoing numerous 'challenges to representationalism'. Gergen notes that the language of scientific psychology has moved from a representational one, assuming a fixed or determinate connection 'between words and world' (1994: 412), to a relational one that opens the way for multiple realities, languages and dialogues on the self. Diverging from Cushman, Gergen argues that the postmodern deconstruction of modernist identity and certainty 'turns from its nihilistic posture to more promising possibilities' (1994: 413) by describing 'a relational view of language' and constructions of identity that require a thoroughgoing dialogue on the values, ethics and morals with which our theories are imbued.

Gergen suggests that postmodern dialogues on the cultural relativism of theories of self, when espoused in such a way as to lay 'claim to foundational or first moral principles' (Gergen, 1994: 414), simply replace one form of demagoguery (the language of science) with another (the language of postmodernism), having the same oppressive and marginalizing effect on the voice of the contradicting Other. Cushman veers in this direction in quashing the possibility of an essential, unitary self-nature and in dismissing the usefulness of in-depth therapeutic approaches toward the so-called Western malaise of emptiness.

Cushman makes a significant categorical error by conflating two important forms of interiority: the individual and the cultural. While he rightly objects to psychoanalysis extending wholecloth its observations of the individual in the therapist–patient dyad to theories about culture (Cushman, 1996), he also errs in the opposite direction. Like the scientist who takes objective knowledge as an ideal, the postmodernist who asserts the domain of culture as the sole origin of self-experience uses this claim 'as a conversational trump ... [that] disregards or denigrates all hands not dealt in these terms' (Gergen, 1994: 413), e.g., local, historical, situational terms. As such, Cushman ignores the criteria for validity that are relevant to the interior, individual level of experience – namely, sincerity or authenticity of subjective experience – and restricts legitimate methods of observation to an intertextual hermeneutic applied to cultural processes at large.

This conflation is what transpersonal theorist Ken Wilber (1995) terms 'subtle reductionism'. In contrast, Wilber proposes a schema of four distinct domains of knowledge, each with their own criteria for validation of truthfulness. Recognizing the distinctive natures of these four modes of gathering and verifying knowledge is essential, he believes, to developing a complete, holistic or 'holarchic' understanding of human consciousness within an evolutionary framework.

The four domains or 'quadrants' include two 'interior' modes of knowing – one individual and one cultural – and two 'exterior' modes – one individual and one social, each of which utilizes distinctly different methodologies for gathering knowledge. The interior domains concern knowledge and experience acquired 'in depth' and are obscure to external observation: they must be interpreted. The exterior domains concern individual and social behaviours that occur 'at the surface', can be measured and observed, and pertain not to what things *mean* but to what people and systems *do* (Wilber, 1995: 127). The interior domains cannot be appropriately subjected to exterior – i.e. empirically observable, behavioural – modes of validation or authentication without losing the subject for whom dialogical interpretation and meaning are key.

Likewise, although subjective knowledge and cultural knowledge are two forms of interior knowing that rely upon interpretation, or hermeneutics, *the individual subject cannot be collapsed into the 'shared cultural worldspace'* (Wilber, 1995: 137) *even though she or he is embedded within it.* Operating with respect to his or her own experience, the individual seeks to determine its *sincerity* or *truthfulness*: the subject-matter of depth psychotherapies. When interpretation is applied to the cultural sphere, the necessary currency of validation becomes the ability to make interpersonal determinations of 'appropriateness, justness, intersubjective mesh, and/or mutual understanding' (Walsh, 1996: 11). Both interior modes rely upon interpretation, but it is interpretation of two different sorts.

The hermeneutic lens is thus highly appropriate to the examination of intersubjective cultural meanings and local, interpersonal contexts: it is inherently an 'interior' focus, much as Cushman (1990) would like to suggest that cultural hermeneutics focus, in contrast to analytic therapies, on the exterior. Both psychoanalysis and cultural analysis utilize the hermeneutic method – the exploration of meaning *in depth.* The method is, in fact, the most appropriate one for the examination of subjectivity at the individual level, for the interior exploration of personal meanings, the undertaking at the very heart of psychoanalytic practice in its contemporary evolution. Regrettably, Cushman dismisses psychoanalysis's 'ideological' preoccupation with the nature of the subjective self at the individual (and theoretical) level, and blames analytic therapies for an objectifying and capitalistic trend that others have placed squarely at the feet of modernity's love affair with science.

For example, Rothberg (in Wilber, 1995) points out that an overheavy weighting of science to the detriment of art and morality reduced three essential domains of knowing to one, leading to postmodern crisis and criticism.

> The content of the other two worlds (the intersubjective [we] and subjective [I] worlds) was increasingly organized according to the structures of the empirical sciences and instrumental or calculative rationality; Habermas links this unbalanced development especially with the powerful influences of the forces of capitalism. (1995: 417)

Further, Cushman fails to acknowledge that both individual and cultural concerns with meaning and meaninglessness, wholeness and emptiness, interpenetrate in reciprocal directions. That is, cultural forces that drain meaning and constructive values from shared communal life may clearly foster individual experiences of dreaded emptiness. Reciprocally, individual attempts to cohere a stably meaningful sense of self within an internal *or* external worldspace of emptiness may arise from a deeper dilemma in subjectivity than the Western cultural 'romance' with self can account for alone. It would belie centuries of human inquiry across cultures to suggest that the search for self is a purely local cultural artifact, although the way this search manifests will surely take a local shape and colour. In particular, there arises the question of a more universal ontological dilemma: how are we to understand the existence of *a sense of self that is conscious in time and space where no distinction reliably or continuously exists between self and time/space*?

Here, the psychology and philosophy of consciousness flow together as a central human preoccupation. Ernest Becker is one of several philosophers of psychology whose interpretations of cultural concerns are sympathetic to Cushman's critiques, but which extend Cushman's line of inquiry into deeper ontological domains. For example, in his lauded 1973 work, *The Denial of Death*, Becker parses out twin ontological strivings from the welter of subjective and cultural life that closely echo Nietzsche's (cf. Mitchell, 1988: 194): the need to etch out an individual identity with the aggressive joy of erotic love, and the need to merge with the larger cosmos through self-surrender in *agape* love. The horror of emptiness and isolation propels individuals *and societies* toward a self-transcendent communion with the cosmos even as they must strive individually 'to stick out of nature and shine ...' (Becker, 1973: 153).

It can be seen that interpretations that collapse self and culture into a single domain (e.g., Wilber's (1995) cultural worldspace) – as in the statement '[t]here is no universal, transhistorical self, only local selves', (Cushman, 1990: 599) – also collapse the potential for local and universal principles to interlock and coexist. Such extreme deconstructionism obliterates thinking about underlying essences or patterns that may link disparate cultures and voices. A more useful perspective concedes the possibility that both relative and universal, constructed and essential truths may coexist with respect for their distinctions. Such a discriminating and perhaps paradoxical appreciation feels critically needed at this time, however much beyond our scope it may be to accurately perceive or verify universal principles, on the one hand, or to complete a thoroughgoing, contextual analysis of the cultural presumptions that colour our perceptions, on the other. In the upsurge of recent analytic interest in paradox, the continuing attempt in psychoanalysis to articulate between larger possibilities and patterns – including metaphysical ones – and the immediacy of personal and cultural realities appears both necessary and fruitful. Gergen (1994), for one, is optimistic that psychology may avert dogmatism in the name of postmodern discovery, and continue a relational interchange in which local realities and multiple voices interpenetrate.

In my opinion, Wilber's (1980, 1995) work succeeds in deconstructing 'hidden ideologies' that have permeated the histories of philosophy, psychology, the sciences and religion, while seeking to preserve and unify their underlying commonalities. In particular, he offers a view of cultural domains of meaning construction and individual domains of subjectivity as interlocking levels of multiple realities which, furthermore, include states of consciousness that *transcend* interior and exterior, self and other distinctions. We may thus consider states of psychic emptiness not merely as reflections of cultural breakdown or social dislocation, nor of psychic fragmentation, deadness or self-deficit. They may also reflect an inherent aspect of the spatial or trans-substantial nature of human consciousness which we in the West have little experience of tolerating, and about which we may have little understanding. Western psychology and psychoanalysis, evolving primarily within the scientific tradition of dualism and objectification of self and other – Wilber's rational, exterior modes of knowledge – tend to regard forms of emptiness as dreaded absences of identity. Except for a few early voices, psychoanalysis has historically spoken little about the possible generative connotations of psychic emptiness, or on non-pathological self-states and self-boundaries in which fluidity or permeability predominates. There are fewer words yet to suggest the possibility of an evolutionary relationship between a fluid, subjective, individual self-awareness in process of continuous creation and destruction, and an expanded numinous consciousness that inheres in immaterial dimensions of being. It is here that psychoanalysis fails in its depth of vision: while it cradles the pivotal emergence of human subjectivity in a richly textured bed of body and culture, it isolates the bedroom from the cosmos writ large. Even the most recent eloquent writers on what I will broadly refer to as 'spatial' experiences in psychoanalysis consistently interpret such states and their metaphors as repetitions of early (preverbal) affect categories (cf. Bollas, 1987; Modell, 1990; Ogden, 1994) belonging to the *structuring* of the psyche in development: pre-Oedipal, narcissistic, autistic-contiguous, etc.

It is my contention in this chapter that experiences of psychic space and their attendant qualities of emptiness, particularly those I am identifying as of a transcendent nature (expanding beyond or dissolving the separate 'I'-sense, the 'autonomous ego, the pristine inviolable self') are central to the creative process of mental life. Further, they can no longer be sufficiently studied in psychoanalysis only by the tracks they lay down in our internal representational world in the form of God-images, the truth value of which is outside of psychology's domain. The human need to symbolize and thus 'articulate the ineffable' (Muses, 1972), to keep the memory of awe near at hand, close to feeling and touch, increasingly enters psychoanalytic discourse as a viable ontological, rather than infantile, need. The study of our conscious and unconscious image- and meaning-making capacity, as well as of our meaning-splitting capacity, has brought psychology in general and psychoanalysis in particular, to the brink of a new phenomenology of consciousness: one that is capable of witnessing the construction and deconstruction of its own mind-forms, under conditions and in states that are significant alterations – but not necessarily aberrations – of ordinary consciousness.

State of Emptiness in Contemporary Psychoanalysis: The Role of Trauma

Psychoanalysis has long concerned itself with clinical manifestations of the 'empty self', a psychologically deadened or vacuous state. Freud (1917) linked such states to melancholic defences against aggressive impulses toward the lost object: 'In grief the world becomes poor and empty; in melancholia it is the ego itself' (1963: 167). Klein (1935, 1946) saw them as symptomatic of splitting defences, particularly projective identification, employed against annihilation anxiety and the operation of the death instinct:

> The feeling of being disintegrated, of being unable to experience emotions, of losing one's objects, is in fact the equivalent of anxiety ... At such moments it appears ... that when emotions were lacking, relations were vague and uncertain and parts of the personality were felt to be lost, everything seemed to be dead. (Mitchell, 1986: 196–7)

Kohut (1971, 1977) attributed states of emptiness to a core deficit in self-structure brought on by environmental failure: 'The patient will describe subtly experienced, yet pervasive feelings of emptiness and depression ... that he is not fully real, or at least that his emotions are dulled ...' (1971: 16), or ' ... a sense of separation of [his] self experience from [his] various physical and mental functions (1971: 128).

While all of these analytic formulations fail to acknowledge the destructive influence of larger social forces, Cushman's account of the empty self (1990) ignores the 'primitive agonies' and 'nameless dread' that often accompany these states of emptiness in the clinical setting. A sense of leakage or disintegration, a 'hollow' of uncertainty may pervade the individual, as Wrye (Wrye and Welles, 1994: 17) describes vividly:

> For many patients, experiences in space have been like a horrible black hole or hollow, threatening dispersion of self into an annihilating void, without containment, safety, or bodily integrity. Early unreliable contact ... may leave an individual 'high and dry' and 'lost in space,' or drowning ...

Along with or in place of such psychic disorientation can be a profound sense of deadness that, according to Eigen (1996), reflects not only minute splitting defences against anxiety but possible irrevocable damage to the capacity to create fluid *movement* between and through various psychic states, including states of emptiness.

> There can be not only the lack of capacity to generate, sustain, and process emotions but also the lack of capacity to sustain and process gaps, empty times, nothingness moments. Ideally, one is able to move between states, now full and now empty, using all the organ stops one can. But individuals get trapped by emptiness, or addicted to fullness, or wiped out by oscillations. (Eigen, 1996: 35)

Even more severe is the destruction of a sense of aliveness recounted in Bion's work. Eigen chillingly describes ' ... a force that goes on working after it destroys existence, time, and space', and that '*includes the destruction of anxiety and emptiness*. Obliterating states can be obliterated. There is no end to nulling' (1996: 35 emphasis added).

This stifling of movement, endless nulling or breakdown in the capacity to psychically alter states that have become hollowed out, frozen or rigid, often triggers urgent manoeuvres to sharpen the edges that distinguish inner from outer, aliveness from deadness, frantic efforts to give the self an outline in the hollow terror of formlessness. Anzieu (1989), Bick (1988) and Ogden (1989) provide acutely tuned observations on this defensive effort to utilize a 'muscular shell or a corresponding verbal muscularity' to establish a 'second skin' (Bick, 1988: 190) when the psyche fails to constitute or reliably maintain a primary sense of self-boundedness. One cannot rest in the experience of being when threatened with a leakage into non-being or disintegration at the most fundamental level of self-sensory organization. Ogden (1989), following Winnicott, identifies this most primitive level of self-definition – that of the 'skin ego' (Anzieu, 1989) – as the earliest root of subjectivity and, in particular, as 'the beginnings of the feeling of "*a place where one lives*"' (Ogden, 1989: 53 emphasis added). Disruptions to this primary sense of containment leave psychic 'holes in the fabric of the "emergent self"' (Ogden, 1989: 52). That is, they leave the individual deeply insecure about having a stable *place* and *time* in which to locate his subjective experience.

Drawing a cultural parallel, Grosz (1994), in a fascinating and insightful work on social attributions toward bodily flows, ponders the relationship between fluidity and solidity as represented by the genders in what is desirable and what is 'abject' or disavowed. She wonders,

> Can it be that in the West, in our time, the female body has been constructed not only as a lack or absence but with more complexity, as a leaking, uncontrollable, seeping liquid; as formless flow; as viscosity, entrapping, secreting; as lacking not so much or simply the phallus but self-containment – not a cracked or porous vessel, like a leaking ship, but a formlessness that engulfs all form, a disorder that threatens all order? (1994: 203)

Grosz suggests that Western identity representations, based on a muscular model of the male, reflect a deep-seated fear of absorption, and thus the 'projection outward of (women's) corporealities, the liquidities that men seem to want to cast out of their own self-representations' (Grosz, 1994: 203). In this light, one can recognize not only the common clinical phenomenon of defensive hardening of psychic edges in response to diffusions in self-coherence, but also cultural reflections of a broader abhorrence of physical and psychic boundarilessness, for example, in the popular Western adoration of the hard, firm and well-defined body, or in the tendency of ethnic groups faced with the threat of inter-cultural mixing to fixate on narrow parameters in order to secure the boundaries of inclusion in and exclusion from the cultural identity (Volkan, 1995).

The splitting, freezing and rigidifying of the fluid interplay between states of consciousness, and between conscious and unconscious process, binds self-reflective action and severely impairs the mind's ability to construct and deconstruct symbolic forms, leading instead toward disintegration, emptiness and manic efforts at restoration (Klein, 1935). The capacity of the developing individual for the kind of transitional experiencing that allows for the establishment of permeable, rather than rigid, boundaries – the fluid interplay between internal and external, reality and fantasy, male and female – 'hinges on environmental support' (Eigen, 1996: 77), be it the environment provided by parent or *culture* or *cosmos*. That is, psychic fluidity relies on the expectancy that an Other can serve not only as an agent of self-transformation, but more importantly, as a *medium* of such (Winnicott, 1986, Bollas, 1987) when psychic states become static, repetitive, and tightly bounded, emptied of the capacity to reflectively digest or process experience. In chronic trauma, in particular, the dissociative isolation of sensation (Spiegel and Cardena, 1991), affect (van der Kolk, 1987), needs (Sands, 1994) and memory (Herman, 1992) profoundly disrupts the psyche's capacity to meaningfully orchestrate alternating states of self-awareness (Peoples, 1991).

At the latter extreme is the person with a multiple personality, who cannot negotiate between, empathize with or otherwise think about frozen self-states (Schwartz, 1994), because the *medium* for reflecting and sustaining awareness has been lost in the space in between, and space itself has become foreclosed. Often, the only means of effecting psychic movement from one state to another is to traumatically induce it. In severe cases, this breakdown in the psyche's fluidity must be literally written onto the body, onto the 'inscribing surface' (Anzieu, 1989: 40) of the skin: when even manic psychic manoeuvres to break out from one frozen identity and switch to another fail, again and again the skin surface becomes the prima materia upon which the individual goes to work, with knife or razor or hammer, to effect a transformation of a deadened psychic state. The manipulation of the soma and piercing of the concretized skin-ego is an urgent attempt to restore the fluidity that will kick-start creative symbolization, when psychic space has become an airless, immovable vacuum.

Therapists working with transsexual clients who have enacted perhaps the ultimate transformation of the psyche-soma, note their frequent piercing of the skin-ego in bizarre and creative ways, and observe their encapsulation in a deadened psychological space. This deadness may be heavily reinforced by lingering cultural perceptions of fixedness toward identity, especially toward the aspect of gender, which is increasingly understood in psychology to be relatively mutable, and socially constructed. The postmodern view in psychology is not at odds with a Winnicottian argument in favour of a measure of gender fluidity, for cultural room to 'play' with conceptions of gender identity, especially in light of constructionist analysis of gender. Sweetnam (1996) suggests that '*both* fixed *and* fluid experiences occur and ... they occur within the context of each other' (1996: 439), with respect to gender.

While processes of dissociative rigidity, concretization and loss of symbolic function are familiar to psychoanalytic clinicians working at the individual level, it is their collective implications that link deconstructionist views with the concerns of transpersonal theorists in the unfolding dialogue in psychoanalysis on the nature of self. Perhaps, as Cushman (1990, 1991) argues, the self is anything but unitary. But the pressing Western search for unity described so ably by Cushman signals a deep collective insecurity – *not merely a failure of culture* – about the mind's capacity to endure the loss of its objects and, more fundamentally, the loss of its stability in time and space. If an over-generalization can be permitted for the moment, the Western psyche displays a characteristic uneasiness in its relationship to the boundariless condition of formless space and fluid self-states, as Grosz (1994) contends. Embodying at once the most successful and most harmful elements of the positivist dream – the quest for control and mastery over the natural and cosmic realms – we appear increasingly discomfited by silence, stillness and emptiness, confusing them with deadness. Heavily materialistic and bereft not only of meaningful community rituals, but of unifying connections with nature and cosmos (Lifton, 1975) that contain and transform our fragmenting losses, we hurl ourselves with the urgency of the multiple toward a means to break into an open space of potentiality, where going-on-being may be restored. Here Cushman's criticisms find their precise mark.

Recontextualizing Emptiness: The Transcendent View

In contrast to the deadening emptiness and fragmentation processes so in the forefront of contemporary analytic thinking, and on the firing line of social constructionism, are alterations of psychic states that enhance an enlivened sense of meaning and connectedness with life while, paradoxically, rendering the internal object world less fixed and patterned, even 'emptied out'. Reported throughout the meditative literature from a remarkable range of cultures, are experiences in which the usual construction of identity or organization of self is dissolved or falls away, and self-awareness as a numinous emptiness that is full and effulgent, a conscious presence without personification, identity or location, appears.

Central to these states is the dissolution of key referents for *locating subjectivity in time and space*. While subjectivity is not destroyed *per se*, it is not anchored to objects internal or external, nor to the flow of objective temporality. In particular, the core self-sense of 'I-ness' is radically undone, while agency nonetheless remains intact, yet depersonified. In such states, referred to as 'samadhi' in both the Hindu and Buddhist traditions, the psychic energy that, in a habitual and pre-reflective manner, has been sustaining the continuity of internal and external representations is loosened, radically undoing their structured patterning, at least temporarily (Epstein, 1986, 1988, 1995; Suler, 1993; Wilber *et al.*, 1986). The result is often a much diminished power of representations to captivate the mind; conscious, preconscious and unconscious representations become more accessible and transparent to observation, and thus to diffusion.

This is not unlike the effect psychoanalytic treatment can have upon unconscious complexes and identity fixations, but its consequences are more far-reaching. What distinguishes psychoanalytic aims from those such as meditation or spontaneous transcendent experiences (Segal, 1996) that bring about this type of emptiness is that the very premise of identity as a solid or enduring structure is undercut. The deconstruction of the self goes far beyond the bounds to which Gergen, Cushman and other postmodern writers venture. For it is not just the sense of psychic unity or continuity that is undercut; the entire prereflective premise of the sensory and conceptual world as solid or stable is shaken. (See Brown: 219–83, in Wilber *et al.*, 1986, for a detailed review of the more extreme stages of perceptual deconstruction that occur in certain meditative practices.)

With repeated experiences of this type, structures of psyche, of identity, of time and of internal objects appear increasingly transparent against the greater backdrop, or backlight – if you will – of the boundariless awareness that informs them. In its most rarefied manifestations known as sahaj samadhi (Wilber, 1995), the subtle distinctions between observer and observed are dissolved into a state of profound openness:

> No objects, no subjects, only this. No entering this state, no leaving it; it is absolutely and eternally and always already the case: the simple feeling of being, the basic and simple immediacy of any and all states, prior to ... the split between inside and outside, prior to seer and seen, ... ever-present as pure Presence ... empty awareness as the opening or clearing in which all worlds arise, ceaselessly ... (Wilber, 1995: 309–10)

Familiar to every culture and carried through time by poets and sages, this 'emptiness of I' is neither strictly situational, nor strictly historical, but appears as both an essential *process* and an integral *condition* of human consciousness. While infant and ethological research suggests strongly that primate – especially human – brains are pre-wired to organize perceptual fields into patterns and 'islands of consistency' when provided appropriate environmental opportunities (Acredolo and Hake, 1982; Schwartz and Rosenblum, 1982; Stern, 1985), voluminous amounts of meditation research attest to the possibility of redirecting, even unravelling, this innate neural organizing tendency (cf., Wilber *et al.*, 1986). When the focus of concentrated attention is shifted from the foreground of apparently solid objects, ideas and events and allowed to diffuse, to rest (as it were) on the background cracks in time and space, one begins to see a mind – and a world – in a ceaseless flux that can be deeply unnerving. As Anzieu (1989: 38) remarks: 'Every figure presupposes a background against which it appears as a figure: this elementary truth is easily forgotten, for our attention is normally attracted by the figure which emerges and not by the background from which it detaches itself.'

Disintegration vs. Unintegration

Perhaps the key distinction between states of emptiness of the sort Cushman describes, those coloured by dread or deadness, and states of creative or transcendent emptiness, lies in the distinction between disintegration and unintegration. The former destroys meaning and the capacity to create it, while the latter allows for the nascent metamorphosis of meaning. Winnicott was one of the first in the analytic field to make this distinction, emphasizing the need for a 'non-purposive state ... of formlessness' (in Eigen, 1996: 79) in which new experience might arise.

Arriving at a similar understanding from a different starting point, Loewald (1980) is one of the few psychoanalytic writers until the recent decade to elaborate this distinction in terms strikingly similar to accounts in the meditation literature. Noting the common suspension of time-sense in the experience of both types of emptiness, he writes:

> At one extreme is the experience of eternity where the flux of time is stayed or suspended ... At the other pole of time is the experience of fragmentation, where one's world is in bits and pieces none of which have any meaning ... While in the experience of eternity – which objectively may last only for a small fraction of time – temporal relations have vanished into a unity which abolishes time, *in the experience of fragmentation time has been abolished in the annihilation of connectedness.* (1980: 142; emphasis added)

On a collective level, the human story includes an intimate tracing of 'ruptures of the ordinary' (Eliade, 1959), *generative* rather than disintegrative experiences of the needed (if temporary) dissolution of psychic, somatic, personal and non-personal boundaries. Many of these experiences of generative boundary loss are well researched in psychology and psychoanalysis; for instance, the powerful absorptive pull of romantic love, or the infant's (presumed) psychic immersion into and at-one-ment with maternal holding. At the cultural level, rituals for the dramatic enactment of breakdown and dissolution – even dismemberment – and restoration have been played out for centuries. The experience of being undone, then recohered, facilitates confidence in one's psychic medium, faith in the fluid forming and reforming of various self-states. Generative disruptions restore hope in the escape from entrapment, in the finding again of *self-movement with self-awareness.*

The relief in restored movement evokes in us, according to Bollas (1987), feelings of supplication and the wish to surrender to that 'transformational other' as if to a god. Psychoanalysis has traditionally taught that the intense co-minglings of wonder and gratitude this god-parent evokes for its power to unbind and reorganize us are at the root of later-life experiences of religious awe and aesthetic appreciation. Bollas notes, importantly, that such 'aesthetic moments' are 'registered through being rather than mind' (1987: 32; emphasis added).

I could not agree more with Bollas's contention, for it is the distinction between consciousness of *being* and *structures* of mind that is the hallmark of aesthetic or transcendent moments. However, Bollas treats these in a fashion characteristic of psychoanalysis, signifying them as vestiges of the infantile unconscious. In contrast, Ghent (1990: 17) suggests there may be 'something like a universal need, wish or longing for surrender' of self-boundaries. He wonders whether its deflection or repression *culturally* may surface in the familiar dread of annihilation seen clinically. For it is the surrender of self-control under an attitude of faith that opens the way for the moment in which time, space and identity may be unbound. The healthy longing for surrender that reveals its shadow side in masochistic submission reflects, according to Ghent (1990) 'a hope for unfreezing', for being released from psychic emptiness and deadness that have held one static and unmoving for too long.

The crucial question as to whether breakups in solidified self-states lead to defensive dissociation, the hardening of a psychic shell and interior deadness or to a heightened state of enlivened presence is dependent at the *individual* level on the psychic and somatic relationship between the *contents* of the body-mind, the *experience* of the body-mind as distinct from its contents, and *awareness* of the capacity to flexibly navigate between the two. This capacity for flexibility is, in turn, dependent upon fluidity and receptivity at intersubjective and collective cultural levels as well. Identity constructs cannot become permeable, safely surrendered and reworked when the unknown space of the unconscious, or the collective space of the cultural consciousness, freezes the interplay of different selves and voices.

A radically deconstructed universe threatens to unhinge what infant researchers like Stern (1985) (another of Cushman's (1991) targets of romantic ideology) define as the core somatic self, the feeling of being subjectively situated or seated in a bounded bodily locus of time and space. More profound than the temblor stirred by experiences of physical or emotional helplessness is the need to depend on our ability to establish a coherent and consistent perceptual universe. Flying in the face of this boundedness, the transsexual noted above serves as a scribe for the culture, writing in bold strokes on his skin a collective dilemma about Grosz's 'formless flow' (1994), embodying both the fear and the yearning to disassemble, deconstruct and re-make the self. The skin-piercer walks into our fearful uncertainty of psychic survival in the boundariless states to which disassembling leads us. This uncertainty, felt in the roots of our hair standing on end, reflects a crisis in faith, a fear that creative life will not be resurrected and restored in the aftermath of the dissolution of form. What is it that enables a Kierkegaard or a William James, faced with the terror of the void, to withstand their withering uncertainty of self in the vast space of an empty cosmos? To find a presence in the seeming absence of the void?

While psychoanalysis is intimately familiar with the fears that arise for the analysand as he lies back on the couch, faced with the surrender of secondary process thought to the primary process of the unconscious, as well as to the mind of the analyst, it is much less familiar with the kind of surrender I am attempting to describe here. Psychoanalysis continually presses the boundaries and limits, as it were, to explore the dimensions of the unknown and the 'unthought known' (Bollas, 1987) realms of psychic life, to forge pathways between the incommunicado and the symbolizable, to reach forward into the ineffable. Nonetheless, psychoanalysis remains primarily preoccupied with the workings of unconscious *fantasy*, with *structures* of the mind. In contrast, the profound surrender or shattering of self organization in both traumatic and transcendent states illuminates the spaces of silence between the mind's incessant workings, to the 'elementary truth' of the mind's silent background space: '... [n]ot known, because not looked for But heard, half-heard, in the stillness Between two waves of the sea' (Eliot, 1971: 59). Is this background the potential space of the prereflective, infantile mind in all of us, acquiring an emergent sense of safety in the soft contiguity of sensation and being, as Ogden (1989) suggests? Or is this potentially a reflective space that contains *but is not identical to* the currents, rhythms and dim shapes within it, closer to what theologian Paul Tillich (1967) has called 'the ground of being'? (See Segal, 1996 for a powerful personal account.) Where contemplative awareness can be brought to bear on the dissolute, in the analytic encounter even the most primitive workings of mind may begin to yield, to reveal this 'ground' Tillich speaks of. In such moments, the ordinary boundaries of the clinical hour become the guardian of a liminal or sacred process that transforms both participants in it.

Bion (1977a, 1977b), in his reflections on 'O', and Loewald (1980), in his essays on time and memory, might be considered the forerunners of contemporary psychoanalytic thinking on self-transcendent states. Both writers speak to states of being that are distinct from the internal representation and registration of phenomena. Rothenberg (1997) draws elegant, insightful parallels between Loewald's conceptions of psychic time and space and Judaic holy texts on the animated and permeable nature of past–present–future, and of self–other–God. Loewald's own words beautifully capture the distinction between psychic dissolutions that *give rise* to meaning (i.e., creative symbolization) from the fragmentation of time and structure into meaningless emptiness. Loewald (1980: 144–5) states:

> In the experience of fragmentation the reciprocal relationship between past, present, and future, taken as active agents, is broken, and the three words no longer carry meaning. What is experienced is a meaningless now, not a present as element in a temporal context. In the experience of eternity that context is not broken up but ceases to exist as a nexus by virtue of a fusion of its elements into a unitary now. *This now does not lose but overflows its meaning*, goes beyond meaning in the accepted sense in which meaning comes into being by connections, linkings between elements. (emphasis added)

Whereas Bollas (1987) sees such unitive moments as an *illusion* of fitting with an object, it is actually the separateness or independent nature of the self that is recognized to be a powerful illusion in the transcendent moment. Bion (1977a) stymies analytic efforts to collapse such transcendent moments into infantile states of mind. He emphasizes the need for the *analyst* to surrender herself to a state of receptivity in which memory and desire – that is, mental objects or structures – are suspended, and in which the focus of attention is on O, 'the unknown and unknowable', a condition the analyst must '*be*' (1977a: 27). On this difficult task Bion muses:

> It may be wondered what state of mind is welcome if desires and memories are not. A term that would express approximately what I need to express is 'faith' – faith that there is an ultimate reality and truth – the unknown, unknowable, 'formless infinite' ... The *objects* of awareness are aspects of the 'evolved' O ... For them faith is not required; for O it is. (1977a: 31; emphasis added)

Bion extends psychoanalytic inquiry into domains that many consider to border on the mystical, denoting O to be 'that which is the ultimate reality, absolute truth, the godhead, the infinite, the thing-in-itself ... *It is darkness and formlessness* ...' (Bion, 1977a: 26,;emphasis added).

In a contemporary extension of the ideas of Winnicott, Loewald, Bion and Lacan, Michael Eigen (1981, 1992, 1996) seeks to chart a course between 'different *orders* of experience' and the *objects* of those experiences. He distinguishes the objects of creative experiencing or idealization from the 'radical encounter with what is the primary quality of experiencing as such: its *intangibility* and *immateriality*' (1981: 430; emphasis added). Like others before him, Eigen (1981) argues that the human capacity for transitional *experiencing* should not be conflated with early infantile *objects* or *stages* of development. Addressing the problem of equating God with father, as in Freud, or with mother, as in Klein, Eigen (1981) acknowledges the complex task with which patients and analysts are faced in distinguishing infantile object representations, endowed as they are with omnipotent fantasy, from experiences that reflect subtle, non-regressive states of self-transcendent consciousness.

Numerous transpersonal theorists have tackled this challenging task of discrimination in recent years (cf. Almaas, 1996; Epstein, 1986, 1988; Peoples and Parlee, 1991; Suler, 1993; Vaughan, 1995; Wilber, 1980, 1995; Wilber *et al.*, 1986). The most prolific and comprehensive of these has been Wilber (1995) in his critical discourses on the way *pre*egoic (i.e., prereflective, infantile) states of merger have been conflated with *trans*egoic (self-reflective) states of boundarilessness. The difficulty in making this discrimination lands us squarely in the arena of paradox that so holds our attention in the post-Freudian analytic century and at the end of this millennium. Central to this issue is the supposition I am offering here, in agreement with Eigen, Winnicott and Bion, that a superordinate, indeterminate and inherent quality of being suffuses psychic life, one that both substands, gives shape to and paradoxically transcends the symbolic contents within it, and that is, by definition, the ground in which transformations occur in consciousness and in the unconscious. This 'area of faith', states Eigen, 'is expressive of a primary creative process *at the* *origin* of symbolic experience and is itself a vehicle for creative experiencing' (Eigen, 1981: 414; emphasis added). A transitional state in which internal attributions and their linkages to external objects are fluidly created, discovered and dissolved, it exists as an enduring and ever-maturing capacity in consciousness, according to Eigen and Wilber. While it may be analogous to the infant's transitional experience in potential space first described by Winnicott (1971), it continually surfaces at higher turns of the developmental spiral (Washburn, 1988, 1996) when self-reflective disidentification from introjects replaces preconscious identifications and fragmenting dissociative processes. Referred to as the 'witness consciousness' (Epstein, 1986; Wilber, 1986) it is a more highly developed and refined cousin to the observing ego capacity that emerges in effective psychoanalytic treatment (cf. Rubin, 1985), and it entails a conscious flexible capacity to track the barely perceptible movements in consciousness (and preconsciousness) that signal identification with or disidentification from perceptions, cognitions, affects, and other psychic structures.[1] Identification, according to Bion, actually excludes the state of being in O: 'Being identified with ... (O) is a measure of distance from it' (1977b: 140).

In this heightened state of 'witnessing' referred to earlier as 'meta-awareness' the experience of psychic spaciousness begins to open up as a generative universe of mind. It is here, paradoxically, that both the unitary and multiple nature of self-identity, of continuity within discontinuity and non-duality within duality, can be discovered with astonishment as something new and yet already known, something continually coming into being and yet dissolving. From this ground the seer and shaman, the mystic and poet speak, at the centre of what is neither creation nor uncreation. The eleventh-century Zen master, poet and philosopher Dogen wrote with great eloquence about this difficult state to articulate:

> Truth is perfect and complete in itself. It is not something newly discovered; it has always existed. Truth is not far away. It is nearer than near. ... For the place, the way, is neither large nor small, neither self nor other. It has never existed before, and it is not coming into existence now. It is simply as it is. (Mitchell, 1991: 98–9)

Liminality and Ritual: Culture as Potential Space for Emptiness

Attempts to identify similarities between industrial Western cultures and non-industrial cultures, as hermeneutic writers point out, is a dangerous if not impossible game. Possibilities for misinterpretation, not to mention romanticization, are rife. Yet discriminating scholars studying the comparative rituals of tribal cultures with highly developed sacred cosmologies – for example, the Tibetan and the Navajo (Gold, 1994) – have consistently recognized the use of initiatory ritual to serve the initiate's passage into and out of liminal or threshold (transitional) states. During such rituals, the unique function of the tribe's shaman or 'seer' is as an adept navigator in as well as a vessel of this potential, transformative space, crossing to and fro the invisible threshold between the seen and the unseen, material and immaterial, the known worlds and the unknown. This is the liminal individual appearing in every culture; in some to be revered, in others feared and marginalized (cf. Schapira, 1988).

The traditional shaman, in order to serve as such a vessel, typically must surrender to states of psychic dismemberment, destruction and death – i.e., *trauma* – often symbolized by a visionary breaking of bones in a charnel ground (Halifax, 1982). Here, a ritual deconstruction of identity and contiguity – *of self in relation to the ordinary nexus of time, space and bodily boundaries* – occurs as the visionary healer surrenders to being 'emptied' of frame of reference and point of view, and intentionally invokes liminality, the crossing of a threshold – i.e., through the alteration of ordinary consciousness into states of intense absorption via prayer, meditation, ritual ceremony, dance, and/or ingestion of psychoactive plants.

Such occasions of surrender, invocation and meditative absorption, carried out throughout human history, announce and inscribe in collective consciousness a human relationship to the natural universe as transitional or 'liminal' experience itself (Eliade, 1959). They establish an 'I–Thou' form of relatedness (Jones, 1991, following Buber) with a larger order, in which the 'I' and the 'Thou' stand in a paradox of identical and separate natures toward each other, and in which Eros and Agape are in harmony rather than conflict.

Becker (1975) has observed that ritual, in Western as well as non-Western cultures, has historically served the apotheosis, initiation and sacralization of the human being, connecting the individual with the cosmos for his mirror, expanding the limited reflections offered up in the glass of mundane eyes. Ritual creates the conditions by which a hierophany may present itself: that is, a rupture in the seeming seamlessness of profane or ordinary time and space, through which the numinous may flow (Eliade, 1959). Ruptures of ordinary space, like the crevice in the ground at Delphi out of which oracular wisdom is said to have poured (Schapira, 1988), are paradoxical: they reveal to the culture an extra-ordinary phenomenon, one that stands uncannily outside of ordinary time and space even as it exists simultaneously in mundane form, such as a rock, tree or mountain.

As with Winnicott's baby, we do not ask the seer or shaman: 'was the cosmos revealed to you or did you create it? Did you discover this sacred opening here, or did you make it?' Throughout millennia, human cultures have practised rituals for entering and exiting the liminal. States of surrender appear crucial to this process: we are not free to choose the sacred site, yet we can at times evoke it through acceptance of our lack of dominance over the very cycles of creation and destruction that mark our initiation into a new psychic order. Surrender appears central to helping create the conditions for the 'breaking through' of the Real, that 'endlessly daunting power which supersedes the already very considerable power ... [of] the Symbolic' (Bowie, 1991: 95), as Lacan meant the Real, in all its chaos and disorder, its ineffability and unpredictability. And as Ghent (1991) has so poignantly elaborated, submission may become an obsessively ritualized pathway in the search for a transformative surrender.

Passages through and into liminal space are often of such intensity they carry parallels to psychic trauma: fragmenting, disassembling and disorienting familiar landmarks of habitual identity structures, and opening the way for a new emergence of being. The passage is typically – perhaps necessarily – overwhelming. It temporarily breaks apart the traveller's vessel, no less so for the analyst than for the shaman. 'God is a trauma', Mogenson (1989) suggests, because the ruptures of ordinary time–space not only rend the fabric of the known and familiar, but – more importantly – upend for the moment the one capacity by which we distinguish ourselves as *human* beings: the capacity to symbolize.

One can suddenly be thrown into transitional, liminal states by such ruptures and, at the same time, be stripped of one's capacity to create meaning in this new space. In this sense, liminal space (Schwartz-Salant and Stein, 1991) seems very similar to the primitive, presymbolic 'autistic-contiguous' position of the infant mind (Ogden, 1989). For this reason, perhaps, in the aftermath of surviving an intense rupture of ordinary reality – such as a close brush with death – the return of the symbolic often ushers with it *both* grandiose (i.e., regressive) self-inflation *and* generative self-transcending insight into the fluid, insubstantial or permeable quality of identity.

This paradox is beautifully portrayed by Jeff Bridges in the film *Fearless*. Descending toward a certain crash with other passengers and crew in a jumbo jet, Bridges is hurled into a trance-like state of terror in which he is shattered by, then profoundly surrenders to, the immanent inevitability of his death. Before the plane ever hits the ground, Bridges psychically dies, enters liminal space, then is restored deeply changed. Walking from the wreckage unhurt, in a state of awe that he has undergone and survived the destruction of his mind, Bridges gains a completely new, and fresh, lived experience of his world. Old identity patterns and behaviours spawned by fear, such as a lethal allergic reaction to strawberries, tangibly, physically evaporate as a result of having survived this death of self in his own mind. At the same time, Bridges is traumatically dissociated from the ordinary, and his transcendent state is interwoven with an inflated, grandiose encapsulation.

A culture's ability to maintain and safely steward *ritual deconstruction*, rather than traumatic destruction, appears to be an essential means by which a society may attempt to commune with the borders of the Real, the chaotic, the ineffable, and by so doing gain facility in traversing the connection to the symbolic realm. Rituals are, of course, problematic: they easily become formalized, rote and deadened, truly empty of vitality and spontaneity. Properly stewarded ritual space (Moore, 1991) provides both the freedom to explore states of unintegration and formlessness, along with containment of the processes of destruction and deconstruction. The degree to which an individual, or a culture, lacks such ritual space appears correlated to the degree to which rigid dynamics of domination and submission hold sway (Peoples, 1992). In the fear of being overwhelmed by the numinous power of the unconscious or transcendent consciousness in boundariless space, tendencies toward dissociation and omnipotent control replace the here-and-now immanence that refined self-reflective awareness can bring.

It would be as misguided to idealize such paradoxical states of emptiness or selflessness as it has been to idealize modernity's notions of certainty and truth. Rubin (1994) and Spezzano (1994), for example, critique the way in which Winnicott's reflections on paradox and transitional experiencing have become romanticized and reified in the analytic literature. Nonetheless, both within and outside of psychoanalysis there is overwhelming evidence of a type of radical psychic deconstructing of a non-psychotic, non-fragmenting nature that presses for our serious attention, even as we wrestle with vexing concerns about its idealization, on the one hand, or devaluation on the other. A number of analytic writers have pointed out that, with respect to the postmodern view, the slippery, indeterminate nature of unity and multiplicity of self, and of local (cultural) and universal (essential) truths, can be engaged without a collapse into nihilistic rumination. Elliott and Spezzano, in Chapter 1 of this book, emphasize that the decentring of individual identity from its pedestal 'should not be equated with a disintegration of the human subject. The criticism that the postmodernist decentring of selves amounts to a wiping out of subjectivity is perhaps better seen as a defensive reaction to the dislocation of modernist fantasies of self-control and mastery' (p. 28).

Is the division between psyche and cosmos, a vestige of which psychoanalysis has clung to since its early strivings for scientific legitimacy, intrinsic? Is it mere hubris to contemplate an untangling of our narcissistic propensities toward omnipotent self-inflation and self-reification from a relationship to consciousness that transcends static identifications in time and space? If liminal or ritual space can be a containing ground through which both individual and culture may constructively 'play' with the creation and destruction of forms of identity, as suggested here, then how is the liminal to be engaged or recognized in psychoanalysis – and in the culture – especially if, like sacred space, it cannot be willed, and must not be imposed? It appears that in the consulting room, as Bion (1977a) urges, the therapist's self-surrender is essential to the potentiality of liminal space coming into being, if it is to arrive at all (cf., Alifano, 1995). Respect is essential to the safe containment of the tremendous potency of the numinous. As Moore (1991: 17) notes, '… the establishment and maintenance of the boundaries of a sacred space … is the sine qua non for a proper relationship to sacred space and the primary condition for being benefitted and not harmed by contact with it'. Similarly, Modell (1990) draws a parallel between the ritual space of the shaman and the demarcated frame of the psychoanalyst as a ground set apart from the ordinary, in which transitional or liminal experiencing – the interplay of multiple levels of reality – can occur.

As therapists and psychoanalysts in Western culture, it is perhaps our dearth of well-stewarded collective rituals that have brought so much psychoanalytic thinking to bear on the intimate ritual of the analytic space. It is also, perhaps, our relative 'emptiness' as a culture of opportunities for communion with the liminal that bolster Cushman's call for the restoration of meaningful rituals and traditions in the context of community. There is a clear need for balance to the 'interiority' of the therapeutic focus by applying psychoanalytic knowledge and skills to the larger social conditions that generate the dreadful emptiness and psychic deadness from which so many suffer. We are seeing this to some extent in psychological responses to societal traumas – cultural 'ruptures of the ordinary'. Yet such 'exterior' measures would surely fail if the search (frequently through the contemporary ritual of psychotherapy) for a fluid and presenced 'interior' space of awareness is devalued by deconstructionist polemics.

Unnervingly, deconstructive hermeneutics dismantle cherished modern ideas of self that are deeply ingrained in Western consciousness. Similarly, information filters to the West from cultures that have radically different views on the nature of the self. Postmodern discoveries in physics continually redefine our understanding of material and immaterial dimensions to our universe. All of these test the resiliency of Western consciousness to stretch itself, to tolerate the break-up of familiar personal – and core *cultural* – presumptions of the unity and solidity of identity. With fuller cross-cultural and multi-disciplinary dialogues, there is perhaps an 'area of faith' that can be carefully carved away from idealization and illusion, and from which Western psychoanalysts might better observe and understand the often terrifying, often awe-inspiring experience of boundary dissolution and transcendent emptiness without presuming it reflects the emergence of or regression to primitive, infantile states of consciousness.

Continuing the quest to comprehend the relationship of psychic forms and formlessness, of identities and space, of continuities and discontinuities in the material and psychic realms, may give rise to a faith in the reflective awareness that seems to be our uniquely human gift and curse: our self-reflective awareness. The very awareness that we are aware may give us a 'purchase' (however ephemeral) in emptiness that is neither purely absolute nor simply relative, but – like the sage Ramakrishna – dances in the 'not-two'-ness (Hixon, 1992). Perhaps we may thus ride through the end of the millenium and the decades that follow with a modest easing of the fear, culturally and individually, that primes the West's excessive Eros drive toward individuation, isolation and boundedness. With greater balancing awareness of the shifting, multiple, situational vagaries of identity, and increasing faith in the spaciousness of direct awareness, perhaps greater compassion for the fragile – and precious – impermanence of all forms, including our own, may slowly begin to arise.

Note

1. This emphasis on healthy disidentification is not meant as support for detachment or disconnection. Rather, the capacity for disidentification discussed above typically enhances, rather than undermines, a quality of enlivened engagement with the world. Clinically, it is often difficult, especially for the traditionally trained analyst unfamiliar with the varieties of meditative experience, to help patients distinguish subtle dissociations from healthy disidentification. Rubin (1997) provides a valuable in-depth case example toward this end.

References

Acredolo, L. and Hake, J. (1982), 'Infant perception', in B. Wolman (ed.), *Handbook of Developmental Psychology*, New Jersey: Prentice-Hall, Inc.

Alifano, R. (1995), 'Empathic surrender from the perspective of the therapist: a phenomenological investigation', Doctoral dissertation at the California Institute of Integral Studies, *Dissertation Abstracts International, 95*, 20990.

Almaas, A.H. (1986), *The Void: A Psychodynamic Investigation of the Relationship Between Mind and Space*, Berkeley, CA: Diamond Books.

— (1996), *The Point of Existence: Transformations of Narcissism in Self-realization*, Berkeley, CA: Diamond Books.

Anzieu, D. (1989), 'The notion of the skin ego', in *The Skin Ego*, New Haven, CT: Yale University Press.

Becker, E. (1973), *The Denial of Death*, New York: The Free Press.

— (1975), *Escape From Evil*, New York: The Free Press.

Bick, E. (1988), 'The experience of the skin in early object-relations', in E. Bott Spillius (ed.), *Melanie Klein Today*, Vol. 1, London: Routledge.

Bion, W.R. (1977a), 'Attention and interpretation', in *Seven Servants*, New York: Jason Aronson.

— (1977b), 'Transformations', in *Seven Servants*, New York: Jason Aronson.

Bollas, C. (1987), *The Shadow of the Object*, New York: Columbia University Press.

— (1989), *Forces of Destiny*, Northvale, NJ: Jason Aronson.

Bowie, M. (1991), 'Symbolic, imaginary, real ... and true', in *Lacan*, Cambridge, MA: Harvard University Press, pp. 88–121.

Bromberg, P. (1994), 'Speak! That I may see you. Some reflections on dissociation, reality, and psychoanalytic listening', *Psychoanalytic Dialogues* 4 (4): 517–47.

Brown, D. (1986), 'The stages of meditation in cross-cultural perspective' in Wilber, K., Engler, J. and Brown, D., *Transformations of Consciousness*, Boston: New Science Library, pp. 219–83.

Cushman, P. (1990), 'Why the self is empty', *American Psychologist* 45 (5): 599–611.

— (1991), 'Ideology obscured: political uses of the self in Daniel Stern's infant', *American Psychologist* 46 (3): 206–19.

— (1995), 'Hermeneutics, history, and the present psychoanalytic moment', *Fort da* 1 (1): 20–2.

— (1996), 'More surprises, less certainty: Commentary on Roland's paper', *Psychoanalytic Dialogues* 6 (4): 477–88.

Deikman, A. (1982), *The Observing Self: Mysticism and Psychotherapy*, Boston: Beacon Press.

Eigen, M. (1981), 'The area of faith in Winnicott, Lacan and Bion', *International Journal of Psychoanalysis* 62: 413–33.

— (1992), *Coming Through the Whirlwind*, Wilmette, IL: Chiron Publications.

— (1996), *Psychic Deadness*, New Jersey: Jason Aronson, Inc.

Eliade, M. (1959), *The Sacred and the Profane*, translated by Willard R. Trask, New York: Harcourt Brace Jovanovich, Inc.

Eliot, T.S. (1971) [1943], *The Four Quartets*, New York: Harcourt, Brace & World, Inc.

Epstein, M. (1986), 'Meditative transformations of narcissism', *Journal of Transpersonal Psychology* 18 (2): 143–58.

— (1988), 'The deconstruction of the self: ego and "egolessness" in Buddhist insight meditation', *Journal of Transpersonal Psychology* 20 (1): 61–70.

— (1995), *Thoughts Without a Thinker*, New York: Basic Books.

Freud, S. (1963) [1917], 'Mourning and melancholia', in P. Rieff (ed.), *General Psychological Theory: Papers on Metapsychology*, New York: Collier Books, pp. 164–79.

Gergen, K. (1994), 'Exploring the postmodern: perils or potentials?', *American Psychologist* 49 (5): 412–16.

Ghent, E. (1990), 'Masochism, submission, surrender', *Contemporary Psychoanalysis* 26 (1): 108–36. [Quote from prepublication draft: 17]

Gold, P. (1994), *Navajo and Tibetan Sacred Wisdom: The Circle of the Spirit*, Rochester, VT: Inner Traditions.

Grosz, E. (1994), 'Sexed bodies', in *Volatile Bodies*, Bloomington and Indianapolis: Indiana University Press.

Halifax, J. (1982), *Shaman: The Wounded Healer*, London: Thames and Hudson Ltd.

Herman, J. (1992), *Trauma and Recovery*, New York: Basic Books.

Hixon, L. (1992), *Great Swan*, Boston, MA: Shambhala Publications, Inc.

Jones, J. (1991), *Contemporary Psychoanalysis and Religion: Transference and Transcendence*, New Haven, CT: Yale University Press.

Klein, M. (1935), 'A contribution to the psychogenesis of manic-depressive states', *International Journal of Psycho-analysis* 12: 145–74.

— (1946), 'Notes on some schizoid mechanisms', *International Journal of Psycho-analysis* 27: 99–110.

Kohut, H. (1971), *The Analysis of the Self*, New York: International Universities Press.
— (1977), *The Restoration of the Self*, New York: International Universities Press.
Lifton, R.J. (1975), 'On death and the continuity of life: a psychohistorical perspective', *Omega* 6 (2): 143–59.
Loewald, H. (1980), *Papers on Psychoanalysis*, New Haven, CT: Yale University Press.
Mitchell, J. (ed.) (1986), *The Selected Melanie Klein*, New York: The Free Press.
Mitchell, S. (1991), *The Enlightened Mind*, New York: HarperCollins Publishers.
Mitchell, S.A. (1988), 'The wings of Icarus', in *Relational Concepts in Psychoanalysis*, Cambridge, MA: Harvard University Press.
— (1993), *Hope and Dread in Psychoanalysis*, New York: Basic Books.
Modell, A. (1990), *Other Times, Other Realities: Toward a Theory of Psychoanalytic Treatment*, Cambridge, MA: Harvard University Press.
Mogenson, G. (1989), *God is a Trauma*, Dallas, TX: Spring Publications.
Moore, R. (1991), 'Ritual, sacred space, and healing: the psychoanalyst as ritual elder', in Schwartz-Salant, N. and Stein, M. (eds), *Liminality and Transitional Phenomena*, Wilmette, IL: Chiron Publications.
Muses, C. (1972), *Consciousness and Reality*, New York: Outerbridge & Lazard.
Ogden, T. (1989), *The Primitive Edge of Experience*, Northvale, NJ: Jason Aronson.
— (1994), *Subjects of Analysis*, Northvale, NJ: Jason Aronson.
Peoples, K. (1991), 'The trauma of incest', in *The Evolution of Self Psychology*, Hillsdale, NJ: Analytic Press.
— (1992), 'Unconscious dominance and submission: internal gender politics of trauma', paper presented to the American Psychological Association, Mini-Convention on Consciousness, Washington, DC.
— and Parlee, B. (1991), 'The ego revisited: understanding and transcending narcissism', *Journal of Humanistic Psychology* 31 (4): 32–52.
Rivera, M. (1989), 'Linking the psychological and the social: Feminism, poststructuralism and multiple personality', *Dissociation* 2 (1): 24–31.
Rothenberg, D. (1997), 'Formulation, psychic space and time: new dimensions in psychoanalysis and Jewish spirituality', in *The soul on the couch*, Hillsdale, NJ: Analytic Press.

— (1994), 'Does the true self really exist: a critique of Winnicott's true self concept', unpublished manuscript.

— (1985), 'Meditation and psychoanalytic listening', *Psychoanalytic Review* 72 (4): 599–613.

Rubin, J. (1997), 'Psychoanalysis is self-centered', in *The Soul on the Couch*, Hillsdale, NJ: Analytic Press.

Sands, S. (1994), 'What is dissociated?', *Dissociation* 7 (3): 145–52.

Schapira, L. (1988), *The Cassandra Complex: A Modern Perspective on Hysteria*, Toronto, Canada: Inner City Books.

Schwartz, G. and Rosenblum, L. (1982), 'Primate infancy: problems and developmental strategies', in B. Wolman (ed.), *Handbook of Developmental Psychology*, New Jersey: Prentice-Hall, Inc.

Schwartz, H. (1994), 'From dissociation to negotiation: a relational psychoanalytic perspective on multiple personality disorder', *Psychoanalytic Psychology* 11 (2): 189–231.

Schwartz-Salant, N. and Stein, M. (eds) (1991), *Liminality and Transitional Phenomena*, Wilmette, IL: Chiron Publications.

Segal, S. (1996), *Collision with the Infinite: A Life Beyond the Personal Self*, San Diego, CA: Blue Dove Press.

Spezzano, C. (1994), 'Illusion, faith, and knowledge: commentary on Sorenson's "Ongoing change in psychoanalytic theory"', *Psychoanalytic Dialogues* 4 (4): 661–5.

Spiegel, D. and Cardena, E. (1991), 'Disintegrated experience: the dissociative disorders revisited', *Journal of Abnormal Psychology* 100 (3): 366–78.

Stern, D. (1985), *The Interpersonal World of the Infant*, New York: Basic Books.

Stolorow, R. and Atwood, G. (1992), *Contexts of Being: The Intersubjective Foundations of Psychological Life*, Hillsdale, NJ: Analytic Press.

Suler, J. (1993), *Contemporary Psychoanalysis and Eastern Thought*, New York: State University of New York Press.

Sweetnam, A. (1996), 'The changing context of gender: between fixed and fluid experience', *Psychoanalytic Dialogues* 6 (4): 437–59.

Tillich, P. (1967), *A History of Christian Thought*, New York: Simon & Schuster.

van der Kolk, B. (1987), *Psychological Trauma*, Washington, DC: American Psychiatric Press.

Vaughan, F. (1995), *Shadows of the Sacred*, Wheaton, IL: Quest Books.

Volkan, V. (1995), *Mind and Human Interaction* 6 (3), August.

Walsh, R. (1996), 'Development and evolutionary synthesis in the recent writings of Ken Wilber', *Re-Vision* 18 (4): 9–24.

— (1988), *The Ego and the Dynamic Ground*, Albany, NY: State University of New York Press.

Washburn, M. (1996), 'The pre/trans fallacy reconsidered', *ReVision* 19 (1): 2–10.

— (1980), *The Atman Project: A Transpersonal View of Human Development*, Wheaton, IL: Quest Books.

Wilber, K. (1995), *Sex, Ecology, Spirituality*, Boston: Shambhala Publications.

Wilber, K., Engler, J. and Brown, D. (1986), *Transformations of Consciousness: Conventional and Contemplative Perspectives on Development*, Boston: Shambhala Publications.

— (1965), *The Maturational Process and the Facilitating Environment*, New York: International Universities Press.

— (1971), *Playing and Reality*, New York: Basic Books.

Winnicott, D.W. (1986), *Holding and Interpretation*, New York: Grove Press.

Wrye, H.K. (1993), 'Hello, the hollow: deadspace or playspace', *Psychoanalytic Review* 80 (1): 101–22.

— and Welles, J.K. (1994), *The Narration of Desire*, Hillsdale, NJ: Analytic Press.

10 The Struggle to Imagine

Charles Spezzano

This chapter does not so much make the claim that psychoanalysis is or should be postmodern as it does show some of the tensions in psychoanalysis to be of a type that is emphasized by various authors who have been labelled postmodern. This itself, however, can be misleading since those tensions are not newly identified. They can be traced back throughout the history of Western thought and are not the invention or discovery of authors alleged to have launched a revolution in contemporary thought called postmodernism. At the same time, these longstanding tensions in our attempts to talk about ourselves have been collected and elaborated in interesting and useful ways during the last few decades. In various forms and guises they have shown up in discussions of the relativism of theories and values, in notions about the arbitrariness of signifiers, in theories that emphasize how discourse is a social construction and all knowledge is mediated, and in formulations of the self as a process. Such aspects of contemporary psychoanalytic discourse tensely coexist with beliefs and ways of working that rest on the truth of interpretations and the stability of each person's unconscious psychology.

Looked at in light of this brief characterization of postmodernism, my chapter is postmodernism 'lite', I do not view the interpretive act as hopelessly relative and contextual. I do think we discover truths about our patients. I even judge the analyst to be capable of viewing the patient objectively enough to talk as if we know something about the patient, even though I also believe my understandings to have been jointly constructed with patients, to be filtered through my own subjectivity, and to be open to updating and improvement in every instance. What is emphasized in this chapter that does conflict with other views of the analytic process that might be seen as less postmodern (or eschewing anything postmodern) is my implicit and explicit claim that many understandings emerge into the analytic dialogue in ways that cannot be adequately captured by the notion that we observe, hypothesize, offer our hypotheses as interpretations, assess patients' reactions and generate new hypotheses that bring us closer to the truth. Especially in describing my readings of Winnicott and Bion, I can be easily seen to insist that the traditional empirical hypothesis-testing project is always only part of how we and patients discover truths about mind operating unconsciously. I think it is there that I have added, or highlighted, an ingredient of psychoanalytic discourse, at least since Winnicott and Bion, that resonates with notions put forward in postmodern texts.

Making Affect Central

What draws me to Winnicott and Bion and what leads me to treat the empirical as only part of what we do is my sense that we are in our clinical work seeking to capture and change with our verbal interpretations aspects of psychological life that are not intrinsically linguistic. As Bion (quoted in Limentani, 1986) once suggested, affects are the 'facts' of psychoanalysis. Patients can never perfectly capture in words or actions an affective state they have experienced and the analyst can never perfectly grasp it either, neither as an affective state nor an idea within her. Nonetheless, with the occurrence of each affective state something has happened. More specifically, for an affective state to occur there must have been unconscious mental activity. The closer we get to capturing that activity (as well as to its intrapsychic and interpersonal origins and vicissitudes) with our words, the closer we get to the truth that is of central interest in the ongoing psychoanalytic conversation.

Affect and Truth

Psychoanalysis pursues *the affective truth* about each human life that comes under its scrutiny. This is a type of truth that overlaps with scientific and hermeneutic truth but is also different from them. It is scientific, in part, because what it studies are psychological experiences that occur at specific moments in time and exist independently of our attempts to know them. It is hermeneutic, in both the ontological and methodological senses of that broad term.[1] Methodologically, psychoanalysis overlaps with hermeneutics because it has always emphasized the key role of interpretation in its version of the scientific method. Ontologically, psychoanalysis casts the human being in a hermeneutic mode in the sense that the psychoanalytic individual constitutes his existence interpretively. Last, however, but certainly not least, psychoanalysis is psychoanalytic – that is, psychoanalysis is distinctively itself – because it emphasizes the ways in which 'wired-in', pre-experiential *affective* meaning categories are immanent in all immediate human experience. One might say, in fact, that what distinguishes psychoanalysis from hermeneutics is that where hermeneutics tends, in general, to point first to culture and language as the major pre-experiential mediums for the basic constitution of human experience, psychoanalysis points first to affects.

The Analyst's Ability to Grasp Affective Truth

An affective state is a complex human experience that can be consciously and introspectively scrutinized, can be described, and can be communicated. Psychoanalysis draws a distinction between describing one's affective state to another and communicating it to another. The receiving person feels the communicated affective state and might hold it or react to it with some other affect. Such affective exchanges constitute a primary form of human communication. The analyst is not a perfect instrument for observing and capturing the affective states of the analysand. Nonetheless, what he observes and imperfectly captures does exist. Its existence is not automatically called into question because of the limits of either introspective or external scrutiny of it.

Yet the imperfection of the mind of one person as an instrument in its attempts to capture the affective state of another is precisely what adds a hermeneutic dimension to psychoanalytic truth. The unconscious processes that produce affective states are never fully available even to the conscious scrutiny of the patient in whom they have occurred. They are, in turn, even less immediately available to the analytic observer and listener. The analyst will inevitably receive the affective product of these processes with her own unconscious and will then be limited to scrutiny of what emerges into her own preconscious–conscious flow of psychic events. It is out of this imperfect scrutiny, however, that there will emerge usable information about, first, the affective state of the patient and, second, those unconscious processes out of which it originated.

The analyst is also limited in her ability to make use of the unconscious affective communications of the patient by her ability to hold them in herself – to hold especially those particular blends of disturbing affects that the patient is forced to project, enact, or crumble under. Further, this holding must persist long enough for the analyst to be able to identify the affects, think about them, and say something useful based on them. To the extent that the analyst cannot hold very well a particular affect or set of affects, to that extent she will be limited in her ability to make therapeutic use of certain events and communications in the analysis. And she will, very likely, proceed in ways that constrain the patient from generating or communicating those affects. In that sense, the analyst as an affective container limits where on the human affective landscape she and the analysand can usefully go together.

There is another property of the psyche of the analyst that plays a significant role in determining the course of that carefully *annotated affective exchange* we call an analysis. Each analyst by virtue of her own analysis, supervisions, and study of the literature has had her unconscious transformed into a psychoanalytic unconscious. The ideas that reach consciousness no longer reflect only her personal, familial, cultural and linguistic meaning systems but also a psychoanalytic meaning system. It is not simply that an idea occurs to her and she then works it over through her conscious awareness of psychoanalytic theory – although that sort of activity certainly plays a role in every analysis – but also that her immediate experiencing of the patient's communications is performed by an unconscious that has been reshaped by her tripartite (personal analysis, case supervision, and didactic) training. The way in which this happens for each of us in training is only partly available to our conscious recall and scrutiny. Many of us will be aware most vividly of the large influence that certain ideas or interactions from supervision and our own personal analyses have had on our conscious reviewing of analytic material. This leads often to the expectation that one will learn to be a more effective therapist or analyst *only* by various forms of exposure to case material – specifically to hearing and discussing exactly what psychoanalysts say to analysands – as if the learning process in our field was largely, if not exclusively, the result of stockpiling things to say to patients under various circumstances. Yet, this outlook contradicts the description we would ordinarily give about how changes are assumed to take place in the unconscious of an analysand. There we would usually assume that a gradual transformation, or working-through, is the rule. The same applies to the creation of a useful, that is, therapeutic, psychoanalytic unconscious in each analyst. All forms of immersion in psychoanalytic language, thought and experience gradually shape this unconscious. More and more automatically, as experience accumulates, this unconscious yields ideas that turn out to be useful to the analytic work. Each analyst comes to trust more and more this process which Freud believed constituted the bulk of human psychic activity, that is, unconscious psychic activity yielding feelings and thoughts into the preconscious–conscious flow of psychic elements to which we then have access. Rapaport (1953: 177) emphasized: 'it goes without saying that in his everyday work the transference affects are the guide of the therapist'; and the response to those transference affects that occur in the mind of the analyst is the stuff out of which useful interpretations are formed.

The postmodern edge of this process through which the analyst is able to form interpretations was first identified in the work of Bion. In the view that emerged from his writings, the analyst cycles through states of having an interpretation in mind, then having the capacity for understanding fall apart. During the latter state, the analyst is more aware of feelings, sensations, images and fragments of often contradictory ideas. The next interpretation that will form is both a coming together again of the analyst's mind and an observation made by the analyst's mind of the patient's mind. So, patients have to find themselves in these interpretations by thinking about not only the words but also the feelings they evoke.

An essential component of clinical work is the elaboration of the patient's affective states to the point where the patient can usefully think about and through them. The identification, description and explanation of affective states, especially those arising in the transference, are the truth in which psychoanalysis has always been most interested, regardless of which school of analysis is taken as a case in point. Analysis assumes the possibility of accurate introspection into the vicissitudes of one's affective states, while studying all the factors that interfere with it.

Affect as the Core of Subjective and Intersubjective Reality

Affect theory provocatively suggests a synthesis, elaboration and clinical adaptation of a radical philosophical theory of mind first presented in modern form by Hans-Georg Gadamer (in German in 1960 and in English translation in 1975) and more recently by Jonathan Lear. Gadamer, in turn, had partially derived his perspective from the earlier work of Edmund Husserl and Martin Heidegger. Husserl's key insight was that 'meanings are structures which a person lives before he thinks about them' (Howard, 1982: xii). A central premise of affect theory is that these essential human meaning categories are best understood as feeling states.

In *Being and Time* (originally written in 1927 but not translated into English until 1962), Heidegger elaborated Husserl's theory into the fundamental ontological idea that the psychological essence of each individual human life at any moment in time is the outcome of neglecting or realizing specific domains of possibilities. These domains of possibilities are, in turn, 'fore-meanings', meaning categories that exist prior to the individual. Ultimately, these meaning categories are most usefully understood to be precisely those affects emphasized by the major psychoanalytic theorists. For Freud, they were sexual excitement and rage: on the one hand, in a dialectical relationship with each other; on the other hand, as a pair of basic desires in perpetual dialectic tension with anxiety and guilt. For Greenberg similar dialectics revolve around the human desires for feelings of safety and effectance. In the broader context of affect theory *shifting dialectical arrangements of affective states* is a more useful way to capture the nature of human psychology.

Gadamer used Heidegger's work to resurrect and update nineteenth-century ontological hermeneutics which had raised the possibility of there being a knowing human subject intrinsically led to generate useful ways of understanding different from the theories of explanation prevalent in physics and chemistry. Most directly relevant to our discussion of contemporary psychoanalytic affect theory is Gadamer's premise that there is a kind of truth that 'happens to us over and above our wanting and doing' (1975). Clinical psychoanalysis suggests that this 'kind of truth' is affective truth. Affective truth is not something we find; it finds us (Howard, 1982). As the American philosopher Roy Howard has elegantly summarized this theory of Gadamer's, such 'truth appears with its own authority in consciousness, and consciousness is, to a degree, passive in this reception' (1982: 124).

Jonathan Lear's (1990) reading of psychoanalysis can best be understood against the backdrop of these earlier philosophical efforts. He has taken the position that 'archaic' or 'primitive' mental activity (Freud's primary process thinking) is the core of psychic life. Archaic mind is, thus, Lear's candidate to be the source of that crucial kind of truth that happens to us and emerges into consciousness. What Lear adds to the discussion, from his reading of Freud, is the implication of an organic relationship between primary and secondary process thinking, between archaic mind and mature mind. In doing this, Lear treats these two minds as two subjectivities interacting with and constantly reshaping each other – in the way Lacan construes the mind to be created from subject and Other (desire) in a dynamic and dialectic arrangement (spawning an imaginary I, ego, in imaginary relationships with imaginary objects). Not only, therefore, does archaic mind influence sophisticated mind in ways that are interpretable but, as we scrutinize and rework our archaic thinking, it (the archaic mental activity) responds to these efforts and is transformed by them. In fact, it is precisely the apparent 'responsiveness of this archaic mental activity to the mind's own attempt to understand it' (Lear, 1990: 7) that persuades Lear of the legitimacy of talking about it as a dynamic form of mental functioning rather than, say, as an unchanging biological organ.

What Lear is getting at is the recognition that those unconscious processes out of which affects emerge can actually be reshaped by the act of interpretation. As mind struggles for expression, it is specifically affect that can transform itself into idea, talk, creativity and relationship. These human activities constitute a full expression of the individual's affectively-originating subjectivity into and onto the world. Psychoanalytic interpretation is a natural extension of these activities. And, Lear (1990: 62) makes clear, it is specifically affect, in its effort to 'express an explanation and justification of its own occurrence', that embraces the analyst's interpretations as a potential vehicle for its full development.[2]

This full development of affect is what psychoanalysis seeks. The analyst becomes a part of this psychic process, its ally against any forces that would mute, distort or misread affect as it attempted to elaborate itself into idea and beyond. Psychoanalysis is grounded in the assertion that, by definition, the closer we get to open, honest, uncoerced discourse between two people the closer we get to the affective truth that psychoanalysis seeks.

The truth that matters in each individual's struggle for psychological survival is affective truth – not scientific or hermeneutic truth. The possibility of capturing this truth is opened up when no intrapsychic or interpersonal domination or coercion is working to distort or inhibit it from being elaborated out of affect and into thought, word and deed. A major thread in the evolution of psychoanalytic clinical theory can be understood as the continual effort to identify the many obvious and subtle sources of intersubjective interference with the elaboration of affect and to systematically eliminate these from the analyst's activities. Similarly, the evolution of psychoanalytic theories of psychopathology can be understood as attempts to specify the seemingly endless ways in which the patient is unable or unwilling to elaborate the truth – in its full affective, ideational and relational expression – in the analysis. This understanding of psychopathology is then also carried over into clinical theory in the form of propositions about what the analyst can do to help the patient stop interfering with the elaboration of her affective states.

The Interpretive Regulation and Elaboration of Affect

All relationships offer opportunities to use the other to maintain or generate certain specific affective states in oneself or to evacuate them from oneself. The analytic relationship heals by drawing into itself those methods of processing and regulating affect that are relied upon by the patient for psychological survival and then transforming them. The mechanism of these transformations is the regulation of affect in a better way within the analysis than it had previously been managed by the patient and the subsequent modification of what, in the classical language of structural change, might be called the patient's unconscious affect-regulating structures. Interpretation of affect is a key component of the analytic way of regulating it. There has been, however, increasing attention to the possibility of permanent change in unconscious affect regulating 'structures' by internalization, not only of the analysing function of the analyst but also by internalization of the therapeutic relationship itself, insofar as it has functioned as an effective affect-regulating 'structure'.

What happens in every good analysis is that a wide variety of events increases the analysand's capacity to hold (keep alive in himself) certain affective states long enough to be able to think usefully about them (that is, long enough to be able to use them as information about the nature of one's unconscious processing of one's position – the position of the self – in one's object world at that moment and one's options for action within that world). What also happens is that useful thinking about affective states actually takes place. At first, this takes the form of interpretations by the analyst.

The analyst's interpretations serve several affective purposes. They begin the process of elaborating rather than abolishing, truncating and warding off the analysand's affects. They also capture real aspects of the truth about the analysand's affective states, as they occurred in the analysand. Finally, what also happens in every good analysis is that the analyst's interpretations serve as a bridge to the transformation of the unconscious affective links between various versions of the self and the objects in the patient's representational world. Although the self and object representations are also changed, I believe those changes, while very closely intertwined with changes in the links between self and object, actually follow rather than precede the changes in these affective links.

Within the analytic holding environment, the analysand gets a second chance to achieve competence in using affects as information about his unconscious psychic activity, especially his processing of contacts with others. Repetitive experiences of competent affect-regulation within the transference gives the patient the material with which to construct a self-representation that sustains a sense of perceived affective competence. And, the sense of conviction that one can competently regulate one's affective life is a state of well-being.

The Intersubjective Regulation and Elaboration of Affect

The issue of holding and interpretation can be viewed from still another perspective that adds an important dimension to our understanding of each analysand's affective experience. To assume this perspective it is necessary to recast Freud's core theory as a dialectic of affects: *Freud's structural theory is a model of sexual excitement and rage in a dialectic with anxiety and guilt.* To minimize the amount of anxiety and guilt we feel we must develop useful defensive ways of thinking (and not thinking) about our own sexual excitement and rage. These defensive ways exist in a hierarchy that reflects their developmental origins, beginning with the denial by the very immature ego and ending with sublimations by the mature ego. The analyst working from this affective model watches the internal struggle of the analysand as the analysand moves through moments of not thinking about, thinking defensively about, and thinking less defensively (even if, at first, more anxiously and guiltily) about his sexual excitement and rage. The analysand will gradually spend more time thinking usefully and adaptively about these affective states as clues to a sustaining and satisfying life agenda. This agenda involves the elaboration (sublimation) of sexual excitement and rage into thoughts, words and acts which do not then produce so much anxiety and guilt, but rather more excitement and fulfilment.

Gradually, however, an increasing awareness of the extent to which people use other people in their attempts to elaborate and regulate their affects began to contaminate this clear clinical theory. Both analyst and analysand are today thought of as unavoidably using each other in these affect-regulating efforts. Further, just as we are all doing all the time, what the analysand will pay most attention to in the clinical situation is (1) the ways in which the analyst is willing (or unwilling) to be used in the analysand's efforts to elaborate and regulate his affects; (2) the ways in which the analysand experiences the analyst using him to elaborate and regulate her affective states or avoiding engaging some aspects of him as a way of doing this regulating. So, for example, breaking a silence with a correct interpretation of what the patient was saying just before the silence might also be an attempt to disengage from the affective state the patient was trying to communicate to, evoke in, or put inside the analyst through the silence. Then the patient's experience of the interpretation might not matter as much as his experience of the interaction, the act of disengaging from an uncomfortable affective state. The patient might be heard to say: 'Yes, you are correct in your understanding of one latent meaning of what I was saying before I fell silent and how that might help us understand why I stopped talking. But what matters more to me right now is your unconscious message that you could not tolerate the affective state my silence catalysed in you. It is that very affective state that I seek to avoid. If you cannot tolerate it either, how will we ever understand it?'

This way of understanding the analytic situation has its roots in the writings of authors going to back to Ferenczi but in its contemporary resurrection it is most often associated with the work of

Donald Winnicott. What Winnicott called the analytic holding environment can be understood as a temporary substitute for the patient's intrapsychic and defensive self-holding of affective states. In other words, the analytic holding environment makes less necessary the patient's truncating of positive affects for fear that they will lead eventually to danger and pain and his warding off of painful affects instead of thinking about them.

Winnicott *explicitly* contrasted holding with interpreting and in so doing gave rise to the current incarnation of the longstanding controversy over the therapeutic impact of interaction versus interpretation:

> In treatment of schizoid persons the analyst needs to know all about the interpretations that might be made on the material presented, but he must be able to refrain from being side-tracked into doing this work that is inappropriate because the main need is for an unclever ego-support, or a holding. (1963: 241)

This technical recommendation can be understood as an amendment to the prevailing Freudian and Kleinian clinical theories in the context of which Winnicott's theories developed.

Freud's clinical theory as it evolved into an ego psychology in the 1920s remained essentially an elaboration of his 1914 paper on 'Remembering, Repeating and Working Through'. The patient is given the instruction to report whatever 'comes into his head' (Freud, 1926: 188). As the patient does this she will remember certain past affective events, but not others. Access to some of these affective events – specifically to the memory of certain affectively disturbing psychic moments – will be 'held back by resistance' (Freud, 1925: 40). What the patient will not remember she will repeat in the transference. She may repeat it in other relationships as well but its repetition in the transference constitutes the core resistance and the point of leverage in working through the resistance. The analyst interprets who, what, when, where, why and how the patient is resisting. As a result, the patient eventually gains insight into her resistances and remembers (or reconstructs) the affective events. This should lead to changes not only in the analytic relationship but also in the patient's loving and working among other persons in her life. If this does not happen then further analysis of resistance is required. These previously hidden resistances are often the toughest to analyse and working through them, Freud wrote, is both 'an arduous task' for the patient and 'a trial of patience for the analyst' (1914: 155).

Klein's clinical theory was the other major clinical theory against which Winnicott was positioning himself with his theory of analytic holding. Klein argued for the analyst to directly interpret early anxiety-situations (such as phantasies of attacks on the mother's body, with retaliation and loss of the internal loved object) in order to pull them toward fuller elaboration and consciousness. The patient envelops the analyst in a web of affects, object-relations, and defensively initiated projections and introjections. The analytic situation itself then becomes a struggle for emotional survival just as the patient's childhood had been. By interpreting 'deeply', the analyst is managing in a new way – and in the most useful way possible – the transferential versions of those tormenting anxieties against which the patient has been entrenched in psychic warfare.

It is in relation to these Freudian and Kleinian theories of interpretation that Winnicott's argument for holding must be understood. To understand it fully, we must also, I think, consider that as Winnicott was developing his idea, Wilfred Bion was developing his companion theory of containment. Winnicott made clear that the infant needs a mother who can take in and hold his terrors, anxieties, and affective pains and disturbances. So too the patient needs an analyst whose mind is capable of such mental activity. Bion added that the mother must think developmentally about what she holds in her mind. So too the analyst must think analytically about the patient's affective projections. In Bion's hands the Kleinian theory of unconscious communication becomes one in which we will all, at various times, seek to move unbearable affects into others as if to say: 'This is driving me mad. Do something with it and then give it back to me in a form I can use; or, if not, then just take it and keep it.'

Winnicott followed the evolution of Bion's ideas and, in fact, once wrote to Bion that he imagined Bion would become the new leader of British psychoanalysis, if, Winnicott added (prophetically, we now know), Bion could avoid embroiling himself in too much conflict. Winnicott and Bion were grappling with the same problem: the unconscious communication of affective states. Winnicott focused on the acts of communicating and receiving communications. Bion focused on the mental activity required of the communicators to make the communication useful. The analyst must allow his mind to fall apart in response to the patient's affective communication. If the analyst can then reintegrate his mind with the new experience included, then an interpretation that will allow the patient to integrate into his thinking a key fact about himself. Through such genuine knowing, growth takes place developmentally and analytically.

The notions of Winnicott and Bion seem to weave in and around each other. Attempts to strongly differentiate their contributions seem as much political as scholarly. Both seem to be developing the postmodern edge of analysis. Here the model of analysis in which the analyst offers hypotheses and observes the patient's response gives way to analyst and patient falling into and emerging from intense emotional contacts during which knowing breaks down and then re-emerges out of joint mental activity. So too, the interplay between Winnicott and Bion may have been more synergistic than is usually described. For example, in a letter he wrote to Bion in October of 1955, in response to his hearing Bion's paper on the 'Differentiation of the Psychotic from the Non-Psychotic Personalities', Winnicott wrote to Bion that while Bion's interpretation was 'right', he would still have preferred to have interpreted the nature of the communication from the patient to the analyst about the immediate analytic interaction. If a patient of his was moving around on the couch in the way Bion's patient had done, Winnicott told Bion, and had then remarked that he ought to have telephoned his mother, he would know that the patient 'was talking about communication and his incapacity for making communication' (from letter dated 7 October 1955, in Rodman, 1987: 91). Winnicott then provided the interpretation of the communication that he would have made:

> A mother properly oriented to her baby would know from your movements what you need. There would be a communication because of this knowledge which belongs to her devotion and she would do something which would show that the communication had taken place. I am not sensitive enough or oriented in that way to be able to act well enough and therefore in this present analytic situation fall into the category of the mother who failed to make communication possible. In the present relationship therefore there is given a sample of the original failure from the environment which contributed to your difficulty in communication. Of course you could always cry and so draw attention to need. In the same way you could telephone your mother and get a reply but this represents a failure of the more subtle communication which is the only basis for communication that does not violate the fact of essential isolation of each individual.

Winnicott makes it clear in this clinical example what he was suggesting as an alternative to (or, more accurately, a special, 'unclever' version of) interpretation in certain clinical situations. Had he recognized the patient's restlessness on the couch as an attempt at communication he would have labelled it as such. He might have said: 'I think you are trying to communicate to me some disturbance you are feeling but which you cannot put into words.' He is arguing that this is not, technically speaking, an interpretation of either resistance or unconscious content, but the creating of a holding environment for the disturbance the patient is experiencing.

One can imagine that he is saying to the Freudian analyst that although the patient's silence and translating of affect into activity might be validly viewed as a resistance, it is, more crucially at the moment, an attempt at forging a channel of communication – an affective link, through unconscious communication, with the analyst. The analysand will experience this link as being held. He is no longer alone with his affective disturbance. 'Whenever we understand a patient in a deep way and show that we do so by a correct and well-timed interpretation we are in fact holding the patient, and taking part in a relationship in which the patient is in some degree regressed and dependent' (Winnicott, 1986: 192).

Paradoxically, he is simultaneously saying to the Kleinian analyst that an interpretation that does not directly capture the most intensely anxious rage – that simply captures the nascent effort of the analysand to communicate – is sometimes what is needed and what is possible. Interpretation of the attempt at communication of affective disturbance is a way for the analyst to interact with the disturbance. Through such interpretation the analyst enters into the disturbance with the patient. The analyst communicates that he is there and ready to help hold the disturbance, help wrestle with it, and help keep it alive without its becoming overwhelming.

If, however, Winnicott had not quickly enough recognized the restlessness as a communication of affective disturbance, he would now acknowledge to the analysand that this failed attempt at communication had apparently catalysed a second wave of disturbance. He would treat this second wave as something arising out of the analysand but also out of the interaction between them in which the first wave of disturbance went unrecognized (or *unmet*, as Winnicott liked to phrase it).

The fantasy of calling his mother was the patient's last-ditch effort to contain the combined disturbances. What would one call the extended comment that Winnicott told Bion he would have said to Bion's analysand in the face of this disturbance? It is not an interpretation of either resistance or unconscious content, yet it is an interpretation of the missed opportunity for communication and the second wave of disturbance that generated in the patient. At the same time, it is also, for Winnicott, something more than an interpretation. It might be understood as an implicit *suggestion* to the analysand to hold the disturbance. It might also be understood as a *holding–containing interaction*, that is, a reaching out to join the analysand in holding and thinking about that second and more intense disturbance to the origin of which Winnicott would have contributed.

No Such Thing as an Act by the Analyst that is Non-Interpretive

So, although Winnicott *explicitly* contrasted holding with interpreting, he *implicitly* suggested that there is no such thing as a non-interpretive act by the analyst. Everything he recommends doing is intended as an interpretive communication to the analysand. More than that, nothing the analyst says or does can help but be an interpretive communication. It will always be based upon her reaction to and understanding of the affective state of the analysand and it will communicate this – implicitly or explicitly. It will also represent her assessment of what the analysand can use at that moment. And that too will be communicated to the analysand by what is or is not said or done. Unless we narrowly restrict the use of the word 'interpretation' to statements that capture and elaborate affect only in one specific way (such as genetic constructions, explanations of compromise formations or unconscious self-object representations), the analyst will always be seen as interpreting. And, ultimately, every one of these interpretive acts (including silences) and statements is intended to increase the analysand's tolerance for and competence in the expression of a broader and more finely discriminated array of affects. The debate among analysts is over how to accomplish that.

Freud had begun by arguing that the anxiety observed in the transference and the anxiety that had initially led to the defences now made manifest in the patient's resistances was Oedipal anxiety. Partly after Otto Rank made the alternative argument that all such anxiety was due to birth and separation traumas, Freud expanded his position developmentally and argued that the infantile situations of anxiety went through a series of stages. Nonetheless, Freud did not recommend a different technique for analysing these earlier anxieties. Klein did, and Kleinian theory has evolved into a method for analysing the flow of anxiety during an analysis, especially as it moves back and forth between paranoid-schizoid anxiety (over attacks on the mother's body and retaliatory parental counter-attacks) and depressive anxiety (over the loss of the internal loved object). Kleinian technique has been summed up by Etchegoyen in a single sentence: 'It consists in interpreting with no other commitment or goal than that of making the unconscious conscious, without allowing oneself ever to be led by complacency and weakness, without fearing the consequences of saying what the analyst considers is happening in the mind of the analysand and which he ought to express' (1991: 416).

Unrepresented Affective States

Resistance and communication define a fundamental dialectic in clinical theory. Resistance to an affective state implies that the affects have been represented mentally and can, therefore, be warded off by the warding off of their representations. Certain early affective experiences, however, do not get represented. Yet they maintain a persistent and peremptory presence in the psychic life of the analysand. One might say that a category of early affective experience takes the form of a painful, lonely, enraged, anxious or depressed mood (an ego state in Bibring's terms) that inhabits the analysand's psyche.[3] *The affect becomes the world.* Hubert Dreyfus and Jerome Wakefield (1988) allude to a similar developmental process. They describe how 'a child's anger at how his father is treating him becomes anger at how his father always treats him, and even rage at how everyone has always treated him' (1988: 278). Even they portray it here as more of a representational process than I want to do. I am trying to get at a different situation from the one in which a representation of the father or mother becomes the prevailing object representation and so casts an emotional tone on the child's whole psychological life. I'm staying closer to Winnicott's notion of the mother as the child's environment. It's as if the heat of south Florida could get inside a child who grew up in such a climate and transform his bodily thermostat so that wherever he lived after that he would always feel oppressively hot. If a child's pain, loneliness, anxiety or grief is allowed to persist too often and too long then that affect or blend of affects comes to be the way that child feels all the time. Dreyfus and Wakefield do agree that such terms as belief, representation or schema do not adequately capture the automatic and chronic character of such an affective state. Christopher Bollas, however, has effectively captured the sense we sometimes have of ourselves as flowing inexorably into such states without consciousness, foreknowledge or will. He roots such experience developmentally in the original experience of the mother as transformational object. The mother is the child's environment and so the transformational object is simply a name Bollas gives to the basic vicissitudes of the infant's affective life with the mother. It is not an object known cognitively. It is what the hermeneutic and existential philosophers have called a person's fundamental way of being in the world, and Bollas acknowledges that he sees it as an existential way of knowing.

Philosopher Maurice Merleau-Ponty provided one of the most powerful statements of this idea. Talking about the same phenomenon as Bollas, he wrote in 1962: 'One present among all presents thus acquires an exceptional value; it displaces the others and deprives them of their value as authentic presents' (1962: 83). This present is an affective present, the affective signature of the relationship between that mother and child. Dreyfus and Wakefield, in fact, directly acknowledge that the roots of their thinking about unrepresented affective states lie in the work of Merleau-Ponty. They emphasize his explanation of such a prevailing mood as an affective emblem that has the effect of reorganizing the background or clearing in which all representations thereafter appear.

The Analysand's Desire for Affective Transformation

Each analysand wants the frustrating and painful components of his emotional fingerprint or emblem to be transformed by the analyst, wants the analyst to have the power that the transformational object once had, wants his affective core to be open again to direct and immediate transformation by the other. As one analysand put it: 'I most value something if it immediately changes the way I feel.'

It is on this prevailing affective state that the entire atmosphere of the analysis exerts its influence, either further solidifying it or loosening the glue that holds it together. The setting of the fee, the message that 'we will do together what you cannot do alone', and, in general, the making of what Winnicott called 'active sensitive adaptation' to the fluctuating capacity of the analysand to tolerate, express and think about specific affective states – all these interactive elements gradually recolour the analysand's prevailing mood and gradually reshape the basic unconscious processes out of which affective states arise.

Adaptation or Subversion?

There is more to the dialectic tension between British object relational and American ego psychological elaborations of psychoanalysis than their 'interpret resistance' versus 'interpret unconscious communication' emphases. What underlies this tension can be understood by contrasting what are arguably the major post-Freudian and post-Kleinian ego psychological and object relational theoretical shifts. Heinz Hartmann added the concept of adaptation. Donald Winnicott added instead the concept of creative imagination. The following quote from Winnicott (1974: 76) could in fact be read precisely as a response to Hartmann's new emphasis on adaptation:

> The creativity that we are studying belongs to the approach of the individual to external reality ... Contrasted with this is a relation-

> ship with external reality which is one of compliance, the world and its details being recognized but only as something to be fitted in with or demanding adaptation ... In a tantalizing way many individuals have experienced just enough of creative living to recognize that for most of their time they are living uncreatively, as if caught up in the creativity of someone else, or of a machine.

The emphasis on interpreting resistance is a direct reflection of the underlying emphasis on adaptation as the ultimate psychological agenda. The emphasis on interpreting unconscious communication is, by contrast, a direct reflection of the underlying emphasis on subversion of reality as the ultimate psychological agenda. As resistance is analysed, the analysand becomes increasingly aware of bits and pieces of his unconscious fantasy life. As fantasy comes up against reality it surrenders. The payoff for the analysand is, from the point of view of the structural theory of technique, to 'increase the opportunities for realistic pleasure' (Boesky, 1988: 307). Of course, the ego psychological patient also becomes increasingly aware – in fact, especially becomes aware – of his resistances. They become ego dystonic. His character softens, its appeal lessened, and as a byproduct of this he becomes increasingly aware of his psychic pain, his anxiety, his depression, as well as his wish for pleasure of various kinds, both realistic and unrealistic. He will more often chose the realistic ones. The ego psychological analysand suffers, then, from both his resistances and his fantasies. His potential for more conflict-free pleasure lies in his enhanced attunement to the realistic pleasures that the world allows.

On the other side of the clinical dialectic, the Winnicottian analysand suffers at least as much, if not more, from a lack of imagination. It is the ego function of imagination that elaborates affect in ways that are unique to this analysand and subverts the existing world of other subjectivities into which this analysand was born. That is why the psyche of the mother resists the child's growing imagination and why he himself resists it. It is intersubjectively subversive, not adaptive. It threatens both he and the mother with a new reality for which neither can know how well they are prepared. And this is precisely the dilemma of the Winnicottian analyst. Each analysand threatens her too with the subversion of her subjectivity, with a new reality.

Both the ego psychological and the Winnicottian analysand are urged by the analytic process to expend less psychic energy on fantasy. It is where he is supposed to turn from there that differs. The ego psychological analysand is returned to reality. The Winnicottian analysand is returned to her imagination. It is through imagination, in fact, as the British analyst Charles Rycroft (1968) summed it up in his collection of papers *Imagination and Reality*, that the analysand will achieve his most useful appreciation of both reality and fantasy. And in 1985 he added:

> A necessary precondition of all imaginative activity seems to be what Keats called 'negative capability', the ability to allow oneself to be 'in uncertainties, mysteries, doubts, without any irritable reaching after fact and reason'; in other words, the ability to abandon Hartmann's 'theoretical ideal of rational action' and to stop trying to 'master reality' in favor of letting oneself happen. (1985: 272)

Rather than the master of reality Winnicott hoped that his analysands would become masters of what Stephen Robinson (1984: 122) has called 'the art of the possible' in an essay of the same title. Robinson expands upon Rycroft and Winnicott in differentiating imagination and fantasy. 'Fantasy belongs to the realm of impossibility. It cannot be subversive – unlike imagination, which always is ... Imagination is the vehicle of hope; fantasy is the vehicle of despair' (1984: 124–5). We might, in fact, say, in this context, that Winnicott's true self is the creation of imagination, while the false self is strictly the product of fantasy.

What the imagination elaborates first is body and affect.

> The psyche begins as an imaginative elaboration of physical functioning, having as its most important duty the binding together of past experiences, potentialities, and the present moment awareness, and expectancy for the future. Thus the self comes into existence. (Winnicott, 1988: 19)

Without this imaginative elaboration 'crude expression of appetite and of sexuality and of hate would be the rule' (1988: 60). It is inside his crude fantasy elaborations of affect that the analysand has imprisoned himself in safety and despair. And he has turned to such fantasy because he has found himself unable to use the object for imaginative elaboration of his excitement and desire or for regulation of his pain, loneliness and anxiety. Instead the object has intruded into him, trying to desperately use him for its own affective purposes, terrifying him and filling him with disgust. He can relate to the object through a false self or through crude fantasy elaborations of his sexual excitement and rage, but he cannot use the object imaginatively. Thus, Winnicott (1974: 33) wrote (elaborating a idea that originated with Fairbairn, 1952), we can understand 'the relationship between fantasying and the abandonment of hope in (object) relating'.

The natural trajectory of this trend in psychoanalytic writing leads to an affect theory that allows for a full understanding of the clinical situation and the psychoanalytic process; and that radically frees both from the narrow confines of that extreme ego psychological framework in which the analysis of resistance is believed capable of encompassing everything useful at the level of clinical theory and the theory of technique. In this intersubjective-affective psychology, *the holding, communicating, containing and interpretation of affect fully define the psychoanalytic situation and process. The analyst and the analysand share the work of keeping alive, imaginatively elaborating, and thinking about the full range of human affective states as these emerge in each of them during the analytic hours.*

Interpretation expresses the analyst's thinking about the affects emerging in him and the analysand, and his thinking about the unconscious processes out of which these affects have emerged, as well as about the ways in which they have been communicated between them. Because it is the analyst's thinking, the analysand must always at least partly resist it. This resistance is not a resistance to knowing but a resistance to repeating the intrusion of the thinking of the other. It must be distinguished, for example, from compulsive associating which is a refusal to think about an affective state that has emerged.

Affects compete with language and culture as expressions of human unconscious processing. The affective life of the individual is the truest expression of his unconscious processing, his genuine subjectivity. Language and culture are the expressions of the collective other into which he is forced to try to fit his excitement and his anxiety, his sexual excitement and his rage. The interpretations of the analyst are also expressions of the unconscious processing, the affective states, and the thinking of an other. It always elicits some refusal and some hatred. Klein, in fact, thought that all resistance was a manifestation of a negative transference (Hinshelwood, 1991: 418) which, in turn, is an expression of the death instinct. Lacan, by contrast, saw this as always, at least in part, the result of the analysand's inevitable relation to the other:

> Obliged to fashion himself with reference to and rivalry with the other, obliged to wait for recognition from or judgment by the other, man is naturally inclined to a whole range of aggressive behaviour, from envy, morbid jealousy and real aggression to mortal negation of self or other. (Lemaire, 1981: 181)

Winnicott seems to have had an intuitive grasp of this dilemma and of the analysand's wish to restore his fragmented subjectivity – fragmented by the intrusion into his psyche of the subjectivity of the other.

Winnicott, however, softened the emphasis on hatred that Klein and Lacan maintained. The patient described in *Holding and Interpretation*, whose internal and dialogical 'chatter' bored both Winnicott and himself, was not, in Winnicott's view being hostile to him. He was simply protecting the integrity of his affective states. Winnicott's evidence for this was that the analysand accepted the basic clinical situation of the analysis and the psychological space it opened up for him and Winnicott. At the same time the patient refused to relate to Winnicott in the sense of trying to use him and refused to play with his affects himself through imaginative elaboration of them. One might see in this an expression of ambivalence. Masud Khan (1987: 15) argued, however, that 'to have seen it in conflictual terms of ambivalence would have been a false over-simplification'. It was simply a 'paradox'. He wasn't loving and hating – working with and resisting – Winnicott. He was entering the analytic space but without any experience of either having his affective states usefully elaborated by the other or by himself. He was looking for the capacity to imaginatively elaborate his affects but he could not take the risk of giving them over to Winnicott to see what would happen.

The Analyst's Uncertainty

The analyst cannot know in advance how the analysand will eventually come to *usefully* think about her own affective states. This thinking will develop during the analysis, as the analysand moves from not thinking, to being interested in the analyst's way of thinking, to inventing her own way of thinking. The analyst may experience the refusal of the analysand to think in his way about her affects as a resistance, but the resistance is always to developing her own way of thinking about her affects. To refuse to think about one's affects in the way the analyst thinks about them is not resistance. To refuse to think playfully and imaginatively about one's affects is resistance. About the analysis he reported in *Holding and Interpretation*, Winnicott (1986) wrote of his analysand: 'it seemed that an observer of life came and talked with me ... We sometimes talked of the patient' (quoted by Khan, 1987: 12).

Commenting on this case report Khan (1987: 14) suggested considering this patient's unconscious communication to his analyst to have taken the form 'I refuse, therefore I am.' The refusal, in my view, was a refusal to think about his affects or to communicate them so that Winnicott could think about them. This is how he keeps them alive and protects them. He expects Winnicott to destroy them if he gets hold of them, to take them and return affects of his own. One must assume this to have been his basic experience of life, that affects thought about and communicated will be taken in and violently transformed into something foreign and unusable. An analysand of the self psychologist Anna Ornstein (1991) put this fear to her directly: 'I am afraid of what will happen to my good feelings in therapy.'

What all analysands share in common with these analysands is the need to have their affective states not only empathically grasped but also to have the analyst say something *useful* about them. To be useful, an interpretation must communicate back to the analysand both an affective state that he can take in and a way of thinking about it in which he can engage. The analysand never totally refuses such an interpretation, although it may often not be clear to the analyst what the analysand has done with it. This uncertainty about the fate of his interpretive creation is part of what the analyst must tolerate in giving it to the analysand.

In the Winnicottian brand of psychoanalysis (which, among British theories, comes closest to the affect theory offered here) the analyst will interpret in ways that will appear to be wildly analytic when viewed by the American ego psychological analyst – and especially to the analyst who relies almost exclusively on resistance as the key therapeutic reference point. What 'wild', however, actually means here is that the analyst remains on more uncertain ground for longer periods of time. More 'mistakes' are made along the way in attempting to grasp, contain, and interpret in the deep way that both Klein and (more temperately) Winnicott openly advocated. The analyst will probably just as often give the analysand something he cannot use as something he can use. This tendency in itself, however, Winnicott (1988) argued, contributes to the analysand's gradual recognition of the idealized and the very bad other (analyst). This recognition, in turn, catalyses a 'gradual acceptance on the part of the patient of the good and bad in the self, of the hopelessness and of that which is hopeful, of the unreal with the real, indeed of all the contrasting extremes' (1988: 142). It is in his attempt to elaboate imaginatively the affective states of the analysand – getting them wrong, that is, offering unusable interpretations of them, as often as getting them right – that the analyst is adapting to the analysand while, paradoxically, allowing the analysand not to have to adapt but to be increasingly free to be subversive to the analyst's subjectivity while imaginatively elaborating her own. The analyst is not interested in getting it right all the time but in doing it (the imaginative elaboration of his own and the analysand's affective states and their unconscious communications about these states). It is with his risk-taking willingness to do it that the analysand will identify, not his perfection in doing it (his perfect empathy or attunement). In fact, what the Winnicottian analyst is, again paradoxically, not willing to do in his willingness to interpret in the deep way Winnicott suggested is to try to worry about being perfect for the analysand. 'At the end,' Winnicott (1988: 142) wrote, 'if all goes well, there is a person who is human and imperfect related to a therapist who is imperfect in the sense of being unwilling to act perfectly beyond a certain degree and beyond a certain length of time'. At the end, I would add, if all goes well, there are two people whose capacity for imaginative, playful, fully human elaboration of their affective states is greater than the absence of their resistances and greater than the reality outside the analysis has wanted and will want to allow. But that is the analysand's postanalytic struggle – one always carried on with both hope and despair – and it is in this struggle that the analysand will be most fully alive.

Notes

1. There are many 'faces' of hermeneutics (Howard, 1982). The term applies to a family of philosophical positions and agendas – related through a common interest in intersubjective understanding, that is, how we ever have the conviction that we know one another or that we have understood the origins and vicissitudes of any human activity. One branch of the hermeneutic family focuses on epistemological methods. Used in this way, hermeneutics refers to an effort to specify the criteria for the reliability of knowledge obtained through interpretation. It rests on the proposition that there is no one best way to know every aspect of the world. The logical positivists of the Vienna Circle argued that the methods and the 'thing language' of physicists were the best tools for knowing any aspect of the world. Hermeneutic philosophers, by contrast, argue that the activity and language of interpretation are the best methods for understanding human subjectivity and the flow of immediate human experience. A second branch of the hermeneutic family is ontological hermeneutics. Calling a particular discipline ontologically hermeneutic is a way of saying that it is intrinsic to that discipline to construe the knowing human subject as an inherently interpreting creature. The ultimate knower is not a judge of facts but an interpreter. The German philosopher Hans-Georg Gadamer resurrected an interest in ontological hermeneutics. A student of the well-known

philosopher Martin Heidegger, Gadamer took the position that we live through innate and universal meaning categories even before we are developmentally able to think or talk about them. (I consider these meaning categories to be our endowment of affective potentials.) Central to Gadamer's theory was the proposition, as Roy Howard (1982: xii) has summarized it, that 'an individual, by the fact of his human existence itself, was already a special decoder of reality, already an active interpreter of a peculiar kind'. Affect theory suggests that each of us is first and foremost an affective interpreter.

2. In putting it this way, Lear is implicitly equating affect with Lacan's Other – that voice within us that exists in dialectical tension with the voice which we call the I, but which, paradoxically, we have constructed largely from the affective agenda of others. The Other, actually the affectively true desiring-subject self, is treated by this false I as a haunting and threatening presence.
3. Bibring theorized that a feeling state can become a prevailing ego state. As such it will characterize the person's immediate experience, his perception of life, and the options for action in the world of his objects that he will be able to consider as possible. The domination of a patient's representational world by a specific pathologic version of self and object always represents a developmentally chronic affect state. The patient has conceptualized such affective states into versions of self and object which then, in turn, keep each affective state (which Bibring calls an ego state) omnipresent in the patient's psychic life. I agree with Bibring's implication (as Rapaport also appeared to have done), that it is this affective state that causes him to see his current interactions as further confirmations of the existence in the external world of people who conform to his objects.

References

Boesky, D. (1988), 'Comments on the structural theory of technique', *International Journal of Psycho-Analysis*, 69: 303–16.

Dreyfus, H. and Wakefield, J. (1988), 'From depth psychology to breadth psychology', in S. Messer, L. Sass and R. Woolfolk (eds), *Hermeneutics and Psychological Theory*, New Brunswick, NJ: Rutgers University Press.

Etchegoyen, R.H. (1991), *The Fundamentals of Psychoanalytic Technique*, London: Karnac.

Freud, S. (1914), 'Remembering, repeating and working-through', *SE* XII: 145–56.

— (1925), 'An Autobiographical Study', *SE* XX: 1–74.
— (1926), 'The Question of Lay Analysis', *SE* XX: 77–174.
Gadamer, H. (1975), *Truth and Method*, New York: Seabury Press.
Heidegger, M. (1962), *Being and Time*, trans. J. Macquarrie and E. Robinson, London: SCM Press.
Hinshelwood, R.D. (1991), *A Dictionary of Kleinian Thought*, London: Free Association Books.
Howard, R. (1982), *Three Faces of Hermeneutics*, Berkeley: University of California Press.
Khan, M. (1987), 'Introduction', in *Holding and Interpretation*, New York: Grove Press.
Lear, J. (1991), *Love and Its Place in Nature*, New York: Farrar, Strauss & Giroux.
Lemaire, A. (1981), *Jacques Lacan*, London: Routledge & Kegan Paul.
Limentani, A. (1986), 'Affects and the psychoanalytic situation', in G. Kohon (ed.), *The British School of Psychoanalysis*, New Haven: Yale University Press, pp. 214–36.
Merleau-Ponty, M. (1962), *Phenomenology of Perception*, New York: Humanities Press.
Ornstein, A. (1991), 'The nature of selfobject transferences', presented at scientific meeting of the Northwest Alliance for Psychoanalysis, Seattle, WA, 15 March 1991.
Rapaport, D. (1953), 'On the psychoanalytic theory of affects', *International Journal of Psycho-Analysis*, 34: 177–98.
Robinson, S. (1984), 'The art of the possible', *Free Association*, Pilot Issue, 1984, p. 122.
Rodman, F.R., (ed.) (1987), *The Spontaneous Gesture*, Cambridge, MA: Harvard University Press.
Rycroft, C. (1968), *Imagination and Reality*, London: The Hogarth Press.
— (1985), *Psycho-Analysis and Beyond*, Chicago: University of Chicago Press.
Thompson, G. (1985), *The Death of Desire*, New York: New York University Press.
Winnicott, D.W. (1974), *Playing and Reality*, Harmondsworth: Penguin.
— (1986), *Holding and Interpretation*, New York: Grove Press. 1987 Reprint. Originally published London: Hogarth Press, 1986.
— (1988), *Human Nature*, New York: Schocken.

Index

Compiled by Sue Carlton